Violence, Nonviolence, and the Pa[lestinian]
National Movement

Why do some national movements use violent protest and others nonviolent protest? Wendy Pearlman shows that much of the answer lies inside movements themselves. Nonviolent protest requires coordination and restraint, which only a cohesive movement can provide. When, by contrast, a movement is fragmented, factional competition generates new incentives for violence and authority structures are too weak to constrain escalation. Pearlman reveals these patterns across nearly one hundred years in the Palestinian national movement, with comparisons to South Africa and Northern Ireland. To those who ask why there is no Palestinian Gandhi, Pearlman demonstrates that nonviolence is not simply a matter of leadership. Nor is violence attributable only to religion, emotions, or stark instrumentality. Instead, a movement's organizational structure mediates the strategies that it employs. By taking readers on a journey from civil disobedience to suicide bombings, this book offers fresh insight into the dynamics of conflict and mobilization.

Wendy Pearlman is the Crown Junior Chair in Middle East Studies and Assistant Professor of Political Science at Northwestern University. She graduated magna cum laude with a B.A. in history from Brown University and earned her Ph.D. in government at Harvard University, where she was the Karl Deutsch Fellow. Pearlman is the author of *Occupied Voices: Stories of Everyday Life from the Second Intifada*. She has published articles in *International Security* and *Journal of Palestine Studies*, chapters in several edited volumes, and commentaries in the *Washington Post*, *International Herald Tribune*, *Christian Science Monitor*, *Boston Globe*, and *Philadelphia Inquirer*, among other newspapers. Pearlman was a Fulbright Scholar in Spain, a Junior Peace Fellow at the United States Institute of Peace, and a postdoctoral Fellow at the Belfer Center for Science and International Affairs at Harvard's John F. Kennedy School of Government. She was the winner of the 2011 Deborah Gerner Grant for Professional Development.

Violence, Nonviolence, and the Palestinian National Movement

WENDY PEARLMAN

Northwestern University

CAMBRIDGE
UNIVERSITY PRESS

CAMBRIDGE
UNIVERSITY PRESS

32 Avenue of the Americas, New York NY 10013-2473, USA

Cambridge University Press is part of the University of Cambridge.

It furthers the University's mission by disseminating knowledge in the pursuit of education, learning and research at the highest international levels of excellence.

www.cambridge.org
Information on this title: www.cambridge.org/9781107632493

© Wendy Pearlman 2011

First published 2011
Second Edition 2012
Reprinted 2013
First paperback edition 2014

A catalogue record for this publication is available from the British Library

Library of Congress Cataloguing in Publication data
Pearlman, Wendy.
   Violence, nonviolence, and the Palestinian national movement / Wendy Pearlman.
      p.   cm.
   Includes bibliographical references and index.
   ISBN 978-1-107-00702-4 (hardback)
   1. Palestine – History – Autonomy and independence movements.   2. Arab-Israeli
   conflict.   3. Nationalism – Palestine – History.   4. Violence – Palestine – History.
   5. Nationalism.   6. Nonviolence.   I. Title.
   DS119.76.P44   2011
   320.54095694–dc22   2011007344

ISBN   978-1-107-00702-4 Hardback
ISBN   978-1-107-63249-3 Paperback

To my parents

Contents

Preface

The inspiration for this research stemmed from my experiences living in the West Bank, the Gaza Strip, East Jerusalem, and Tel Aviv for a total of more than three years between January 2000 and August 2008. I was already hooked on Middle East politics before that journey began, as I had lived in Morocco and studied Arabic for five years. Yet my first trip to Israel and the Palestinian territories captured my heart and mind in a new way. At the turn of the millennium I did a tour of Israel and then spent five months in the West Bank, where I studied at Birzeit University and worked at a local organization. The following summer I lived and worked in the Gaza Strip. During the years that followed, I returned every chance I got. When afar, I monitored day-to-day events with what became an unhealthy addiction to the news. People often asked me what my Jewish family thought about their daughter giving so much attention to the Palestinian situation. I would explain that my grandmother's only regret was that I had been a more interesting person before I became an "all Israel–Palestine all the time" channel.

Three months into the second Intifada, I conducted interviews with about two dozen Palestinians in the West Bank and Gaza Strip. These were published in 2003 as the book *Occupied Voices: Stories of Everyday Life from the Second Intifada*. I undertook that project both to help myself understand the experiences of ordinary people enduring a terrible conflict and to bring their voices to a larger audience. As I gave book talks around the United States, however, I found that discussions repeatedly ended with the same query. Over and over, people said that they were moved by the personal stories but had trouble understanding why Palestinians carried out violence against Israelis. Even those who supported Palestinians' quest for statehood were perplexed. "Don't Palestinians see that suicide bombings only undermine sympathy for their cause?" people asked. "Why don't they use nonviolence instead? Where is the Palestinian Gandhi?"

The answers at my disposal fell short. I knew from my study of history that Palestinians *had* used nonviolent as well as violent protest, but I lacked a convincing explanation of why they had done so to different extents at different times. My conversations in the West Bank and Gaza had shown me why many people believed that protest was necessary and justified. Yet this did not account for why protest took certain forms. By then I was a doctoral student in political science, so I turned to scholarly theories of rebellion and insurgency for answers. Influential studies attributed political violence to factors ranging from manipulative elites to religious fundamentalism to cold calculations of costs and benefits. Though these were often validated by cross-national statistical tests, they misrepresented or oversimplified what I had seen on the ground. Furthermore, they had more to say about how conflict escalates to bloodshed than about the circumstances under which it remains unarmed.

I made this question the topic of my dissertation. My motivation was to satisfy my own desire for understanding and to contribute to others' understanding as well. Knowing that any viable explanation of violent or nonviolent protest should account for ebbs and flows in both, I extended the scope of my research to cover the history of the Palestinian national movement. I studied Hebrew to increase my appreciation of the Israeli experience, as well as methodologies of quantitative and qualitative research to bring greater rigor to my analysis. I also returned to live in Israel and the Palestinian territories from June 2004 through August 2006 to carry out field and archival research.

I strove to bring diverse forms of evidence to bear upon my question. My analysis of Mandate Palestine drew on original material from the Israel State Archives, namely the collections of Chief Secretary's Office Papers, Palestine Government Arab Documents, and George Antonius Papers. I scrutinized the reports of the official commissions of inquiry into the disturbances of 1921, 1929, and 1936, the British high commissioner's monthly reports, periodic reviews, and telegrams, and the writings of district commissioners detailing events in the areas of Palestine under their purview. I also made use of memoirs of Palestinians and Arabs involved in nationalist activity at the time.

For later eras, I incorporated other materials. I consulted the wealth of primary documents collected and published by the Institute of Palestine Studies in English and Arabic. I used press reportage, some obtained from the press archive at Tel Aviv University's Moshe Dayan Center. I examined quantitative data from the statistics kept by B'Tselem (the Israeli Information Center for Human Rights), the ICT-Merari terrorist incidents database of the Institute for Counter-Terrorism at the Interdisciplinary Center in Herzliya, Israel, and a comprehensive database on violent events compiled by Mohammed Hafez of the Naval Postgraduate School. I also scrutinized more than a decade of public opinion polls conducted by three Palestinian research institutes: the Palestine Center for Survey Research, the Jerusalem Media and Communication Centre, and the former Center for Palestine Research and Studies. In addition, I relied upon more than three dozen human rights and investigatory reports authored by Israeli, Palestinian, and international organizations. I gained appreciation for the primary data contained in such on-the-ground documents when I helped translate them during my own internships in two Palestinian human rights groups, the Palestinian Independent Commission for Citizens' Rights in

Ramallah and the al-Mezan Center for Human Rights based in the Jabalya
refugee camp in the Gaza Strip.

Finally, my twenty-six months in Israel and the Palestinian territories built
on my previous experience and enabled me to continue to hone my understanding of both peoples by living among them. I observed interactions,
developed lifelong relationships, absorbed daily media in two languages, and
paid attention to the political talk that is the sound track of life on both sides
of the Green Line. I had countless informal conversations with Israelis and
Palestinians about the conflict and conducted forty-eight formal interviews,
six of which were in the Gaza Strip (between July and August 2005), four in
Israel (June–August 2006), and thirty-eight in the West Bank (June–August
2006, January 2007, August 2008). I carried out interviews in either Arabic or
English, and tape-recorded, transcribed, and translated nearly all of them. In
the interest of taking the strictest precautions to protect human subjects from
any kind of harm or discomfort, I have not identified interviewees by name.
I have, however, helped readers situate their comments by briefly indicating
their occupation or affiliation, as well as the place and date of the interview.

I could not have carried out this project without the help of many people.
My dissertation benefited immeasurably from my advisers, Jorge Domínguez,
Devesh Kapur, Roger Owen, and Stephen Rosen. I thank each of them for
challenging my project in a different way. Their combined abilities to pierce
through my often murky ideas taught me not only how to think and write,
but also how to teach. I learned no less from wonderful graduate school class-
mates. In them I have been fortunate to find a community of scholars and
friends for the long haul.

I am indebted to several institutions that funded my research. My field-
work was made possible by a United States Institute of Peace "Peace Fellows"
Dissertation Fellowship and a grant from the Palestinian–American Research
Center. A Harvard University–Hebrew University Graduate Fellowship and
Foreign Language and Area Studies Award enabled me to study Hebrew and
other topics for twelve months at the Hebrew University of Jerusalem. A Starr
Foundation Fellowship at the Center for Arabic Studies Abroad provided for
twelve months of advanced Arabic training at the American University in Cairo.
I was able to get a start on revising my dissertation as a postdoctoral fellow at
the Belfer Center for Science and International Affairs at the John F. Kennedy
School of Government. There I learned tremendously from top-notch scholars
of conflict, both experienced and up-and-coming. They gave me invaluable
feedback on my work and inspired me through exposure to their own.

Now an assistant professor at Northwestern University, I am fortunate to
have benefited from the tremendous generosity of the Crown family and its
dedication to Middle East studies, as well as from Weinberg College's support
for junior faculty. I could not imagine colleagues better than those whom I
have found in the Department of Political Science. I thank them all. A vibrant
working group of faculty studying the Middle East and North Africa has provided the icing on the cake of a terrific intellectual home.

Over the years, I have presented various pieces of this research at Northwestern, Harvard, the University of Chicago, and the Northeast Middle East Politics Workshop, among other conferences. I am appreciative of all who shared their time and thoughts with me in those forums. The deepest gratitude goes to those who read chapters or sometimes much more of the manuscript-in-preparation: Nathan Brown, Rex Brynen, William Gamson, Jeff Goodwin, Ylana Miller, Aldon Morris, Rosemary Sayigh, Yezid Sayigh, Charles Smith, Hendrik Spruyt, Salim Tamari, Mark Tessler, Mary Ann Weston, and the late Gil Friedman. I am indebted to their generous giving of expert knowledge and fantastic insight. I can only hope that my revisions do some justice to the acumen of their suggestions. I am also very grateful to those who offered counsel in navigating the path from dissertation to published book, especially Jamie Druckman, Dennis Chong, Devesh Kapur, Dan Galvin, Ben Page, Jim Mahoney, Monika Nalepa, Jillian Schwedler, and Victor Shih.

Innumerable people assisted my field research in the West Bank, Gaza Strip, and Israel. Their kindness continually humbled me, and I regret terribly that I cannot honor them all by name. I am especially grateful to Aboud and Rodaina Abdullah and family, Bradley Brigham and Ghaith Omari, Ali Jarbawi, the Jarrar family, Laura Junka, Lucy Mair, the Muna family, Charmaine Seitz, Jamila and Yasaar Shrafi and family, Ghada Snounu and family, Issam Younnis, and my incredible neighbors in the old city of Jerusalem. I lack the words to express my particular debts to Iman Ashur, Jehan Jarrar, Suzanne Jarrar, and Alberto Spektorowski.

I thank wonderful friends, new and old, for their wisdom, humor, and patient encouragement: Mirna Adjami, Diana Allan, Sa'ed Atshan, Theo Christov, Lara Deeb, Sarah Eltantawi, Lora Gordon, Dan Ho, Manal Jamal, Jana Lipman, Emily Maguire, Jen Marlowe, Sreemati Mitter, Marcy Newman, Alison Post, Tamara Qiblawi, Almas Sayeed, Rashmi Tiwari, Elina Treyger, and Sean Yom. I have unbound gratitude for my family, Alicia Pearlman, Charlie Pearlman, Judy Kolker, and Judy Schwab, for their unconditional love and support. My grandmother Margaret Pearlman continues to be my rock and inspiration.

My father, Michael Pearlman, has showed an unparalleled knack for lifting my spirits, often by reminding me not to take myself too seriously. My mother, Lois Pearlman, passed before I began postgraduate studies. Yet her example of compassion, creativity, and courage lit my every step and always will. It is to them that I dedicate this book.

Acronyms

AE	Arab Executive
AHC	Arab Higher Committee
ALF	Arab Liberation Front
AMB	al-Aqsa Martyrs Brigade
ANC	African National Congress
ANM	Arab Nationalist Movement
AOLP	Action Organization for the Liberation of Palestine
BSO	Black September Organization
COSATU	Congress of South African Trade Unions
DFLP	Democratic Front for the Liberation of Palestine (formerly PDFLP)
EC	Executive Committee of the Palestine Liberation Organization
IRA	Irish Republican Army
LNM	Lebanese National Movement
MCA	Muslim–Christian Association
MK	Umkhonto we Sizwe (Spear of the Nation)
NGC	National Guidance Committee
NICRA	Northern Ireland Civil Rights Association
NIFHC	National and Islamic Forces Higher Committee
PA	Palestinian Authority
PAC	Pan-Africanist Congress
PDFLP	Popular Democratic Front for the Liberation of Palestine (later DFLP)
PFLP	Popular Front for the Liberation of Palestine
PFLP-GC	Popular Front for the Liberation of Palestine – General Command
PLA	Palestine Liberation Army
PLC	Palestinian Legislative Council
PLF	Palestinian Liberation Front
PLO	Palestine Liberation Organization
PNC	Palestinian National Council

PNF	Palestinian National Front
PPSF	Palestinian Popular Struggle Front
PRCs	Popular Resistance Committees
SDLP	Social Democratic and Labour Party
SMC	Supreme Muslim Council
UDF	United Democratic Front
UNLU	United National Leadership of the Uprising
UNSCR	United Nations Security Council Resolution
UNRWA	United Nations Relief and Works Agency for Palestine Refugees in the Near East

The Organizational Mediation Theory of Protest

April 1936: Palestine erupts in revolt. For years, the indigenous Arabs of Palestine have engaged in pressure politics. Their goal is to convince Great Britain to abandon its support for the establishment of a Jewish national home in Palestine. After a decade of such protest fails to bear fruit, however, Palestinian Arabs launch a rebellion. The "Great Revolt" begins with broad-based participation in unarmed activities such as a general strike, popular demonstrations, and boycotts. Sporadic armed attacks become more frequent as rural bands carry out sniping and sabotage. The rebellion enters a hiatus and then becomes more dramatically and exclusively violent when it resumes in the fall of 1937. Rebel bands battle with British troops, and thousands die before the rebellion collapses into internecine fighting.

March 1988: The first Intifada against Israel's occupation of the West Bank and Gaza Strip is in its third month. For weeks on end, Palestinian youths clash with Israeli troops by throwing stones, blocking roads, burning tires, and defying curfew. Each day registers acts of nonviolent protest, including sit-ins, boycotts, commercial strikes, refusal to pay taxes, mass resignation from Israeli institutions, and the organization of community-based alternatives. Women lead huge demonstrations on International Women's Day. On "Land Day," an annual protest against land confiscation, Palestinians inside Israel march in solidarity with the occupied territories. Tens of thousands of Palestinians have been arrested, injured, or killed. Nonetheless, their use of lethal violence against Israel remains very limited.

March 2002: A second Intifada is in its second year. With violence claiming the lives of 246 Palestinians and 113 Israelis, the month is among the bloodiest in the history of the Israeli–Palestinian conflict. Palestinian activists open fire on Israeli civilians, infiltrate settlements, detonate bombs at bus stops, fire makeshift rockets, and set off a roadside bomb that destroys an Israeli tank. Israel's repression of Palestinians is likewise violent and severe. On March 27, a suicide bombing, the 37th of the Intifada, leaves scores dead and wounded at a Passover dinner. The Israeli army responds with a sweeping and bloody operation whereby it reoccupies most West Bank towns. That day, an 18-year-old girl becomes the youngest Palestinian female suicide bomber.

Why do social and insurgent movements employ the strategies and tactics that they do? Focusing on the vexing problem of political violence, scholars have produced theories about the targets, timing, and intensity of a group's use of arms. Yet as the history of the Palestinian national movement demonstrates, violence is only one form of protest and contention. The question of why movements use violent means, therefore, is inextricable from the question of why they do or do not use *nonviolent* means. This book takes up this query. I argue that while the paths to violence are multiple, there is one prevailing path to nonviolent protest: a path that requires a movement to have or create internal cohesion. When a movement is cohesive, it enjoys the organizational power to mobilize mass participation, enforce strategic discipline, and contain disruptive dissent. In consequence, cohesion increases the possibility that a movement will use nonviolent protest. Inversely, when a movement is fragmented, it lacks the leadership, institutions, and collective purpose to coordinate and constrain its members. Its very internal structure thus generates incentives and opportunities that increase the likelihood that it will use violence.

This argument is straightforward, yet its implications pose a challenge to existing analyses. Scholars and commentators propose a plethora of explanations for a movement's conflict behavior, from religious values to access to weapons, and from the escalatory effect of state repression to stark calculations of what is needed for success. My emphasis on movement cohesion and fragmentation suggests that there is no simple one-to-one correlation between any of these factors and movement protest. Rather, their influence is mediated by a movement's internal structure. Movements are not machines, propelled automatically by instrumental calculations, ideology, or all-powerful elites. Nor are they akin to billiard balls, pushed in one direction or another by external impetuses or pressures. There are instead distinctly internal and organizational reasons for their strategic choices.

I call my analytical approach the "organizational mediation theory of protest." While this approach can shed light on a variety of movements for social and political change, I apply it here to self-determination movements. Struggles of ethnic or national groups for autonomy or independence are among the world's most common sources of bloody conflict. Yet most self-determination movements are not violent. Of the 132 self-determination movements active as of 2006, only 18 engaged in armed hostilities.[1] Even movements that do engage in violence do not do so consistently over time. Of the 71 self-determination movements that waged armed struggle at some point since the 1950s, more than half no longer rely on violent strategies.[2]

The need to understand the conditions under which protest is violent or nonviolent is pressing for scholars and policy makers alike. There is perhaps no better case with which to explore this puzzle than the Palestinian national movement. Many find it difficult to explain Palestinians' strategies, including those who sympathize with their goals. Witnessing lethal attacks, some wonder why there is no "Palestinian Gandhi." They suggest that nonviolent means might better help Palestinians win international sympathy or convince Israelis that painful concessions would not diminish their security. This book suggests why these questions are off the mark. Launching nonviolent protest is not simply a matter of leadership or utilitarian calculations. A movement's organizational structure is itself sufficient to make unarmed methods highly improbable, regardless of other impetuses or motives for such a course.

The Palestinian case is anomalous in many respects, such as its diasporic dispersal, complex interpenetrations by Middle East regional politics, and attraction of vast attention from across the world. Compounding this is the particular intractability of the conflict between Israeli and Palestinian claims to a nation-state in the same land. Given its peculiarities, much of the research on comparative conflict processes does not address the Israeli–Palestinian situation. At the same time, the literature specifically on this case tends to fall in the realms of journalism, history, and policy analysis more than in that of the social sciences. These tendencies forfeit valuable opportunities to scrutinize the Palestinian experience for generalizable insight.

While the larger circumstances of the Palestinian national movement are exceptional, many of the dynamics shaping its protest behavior are not. Palestinians share with other social and self-determination movements two basic challenges: overcoming multiple sources of internal division in order to mobilize collective action and choosing among available strategies for challenging a status quo. Many scholars of Palestinian politics are sensitive to the link between internal divisions, on the one hand, and strategy, on the other. Nearly all note that this relationship has inhibited the success of Palestinians' struggle.[3] Yet none to date have systematically theorized and analyzed its effect on their very *forms* of struggle. In undertaking that task, I seek to make a unique contribution to understandings of the Israeli–Palestinian conflict, while also countering treatment of the Israeli–Palestinian conflict as categorically unique. To further this end, I also show how patterns in Palestinian history can help us understand the South African antiapartheid struggle and Northern Ireland republican movement and how these movements can in turn elucidate the Palestinian experience.

LIMITS OF CONVENTIONAL EXPLANATIONS

Protest is the act of challenging, resisting, or making demands upon authorities or power holders.[4] Violent protest entails the exertion of physical force for the purpose of damaging, abusing, killing, or destroying. Nonviolent protest does not entail physical force. Gene Sharp identifies three kinds of nonviolent action: acts of protest and persuasion, such as marches or the display of signs and slogans; noncooperation, such as strikes and boycotts; and nonviolent intervention, such as sit-ins, hunger strikes, and other deliberate refusals to observe law or social custom.[5] As analysts look across cases, these criteria can help them categorize protest as either violent or nonviolent. The application of these criteria, however, demands attention to context. For movements that espouse armed struggle, a shift toward stone throwing represents a decrease in the violent character of protest. For movements committed to electoral politics, the opposite is the case.

Movements rarely use violent or nonviolent protest to the complete exclusion of the other. Yet what explains the relative prominence or intensity of either in a movement's repertoire of contention? Scholarship on social movements has shed light on the conditions under which people overcome problems of collective action to launch sustained challenges to authority. While an earlier generation of thinkers attributed collective behavior to systemic strains and psychological discontent, the resource mobilization approach emphasized the role of external allies and funds in enabling activists to form organizations. The political process approach then redirected attention to the shifting environmental conditions that generate "political opportunity structures" conducive to direct action. Such shifts produce social movements when aggrieved groups mobilize through networks and organizations and adopt frames that inspire and legitimate such mobilization.[6] Recent work criticizes political process models for being overly structural and ignoring the creativity and emotion entailed in collective protest.[7] The sum of this research offers an important foundation for any study of protest. Nevertheless, its diverse strands tend to debate the sources of movements' emergence more than the strategies that movements undertake.[8] Some critics attribute this oversight to scholars' view of protest as a mechanical outcome of conflict between states and challengers rather than a puzzle in its own right.[9]

Nonetheless, existing research on social movements and other forms of contentious politics points to a range of possible explanations why movements engage in violent or nonviolent protest. One perspective holds that protest is a strategy that movements choose instrumentally in interaction with the adversary from which they seek concessions.[10] According to this view, states' exclusion of certain groups or issues from conventional processes of decision making pushes people to disrupt the system through dissent.[11] The basic asymmetry of institutional and material power leads movements to seek any leverage against ruling authorities. Some turn to nonviolent protest to deny governments the obedience and compliance on which their rule depends.[12] Others embrace violence on the rationale that only stiff costs can compel states to make concessions. In this context, some analysts believe terrorism to be a rational "weapon of the weak" because it gives groups an impact far larger than their small size or resource endowment.[13] Empirical findings suggest that terrorism has also proved effective, particularly in coercing democracies to relinquish territory.[14]

Turning from state structures to state policies, other research considers the particular effect of repression on the likelihood that protest will be violent or nonviolent. Many case studies demonstrate that repression generates individual-level motivations and group-level pressures that radicalize rebellion.[15] Nevertheless, comparative findings are inconclusive,[16] which suggests that it is variations in the application of repression that trigger variation in protest. Some research finds that indiscriminate repression drives movements from nonviolent to violent protest; when protestors perceive that they are punished regardless of whether their strategies are moderate or radical, they opt for that which inflicts higher costs on their opponent.[17] A similar dynamic ensues when regimes respond to nonviolent protest with coercion rather than concessions, after which rational rebels conclude that nonviolence is ineffective and a stronger course of action is necessary.[18] Inconsistent repression can have the same effect, insofar as it sends a signal that the regime is weak and vacillating. For protestors, therefore, tactical escalation can appear to be the coup de grâce that snatches victory.[19]

These arguments show that protest is the outcome of a dynamic process of rational action, reaction, and anticipation. Nevertheless, the strategic interaction paradigm does not explain why movements sometimes take steps that are suboptimal or even haphazard. Nor does it tell us why they continue with a strategy after it fails to bear fruit. Reflecting that critique, an alternative approach holds that a movement's repertoire of protest is not simply instrumental, but shaped by culture, religion, ideology, or the nonrationalistic "shared understandings" that bring a group together.[20] According to this view, movements that reject nonviolent forms of protest may be driven by ideas and identities that render militancy a value in and of itself. Such arguments are particularly prevalent with regard to Middle East cases, as some suggest that there is something in Islam or Arab culture that disposes people to violence. Along these lines, one commentator attributes suicide bombings to "the thirst for vengeance, the desire for religious purity, the longing for earthly glory and eternal salvation."[21] Others agree that a "culture of martyrdom" can shape protest tactics, but argue that this is a culture of despair among victims of protracted violence who only then become perpetrators.[22]

These explanations remind us that values and beliefs mold collective behavior in ways irreducible to mechanical computations of effectiveness. Yet these claims are often ad hoc. Most cultures are sufficiently rich and complex to legitimate either violent or nonviolent protest. Furthermore, culture per se cannot explain why a single population might engage in different kinds of protest at different points of time. Toward a better account, another line of ideational explanation shifts focus to dynamic processes of framing. Framing is the creative endeavor by which entrepreneurs construct ideas and representations that inspire people to take part in collective action.[23] In this regard, many emphasize the role of movement elites in convincing their communities to engage in one or another kind of protest. Works on the history of nonviolent protest often stress the centrality of leaders such as Mahatma Gandhi and Martin Luther King Jr., who toiled to frame their struggles in ways that persuaded others of the value of unarmed means of resistance and social change.[24] Along similar lines, leaders can also invoke shared values and beliefs in ways that promote violent collective action. A large body of research on ethnic and nationalist conflict examines how leaders incite their populations to arms, often in a self-interested bid to outsmart opponents, distract attention from political ills, or otherwise preserve their grip on power.[25]

Arguments emphasizing elites highlight the role of agency and contingent choice in shaping forms of protest. Nevertheless, in implying a direct link between particular leaders and collective behavior, they neglect how contentious politics unleashes social processes beyond the control of any single individual. Recasting protest as such a process, other scholars propose that movement tactics evolve in stages that form a predictable "protest cycle." Sidney Tarrow argues that movements gain pace in an initial mobilization phase, during which early risers escalate tactics, new actors come to the fore, and novel repertoires of framing and contention diffuse.[26] As the costs of protest accumulate, crowds withdraw in exhaustion and a demobilization phase ensues. At that point, the government often selectively accommodates the demands of movement moderates while repressing those of radicals. The outcome is sporadic acts of militant violence amid a general decline in mass mobilization.

The protest cycle model reminds us that the use of violent or nonviolent protest cannot be divorced from fluctuations in movement momentum, which evolve organically over time.[27] Nevertheless, cyclical formulations are more useful as description than explanation. Furthermore, Tarrow's observation that movements split when they demobilize generates as many questions as answers. Do rifts among movement members percolate only during the decline of protest, or can they occur at its outset or upsurge? After all, as Mark Lichbach writes, "Competition, not cooperation, is the norm among dissident organizations."[28] Casting a spotlight on this competition, a growing trend in research on insurgency focuses on intra-group influences on inter-group hostilities. Various studies demonstrate how rivalries within a single identity group can feed motivations for violence against an external adversary. Research on ethnic politics has long upheld the argument that vying camps intensify their demands to "outbid" each other for popular support.[29] In the context of insurgencies, the same dynamic goads movement factions to escalate violence against the state.[30] Intra-group competition takes on other dimensions when moderate insurgents enter into peace processes. In that context, their more radical rivals often act as "spoilers" who initiate attacks to undermine negotiations.[31] In civil wars, these and other intra-group contests can develop into a complex web. A multiplicity of overlapping interests and identities belie the notion that civil wars follow a binary cleavage between two national adversaries.[32]

Several works on intra-movement influences on violence invoke the Palestinian case to illustrate their claims.[33] However, these scholars frequently bias their conclusions by truncating their empirical purview to moments of heightened violence and neglecting periods in which Palestinians engaged in nonviolent protest or little open protest at all. What was the relevance of intra-group competition during those times in which the guns were relatively silent? Existing research typically ignores this question because it takes cases characterized by both internal rivalries and external violence and asks how the former affects the latter. In failing to allow the independent and dependent variables to vary, it is unable to assess the kinds of strategic action that result when movements are less internally divided. Nor does it explain why some factionalized movements, among them the Palestinian movement, at times use unarmed protest or sustain diplomacy.

To understand how internal processes affect the prospects for either violence or nonviolence, researchers cannot assume unbridled escalatory competition among factions within a movement. Rather they must investigate the structural conditions under which those who share some collective goals are able to reconcile their differences. They can then trace the impact of such reconciliation on the contours of collective action. This approach shifts analytical focus from activists' rival preferences to the ways in which movements as a whole are organized. A movement will always have members with more "radical" or "moderate" leanings. The question is how the system of relationships internal to a movement variably constrains or unleashes their ability to pursue those inclinations unilaterally. The dynamics of outbidding and spoilers are less analytically valuable as complete theories of conflict than as two of many possible mechanisms through which different levels of movement cohesion shape protest. Building on this view, the organizational mediation theory of protest takes as its starting assumption what scholars of conflict increasingly posit as their conclusion: movement members interact with both an external power and others in their own community. The puzzle is not whether a movement is engaged in two-level games. It is how the structure of those games, and with them forms of movement protest, vary over time.

The organizational mediation theory of protest is not the first to focus on the relationship between a movement's internal structure and its external strategy. Charles Tilly, for example, discusses how the organization of a population shapes its repertoire of collective action. Yet he invokes this relationship mainly to differentiate types of groups such as religious confraternities or trade unions.[34] He does not consider variation in internal organization within any single kind of group, such as movements for self-determination. By contrast, Jeremy Weinstein focuses on rebellions and contrasts groups in which people participate due to commitment to the cause with groups organized around material incentives. It is in the latter that fighters are most prone to engage in looting, indiscriminate force, and violence against civilians.[35] This distinction calls attention to the effect of organization on patterns of insurgent violence. Yet it leaves us to wonder how organization shapes the very turn to violence, as opposed to nonviolent protest, in the first place.

COHESION AND FRAGMENTATION

Existing scholarship thus identifies a plethora of variables that affect protest. The organizational mediation theory of protest is not a monocausal theory intended to replace these mono- or multicausal theories. It is a new approach that focuses on how the factors that we typically think of as driving protest are filtered through a movement's internal dynamics. Their effects cannot be understood in isolation from the matrix of conflict or cooperation among movement members. Movements sharing the same emotional push toward violence or facing the same rational payoff for nonviolent protest will be more or less likely to use these strategies depending on their organizational structure.

In the context of this study, organizational structure refers to the system of relationships and rules that integrate members of a movement for the pursuit of collective aims. While various dimensions of organizational structure merit attention, one key characteristic is the degree to which that structure is cohesive or fragmented. Political scientists invoke the term "fragmentation" to gauge divisions in a polity or political system. Fragmentation thus typically refers to the distribution of seats in a legislature, the total veto points in a policy-making process, or the number of ethnolinguistic groups within certain geographical borders.[36] Scholars measure these kinds of fragmentation through a count of relevant subunits, adjusted for size or salience. Such measures have the benefit of replicable quantification. However, they offer a thin view of the diversity of objectives or dispersion of authority within a collective. They focus attention on the number of fragments within a unit at the expense of larger questions about the character of their interaction, the controls on their behavior, the compatibility of their preferences, and the formal and informal rules according to which power is distributed among them.

These issues are pertinent to movements for self-determination. Many movements are made up of multiple and fluid subgroups that bargain over strategy, ideology, institutions, and resources. These nonstate groups face some of the same burdens of states, such as creating social order and centralizing decision making. Yet they lack the powers of states, namely a successful claim of monopoly on the legitimate use of violence within a given territory.[37] The combination of domination vis-à-vis citizens and sovereignty vis-à-vis strangers enables states to regulate political fragmentation within their borders. In nonstate entities, however, fragmentation takes on different dimensions. Standard indexes of fragmentation do not capture this complexity because they imply premises, such as binding laws or deep-seated ascriptive divisions, which do not apply. Furthermore, these indexes assume that identified subunits are coherent and stable. In movements and insurgencies, however, political factions often splinter, proliferate, merge, and splinter again.

Sources of fragmentation in self-determination movements are numerous, shaped by context, and concurrent at various levels of population. In developing an instrument for assessing fragmentation, it is therefore less helpful to enumerate and measure all sources of division than to identify the means by which movements achieve some degree of unity, despite the many pressures working against it. This logic is similar to the argument that fragmentation in political party systems is not inherent in particular types of social cleavage as much as it is produced by the ways that institutions manage those cleavages.[38]

I extend this insight to a new conceptualization of movement cohesion. Here it is useful to consider the definition of cohesion used in the natural sciences. In geology, physics, and chemistry, cohesion is the attraction by which the elements of a body coalesce into extended states.[39] Those who study cohesion in these contexts do not count composite units, but examine the origins and manifestations of forces that cause or oppose their attraction. In crafting the organizational mediation theory of protest, I adapt this notion to the social world. I define cohesion as the cooperation among individuals that enables unified action. As with atoms or molecules, cohesion results when the forces assisting cooperative behavior exceed the forces encouraging competitive or antagonistic behavior. It is the capacity for internal command and control that enables a composite social actor to act as if it were a unitary one.

The difficulty of building a cohesive organizational structure is attributable to the multiplicity of potential equilibriums when people bargain on many policy issues simultaneously.[40] In such contexts, no ex ante collective choice is equally desirable to all.[41] Decision making by composite political entities, be they congressional committees or social movements, is thus fundamentally different than decision making by individuals. For a movement, the task of choosing a protest strategy is not simply a matter of ranking preferred outcomes, recognizing constraints, and selecting the most efficacious option. Strategy cannot be automatically derived from the logic of purposeful interaction with an external adversary. Instead, it is produced through a process of internal bargaining, compromise, and coercion.

The implication is that scholars must be wary of reifying composite actors, be they political parties, firms, states, or nonstate entities. Gary Cox and Kenneth Shepsle explain, "We know these collectives are not unitary on the one hand, and that adding up the heterogeneous tastes comprising their memberships is problematical on the other ... 'it' is not really an it."[42] I conceptualize a movement's cohesion as the degree to which it, which is not actually an "it," acts as if it were. Fragmentation is the degree to which it does not. I assess a movement's level of cohesion or fragmentation by qualitatively measuring factors that facilitate cooperation among individuals and enable unified action. Three factors are particularly important: leadership, institutions, and the population's sense of collective purpose.

Leadership, as defined by John Gardner, is the "the process of persuasion and example by which an individual (or leadership team) induces a group to pursue objectives."[43] I assess leadership by assessing if a movement has one unified leadership body rather than several. I also gauge the extent to which that leadership is perceived by movement adherents as legitimate. Leadership contributes to a cohesive organizational structure by clarifying goals and inspiring people to cooperate for their achievement. In game-theoretic terms, leaders are "agenda setters" who use political skill and artistry to influence people's preferences. They thereby produce collective choice equilibriums where they might not otherwise occur.[44] This function of leadership comes to the fore in critical choices made at particular turning points. For example, leaders' decision to suppress unruly dissent at a decisive juncture can send a powerful warning to other would-be rebels and consolidate the decision-making authority of the political center. On the flip side, a decision to excuse insubordination or bow to external intervention can embolden and empower rebellious forces. With time, a central leadership may find itself increasingly unable to impose its will. The crucial nature of these decisions is not always evident at the time. One testimony of leadership is the ability to anticipate them and act in ways that bolster cohesion over the long term.

Institutions are the structures and norms that govern social interaction. They are the "rules of the game" that pattern behavior for both individuals and groups.[45] Adapting Samuel Huntington's criteria for institutionalization, I evaluate the strength of institutions according to the extent to which they acquire value and stability by becoming increasingly adaptable, complex, autonomous, and coherent.[46] Institutions undergird a cohesive organizational structure. In William Riker's terminology, they systematically include or exclude certain opinions or values from decision-making processes and thereby give rise to collective choices that are more than "random embodiments of peoples' tastes."[47] Institutional design can create compromise and order even in populations divided by diverse preferences. Institutions are particularly critical in producing inter-elite and interfactional cooperation. When internal rivals submit to the same set of political rules, they accept limits to the pursuit of their ambitions and ideal outcomes. They thereby surrender some autonomy and forge a basis for collective action.

Finally, collective purpose is the extent to which a population agrees on clear objectives, that agreement crosses social, economic, and other cleavages, and commitment to those objectives is strong. Collective purpose is the ultimate guarantor of a movement's cohesion because it guarantees the movement itself. The effect of collective purpose in creating movement cohesion may be a top-down process. Leaders can explicitly invoke ideas that resonate with people's shared identities and interests, and thereby bolster unity in the struggle for goals that they hold in common. In doing so, they can leverage popular backing to isolate and thwart rivals, which may consolidate their authority and control. By contrast, collective purpose can generate movement cohesion from the bottom up. To the degree that rival groups seek popularity, society's sense of collective purpose shapes the incentives and constraints under which those groups operate. A collective purpose among the population can thus compel bickering factions to resolve their differences. In the face of a general consensus on goals and means, activists stray from public opinion at their political peril. When the population lacks a collective mission, however, the political arena can become a free-for-all in which any actor pursues private interests with no loss of public support.

As empirical indicators, leadership, institutions, and collective purpose shape each other in complex ways. Agreement among adherents of a movement can compel an ambivalent leadership to champion a clear collective purpose. Institutions can synchronize behavior in the absence of popular consensus on clear objectives. Effective leadership can create consensus where it would otherwise not exist and inspire people to act in unison where institutions do not. For the purposes of this book, I do not theorize the distinction between a situation in which collective purpose is strong but institutions are weak from a situation in which institutions are strong and collective purpose is weak. Nonetheless, I anticipate that, the more that a movement's cohesion relies solely on any one of these elements at the expense of others, the more vulnerable it is to breaking down under fatigue or exogenous pressures.

I conceptualize cohesion and fragmentation as ideal typical points on a spectrum. A movement can be considered to be cohesive when a sufficient portion of adherents is governed by a single leadership, institutional framework, and sense of collective purpose. Under such conditions, the movement can develop a threshold of effective command and control. Leaders are able to direct human and material resources authoritatively and dissidents lack the capacity to thwart them. This does not mean that movement cohesion indicates uniformity of opinion. Fragmentation is not the absence of pluralism, but pluralism without rules or mechanisms for generating cooperative behavior.

ARGUMENT

It may not be controversial to suggest that a movement's degree of cohesion affects the probability that it will mobilize collective action or that collective action will be successful. What this book proposes, however, is that cohesion also affects the very form that collective action can or is likely to take. The following discussion elaborates a two-part argument: a movement must be cohesive to use nonviolent protest, and fragmented movements are more likely than cohesive ones to use violent protest.

1. Cohesion Increases the Possibility of Nonviolent Protest

Internal cohesion increases the possibility that a movement will use nonviolent protest for three reasons. First, cohesion facilitates mass mobilization. To the degree that a movement has a unifying sense of collective purpose, it will be more capable of rallying a broad base of the population rather than merely narrow sectors or select recruits. For that participation to constitute meaningful collective action, some kind of leadership or institutional framework must exist or emerge to steer it. Mass mobilization is more critical for strategies such as civil disobedience and labor strikes than for armed struggle. A single person with a gun is sufficient to execute an attack. A tiny cell of militants can carry out terrorism that alters the course of a conflict decisively. A small group of people going out into the street, however, does not make a protest event, much less a protest campaign. Activities such as demonstrations, work stoppages, and boycotts constitute strategies of dissent only if they enlist large numbers for long enough to have the potential to undermine state power and alter decision makers' calculations.[48] Mass mobilization is not as essential for the use of lethal force because weapons amplify the disruptive capacity that any individual can generate with his or her own person. Due to this "force multiplier," the deployment of arms reduces the need for a sizeable deployment of people.

Second, cohesion is vital for discipline. Command and control is the bulwark against principal-agent problems that undermine effective authority in any organization. Discipline is vital for nonviolent protest, which ceases to be nonviolent when participants attack bystanders or destroy property. Discipline also features prominently in Peter Ackerman and Christopher Kruegler's principles of strategic nonviolent conflict because it reinforces morale, encourages restraint on the part of the opponent, and gives a protest campaign credibility, stature, and power.[49] Discipline is not as essential for violent protest. Certainly, lack of restraint can undermine the efficacy of armed insurgencies. Unruly behavior can impair operational effectiveness, alienate would-be supporters, or squander limited resources. Yet it need not undermine the occurrence of armed protest. Even without discipline, protestors can mobilize violent means and sustain them.

Finally, cohesion improves a movement's ability to devise and implement coherent strategy. Without leadership, institutions, and collective purpose, it is difficult for a movement to act logically and consistently toward a collective objective. Such strategic coherence is vital for motivating participation in nonviolent protest and for that participation to be sustainable. Large numbers of ordinary people are unlikely to join in civic action unless they believe it will be effective. Due to its mass character, nonviolent protest is rarely able to offer participants incentives other than the promise of public goods. If people sacrifice their time, energy, and perhaps safety to participate in nonviolent protest, therefore, they typically expect it to fulfill their collective aspirations. By contrast, violent protest can persist even when it is not effective at the movement level. Participants in violent insurgencies may be recruited by either particularistic or collective inducements. Furthermore, insurgencies often generate self-sustaining dynamics quite distinct from their ability to deliver the public goods with which they are legitimated. Taking up arms gives participants coercive power to use for a variety of private benefits. Those who fight often develop vested interests in militancy or face disincentives for exiting, regardless of the capacity of that militancy to deliver improvement for the population as a whole. Recruitment on the basis of opportunistic rather than social goods can undermine the effectiveness of violent protest no less than nonviolent protest. However, it can coexist with protracted violence in ways that are nearly impossible with protracted nonviolent action.

Mass mobilization, discipline, and strategic coherence are beneficial for the success of either violent or nonviolent protest. Nonetheless, they are requisite for the very *occurrence* of most forms of nonviolent protest in ways that they are not for violent protest. All three of these features are facilitated by movement cohesion. Internal cooperation helps a movement rally extensive and cross-cutting recruitment, manage it, and sustain it in the face of obstacles and repression. It also enables the design and execution of a sound plan of action. By contrast, a fragmented movement will face problems in organizing, directing, and disciplining its members. When a movement lacks command and control, it will be unable to craft tactics with a reasonable expectation of convincing its opponent to make concessions.

The history of nonviolent resistance movements illustrates the critical role of cohesion. In its 1930–1931 nonviolent campaign, the Indian independence movement gained cohesion from institutions, leadership, and a sense of collective purpose. The National Congress Party helped enable and discipline nationwide participation by introducing an institutional element into a previously diffuse effort. Its nearly all-India framework encompassed a large stretch of political life and gave it the stability and authority to act akin to an alternative government. In addition, Mahatma Gandhi led the creation of a structure for decentralized participation. Within this framework, villages took part in resistance by engaging in self-governance. Gandhi's charisma and skill contributed to building a political coalition and inspiring millions to follow the goal that he articulated. Although inter-elite and interreligious tensions were never absent, large stretches of the country exhibited strong commitment to the goal of independence. This sense of collective purpose across cleavages was crucial for a campaign of broad-based civil disobedience and noncooperation.

The American civil rights movement from the mid-1950s to mid-1960s offers additional corroboration. The backbone of the movement's cohesive organizational structure was networks of black churches.[50] These networks nourished lines of communication and coordination within which leaders framed their collective purpose and planned and implemented tactics of direct action and civil disobedience. The link between organization and nonviolence came to the fore when activists in Montgomery formed an association to coordinate a yearlong boycott of segregated busses. From this, the Southern Christian Leadership Conference emerged as a formal vehicle to promote the Montgomery model throughout the South. Conference President Martin Luther King, Jr. offered leadership to the civil rights movement at large. Invigorating his ability to inspire mass participation was the moral resonance of his framing of the movement's collective purpose. With this organizational and leadership base, the movement's nonviolent campaign expanded geographically and innovated tactically from boycotts to sit-ins, freedom rides, mass marches, and community campaigns.[51] Strategic differences and competitive dynamics grew among the movement's various subgroups over time. In its early phase, however, a cohesive organizational structure was the essential foundation for nonviolent protest, as well as the peaceable discipline with which protestors gave themselves up for arrest by the thousands.

Similar patterns are apparent in nonviolent mobilization in East Timor.[52] The National Council of Timorese Resistance served as a nonpartisan umbrella organization that brought together formerly warring factions and maximized country-wide coordination. Wielding a legitimate claim to represent all East Timorese, Xanana Gusmao offered effective leadership by articulating a clear objective and maintaining close relationships with the grass roots. These elements, together with sweeping popular support for the goal of ending the Indonesian occupation, made possible the nonviolent independence campaign of 1988–1999.

Finally, institutions, leadership, and collective purpose coalesced to aid nonviolent protest among ethnic Albanians in Kosovo, particularly from 1988 to 1989. A measure of institutionalization emerged in the centralized Democratic League of Kosovo, which used preexisting networks to enlist mass membership and establish a province-wide bureaucracy. It also enabled disengagement from the state through a system of autonomous political, health, and educational institutions. Ibrahim Rugova gave this encompassing framework a clear leader and diplomatic representative. With the popular goal of reinstating their constitutionally guaranteed autonomy, Kosovar Albanians participated in such nonviolent protest activities as general strikes, mass marches, political funerals, and symbolic lighting of candles and honking of horns.[53]

Movement cohesion approximates a necessary condition for nonviolent protest, *not* a sufficient one. A cohesive movement may make war as well as peaceable protest, as the Vietnamese liberation, Tamil separatist, and other movements have shown. A movement is highly unlikely to undertake nonviolent protest on any broad scale, however, unless it is cohesive. Observing movements that use arms when unarmed methods might be more effective or compatible with international norms, many commentators are quick to blame ideological fanaticism or militants' pursuit of particularistic benefits. Too often ignored is how a movement's own organizational structure makes unarmed methods improbable.

2. Fragmentation Increases the Likelihood of Violent Protest

Fragmentation in a movement's organizational structure not only decreases the possibility that it can use nonviolent protest. It also gives rise to dynamics that increase the chances that the movement will engage in violent protest. These dynamics are described here in turn.

Fragmentation Generates Motivations for the Use of Force Apart from Collective Goals

To the degree that a movement is divided into contending actors or factions, it is not uncommon for internal rivals to compete against each other by radicalizing protest against the movement's external adversary. Within a movement, elites and aspirants may find that violence is useful for winning public support and securing a reputation for superior nationalist commitment. It is thereby a tool in their effort to outflank others in the contest for political power or limited resources.

Fragmentation is the organizational structure in which intra-group competition spurs violent protest. Illustrations abound. In Italy and Germany, the aspirant "New Left" adopted more militant strategies in attempt to distinguish itself from its "Old Left" predecessors.[54] In the throes of the 1979 Iranian revolution, radical students seized American hostages at least in part to assert their primacy over other forces within the movement that overthrew the shah.[55] In the conflicts that ravaged Yugoslavia, Rwanda, Sri Lanka, and Sudan in the later decades of the 20th century, power struggles internal to one national community were an important factor that induced "ethnic entrepreneurs" to spur violence against another community.[56] In some cases, these dynamics mirror familiar models of ethnic outbidding. What is new in my treatment of this phenomenon is a focus on the organizational structure within which such processes become more or less probable or intense. Factional competition does not always result in outbidding. It is when competition is unleashed from an authoritative vision or decision-making procedures that internal battles are prone to escalate violence against an external foe.

In addition, movement fragmentation generates incentives for violence that cannot be reduced to outbidding. Movement members may turn to militancy not to "up the ante" against the state as much as transfer internal contestation from realms in which they lack resources to realms in which they enjoy comparative advantage. Those who possess the ability and will to take up arms may militarize protest to launch themselves to the forefront of their communities. In this case, insurgents using violence are not extremists advancing uncompromising goals. They are parties taking advantage of their military capacities in order to shift the modalities of domestic competition in their favor and thereby leave less militarily capable rivals behind. Those rivalries might stem from intergenerational tensions, socioeconomic gaps, personal rivalries, or other cleavages unrelated to the "master cleavage" of the broader conflict.

Evidence of this dynamic can be found in Iraq after 2004. An important impetus for the antioccupation activity of cleric Muqtada al-Sadr was the resentment of relatively impoverished Shi'a toward the traditional Shi'i elite. When that elite allied with the United States, taking up arms against Coalition forces gave disenfranchised Shi'a a source of counterinfluence in the struggle for power within the Shi'i community.[57] Sadr did not embrace militancy with the aim of outstripping others in the race to claim responsibility for attacks. Rather, his aim was to distinguish himself as an alternative representative of his co-religionists. Violent protest offered a vehicle for doing so.

Fragmentation Weakens Constraints on Escalation

A movement's organizational structure mediates members' motivations for carrying out violence. It also influences their opportunities to act on those motivations. To the degree that movement cohesion integrates decision making, it circumscribes individuals' capacities to diverge from collective to private objectives. These private motives might include an instrumental interest in exploiting conflict for power or material gain. They might also entail noninstrumental impulses to act on anger, vengeance, obligations of social solidarity, kinship feuds, personal animosities, the desire to assert personal dignity, or a yearning for prestige. No movement can eliminate members' particularistic goals. However, a cohesive movement can subject members' behavior to the constraints of leadership, institutions, and an overriding sense of collective purpose. A fragmented movement lacks authoritative means to set parameters on when, where, and against whom violence can be used. Fragmentation invites a slippery slope from a situation in which a consensus strategy governs collective behavior to one in which multiple strategies compete. It can eventually generate conditions in which acts carried out in the name of collective goals reflect only the ends of those who commit them.

Fragmentation Divides a Movement into Smaller Subgroups That Are Well Situated to Sustain Radical Agendas

Intra-party battles may be as explosive as inter-party battles in any political system, and these battles carry some possibility that a single group will split into two or more. This possibility is particularly strong in the fluid context of statelessness, however, because members face fewer institutional barriers to establishing splinter groups. They need not register a new political party with an official agency or win elections to claim legitimate leadership. As the annals of self-determination struggles have shown, dissidents can simply declare themselves to constitute a new organization. While the possibility of splintering always exists, it is less likely in movements with a cohesive organizational structure. Strong leadership, institutions, and collective purpose can generate social and political incentives for cooperation among adherents even when they disagree on particular issues. Otherwise, any dispute invites factions to splinter.

These relationships are pertinent to protest because splinter groups are well suited for violence. They tend to be small, which enables them to maintain radical agendas that large, inclusive organizations cannot. In competitive settings, the more a group seeks to appeal to a large range of constituents, the more it downplays ideological specificity and becomes a "catchall party."[58] By contrast, the more narrow a group, the more militant it can afford to be. Hence, regardless of goals or ideology, the very organizational character of a splinter group prepares it to be an agent of political violence. These patterns come to the fore during peace processes. A movement leadership's entry into talks with a former adversary nearly always entails some compromise on rhetoric or goals. Leaders who manage fragmentation can forestall breakaway groups from carrying out violence against negotiations. Those who cannot may find their strategy at the mercy of spoilers.

Movement fragmentation generates structural circumstances conducive to splinter groups as well as impetuses to internal competition. It can also give rise to a new political formation: the "semi-splinter group." When mainstream leaders seek broad-based popular support, they have incentives to avoid controversial stances. This is especially pressing if they aspire to recognition from external forces. Nonetheless, leaders will have difficulty reining in militancy if radical members within their ranks have the organizational space to make demands freely. If mainstream leaders openly endorse extremist strategies, they risk losing the general appeal that comes from a middle-of-the-road stance. In addition, they might invite retaliation, jeopardize support from more conservative patrons, or doom a quest for international legitimacy. If leaders ignore more radical constituents, however, they risk watching a dissatisfied faction leave to join a rival party or create an independent entity.

As a compromise solution, leaders may decide to turn a blind eye to the creation of a semi-splinter group. It will thus allow their radical cadres to form their own grouping and claim responsibility for their actions with a distinct name. These individuals will not sever their affiliation with the original organization, which may grant it tacit approval and covert financial support, even as it disavows any connection. The creation of a semi-splinter group is instrumentally rational. For the parent group, it provides a safety valve for restive members without discrediting the movement's moderate image. For militant cadres, it offers both freedom of action and funding, while saving them the start-up costs of establishing a completely autonomous organization. The establishment of a semi-splinter group therefore offers a comfortable middle ground when cadres' attempt to change their group's strategy through "voice" comes to no avail, yet they do not wish to pay the price of full "exit."[59]

In principle, a semi-splinter group is a convenient resolution to a political predicament. In practice, it is risky. Born from an organizational structure of weak command and control, the semi-splinter is prone to take on a life of its own. Targets of the semi-splinter's attacks will seek to uncover and punish those responsible, and their pursuit might lead them to the parent organization. This may induce that organization to calculate that the costs of the semi-splinter outweigh its benefits. It might then act to cut off support. Until it does so, however, the semi-splinter is a powerful agent of violence. An organizational formation facilitated by fragmentation, it has the motivations of a small, ideologically united faction, yet can call upon the resources of a much larger and more established organization.

Fragmentation Impedes Attempts to End Hostilities

Another way that organizational fragmentation mediates a movement's use of violence is by hindering efforts to terminate that violence. Lewis Coser argues that it is only when conflict is interest-driven or "realistic," as opposed to psychologically driven and "nonrealistic," that groups are able to calculate that they benefit more by ending violence than by continuing it. Yet not all movements are equally capable of making and enforcing those calculations. A movement must have a minimally cohesive organizational structure if it is to define and pursue political goals, recognize when they are achieved, and adjust its behavior accordingly. Coser explains:

> Since the aim of realistic conflict is to attain specific results, it follows that the contenders have no interest in pursuing it once such results have been attained. Centralization of the internal structure of each contending party assures that once these results are reached, peace can be concluded and maintained.[60]

A centralized internal structure is a necessary condition for a movement's pursuit of collective "specific results," as opposed to members' contradictory aims. Along similar lines, a movement must be cohesive if it is to determine that prospects for achieving those results render circumstances opportune for a transition from conflict to conflict resolution. It must also exercise command and control if it is to prevent members from engaging in hostilities. As such, a movement's organizational structure shapes its ability to make the credible commitments upon which initiatives such as ceasefires or settlements depend. Only when a movement is cohesive does it have the authoritative leadership to make binding decisions, a minimum of popular consensus to legitimize these decisions, and institutional mechanisms to ensure that members conform to collectively agreed-upon terms.

The role of organizational structure in mediating a movement's termination of violent conflict is critical during peace processes. Of the 38 peace accords signed between 1988 and 1998, 31 failed to last more than three years.[61] In those cases in which negotiations resulted in an enduring settlement, the conjunction of leadership, institutions, and collective purpose helped to prevent opposition factions from disrupting them. The greater the proliferation of interests and dispersion of operational capabilities in a movement, the less likely it is to find an arrangement that will convince all actors to put down their weapons. Fragmentation is a situation in which movement members possess multiple purposes and the autonomy to act on them. As an organizational structure of manifold veto points, it invites the unilateral action of those who believe that an agreement will undermine their interests. Hence, it may be difficult for a fragmented movement to terminate its use of violence through processes other than its physical defeat. At the same time, fragmentation can hamper an external adversary who seeks victory on the battlefield because it leaves the movement without a single military "backbone" to break. Even if a state succeeds in repressing such a movement to the point that it can impose a settlement, this fragmentation will undermine stability once the guns go silent. Like putting Humpty-Dumpty back together, it will be arduous to reconstitute a shattered self-determination struggle into a viable society, economy, and political order.

These arguments challenge commonplace assumptions about international bargaining.[62] In Robert Putnam's model of two-level games, politicians involved in inter-state negotiations derive leverage from fragmentation within their own political systems. Facing diverse preferences at home, they demand a more favorable agreement on the claim that otherwise they will not obtain the requisite approval from domestic political bodies.[63] Scholars invoke this logic in cases ranging from trade to war, but few have examined the circumstances under which it does or does not obtain. The organizational mediation theory of protest suggests why fragmentation in one's own camp is not necessarily advantageous. When a movement lacks command and control, leaders are unable to follow through with an agreement. Bargaining is thus not simply a situation in which one party signals its preferences and another responds.

The central problem is not information and balance of power, but implementation. Organizational fragmentation makes dynamics of international bargaining akin to those of labor management. For unions bargaining with employers, internal cohesion is vital because the viability of an agreement depends on the ability to deliver compliance. Standard models of inter-state bargaining falter to the extent that each actor involved in negotiations is a composite of sub-actors. Organizational structure mediates the ability of parties, and particularly nonstate parties, to behave in ways assumed by rational choice theory.

Fragmentation Invites Outside Interference, Which Can Encourage More Fragmentation and Violence

Lacking control over their own territory or domestic economy, self-determination movements frequently seek political, economic, or military assistance from states. In turn, these states attempt to influence movements to their own benefit. Though any nonstate actor is vulnerable to interference, the more cohesive it is, the more impenetrable its internal decision-making processes and political–strategic position will be. The more fragmented, the more outside actors will be able to manipulate persons or factions within the movement to act as their proxies. Just as fragmentation creates opportunities for outside interference, so does interference aggravate fragmentation. External patronage can give opposition factions the resources to act independently of the official leadership or institutional framework. It thus undermines command and control, adding new interests to those already dividing a movement's ranks.

External intervention, as opposed to external solidarity, rarely aids nonviolent protest. Yet the historical record shows that it often increases incentives and resources for militarism that would otherwise be weaker. The cracks in the Kashmiri separatist movement after 1989 invited state patrons to intervene and fund insurgency according to their own interests. A loose and divided organizational structure also gave wide latitude to foreign fighters to form their own factions within the Kashmiri struggle. Fragmentation therefore enabled intervention, which in turn increased fragmentation. The result was a separatist movement encompassing strands with distinct programs and ideologies.

Adding further complexity, external patrons are often divided themselves. Their rivalries can prompt them to intervene in a movement in ways that further fragment its organizational structure and impel engagement in violent conflict. The rivalry between China and the Soviet Union precipitated or aggravated splits in national liberation struggles throughout Africa.[64] During more than a century of conflict in Lebanon, sectarian discord invited rival states to ally with one or another religious–political movement. Antagonism among external patrons compounded antagonism among and within sectarian groups. This intensified their use of violent, as opposed to political or nonviolent, means to advance their interests. At times, this situation even rendered Lebanon a proxy field for regional or international wars.[65] Interstate competition also aggravated the rivalry between Iraq's two main Kurdish parties. Syria, Iran, and Turkey competed in offering military and financial support to each party, driving intra-Kurdish competition to bloodshed at various junctures after the mid-1970s.[66] The Afghan resistance against the Soviet Union during the 1980s saw the *mujahedeen* divided along ethnolinguistic and tribal cleavages, as well as between leaders based inside and outside of Afghanistan. The United States, Pakistan, Iran, and Saudi Arabia seized upon and fueled this fragmentation. In the process, they channeled patronage that buttressed the resistance.[67] In these and other cases, fragmentation enabled outside interference, which in turn contributed to both more fragmentation and to violence.

Fragmentation Motivates Violence with the Aim of Surmounting Fragmentation Itself

Both students and practitioners of guerrilla warfare have argued that unity is one of the greatest assets for any movement seeking to challenge a state.[68] Yet, given all the fragmenting dynamics discussed thus far, unity is difficult to achieve. The task of forging a cohesive front is hence the heart of what Lichbach calls the "rebel's dilemma."[69] Some leaders who face this dilemma have turned to violence against an external enemy in the expectation that this would stitch together divisions within their own population. When diminishing resources and ideological disputes undermined the organizational structure of opposition movements in Europe in the 1960s and 1970s, for example, some groups embraced militancy as the only remaining unifying principle.[70] Many anticolonial struggles exhibited similar patterns. As Frantz Fanon famously asserted, violence offers the "cement and blood" bringing a colonized people together in the struggle for national liberation:

> The practice of violence binds the [the colonized people] together as a whole, since each individual forms a violent link in the great chain.... The armed struggle mobilizes the people; that is to say, it throws them in one way and in one direction.... Violence is in action all inclusive and national. It follows that it is closely involved in the liquidation of regionalism and tribalism.... Their destruction is the preliminary to the unification of the people.[71]

Paradoxically, fragmentation in a self-determination movement can thus impel members to use violence in the hope of eliminating fragmentation itself.

SOURCES AND MANAGEMENT OF FRAGMENTATION

Although this book focuses on the effect of a movement's organizational structure, it is also valuable to consider its sources. Causes of cohesion or fragmentation lie both internal and external to the movement. Internally, divisions stem from the basic competition for limited resources under conditions of uncertainty. They are also fueled by differences of opinion or ideology, personal rivalries, opportunism, physical dislocations, and/or socioeconomic disparities. In addition, divisions are influenced by the social structure of the national community in question. Broadly speaking, factors associated with national integration, such as education, urbanization, and mass media, can encourage cohesion. They do so by facilitating compatible value orientations, correspondence in communication codes and culture, and a dense web of social and economic transactions.[72]

Nonetheless, informal understandings and expectations do not create movement unity in the absence of leadership, institutions, and collective purpose. In the Palestinian case, generations have been bound together by a shared sense of place, history, culture, language, and commitment to the cause of national liberation. Yet this sense of constituting a collective does not alone coordinate collective action. That political factions have appealed to the public with similar slogans and symbols has not rendered them any more or less prone to cooperate in the pursuit of the goals that they all venerate. Indeed, whereas Palestinians' core national identity has arguably strengthened over time, their political cohesion or fragmentation has experienced both ups and downs. It is this organizational structure of the Palestinian struggle as a movement, not the collective consciousness of Palestinians as a people, that has mediated forms of protest.

Other sources of fragmentation come from outside a movement. A movement's cohesion is not immune to the cumulative strain of successive setbacks, an intransigent adversary, or unhelpful stances on the part of international parties. Protracted conflict generates new grievances and demands that can destabilize the relationships that make up a movement's political order. It can unsettle authority structures, collapse coordinating frameworks, and embolden once-contained hardline groups. This shake-up of domestic forces may precipitate splintering within political groups and heighten competition among them. Furthering these trends, states sometimes deliberately provoke or exacerbate divisions in a movement challenger in the hope of defeating it. Nevertheless, conflict and repression will not provoke divisions in all movements equally. Movements that possess leadership, institutions, and collective purpose before the onset of repression will be better positioned to retain their cohesion in the face of repression's fragmenting effects.

To facilitate theorizing in this regard, concepts from the natural sciences are again useful. Chemists study how different materials respond when subjected to the same external force. Some materials, such as rubber, are "resilient" because they resist or recover from the impact of outside shocks. Other materials, such as glass, are "brittle" because they tend to fracture under stress. Resilience and brittleness are preexisting characteristics of the internal composition of the material, but it is external pressure that brings them to the fore. This distinction offers a useful metaphor for the organizational mediation theory of protest. A movement's degree of preexisting cohesion is one factor that determines whether it will be resilient or brittle in the face of external pressures. The more cohesive the movement, the greater will be its ability to bend like rubber in the face of repression, and thereby preserve its organizational structure and strategy. The more fragmented the movement, the more repression will cause it to shatter like glass.

This argument reveals the limits of the truism that fighting with an out-group triggers solidarity within an in-group or that people "rally around the flag" in times of war.[73] Rather than assuming that conventional wisdom, research should probe how a group's organizational structure conditions the effect of external conflict on a movement's internal political dynamics. This logic echoes Coser's insight that external conflict tends to unite a group, yet whether it also results in *centralization* depends on both the nature of the conflict and the group's preexisting degree of consensus.[74] A cohesive organizational structure gives a movement resilience in the face of external pressure. When leaders are arrested or killed, institutions can provide procedures for replacing and regenerating them. At the same time, when a movement's institutions are disrupted, a legitimate leadership can guide people to act in concert. Similarly, when the hardships of a protest campaign accumulate or opportunities expand for the pursuit of particularistic rather than public gains, a strong sense of collective purpose creates pressure for continued commitment to shared goals. Nevertheless, even those movements with robust organizational structures may find it difficult to avert the fragmenting effects of repression as they mount. It is due to the toll of repression upon organizational structure that a movement's degree of fragmentation can be considered to be *embedded* in conflict processes.

In states, fixed electoral rules and governmental structures can make cohesion or fragmentation relatively constant. In nonstate entities engaged in conflict, they tend to emerge or subside in dynamic processes of interdependent decision making. The forces that divide movements are many, and authoritative leadership, institutions, and collective purpose can be difficult to attain. In many movements, therefore, leaders engage in an ongoing struggle against the susceptibility to splits within their ranks. This can be thought of as the *management of fragmentation*. Leaders employ a variety of resources and strategies to that end. They can use personal charisma to rally people behind them or distribute or withhold resources in ways that induce people's allegiance. They can also enact decision-making rules that they anticipate will generate policies that bind the movement as a whole. When other tactics fail, they can try to impose cohesion by threatening or removing dissidents by force. Strategies pursued to manage fragmentation at one point in time carry important, and often unintended, consequences for later eras. As a framework for analyzing these patterns, the organizational mediation theory of protest highlights the role of both path dependence and contingent decisions in shaping a movement's organizational structure. For many self-determination movements, the struggles for internal unity and national liberation are intertwined. The course of each can create enduring legacies, which also have an impact on protest.

The Palestinian movement offers generalizable insight about the sources of movement fragmentation and the consequences of different strategies for managing it. In addition, Palestinians have grappled with a realm of fragmentation that is more unique to their situation. Since the inception of its conflict with Zionism, the Palestinian national movement has been shaped by its complex interconnections with Arab states. In the words of Palestine Liberation Organization (PLO) leader Nayef Hawatmeh, "The historical and fateful link between the Palestinian question and the conflicts occurring in the rest of the Arab world ... distinguishes the Palestine question from any other cause of emancipation or national liberation."[75] The relations between the Palestinian movement and Arab governments have become even more entangled by their overlap with the multiplicity of interests among Palestinians themselves. The chapters that follow show the interpenetration between Palestinians and Arab countries to be a recurrent factor in Palestinians' struggle to build a cohesive organizational structure, on the one hand, and their strategies of protest, on the other.

METHODS AND IMPLICATIONS

The following chapters evaluate these general arguments in the case of the Palestinian national movement. As detailed in the preface, the empirical analysis relies on a range of evidence, including archival materials, government documents, memoirs, newspapers, survey data, and dozens of interviews conducted during years of fieldwork in the West Bank, Gaza Strip, and Israel. When appropriate, I incorporate quantitative data to show patterns or invoke counterfactual reasoning to illustrate how a different organizational structure might have mediated different protest outcomes.[76] My main research methodology is process tracing. I carry out the qualitative analysis of events, contexts, and actors to identify the steps through which various levels of cohesion, as well as different strategies for managing fragmentation, affect the character of protest. This technique reconstructs the constellation of factors and conditions in which movement member's decision making took place.[77] The focus of this analysis is causal mechanisms in Tilly's sense of classes of events that alter relations among elements in similar ways across situations.[78] If the organizational mediation theory of protest is valid, process tracing should demonstrate the causal relationships posited in this chapter. When I observe strategies of nonviolent protest, I should be able to trace this outcome back to the capacity for coordination and restraint generated by a movement's leadership, institutions, and sense of collective purpose. When I observe that a movement lacks such cohesion, I should be able to trace forward to see not only that it does not undertake mass-based nonviolent protest, but also that the very absence of effective command and control increases incentives and opportunities for violent protest.

In-depth examination of a single movement over the *longue durée* is a fruitful research design for evaluating these claims. Analysis of within-case variation is a powerful tool of causal inference that can avert some of the problems of statistical testing.[79] Moreover, the particular structure of this study makes it possible to analyze different types of within-case variation. It encompasses John Gerring's three kinds of case studies. As the unit under study is the

Palestinian national movement, the project as a whole constitutes "observation of a single unit through time." In addition, individual chapters offer a basis for "analysis of within-unit variance at a given point of time," and the juxtaposition of chapters provides a basis for "analysis of within-unit variance over time."[80] These multiple kinds of variation provide many observations while controlling for basic parameters whose divergence can undermine conclusions drawn from cross-national tests. Scrutiny of these data offers a basis for comparing the organizational mediation theory of protest with rival approaches. It also suggests its applicability to other movements. The Palestinian movement is a sound focus for this study because it meets several of Stephen Van Evera's criteria for case selection. It offers data richness, within-case variance, and extreme values on the independent and dependent variables.[81] Furthermore, it holds "intrinsic importance" and "resembles conditions of current policy problems." Indeed, violence in the Israeli–Palestinian conflict *is* one of the world's main policy problems, and it has been for decades.

An organizational mediation theory of protest in the Palestinian case stands to make four broad contributions to scholarship on conflict and contentious politics. First, it critiques the tendency to treat self-determination movements as if they were unitary actors. Observers often refer to *the* Kurds, Tibetans, or Basques, and assume their collective behavior to be a coherent entity's pursuit of clear goals. This assumption is rarely declared and defended, yet it is implicit in many works. Conceptually, it is the context in which scholars identify causal variables that act upon movements rather than probe how variables filter through different internal structures. Methodologically, it is the grounds on which scholars use movements as the straightforward unit of analysis in cross-national statistical tests. Analytically, it is the basis for much theory building influenced by neorealist approaches to international relations. These often neglect domestic politics by instead focusing on balance of power, asymmetry of information, and signaling. The assumption that states and nonstate actors behave as if they were coherent entities is appealing because it simplifies a complex world into variables that can be elegantly modeled. Yet it discounts the ways in which a movement's difficulty in achieving unity is itself a factor that shapes how it behaves. It thus obscures important political processes and risks producing erroneous explanations of strategic action.

Second, this book shifts scholarly attention from the preferences of political actors to the ways in which they organize. The organizational mediation theory of protest challenges the attribution of political violence to culture, emotions, select incentives, or stark utility without consideration of the domestic political relationships from which such violence emerges. In a nonstate setting no less than in a state, frameworks of cooperation or competition systematically shape what people do. The emphasis on organizational structure addresses the issue of potential endogeneity in the relationship between fragmentation and protest violence. It might be said that fragmentation does not increase violence; rather, movements fragment precisely because members differ in their preferences with respect to violence. While this criticism is important, it mistakenly ignores structure and context. Fragmentation is not the automatic result of differences of opinion. It is the absence of the leadership, institutions, or overriding collective purpose that helps people to adjudicate their differences and submit to a compromise plan of action. Furthermore, fragmentation often precedes violence temporally. It also precedes it analytically, driving its escalation and continuation through causal mechanisms specified in this chapter.

Third, this book treats variation in the forms of protest as a question in its own right and thereby draws connections across standard fields of scholarship. Some charge that social scientists ignore the topic of unarmed protest, leaving everyday discourse either to dismiss it as ineffective or romanticize it as a panacea.[82] When nonviolence is studied, it is usually situated in an academic literature on social movements. The study of armed activity, by contrast, is situated in a different literature on conflict. These conventional divisions are both empirically and theoretically suspect. As Tilly argues, violence and non-violence represent a single set of political behaviors to be explained.[83] In James DeNardo's words, "Accounts of radical activity that focus exclusively on one kind of strategy or another are inherently too narrow in focus. Neither mass political violence, nor terrorism, nor peaceful protest, nor nonviolent resistance can be explained in vacuo."[84] The organizational mediation theory of protest offers an approach that examines both violent and nonviolent protest under the rubric of a single framework.

Finally, this research contributes to the growing trend that problematizes the link between conflict in general and violence in particular. As Rogers Brubaker and David Laitin write, violence "should not be treated as a natural, self-explanatory outgrowth of ... conflict, something that occurs automatically when the conflict reaches a certain intensity."[85] Stathis Kalyvas has applied this insight by analytically decoupling the phenomenon of violence in civil war from that of civil war itself.[86] This book likewise decouples the existence of a self-determination conflict from the violent or nonviolent strategies that a self-determination movement employs. Yet it also pushes this distinction further. Just as violence is not simply a result of a high intensity of conflict, so nonviolent protest is not simply the product of a low intensity. It is not the case that groups use nonviolent protest until conflict becomes so heated or intractable that their anger or strategic calculations mechanically drive them to violence. Anger or utility may lead to violence, but the lack thereof does not necessarily lead to nonviolent protest. This is the case because violent and nonviolent protest have different organizational requirements. A movement's organizational structure thus fundamentally mediates the protest strategies that it is able or likely to employ.

It is worth emphasizing the contributions that this book does *not* seek to make. Its objective is neither to predict the success of violent or nonviolent protest nor to judge the morality of their use. Furthermore, it does not aim to elucidate the fact of collective action, meaning why people incur private costs or risks to attain public goods, as much as the form that collective action takes. In addition, this book's already extensive scope has set certain limits on its empirical analysis. For the period after 1948, I focus on the Palestinian struggle for statehood and do not discuss the activity of Palestinian citizens of Israel within that state. For the period after 1987, I concentrate on the national movement based in the West Bank and Gaza Strip, although with the awareness that the majority of Palestinians live outside those areas. Finally, while I examine fragmentation and violence in the Palestinian movement, I do not underestimate the existence of either fragmentation or violence on the Israeli side of the conflict. Both are important topics treated elsewhere. This book can, however, aid analysis of the interaction between fragmentation among Palestinians and fragmentation among Israelis. In both nations, the organizational structure of politics has allowed hardline groups to form, act with a measure of autonomy, and exercise political influence beyond their numbers. In both nations, the official political leadership frequently faces restless minority political opinions and does not always wield complete control over the use of armed force. Political actors on each side of the Israeli–Palestinian divide follow internal debates and power struggles on the other side and strategize about how to use them to their own advantage. Those with maximalist goals may carry out actions in the expectation of stoking their adversary's divisions in ways that obstruct the path to peace. Although this book does not explore these empirical threads in detail, it offers an analytical launching pad for those who wish to do so.

In what follows, Chapters 2 through 6 demonstrate the organizational mediation theory of protest by examining five successive eras of Palestinian history. Chapter 7 suggests the broader generalizability of the argument by applying it to the cases of the South African antiapartheid struggle and the Northern Ireland republican movement. Chapter 8 concludes by discussing the empirical and analytic implications of the research. It argues that the resolution of conflicts involving nonstate groups may be assisted by efforts that aid their building of internal cohesion, or at least by reconsideration of policies that obstruct such cohesion. A peace accord with a fragmented movement has a slim chance of success. Counterinsurgency based on divide and conquer can be counterproductive. By fueling divisions in a rebel movement, the state may succeed in carving the movement into more manageable units. In feeding fragmentation, however, it will encourage the movement's use of violence and contribute to precluding its use of nonviolent protest.

2

National Struggle under the British Mandate, 1918–1948

Some have said that there was no Palestinian people before 1948, or even 1967. Under the Ottoman Empire, the land between the Mediterranean Sea and the Jordan River spanned a number of administrative districts. Yet while there was no political unit called Palestine, the term had ancient roots. Writings of the people of the region testify to the sense that they held a unique place within the Arab world.[1] Commercial, social, and cultural relations linked them to the rest of Greater Syria. Ethnic identity created feelings of an inextricable bond to other Arabic-speaking countries. A commitment to Islam fortified most people's political allegiance to the Ottoman state. A minority in Ottoman Syria came to support Arab independence against the Young Turks' imposition of Turkish nationalism. In the void created by the collapse of the Ottoman Empire in 1918, the call for an independent Greater Syria became the dominant ideology. Nevertheless, European powers carved Arab lands into nation-states at the end of World War I and placed them under colonial trusteeships called "Mandates." In each country, people formed movements to fight for national independence.

The Palestinian national movement was the local manifestation of this Arab nationalist awakening. Its trajectory, however, was set apart due to its confrontation with another people's claims to the same land. The Zionist movement, gaining strength after Theodor Herzl's publication of *The Jewish State*, came to focus on the ancient Kingdom of Israel as the home for a modern Jewish state. On the eve of the first wave of Zionist-inspired immigration in 1882, the traditional, religious Jewish community in Palestine numbered about 24,000, or 5 percent of the population of 500,000. By the conclusion of the second wave in 1914, their number had grown to 85,000.[2] Though most Arabs were unaffected by this development, some peasants and urban merchants felt their interests threatened. This led to written protestations against Jewish immigration and land purchases, and even a few violent clashes, as early as the 1880s and 1890s.[3] Opposition to Zionism became more political and profuse with the lifting of press censorship in 1908. Newspapers warned that Zionism would render Arabs strangers in the land that they considered to be their patrimony.

Palestine's Arabs increasingly referred to themselves as "Palestinians" in that context.[4] Feelings of alarm regarding Zionism intensified in 1917, when the Balfour Declaration announced that the British government "view with favor the establishment in Palestine of a national home for the Jewish people and will use their best endeavors to facilitate the achievement of this object, it being clearly understood that nothing shall be done which may prejudice the civil and religious rights of existing non-Jewish communities in Palestine." For the approximately 90 percent of the population that was Muslim or Christian Arab, this policy not only prejudiced their civil and religious rights. It also precluded their own political right to a national home.

What ensued would become a struggle for self-determination. Following Britain's military occupation of Palestine in 1917, Palestinians' immediate objective was to undo the Balfour Declaration. Once Britain received a Mandate over Palestine in 1920, their focus turned to convincing the colonial power to abandon the commitment to a Jewish national home that was codified in the Mandate's terms. After the Mandate government came into full force in 1923, Arab leaders acted less on the expectation of defeating British policy than on the hope of diminishing its harm. Their goal became more ambitious as other Arab countries made progress toward attaining autonomy or independence. By the 1930s, they increasingly set their sights on gaining control of the Mandatory state.

Palestinians' strategies of protest evolved as did these objectives. They began with political entreaties and intensified to demonstrations, strikes, and ultimately armed rebellion. Leading scholars have not typically problematized these tactical shifts. They agree that Palestinians initially adopted moderate tactics and became more militant as those failed to bear fruit. Anne Mosley Lesch writes, "The national movement that began with petitions and selective noncooperation in the early 1920s had led, as its demands were blocked and its aspirations thwarted, to a bitter revolt in the late 1930s."[5] Yehoshua Porath agrees: "The atmosphere of tension and resentment ... was the foundation from which the idea gradually evolved that in order to preserve the Arab character of Palestine ... the Arabs had to resort to violence."[6] Palestinian writers of the era voiced a similar interpretation. "When people are in despair they ... use whatever weapon they can against very much more powerful forces," Aziz Shehadeh wrote in 1936.[7]

These commentaries are sound, but they tell only part of the story. They highlight motivations for protest yet overlook the mechanics through which that protest took different forms over time. The organizational mediation theory of protest offers a framework for an alternative analysis. It calls attention to the structure of Palestinians' national struggle and demonstrates how weak internal authority and discipline shaped their conflict behavior. This chapter explores these relationships in five sections. The first section examines the early years of British rule, when a basic level of cooperation among traditional Palestinian elites facilitated their preferred strategy of nonviolent protest and diplomacy. The second section evaluates how elite factionalism, against a backdrop of socioeconomic changes and Zionist expansion, hampered both the organization of nonviolent protest and the forestalling of violent riots in 1929. The third section examines how the development of political organizations provided a structure for rallying politicized opinion and pressuring traditional leaders to temper their rivalries. Those means of containing fragmentation aided a general strike in 1936. Its breakdown contributed to unprecedented internal and external violence from 1937 to 1939. The fourth section considers the enduring impact of fragmentation on the events marking the end of the Mandate, and the fifth section concludes the discussion.

FROM OTTOMAN TO BRITISH RULE

The first leaders of the Palestinian national movement were the urban notables who had served as local elites during Ottoman times. Typically hailing from Jerusalem, Nablus, or other large towns, these aristocratic families gained prestige in their communities thanks to tradition, education, property ownership, and positions in governmental or religious institutions.[8] They solidified their influence by serving as intermediaries between the people and the Ottoman state, and extended their social control into the countryside by forming alliances with rural elites. Palestinian notables increased their wealth and power under the Ottoman reforms of the middle to late 19th century. They gained new government posts and new land registration policies allowed them to accumulate more land. In addition, their local influence became indispensable for a new regimen of tax collection. Impoverished peasants increasingly turned to these elites for exorbitant loans, plunging the masses further into destitution and elevating elites' status as patrons.

Although elites lost much of their effective power when the British occupied Palestine, they stood as the default leaders of the Arab population. By 1920 they had taken the lead in forming more than 40 social and political clubs. Many were familial coalitions dominated by a single prestigious clan, yet nearly all were nationalist in upholding the goal of fighting Zionism.[9] In prominent groups such as the Arab Club and the Literary Club, sons of aristocratic families called for the unity of Palestine with Faysal's Arab Kingdom of Syria. Some traveled to Damascus to help make that a reality. Politically ambitious young men, they embraced Arab nationalism as a path to freedom and progress, as a way to forestall the creation of a Jewish national home in Palestine, and perhaps also as a vehicle to obtain their own positions of influence.[10] Many older notables favored Palestinian independence and took a more conciliatory line toward the British, not least because they hoped both would preserve their privilege. The most prominent organization representing that orientation was the Muslim–Christian Association (MCA). In 1919 the MCA brought together 30 delegates from across the country in the first Palestinian Arab Congress. Though disagreements remained, the Congress passed resolutions that called for Palestine, dubbed Southern Syria, to be joined with its

Arab neighbors. Support was unanimous for other resolutions invoking the Wilsonian principle of self-determination and rejecting Zionism.

Debates over pan-Arabism continued until France toppled Faysal's kingdom in 1920. With dreams of Syrian unity collapsed, Palestinian elites came together in Palestine-specific nationalism. The MCA held another Palestinian Arab Congress in which it called for recognition of Palestine as a distinct political entity to be governed by a national government and parliament elected by the Arabic-speaking peoples resident before the war. The Arab Congress declared that the Jewish people held no right to a national home in Palestine, urged a ban on the transfer of lands to Jewish control, and demanded a halt to Jewish immigration. It also proclaimed that Palestinian Arabs' unity took precedence over their other familial, regional, religious, or other loyalties. To represent this unity before the British, delegates elected an Executive Committee of the Palestinian Arab Congress, which became known as the Arab Executive (AE). Musa Kazim al-Husayni, a former Ottoman administrator and mayor of Jerusalem in his 70s, was chosen to be the AE's president. With this, the strata of older, conservative politicians assumed the mantle of the national cause.

The Arab Congress's election of an executive confirmed a measure of leadership, institutions, and collective purpose in the incipient national movement. Leading dignitaries spoke for Palestine with a legitimacy that was a natural extension of their long-standing social status. When colonial authorities expressed doubt that the AE represented the will of the population, organizations such as chambers of commerce and municipalities issued announcements asserting that it did.[11] The AE gained a basic institutional framework by establishing a permanent secretariat in Jerusalem and developing channels of communication and coordination with local MCA branches. This network, as well as links to other clubs and societies, enabled the national movement to reach communities throughout the country and stay abreast of their developments.[12] Three more Palestinian Arab Congresses from 1921 to 1923 brought together a progressively larger number of delegates representing the country's different regions, associations, and religious denominations. Though most members were Muslims, Christians were represented in numbers greater than their approximate 9–12 percent of the total Arab population.[13] Congresses offered regular forums to reaffirm the AE's authority and debate possible responses to the latest political developments. In formally endorsing consensus national platforms, they gave expression to Palestinians' sense of collective purpose.

This rudimentary organizational structure helped leaders carry out their preference for constitutional and nonviolent means of advancing the national cause.[14] During the first years under British rule, nationalist societies presented protest notes and memorandums, convened congresses, delivered speeches, and published articles. They coordinated testimony before the King–Crane commission dispatched by the United States to investigate sentiments in Greater Syria. They also organized delegations to the peace conferences of 1919 and 1920, though the British forbade them to leave Palestine. Upon its formation, the AE continued to submit memos, draft statutes, and petitions. It met with Colonial Secretary Winston Churchill, held repeated conversations with the high commissioner for Palestine, and dispatched three consecutive delegations to meet with members of Parliament and government officers in London. Seeking international support, the AE sent representatives to make the Palestinian case before the Turkish government, the pope, and the League of Nations in Geneva. To mobilize and demonstrate its popular support, it also organized demonstrations, delivered public speeches, publicized its positions in the press, distributed leaflets, and reached out to its constituents in mosques, churches, and cafés. This nonviolent protest was made possible by the AE's basic cohesion. Without an organizational structure to facilitate coordination, political elites would not have reconciled their different opinions enough to agree upon the dispatching of delegations, their composition, or the content of their demands. Petitions and press statements might have communicated disparate messages, and demonstrations might not have rallied people across communities. Movement cohesion not only made possible a nonviolent political strategy, but was also a plank in that strategy. Spokesmen had to show consensus if they were to convince the colonial power that the Arab population was united behind their claims. They had to show command and control if they were to demonstrate that this population constituted a nation that was prepared for self-determination.

Given the context of the times, the young national movement was both cohesive and engaged in nonviolent protest. "A leadership crystallized which was accepted, at least initially, by the entire political public as legitimate," Porath wrote. "Almost the entire public was united around the Executive Committee ... and its parliamentary, legal, and non-violent tactics."[15] Nevertheless, this cohesion, and likewise the nonviolent protest that it mediated, was tentative and weak. The entire political public accepted the AE's legitimacy. However, this public did not include the overwhelming majority of the population, who were illiterate and chronically indebted peasants struggling for subsistence and living, in the words of one British report, "in a state comparable to that of the serfs under the Carolingian dynasty."[16] The population was committed to protecting Arab Palestine. Nonetheless, familial and local loyalties were preeminent in the lives of most Palestinians. The middle class and cross-cutting cleavages remained minimal.

Among urban notables, furthermore strategic and personal tensions continued between older conservatives and younger nationalists. These were compounded by inter-familial rivalries, competition among rural elites, antagonism between urban and rural families, and distrust between clans (*hamulah*s) at the village level. The fact that patron–client ties traditionally connected different urban notable families to different rural *hamulah*s reinforced rifts. Religious heterogeneity and regional differences did likewise.[17] These cleavages led to a proliferation of power centers in society that obstructed the centralization of authority. As Lesch writes, "Each family felt itself to be the equal of the others and therefore found cooperation under the leadership of an individual from any other elite family difficult."[18] Some 50 years later, a leader of the PLO would use similar words to describe fragmentation in the resistance movement: "Each organization regarded itself as superior, and expected other organizations to fall in with its political program."[19]

The national movement's cohesion was particularly precarious due to the "tinderbox" character of Arab–Jewish relations in Mandate Palestine, where nearly any event, rumor, or misunderstanding could spark clashes.[20] Some observers charge that Arab leaders did not act decisively to prevent violent incidents because they did not wish to do so. The organizational mediation theory of protest suggests otherwise. The Palestinian movement managed some impetuses to fragmentation from the top down. Yet leaders were unable to thwart outbreaks of violence propelled from the bottom up. Politicians had influence as spokesmen, not as governors. Arab Congresses represented a loose coalition of elites organized along family lines. Their incipient organizational structure was aimed at marshaling pressure, not activating, integrating, or ruling society.

This organizational structure mediated the course of occasional outbreaks of violence. An examination of the two major incidents during this period demonstrates this effect. The first incident was riots that erupted in Jerusalem in April 1920 during the annual Muslim procession in honor of the prophet Moses (Nebi Musa). Faysal's coronation as king of Syria one month prior inspired an outpouring of nationalist enthusiasm. Against this agitated backdrop, hundreds of Muslim pilgrims on route to al-Aqsa Mosque stopped to hear Musa Kazim al-Husayni and others deliver speeches with patriotic and anti-Zionist slogans. The speeches put the procession behind schedule, and police decided to make up for the lost time by redirecting pilgrims along a shortcut through the old city's Jewish quarter. There, some threw stones and attacked Jewish property and passers-by. Riotous violence ensued, leaving five Jews dead and 211 injured, in addition to four Arabs dead and 21 injured.[21]

A subsequent British commission of inquiry concluded that the violence was spontaneous and driven by anger toward the Balfour pledge.[22] While emotions propelled protest, the organizational structure of the national movement mediated its character. As elsewhere in the Middle East during this era, violence escalated not due to the authority that leaders exercised over the population but due to the lack thereof.[23] Before the events, some leaders had instructed their organizations to take caution to avoid any inadvertent descent into violence. Those who delivered speeches had not known that the procession would diverge from its customary route through Muslim-only areas, and Husayni condemned the riots immediately after they occurred.[24] Elites resolutely preferred pressure politics and nonviolent demonstrations of opposition. Nevertheless, they did not ground their strategy in robust organizations or a popular ideology. Oriented more to high-level diplomacy than to mobilizing their own society, they were unable to prevent grassroots indignation from exploding, on occasion, into violence. At the same time, there existed no other leadership capable of organizing and prolonging violence as an alternative approach. For that reason, violence took the form of a sporadic and short-lived flare-up. It did not develop into a prolonged strategy of struggle.

A second major outbreak of violence erupted in 1921 during the celebration of May Day. A clash between Jewish groups in Tel Aviv led police to fire in the air to disperse the crowd. Believing that Jews were attacking them, Arabs in nearby Jaffa acted with force. They smashed Jewish shops, attacked bystanders, and exploded into an immigrant shelter. Violence spread as rumors proliferated. In the end, 47 Jews were killed and 146 injured, mostly by Arabs, whereas 28 Arabs were killed and 73 wounded, mostly by British security forces.[25] An official inquiry found that, as in the previous year, the disturbances were an unplanned manifestation of Arab opposition to the establishment of a Jewish national home in Palestine. Yet also like the Nebi Musa riots, the character of the May Day unrest was mediated by the organizational structure of the Palestinian national movement. Rumors provided a bottom-up impetus for violence, and the mediating efforts of elites offered some top-down barricade against its expansion. In Jaffa, Arab mayors and members of the MCA condemned violence and toured the town to calm residents. In Nablus and Jenin, local leaders worked with authorities to appeal for calm and discredit rumors that nearby Tulkarem was under attack. After hundreds of men set off to aid Tulkarem's defense, elites rushed to disperse them. Meanwhile in Ramleh and Jerusalem, notables used their social influence to ensure that no disturbances commenced.[26]

The official British inquiry into the disturbances credited these interventions. It concluded that Arab leaders, "whatever their feelings may have been, were always ready to help the authorities in the restoration of order.... [W]ithout their assistance the outbreak would have resulted in even worse excesses."[27] The eruption, escalation, and ultimate expiration of lethal unrest thus bore the stamp of a national struggle whose command and control centered on the personal prestige of a handful of elites. Where their leadership was strong, they could intervene to steer nationalist protest according to their strategic preferences. Where it reached its limits, protest was susceptible to escalate to bloodshed. Even Porath, who argues that the riots were not spontaneous, believes that violence ceased for eight years thereafter due largely to "the fact that the traditional leadership was completely opposed to this method of action and apparently succeeded in influencing the community in this direction."[28] Elites used their general, and not directly contested, sway within their communities to curb violent protest during the first phase of the Mandate. However, they did not build the organizational structure necessary to institutionalize or advance nonviolent protest as a lasting alternative.

RISING TENSION

During the first years of British rule, the Palestinian national movement derived a measure of cohesion from popular deference to the leadership of traditional elites, a basic level of cooperation among those elites, and universal consensus on the need to oppose Zionism. Nonetheless, leaders did not build stable and authoritative institutions. The national movement remained vulnerable to fragmentation from above stemming from elite rivalries. It was also vulnerable to fragmentation from below, as might result from the destabilization of traditional patterns of social order. Moreover, it was vulnerable to fragmentation from the outside, as driven by British policies that intentionally or unintentionally fomented division. Over the course of the 1920s, fragmenting dynamics emerged from each of these sources.

The backdrop to these developments was the failure of the AE to convince the British to abandon the Balfour promise. In 1923 Britain completed its implementation of the Mandate, the text of which reaffirmed commitment to a Jewish national home and made no mention of Arab self-determination. This setback tested the bounds of national unity within and for the AE. Arab Congresses divided between those who advocated bolder forms of civil disobedience, such as refusal to pay taxes, and those who preferred that protest stay within legal bounds. In addition, power struggles intensified. Jerusalem elites, particularly the Husayni and Nashashibi families, began to adopt different positions toward the British as a part of their maneuvers against each other. The British likewise maneuvered Arab elites as a way of staying on top of all of them. The government dismissed Musa Kazim al-Husayni from his post as mayor of Jerusalem after the 1920 riots. In his place, they appointed his leading rival, Raghib al-Nashashibi. Thereafter, the Nashashibis came to be regarded as more pro-British and the Husaynis as more nationalistic.[29]

The Husayni–Nashashibi rivalry peaked again in 1921 when the mufti of Jerusalem died. Nashashibi candidates sought the position, but the British saw to the appointment of al-Haj Amin al-Husayni. In 1922 the government created the Supreme Muslim Council (SMC) to oversee all Islamic institutions and *waqf* funds. The Nashashibis' candidate again floundered and Haj Amin became president. In the years that followed, Husayni developed the SMC's nation-wide networks to extend his influence. He emerged as the most popular figure in country, and one with a reputation for strident anti-Zionism. Meanwhile, the Nashashibis gathered families hostile to the Husaynis into a coalition called "the Opposition" and then the "Palestine Arab National Party." These blocs denounced the SMC as a tool of the mufti's political ambitions. They also criticized the Arab Congress and its AE as Husayni strongholds that lacked authority to speak for all Palestinians. When the AE called a new Arab Congress in 1924, the National Party refused to participate unless it convened jointly with opposition parties. The AE rejected these conditions, insisting that the Congress was not a party but the framework for all parties. When the dispute went unresolved, the 1924 Congress was canceled. Five years passed before another convened.

The national struggle was experiencing what would prove to be a pattern of organizational fragmentation. A nationalist group formed, acquired a following, and effectively became synonymous with the national movement itself. The line was thus blurred between what was one faction among many and what was the organizational structure for all factions. The authority of that organizational structure diminished as other parties gained strength and came to contest the dominant faction. In other words, at an early stage of the movement's development, one political player took on the role of rule maker because no other institution fulfilled that function. At a later stage, other players could not compete in the political game without challenging both the rule maker and its rules. A similar dynamic would occur with the rise of the Fateh movement, first as a resistance faction and then as the force dominating the very terms of the PLO umbrella and the Palestinian Authority. Rival factions found that they could not oppose Fateh without also contesting the overarching national structure with which it had developed a symbiotic relationship. Under conditions of agreement on the basic parameters of national politics, factional competition might have been healthy pluralism. In its absence, such competition invited destabilizing fragmentation.

British policies also contributed to Palestinians' organizational fragmentation. The text of the Mandate endorsed the creation of a public body and self-governing institutions for the Jewish community, or Yishuv. It did not do likewise for the Arab community. Authorities tended to deal with Arabs as either Christians or Muslims rather than as a single nation. The government explained that it instituted religious bodies such as the SMC to maintain the Ottoman system of respect for religious difference. Rashid Khalidi argues that it was a strategy of divide and conquer.[30] Beyond this, the very establishment of the Mandate caught the Palestinians in a web of contradictions. The AE refused to legitimize the Mandate by participating in any official body that fell "short of giving the People of Palestine full control of their own affairs."[31] Yet leaders could not boycott all levels of an apparatus that penetrated and transformed the country as a whole. As a result, thousands of Arab public employees pledged the government their allegiance, would-be employees sought its approval, local communities competed for its services, and traditional elites labored to gain its favor.[32] Those who accepted public office, as did mayors or SMC officials, had to accept the government's condition that they not engage in politics. Thus the public figures who both claimed and were expected to represent Palestinians' national aspirations had personal incentives not to do so. In Khalidi's view, the government deliberately recruited notables into its institutions to undermine their commitment to the struggle for self-determination. "By giving a crucial portion of the Palestinian elite both some control over resources and a measure of prestige, but no access to real state power, these institutions successfully distracted many Palestinians from a unified focus on anticolonial national objectives," he writes.[33]

Between the British preference for maintaining stability through traditional leaders and traditional leaders' interest in preserving inherited privilege, the national movement had little prospect of forging a cohesive organizational structure. Meanwhile, nationalist concerns were becoming dire. From 1921 to 1929, Jewish land possession nearly doubled, dozens of new settlements were established, and Jewish-owned enterprises multiplied.[34] The Yishuv

increasingly acquired the character of a state in the making. It created an
elected national assembly, an armed defense force, and an array of institutions
to manage agricultural collectives, immigrant absorption, and banking. An
encompassing labor union served as an engine of employment, public works,
and economic self-sufficiency. Waves of immigrants brought human and material resources. Effective champions outside Palestine offered both funding and
lobbying with foreign governments.

The Arabs of Palestine neither received such outside support nor experienced such internal institution building. For them, the first decade of the
Mandate was instead one of intensifying crisis. According to British figures,
the Jewish population of Palestine increased from about 84,000 to 175,000
between 1922 and 1931. The Arab population grew from 589,000 to 760,000
during the same years. These burgeoning demographics contributed to a scar-
city of arable land. By 1930 nearly 30 percent of Arab peasants were landless
and another third had plots too small for subsistence.[35] Tens of thousands
of indebted farmers were forced to leave the fields that they had worked for
generations. Moving to shanties on the outskirts of Palestine's budding towns,
they worked as cheap laborers. Hours were long and conditions wretched.[36]
Peasants' dislocation both nourished spaces of volatile bitterness and cor-
roded the ties that traditionally linked them to rural patrons. It also exposed
the chasm between their vital interests and those of the conservative notables who urged prudence toward the government. Meanwhile, elites continued to extract profits from tenant farmers, as some did from the sale of
land to Jews.

As the first decade under British rule came to a close, Palestinian Arabs'
internal tensions were kept in check by a traditional social order that lingered
largely due to the absence of mobilized alternatives. Yet inherited relationships
fell short of an organizational structure to adjudicate contradictory interests
and direct collective action. In 1922 the British proposed elections for a country-wide legislative council in which Muslim, Christian, and Jewish representatives would advise the government. They stipulated that this body work
within the limits of the Mandate, which implied legitimation of the Balfour
Declaration. The ensuing debate revealed the difficulty of crafting a unified
national strategy. The Nashashibi camp advocated participation in the elections and the Husayni camp called for a boycott. While the latter triumphed,
divisiveness continued. During the five-year hiatus in the convening of an Arab
Congress, the country-wide network of MCA branches deteriorated. The AE
approached bankruptcy and its work came to a standstill. Palestinians organized protests against Lord Balfour's visit in 1925 but took no action against
the spike in Jewish immigration and land purchases during the same year
(see Figure 2.1). The AE had engaged in vigorous diplomatic activity during
its more cohesive years before the Mandate's finalization. Between 1923 and
1930, however, it did not send a single delegation to London.[37]

In 1928 the Husayni faction bowed to some opposition demands, creating
conditions in which another Palestinian Arab Congress finally reconvened.

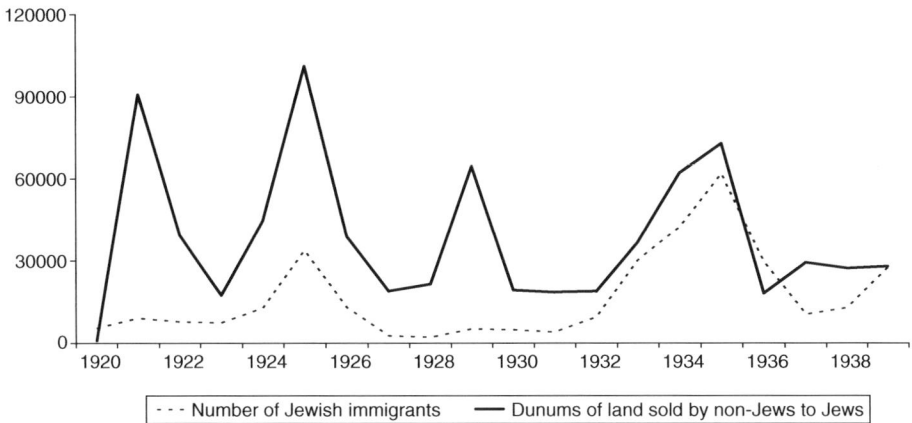

FIGURE 2.1. Jewish immigration and land purchases, 1920–1939.
Data source: The Royal Institute of International Affairs, *Great Britain and Palestine, 1915–1939*, Information Department Papers No. 20A (London, 1939), 56.

It would be the last ever held. The Congress elected an expanded AE led by Musa Kazim al-Husayni with two Nashashibi allies as vice presidents. Nevertheless, the decline of traditional authority and growing strategic disagreements prevented the leadership from exercising diplomacy with the free hand it once had. Musa Kazim al-Husayni and Raghib al-Nashashibi opened negotiations with the British about a representative assembly for Arabs and Jews. Due to fear of militant resistance, they kept the talks secret.[38]

The parties had just reached an agreement in the summer of 1929 when an outbreak of violence exposed the limits of the cohesion that the new AE appeared to rehabilitate. The conflict stemmed from contestation over the Western Wall of what Jews regard as the Temple Mount and what Muslims consider the Noble Sanctuary housing al-Aqsa Mosque and the Dome of the Rock. Under the Ottomans, the holy site was under Muslim control. Britain pledged to maintain this status quo but eased restrictions against Jewish access. Some Jewish worshipers became bolder and in 1928 placed several objects at the site. Muslims protested that they were illegally staking ownership. When the British eventually removed the objects, Jews protested with demonstrations, newspaper denunciations, and a strike. Amin al-Husayni sponsored a counter-protest and an international campaign to mobilize Muslim support, while also authorizing measures that disturbed Jewish prayers. Agitation continued until a Zionist demonstration at the Wall, in the words of the official inquiry, set "in motion a chain reaction." During the next days, Arabs descended on the Wall and destroyed Jewish prayer books and property. An Arab killed a Jewish boy and the boy's funeral transformed into an anti-Arab demonstration. Against a backdrop of rumors, Muslims brought sticks and clubs to Friday prayers at al-Aqsa. They proceeded to a Jewish neighborhood and beat residents at random, sparking mob violence that spread throughout the country. After one week, 133 Jews were killed and 339 wounded; 116 Arabs were also killed and 232 wounded, mostly by British security forces.

Yishuv leaders accused the AE and the mufti of Jerusalem of launching a pogrom. The Shaw commission of inquiry agreed that Arab leaders had failed to quell anti-Jewish feeling, yet exonerated them of responsibility for the killings. It concluded that the engine of violence was, as before, Palestinians' indignation and fear regarding the Jewish national home.[39] Though several historians share this interpretation,[40] they have not explained why violence erupted and spread despite elite leanings to the contrary. The organizational mediation theory of protest offers such an explanation. The SMC and AE led opposition to Zionism, yet lacked the ideological and institutional cohesion to maintain protest within the nonviolent bounds that they preferred.

Several aspects of the events illustrate how the national movement's fragmented organizational structure mediated violence. First, it was not official leaders who instigated unrest, but rivals who disagreed with their moderation and perhaps also pursued their own claims to leadership. Amin al-Husayni did not dictate every action of the religious establishment, and those who disagreed with him acted on their own preferences. In response to the Zionist demonstration at the Wall, Shaykh Hassan Abu Suud, one of the mufti's main competitors among the clergy, delivered a deliberately provocative speech.[41] He and other imams instigated the procession that attacked Jewish property at the Wall while the unsuspecting mufti was away at talks with British authorities.[42] Had there not been among al-Aqsa shaykhs those who contested the mufti's more conservative stance, it is unlikely that sermons from the mosque's pulpit would have helped to spur bloodshed. The Shaw commission recognized this when it noted that nearly all national movements have "an extremist section who are not content with the official policy of the organization to which they belong and whose activities are in consequence directed towards an intensification of that policy."[43] Palestinian leaders might have enforced their official policy, but were inhibited by the limits of the organizational structure within which they operated.

Second, when leaders did exercise authority, it was with the purpose not of instigating but of quelling violence. The day that riots erupted, the mufti discovered the circulation of an incendiary note forged with his signature. Husayni asked the British to increase their police presence and instructed preachers to give pacifying sermons.[44] "Arm yourselves with compassion, wisdom and tolerance," he reputedly told the crowd. "Calm yourselves, go home and leave me to do all I can. The government is not against you, nor the police. It is the duty of the government to maintain order."[45] Far from condemning the mufti, the Shaw commission found that "throughout the period of the disturbances [he] exerted his influence in the direction of promoting peace and restoring order."[46] Indeed, violence was most intense in towns in which the mufti's influence was weak and did not take place in areas in which it was strong.[47] This may have been particularly the case in Hebron, which had strong ties to the Nashashibi camp. It was reportedly Nashashibi affiliates who incited the violence that killed 64 members of the town's traditional Jewish community.[48]

Third, the AE echoed the mufti's cooperation with the government and pleas for calm. On the eve of the riots, three AE members met with representatives of the Zionist Executive at the house of the British chief secretary.[49] After the first day of riots, the AE issued a manifesto in which it discredited false stories about Jewish and British attacks on Arabs and appealed against violence:

> We call upon you, O Arabs, in the interests of the country, which you place above all other considerations, to strive sincerely to quell the riot, avoid bloodshed, and save life. We request you all to return to quiet and peace, to endeavor to assist in the restoration of order, and to turn a deaf ear to such unfounded reports and rumors. Be confident that we are making every possible effort to realize your demands and national aspirations by peaceful methods. Arm yourselves with mercy, wisdom, and patience. For verily, God is with those who bear themselves in patience.[50]

The mufti also signed the manifesto, yet neither the SMC nor the AE was a governance body with the political or military capacity to stop riots once they got under way. Their authority among their constituents was basically moral. As the AE secretary admitted, even this authority was waning. In the wake of events, leaders voiced concern that violence could erupt anew. Haj Amin reportedly requested police protection for fear of assassination.[51]

Finally, and despite the ways in which movement fragmentation absolved the mufti of direct blame, the riots reflected the conflicting interests of nearly all Palestinians who worked with the colonial authorities. On the one hand, Husayni was uncompromisingly opposed to Zionism. On the other, he sought the good graces of the government.[52] Irreconcilable pressures led the mufti to walk an ambiguous middle line, which further narrowed as he faced outbidding from aspirants more radical than he. For the national movement as a whole, such contradictions undermined the crystallization of collective purpose, effective leadership, and strong institutions. It thus hindered the full institutionalization of either legal or rebellious strategies of protest.

The 1929 riots revealed the organizational dilemma of a national movement built around a narrow stratum of elites. The problem was not that notables failed to "control" society, but that the national struggle did not integrate the participation and needs of the population that it represented. This became more acute as the chasm widened between elites' personal ambitions and the threats facing Arab Palestine.

THE ARAB REBELLION

The 1929 violence ushered in a shift, in Lesch's words, from "mobilization from above" to "mobilization from below."[53] By the 1930s, Palestinian society had undergone far-reaching socioeconomic change. Improvements in health led to population growth, and the expansion of transport and infrastructure increased trade. Citriculture, manufacturing, and government employment offered some alternative to subsistence agriculture. The growth of coastal cities such as Jaffa and Haifa brought people together in new forms of exchange and also offered a measure of distance from the bickering politics of the Jerusalem elite.[54] The expansion of education, though lagging behind Palestinian demand,[55] had a similar effect. The percentage of Arab children enrolled in school rose from 20 percent in 1911 to approximately 34 percent by 1946.[56] Education expanded the ranks of a middle class whose ambitions could not be satisfied under the traditional distribution of power. Teachers and civil servants assigned to work in the countryside transmitted political debates from urban to rural areas.[57] The growth of literacy fostered the rise of print culture, which Benedict Anderson famously associated with the spread of nationalism.[58] Giving voice to a small but influential nationalist intelligentsia, newspapers helped Palestinians follow the events transforming their country and region.[59]

Doug McAdam has shown how broad economic and demographic shifts precipitated the American civil rights movement by fostering the establishment of organizations and optimism about the possibility of change.[60] Social transformations in Palestine in the 1920s and 1930s had a similar effect. Activists founded civil society groups such as sports and literary clubs, family-based societies, charitable associations, women's groups, chambers of commerce, and labor unions.[61] Boy Scout troops organized popular demonstrations and patrolled the coast for illegal Jewish immigrants. Middle-class groups, such as the Young Men's Muslim Associations, the Arab Young Men's Association, and the Committee of the Nablus Congress, called for stronger opposition to British policy. In addition, two national political parties were formed in 1932, the Congress of Arab Youth and the Palestine branch of the pan-Arab Istiqlal Party.

Many of these groups had a nationalist orientation. Vocal in protesting the advance of the Zionist project, they denounced what was known as the "Hebrew labor only" movement and accused the British of discriminating against Arabs in wages and law enforcement.[62] Most of all, they called for the government to stem Jewish immigration. As Jews fled rising anti-Semitism in Europe, the Jewish community grew from 11 percent of the population of Palestine in 1922 to 28 percent in 1936. Jewish land purchases increased accordingly (see Figure 2.1). In addition, the character of land transfers became more deleterious. The 1910s and 1920s had seen mostly absentee landlords selling plots that were sparsely populated. By the 1930s, more sales included the fields on which poor Palestinian farmers depended. British reports repeatedly drew attention to the dearth of cultivable land and the need to protect the peasantry, if not restrict Jewish immigration and land purchases as well.[63] Nevertheless, neither these recommendations nor campaigns by the AE, SMC, Arabic press, or the new Arab National Fund alleviated the crisis.

A new generation of professionals and educated activists criticized traditional elites' failure to confront these challenges. Some followed news of

Gandhi's activities and urged Palestinians to carry out civil disobedience.[64] Others formed underground revolutionary cells prepare for military confrontation.[65] Nationalist achievements in neighboring countries stirred Palestinian opinion. Egyptians launched demonstrations that helped push Great Britain to grant independence, while Syrians held protests that forced the French into treaty negotiations. The Arabic press called on Palestinians to follow these examples.[66] Goaded by the Istiqlal Party and others, the AE organized in 1933 its first demonstrations targeting the mandatory government, as opposed to Zionism. Still, the attempt at strident protest came too late to mollify tensions between older and younger politicians. Meanwhile within the Islamic establishment, a battle between the mufti and anti-mufti camps raged in rival newspapers and competing conferences. In 1934 Musa Kazim al-Husayni died, and the leaderless and penniless AE dissolved. Notables formed their own family-based political parties and pressed competing claims to speak for Palestine. As Arab society became increasingly politicized, the loose elite alliance that once sufficed as a way of doing politics crumbled. The national struggle fragmented between conservative elites enmeshed in power struggles, an emergent cohort of more strident activists, and masses on the verge of explosion.

Events in 1935 further heightened the urgency. That fall, a barrel in transit to a Jewish businessman cracked open to reveal smuggled ammunition. The incident confirmed Arabs' suspicions that the Yishuv was arming for a fight to decide the country's future. Meanwhile, a preacher named Shaykh Izz al-Din al-Qassam invoked Islam to mobilize Haifa's poor in an armed struggle against Zionism and imperialism. He secretly trained recruits and in November 1935 lost his life in their first battle against British troops. Qassam's funeral inspired a religious and nationalist outpouring. Palestinians of different backgrounds lauded the sacrifice and courage that distinguished Qassam from traditional leaders. Notables attempted to ignore the Qassamite phenomenon but could not. In the words of writer Ghassan Kanafani, "They discovered that if they did not try to mount the great wave that had been set in motion by Qassam, it would engulf them."[67]

Elites vested their last hope in the British Parliament's consideration of a proposal to establish a legislative council for all inhabitants of Palestine. In the early 1920s, they had rejected a similar proposal because it entailed acceptance of the Balfour Declaration. By the mid-1930s, Arab leaders embraced it as the seemingly only way to slow the imminent move toward Jewish national independence. Yet to their shock, both houses of Parliament voted against the council's establishment. Arab leaders accepted an invitation to dispatch a follow-up delegation to London. As of their last meeting on April 15, however, they were unable to settle quarrels regarding the selection of delegates.[68]

On the same day, Arab gunmen shot three Jews. The Jewish paramilitary Irgun responded by shooting two Arabs, and a Jewish funeral ended in attacks on Arabs. As rumors of atrocities spread, Arabs rioted and attacked Jews. On the evening of April 19, activists in Nablus and Jerusalem met and announced a general commercial and labor strike to commence the following day. On April 20, public gatherings in Jaffa and Nablus called for the strike to continue. Those spearheading this effort were predominantly members of the Istiqlal Party. In mobilizing a strike, they sought to take advantage of popular outrage and push the national movement toward bolder protest. Yet they also sought to discipline and steer that momentum and thereby prevent demonstrations from spinning out of control. Lesch explains, "Fearing intercommunal violence, middle-class Arab professionals and merchants hastily formed local committees which they hoped could organize a nonviolent protest strike to channel the Arabs' explosive anger."[69] Activists understood that, if protest was to be both broad-based and nonviolent, the national movement required cohesion. That is thus what they sought. Istiqlal Party leader Akram Zu'aytir opened the public meeting in Nablus by declaring, "We must decide if ... we will seize this auspicious opportunity and work with a single hand, in a single way, and for the single goal of saving this country from the situation in which it finds itself."[70] Seeking to overcome political divisions, the Nablus group resolved to "go forward on a national rather than a partisan basis."[71] They called their assembly a "National Committee" and contacted other communities and urged them to follow their lead.

Within days, National Committees emerged in nearly all Arab towns. The press called for national unity and participation, and the public responded with robust support. Popular enthusiasm and a network of local committees suggested the potential for new cohesion. The national movement also needed a national leadership in order to transform a tentative patriotic unity into a more robust organizational structure. Those who traditionally played that role, however, were precisely those most resistant to acting against the government. Elite politicians were largely silent as nationalist agitation continued for 10 days. At that point, National Committee representatives from throughout Palestine met and decided to elect their own executive body to guide the general strike.[72] It was only then that elite families and factions, fearful of being cast aside, came together and formed the Arab Higher Committee (AHC). The AHC announced that it would assume leadership of the strike. With Amin al-Husayni as president, the AHC declared that Palestinians would continue the protest campaign until the government established a representative national government in Palestine, ended Jewish immigration, and banned the transfer of Arab land to Jews.

Many commentators then and since have accused Husayni of engineering the 1936 rebellion. An analysis of events in sequence, however, reveals that middle-tier activists were "first movers" who imposed a strategy of protest upon, if not against, hesitant elites.[73] Once protest gathered momentum, remaining on the sidelines would have been political suicide. In this way, the Palestinian movement crystallized a decentralized institutional framework, collective purpose in society, and finally a national leadership. For a brief but historic moment, the national movement moved toward overcoming fragmentation. The resulting organizational structure would mediate the use of nonviolent protest on a scale theretofore unparalleled.

The General Strike

The events of April 1936 launched the three-year Grand Arab Rebellion. From April to October 1936, Palestinian Arabs carried out a general strike, demonstrations, and a noncooperation campaign, as well as armed activity. From July 1937 until mid-1939, nonviolent protest was minimal and violence engulfed the country. At both stages, protest was mediated by the organizational structure of the Palestinian national movement.

At the rebellion's outset, a new level of movement cohesion grew from the elements of leadership, institutions, and collective purpose. The AHC contributed to unity by including representatives of all major parties, among them members of the Christian and Muslim communities and the Husayni and Nashashibi families. Rival elites thus pledged to put aside their differences, at least temporarily, and forge a united front. While never complete, this inter-elite cooperation both represented and encouraged universal commitment. The mufti, the most popular and well-known personality in the country, enhanced its legitimacy. National Committees were the lynchpins of an institutional framework. In each community, committees attended to the daily functioning of the strike by devising strategies, translating them into tactics, communicating directives, and handling difficulties as they arose. Committees rallied and oversaw protest activity in particular localities. Developing lines of communication and coordination among themselves, they constituted an overarching country-wide structure. This institutional framework both inspired and was inspired by a heightened collective purpose in society. Palestinian Arabs voiced strong consensus on the justice and urgency of action against the Jewish national home. The sum of these developments was a striking advance in movement cohesion. Robert John and Sami Hadawi observed, "For the first time, perhaps, there was unity between the entire non-Jewish population of Palestine, as Moslems and Christians, moderates and extremists, united in a resolve to 'continue the general strike.'"[74]

This cohesion enabled a national protest campaign in which diverse sectors of society participated using the nonviolent means at their disposal.[75] The Arab Car Owners' and Drivers' Association halted transport facilities, merchants and city laborers stayed home, prisoners refused to perform penal labor, and schools and factories closed. The Jaffa port ceased operations. Local committees limited farmers' marketing to specified hours. Intellectuals published leaflets, and newspapers urged the public to participate.[76] Men, women, and children of all ages took part in public demonstrations, and families across the country observed a boycott of Jewish firms and products. Boy Scouts and *shabab* – urban young men who would continue to play a key role in resistance activities for generations thereafter – enforced compliance at the neighborhood level. Although Arab civil servants did not go on strike, first- and second-tier public officials came together to submit a memorandum to the government explaining Arab grievances and claims. Many also donated a percentage of their salaries to help the national campaign.

Such broad-based and sustained nonviolent protest would not have been possible without movement cohesion. The secretary of state for the colonies admitted, "Intimidation ... is responsible only in a small measure for the continuation of the strike which clearly has the full sympathy of all too large a part of the Arab population."[77] As would recur in the Palestinian experience, consensus in society facilitated a united stand among otherwise antagonistic political personalities. Elites in turn reinforced popular unity. AHC members toured the country to rally support for the strike.[78] They continued to speak out despite government pressure of the kind that had brought them to acquiesce in years past.[79] National Committees, meanwhile, initiated mechanisms critical for sustaining the strike over time. Leaders in Nablus, for example, established secondary and tertiary "backup" committees to take responsibility should members of the first-order committee be arrested. They divided Nablus into 15 districts and elected committees to oversee protest in each locale.[80] These representatives met continually and agreed upon pragmatic measures to adapt the strike in accord with the needs and problems facing each neighborhood.[81]

The indispensability of cohesion for nonviolent protest was similarly evident in the cooperation of national leaders and local organizations in supporting those who absorbed the most costs to keep the strike going. The AHC's Central Relief Committee solicited and distributed contributions from Arab and foreign sources. National Committees and women's groups managed neighborhood-based fund-raising tasks such as door-to-door requests for donations. Nourishment and supply committees dispersed food staples to the needy and National Committees paid compensation wages to ensure that key groups of striking workers did not return to work. In this way, an organizational structure took shape that managed the potential for fragmentation in order to prevent it from derailing the nonviolent protest effort.

In the absence of leadership, an institutional framework, and collective purpose, it is doubtful that Palestinians could have launched a country-wide strike, motivated the participation of people of various backgrounds, and sustained it for six months in the face of economic hardship and government repression. Cohesion helped generate credible commitments of participation that became reinforcing and self-fulfilling, and thereby institutionalized the strike as a new status quo. After a month and a half, Istiqlalist Muhammad 'Izzat Darwazah noted that "the strike continues and people no longer even talk about the issue of the strike's continuation because it has become a matter of habit."[82] For Zu'aytir, the length of the strike seemed nothing short of a "miracle." The source of the strike's staying power, he wrote, was the fact that "all people without exception were integrated into it."[83]

As in other rebellions, support for greater militancy grew as weeks passed and the government refused to meet protestors' demands. Still, the organizational structure linking national leaders and local groups enabled activists to meet, discuss, and devise ways of escalating protest without exceeding the bounds of nonviolence. Some 150 professionals and intellectuals issued a petition demanding "no taxation without representation" on the grounds that "noncooperation is a peaceful weapon for launching honorable resistance against British colonialism."[84] On May 7, representatives from 20 National Committees met and unanimously adopted the call to stop paying taxes. The AHC endorsed the resolution, rendering it policy for the national movement at large.[85] In this coordinated move, activists managed to bolster and adapt the nonviolent character of protest despite conditions of rapid radicalization. Zu'aytir observed, "The first serious political step that we must take is civil disobedience, meaning refusal to pay taxes. We do this in the knowledge that the country is heading toward armed revolt and revolutionary sentiment is escalating at an astonishing rate."[86]

Nevertheless, the national movement's ability to build cohesion was incomplete. The economic and cultural gaps between the countryside and the cities meant that the committee structure and strike effort obtained predominantly in urban areas. In addition, mutual suspicions continued to plague the movement. These existed among elite parties[87] and between the conservative leadership and more militant nationalists.[88] The AHC did not represent the submission of private interests to an autonomous institution as much as "the temporary suspension of factional politics."[89] Neighborhood committees coordinated demonstrations and relief efforts, but they did not authoritatively dictate the behavior of all people in their communities. The limits of cohesion pointed to the limits of an indefinite commitment to nonviolent strategies. In the first month of the revolt, Arabs carried out dozens of attacks on Jewish people and property. "The committees declared in favor only 'of civil disobedience,'" John and Hadawi observed. "Nevertheless, as in India, acts of spontaneous violence occurred."[90]

The overriding engine of violence was Britain's refusal to accommodate the strike's demands. Still, the effect of government obstinacy in propelling violence was not automatic, but mediated by the national movement's organizational structure. National Committees issued manifestos denouncing lawlessness, but to minimal effect.[91] The AHC's influence was no greater. For both local and national leaders, continued mobilization of nonviolent protest depended on the ability to convince the public that nonviolence would deliver results. Even the high commissioner recognized that Arab leaders "cannot control the extremist element unless they have some concession to offer."[92] When the high commissioner censured Husayni, therefore, it was not for leading armed protest, but for lacking the fortitude to confront public opinion. "The extremists lead," he observed. "They frighten those who, like the Mufti, refuse to stand in the open and declare themselves wholeheartedly for violence or wholeheartedly for acceptance of Government offers."[93]

In mid-May the government flouted the strike by releasing a schedule for new Jewish immigration permits. It also intensified countermeasures, including the deportation and arrest of Arab activists, search and arrest without warrant, and imposition of collective fines and curfew.[94] Demolition of entire swaths of Jaffa's old city left 6,000 people homeless.[95] As authorities cracked down, popular participation in civic protest receded, and bands of armed rebels formed in the countryside. The first rebel bands consisted of people from a single village or clan who came together to shoot or carry out sabotage attacks against British or Jewish targets. Thereafter, bands developed into permanent units of 50–70 regulars led by a commander. They eventually grew into networks in which a single commander directed both a main band and subsidiary bands.[96]

Fragmentation in rural society fed fragmentation in the revolt, which in turn mediated patterns in violence. Competition at the village level created an impetus for military activity. Families formed rebel bands lest they lose status to rival families that were taking up arms or be left vulnerable to their attacks.[97] Clans' antagonism likewise impeded their integration into a single system of command and control. Yuval Arnon-Ohanna explains, "Just as no *hamula* in Palestine had managed to dominate the others and to attain social and political supremacy, so none of the bands was able to impose its will on the others and assume a position of leadership."[98] Different rebel commanders dominated different regions, and it was not until late July that the most prominent commanders met to discuss coordinating their activities.

The power struggle between urban notables likewise fed militant protest as the rebellion became a theater for escalatory outbidding. Raghib al-Nashashibi advocated the radical call for Arab government employees to resign, not least in order to force the mufti to relinquish his public post as head of the SMC. Predictably, the mufti opposed this measure. The Nashashibi camp was also the first faction to offer assistance to rebel bands, perhaps in a bid to sweep away the more timid Husayni. Refusing to be left behind, the Husaynis began sponsoring bands as well.[99] Internal rivalries thus contributed to violence apart from those impetuses stemming from British policy or the overriding conflict with Zionism. Elites used the armed rebellion as a resource with which to challenge each other and to solidify their respective spheres of influence. The AHC assisted some inter-elite cooperation, yet it proved to be not an enduringly cohesive organizational structure as much as a cover for long-standing enmities in the notable class.

Eventually, Nashashibi leaders came to view the military rebellion as futile and reduced their involvement. By contrast, the Husayni camp became more enmeshed. As the armed revolt escalated, the mufti reasoned that he had to assume a leading role if he was to preserve his preeminent standing with the public, which supported rebellion, and with the British, to whom he wanted to demonstrate that he was irreplaceable.[100] After all, if it was he who spearheaded the armed fight, then authorities would need to negotiate with him to end it. Foreshadowing future dynamics, a Palestinian leader attempted to communicate to hostile authorities, "Work with me [and not any alternative leadership], or expect violence to continue."

The effect of the national movement's organizational structure on the politics and protraction of armed rebellion became clear as leaders of neighboring Arab states began to intervene. This was further complicated by divisions among Arab leaders themselves. The Iraqi foreign minister mistrusted the king of Saudi Arabia, who in turn resented King Abdullah of Transjordan. Abdullah amplified Palestinians' own rivalries because his long-standing affiliation with the Nashashibis made him anathema to Amin al-Husayni. His aspiration to integrate Palestine into his own kingdom, moreover, threatened Haj Amin both personally and nationalistically. In July Abdullah urged an end to the revolt without preconditions. The Nashashibi camp voiced its approval. Rejecting the initiative, the mufti redoubled his entanglement in the armed rebellion. Abdullah's proposal for ending violence without further bloodshed could be considered strategically rational in light of Britain's refusal to accommodate the strike's demands. Had the Palestinian movement been more cohesive, it might have reacted differently. Given its organizational structure, however, external intervention only aggravated divisions, which in turn accentuated motives for violence and depleted capacities for unarmed strategies.

The relationship between fragmentation and violence took another turn in late August when Fawzi al-Qawuqji, a former Ottoman military officer, led volunteers from different Arab countries into Palestine and declared his establishment of a central command for the revolt. The Beirut-born Qawuqji divided Palestine into three theaters of operation, organized reserve forces, and built revolutionary courts. Recognizing the revolt's need for improved command and control, he pledged, in his own words, "to end chaos and treason on the one hand, and resolve problems between families on the other."[101] Nevertheless, Qawuqji established relations with the Nashashibi faction and openly criticized the mufti. This partaking in Palestinians' factionalism rendered his quest for a unified military effort impossible. When Qawuqji called a meeting of rebel commanders to confirm his authority as "commander-in-chief of the Arab Revolt in Southern Syria," he did not invite Abd al-Qadir al-Husayni, the mufti's nephew and the commander that he backed.[102] Henceforth, the armed rebellion proceeded on two tracks. The Husaynis oversaw bands in their zone of influence. Qawuqji instituted a separate framework in which Iraqi, Syrian, Druze, and Palestinian Arab commanders oversaw tiers of rebel bands in their respective areas.

Qawuqji's efforts to manage fragmentation affected the character of violent protest in the areas under his auspices. A measure of command and control helped pin military activity to the pursuit of collective objectives and forestall its descent into renegade forms. "For the first time the Palestinian bands are meeting and acting in a singular military formation," Qawuqji recorded in his memoirs. "In adhering to this order, they felt a new spirit and the people of the villages looked upon them with esteem."[103] Still, the factors that divided the rebels continued to undercut those that united them. Fighters bickered over matters from rations to rank, and many Palestinians mistrusted the motives of those from outside Palestine. Furthermore, there was no integration between Qawuqji's military leadership of the rural revolt and the AHC's political leadership of the urban-based strike. On the contrary, Qawuqji acted as if the AHC did not exist.[104]

The revolt continued for six months. By September 1936, the Arab population was exhausted and economic crisis acute. The AHC feared the impending arrival of British army reinforcements, as well as financial devastation should Palestinians lose the approaching citrus harvest season.[105] Seeking an end to the rebellion without admitting defeat, elites asked leaders of Arab countries to pen an appeal for the strike's end. The AHC then met with National Committee representatives and secured their unanimous approval to endorse the appeal.[106] Palestinian newspapers printed the Arab leaders' message with a manifesto indicating the AHC's agreement. With this regional, national, and local coordination, the rebellion came to a halt.[107]

The national movement thus employed whatever organizational cohesion it could muster to terminate the rebellion before fragmentation worsened and the costs of revolt further outweighed its expected benefits. "The strike had become a cruel and heavy load upon all people," Darwazah observed. "Reason and conscience demanded that it be ended in this dignified manner so the nation would not become resentful, reckless, or fractured."[108] Qawuqji also recognized the appropriateness of halting the rebellion. "Today the situation has become fitting for a resolution," he wrote. "The people are in need of nothing save a leader who knows how to extract benefit from their virtues."[109] Perhaps unconvinced that such leadership existed, Qawuqji instructed rebels to preserve their weapons as they waited for the next phase.

The Armed Revolt

The ensuing lull gave Palestinian Arabs some opportunity to recuperate economically and societally. Politically and organizationally, however, the national movement's cohesion continued to erode. Amin al-Husayni and Raghib al-Nashashibi took contrary positions on the major questions facing the national movement: whether the AHC should continue or disband, whether to boycott or cooperate with the commission investigating the rebellion, and whether testimony before that commission should focus on broad or narrow nationalist demands. The Nashashibi camp withdrew from the AHC after an attempt on the life of Fakhri al-Nashashibi, Raghib's nephew and an ardent opponent of the mufti.[110] The leadership body that was once a symbol of national unity was left little more than an instrument of the mufti's faction.

In July 1937, the Royal (Peel) Commission issued its recommendations: partitioning of Palestine into a Jewish state and an Arab state unified with Transjordan, along with a new Mandate over the main holy places. The Yishuv was divided. Arab leaders rejected the plan, which would force nearly one-third of the Arab population, particularly in the Galilee, to come under Jewish rule or be transferred from their homes. District Commissioner Lewis Andrews described the local mood as one of shock. "That the Arab population of Galilee should ever be reconciled to the scheme is clearly too much to hope," he wrote. "Their common feeling … is that they have been betrayed."[111]

In late September, Andrews was assassinated by Arab gunmen and the rebellion recommenced.

The impetus for the second stage of the revolt, like the first, was the loss of confidence in political means to forestall Zionism and preserve Palestine as an Arab country. The national movement's organizational structure, however, had changed. The elements of leadership, institutions, and collective purpose that enabled some nonviolent protest in 1936 were much weakened when protest resumed in 1937. Inter-elite cooperation had dissolved. While the mufti threw his support behind continued rebellion, some Nashashibi affiliates accepted the Peel partition plan and others fled the country. Britain's intensified counterinsurgency provoked further divisions. During the general strike, repression had been limited by the lack of troops on the ground and the high commissioner's belief that harsher action would be counterproductive. Under a different high commissioner by 1937 and after the freeing of British forces in Europe after the September 1938 Munich settlement, however, Britain poured reinforcements into Palestine and brought the area under de facto martial law. Thereafter, official policy sanctioned systematic destruction and vandalism. Unofficial acts of brutality by security force members compounded their impact.[112]

The effect of repression on protest was mediated by the organizational structure of the Palestinian movement. Given the Husayni–Nashashibi split, the collapse of the AHC, and the public's exhaustion, the movement's increasing fragmentation rendered it more brittle than resilient under the brunt of counterinsurgency. Beyond this, repression directly attacked the mechanisms through which any movement regenerates command and control. The government undercut leadership structures when it stripped Husayni of the presidency of the SMC, outlawed the AHC, deported those members it was able to arrest, and prevented those who were abroad from returning to Palestine. The mufti hid in al-Aqsa before secretly escaping to Beirut, where he established a new AHC headquarters. Meanwhile in Damascus, Darwazah and other exiled leaders opened the Central Committee for the Jihad to guide and fund the Palestinian revolt. Exile impeded the centralization of authority and unification of collective purpose in the Palestinian national struggle. It grounded leaders in a distinct political reality and made them prone to develop outlooks different from that of the resident population. It also undermined their ability to influence events on the ground. This relationship between exiled leadership and organizational fragmentation would become a recurring motif in the Palestinian struggle.

Counterinsurgency also gutted the institutional frameworks that had generated cooperation during the general strike. The government banned National Committees and detained about two hundred local leaders. This crackdown netted some who had advocated violence, but it also removed those who had called for Gandhi-inspired civil disobedience, labored to build national consensus, and established grassroots associations. Repression deprived political parties of their vanguard and collective action of its institutional backbone.

As would be the case in subsequent years, the arrest or deportation of top leaders opened a fragmenting power struggle in the movement's lower ranks. As Mustafa Kabha noted, "Every second-tier leader considered himself a candidate to fill the void ... the majority of [whom] had neither the appropriate vision nor the knowledge.... As a result, each tried to impose his own preferences, or that which served his own personal or familial interest, upon the revolt."[113] Arrests removed those most able to channel the popular will to rebel into nonlethal forms of protest. The government was thus left with no "partner" on the other side. In this, Darwazah recognized a pattern familiar today:

> The authorities have made a great mistake in arresting the Higher Committee and abolishing the Higher Committee and other Committees. The members of the Higher Committee and other Committees had the capacity to work to pacify the situation and calm things. But now [the authorities] will face the strange situation in which there is no one to talk to.[114]

Apart from its effect on leadership and institutions, counterinsurgency also undermined national purpose among the population at large. The British imposed collective punishment in a deliberate effort to break civilians' resolve and "comb out" rebels from their midst.[115] They demolished houses, fields, and even entire villages. They carried out sweeping searches during which they held men in wire cages as they destroyed or looted their household possessions. They imposed exorbitant fines on entire communities while also erecting obstacles that kept them from earning the livelihoods with which they might pay those fines. Furthermore, they arrested tens of thousands of Palestinians in arbitrary roundups and subjected detainees to multiple forms of torture.[116] Indiscriminate punishments, apart from two incidents that might be classified as atrocities,[117] created terror among the Arab population. It may have intensified some people's support of the rebels but brought others to distance themselves out of fear or fatigue. Many had both reactions simultaneously. "We think ... that the activities of the gangs are a mistake," one village head told a government official. "But if anybody has been telling you that either I or anybody else do not sympathize with the gangs, they are lying."[118]

Counterinsurgency also weakened popular unity by destabilizing the organizational system that previously helped fund rebellion. During the strike, the AHC and National Committees solicited donations in a fashion that balanced the rebels' needs with the population's means. With the collapse of authority structures in 1937, however, no leadership or institutional checks prevented rebels from plundering as they imposed their own demands on the populace. The Central Committee in Damascus attempted to control such abuses, yet commanded neither disciplinary mechanisms nor consensus on what was and was not permissible in the name of the revolt.[119] Faced with extortion, many of the urban middle classes fled Palestine,[120] while those who remained retreated from the forefront of the national struggle. This removed precisely those whose political sensibilities and organizational experience had been vital in mobilizing nonviolent protest. The initiative thus shifted to peasants and the urban poor, who typically lacked the same preference for civil disobedience and ability to organize it.[121] By late 1938, a district commissioner noted, "Moderate opinion has now lost the last shred of influence it possessed."[122]

In undermining leadership, institutions, and collective purpose, British countermeasures increased Palestinians' organizational fragmentation. This in turn weakened their ability to carry out nonviolent protest. At the outset of the British crackdown, some Palestinian activists called for resumption of the general strike. However, the appeal no longer resonated with mass opinion. Nor was there an organizational structure capable of implementing it. The high commissioner judged the effort to be "never more than a half-hearted affair." After two days, he reported, "The shop-shutting movement had lost whatever momentum it had ever had." By the third day, it "completely petered out."[123]

The absence of civic protest left a void that became filled by action that was more exclusively and intensely violent. Whereas an estimated 900–2,000 fighters participated in military activity during the first stage of the rebellion,[124] the number of fighters rose to as high as 15,000 during the peak of the second stage.[125] By 1938 rebels had taken control of large stretches of the country, rendering roads unsafe for travel. Civil administration was practically non-existent.[126] From the government's point of view, 1938 was "the worst year in the history of the country since the war."[127] Despite military reinforcements, the number of British killed increased from 30 during the 1936 strike to 77 during 1938. The number of British injured rose from 163 to 216 and the number of Jews killed rose from 81 to 255.[128] Walid Khalidi estimates that, out of a total population of 960,000, some 5,000 Palestinian Arabs were killed and 15,000 wounded during the full course of the 1936–1939 rebellion.[129]

With civic protest muted, British forces focused on the rural insurgency. There as well, they sought victory by aggravating fragmentation within rebel ranks. "The constant pressure which is now maintained ... by both the police and the military, has split the brigands into smaller bands," officials reported.[130] Britain also tried to provoke discord among bands by dispatching extortionists who claimed to be genuine rebels and by disseminating rumors that some rebels were collaborating with authorities.[131] The organizational structure of the national movement did not equip it to stop or even manage this fragmentation. The Haifa district commissioner reported, "The leaders in Syria of the Palestinian rebels no longer have the control over the situation which they had in 1936."[132]

This state of affairs defies the common view that Amin al-Husayni single-handedly drove violence. Even historians sympathetic to Haj Amin agree that he became a more ardent advocate of armed rebellion in 1937, whether on strategic or vengeful grounds.[133] Given the organizational structure of the Palestinian movement, however, no exiled figure could prevent the rebellion from developing a logic of its own. On these grounds, Darwazah appealed to Qawuqji to return to Palestine and "use his personality, reputation, and acquired knowledge … to impose a single leadership."[134] Qawuqji refused. The Central Committee succeeded in developing cooperative relations with three commanders in northern Palestine, yet at least a dozen commanders in other regions were beyond its influence. Without a cohesive organizational structure, Damascus-based leaders had few means to assert command and control beyond written entreaties. Darwazah recalled:

> We made great efforts to unite the leadership, but were unable to do so or to impose such unity by force…. Complaints reached us regarding the behavior of commanders and rebels. There were disputes between commanders as well. Each commander defined his area of operations, which he saw as his own sphere of influence. He would be upset if a neighboring leader encroached into his area in any way that he saw as a violation of his jurisdiction. We took pains to send letters to treat this.[135]

In his memoirs, Zu'aytir contrasted the strengths of the first stage of the rebellion with the afflictions of the latter. "The most grave [difference] was the inability of the high political leadership to rein in rebels' insubordination," he wrote.[136] This leadership crisis reverberated to the grass roots. Whereas the organizational structure of the 1936 strike helped inspire cross-cleavage solidarity, the breakdown of this structure after 1937 invited to the fore clan, regional, religious, and other social divisions. Paramount among these was the poor peasantry's resentment of wealthier city folk. Turning the tables on conventional hierarchies, rural rebels forced urban men to replace their Turkish tarbushes with the *keffiyehs* typical of the peasantry.[137] They ordered both Muslim and Christian women to veil, announced a compulsory draft, declared the cancelation of all debts, and demanded that city residents stop using electricity.[138] Fragmentation bred social and political motivations for violence apart from opposition to Zionism. Rebels took up arms as a guise for acting on jealousies and familial rivalries, settling old scores, plundering, or attacking those whom they accused of being traitors or collaborators. Among those abducted or killed were Arab police officers, Communist and union leaders, people charged with selling land to Jews, those who refused to pay taxes to the revolt, and members of the Druze and Christian communities.[139] It was not always clear where the struggle for self-determination ended and internal score settling began. People wondered which rebels were freedom fighters and which were thugs.

By the rebellion's end, approximately one-quarter of Palestinian casualties had been committed by other Palestinians.[140] This was not a strictly internal affair, but also a kind of protest against the British. The government viewed all violence, whether against Arabs, Jews, or itself, as an intolerable breach of law and order.[141] Intra-Arab attacks directly struck the functioning of the Mandate insofar as it sought through intimidation to compel Arabs to abandon public employment. It also convinced authorities of the need to disarm Arab police officers who remained on duty. When the high commissioner admitted that "Arabs fear the terrorists more than they respect the government," he recognized that rebels' use of force against their own community was an effective challenge to the colonial apparatus.[142]

Fragmentation thus contributed to the lethality of protest both by fueling competitive motives for violence and by weakening constraints on its usage. In addition, it inhibited efforts to bring hostilities to an end. The high commissioner recognized:

> Although the rebellion is widespread, there is no unity of command and the leaders tend to squabble among themselves.... [L]ack of cohesion may also mean that the disturbances would not end so promptly as the 1936 troubles if the word were given. Even if the Arab leaders call for a cessation of activity, brigandage and terrorism on a restricted scale will continue sporadically.... Where there is lack of discipline in the field, there will not be discipline during an armistice or a peace.[143]

Palestinian leaders lost the ability to constrain rebels in the field. Moreover, they themselves became constrained by these militants. A commissioner noted, "Doubts have been expressed as to whether the rebel committee in Damascus could stop disorder if it wanted to and that it can only maintain leadership so long as it cheers the rebels on."[144] Even elites with moderate preferences found it wise to assume radical positions lest they lose credibility or risk being targeted for assassination.

Compounding these manifold forms of fragmentation was the resurgence of the Husayni–Nashashibi rivalry in the autumn of 1938. Fakhri al-Nashashibi issued a call for an end to rebellion, claiming that most Arabs blamed the mufti for the revolt's disastrous course.[145] The ensuing struggle between Husayni and his detractors split society between those for and against the rebellion. "A section of the Arabs, long tired of the disorders, now feels sufficiently exasperated to voice an audible protest," the high commissioner reported. "Fakhri Nashashibi is exploiting these sentiments for his own ends, just as Haj Amin for his own purposes plays upon the militant resentment of the other section of Arab opinion."[146] Rebel bands responded to Nashashibi's challenge by intensifying antigovernment violence, leading to a spike in attacks in late 1938.[147] Thereafter, Husayni forces vilified the Nashashibi opposition, the opposition supplied intelligence to the authorities, rebel bands assassinated oppositionists, and oppositionists and the government organized "peace bands" to combat the rebels. The authorities exploited Palestinians' fragmentation in the hope that the rebellion would implode. "With Government encouragement," a commissioner noted, "the struggle between Government and the majority of the Arab population on the issue of the future of the country, may change to a contest with a section only of the Arabs on a question of which Arab party is to predominate."[148]

By the end of 1938, the Grand Arab Rebellion encompassed a face-off between Palestine's leading elite families, a turf war among dozens of rebel commanders, and a disintegrating popular uprising. All of these battles occurred within the context of the clash between Palestinian Arab and Jewish nationalisms, as enacted in a rebellion against Great Britain. Rebel bands fought anti-rebel bands, the army, and each other. In the government's assessment, the revolt thus "lost the characteristics of a national movement and degenerated into a series of crimes of reprisal."[149] Meanwhile, the government stipulated that civilians obtain permits to travel between towns. Rebels responded by threatening violence against anyone who did so. "It appears that the Arab population must sooner or later decide whether to face ruin and starvation owing to their inability to move about to sell their produce, or a problematical death at the hands of the rebels," the high commissioner reckoned.[150]

As the rebellion unraveled, the national movement's fragmentation contributed to violence in yet another way. It hampered the diplomacy that would bring violence to an end. In early 1939, the British hosted separate Arab and Jewish conferences to solicit recommendations for a new policy. When Palestinian Arab elites could not agree on who should attend, Britain invited representatives of other Arab countries to participate on equal footing. When the Palestinian movement had been more cohesive, leaders were able to subordinate such external involvement to their own coherent strategy. Such was the case at the end of the 1936 strike, when the AHC asked Arab leaders to intervene to provide what it could not provide alone: a way of abandoning protest without admitting defeat. By 1939, the movement no longer had an authoritative leadership to direct external involvement or a clear strategy for such involvement to serve. Instead, Arab states intervened to fill Palestinians' leadership vacuum.[151] The effect of external involvement on the national movement was thus mediated by the movement's organizational structure. This would be the case for generations thenceforth. For non-Palestinian parties that believed that they could derive some benefit from the Palestine question, the tears in the Palestinian national fabric created opportunities. Britain's eagerness to work with anyone but the mufti did as well.

In May 1939, Britain issued what became known as "the White Paper," in which it declared that it had never intended to create a Jewish state. Judging that the Balfour pledge had been satisfied, it proposed to restrict Jewish immigration and land transfers, and to grant independence to a unitary Palestinian state in 10 years. The Zionist movement denounced the White Paper, as did many within Britain's own government. It was thus unlikely ever to take effect. Still, Palestinians' reaction is indicative of the impact of organizational structure on strategic action. Most Arab heads of state, Palestinian politicians, and ordinary Palestinians embraced the new British policy as a victory. An English teacher in Palestine noted, "The average Arab one spoke to was triumphant, regarding the White Paper as a concession won by Arab arms."[152] In the words of Qassamite fighter Subhi Yasin, "In principle, there was not a single loyal and perceptive Arab who did not agree with the White Paper."[153] Nevertheless, the Palestinian movement did not have an organizational structure that would enable it to articulate and enforce this majority sentiment. Kabha noted that the people "were not given the right to make their voices heard because, given the divisions among their ranks, no one was capable of speaking in the name of all who participated."[154]

Divisions enabled the minority who opposed the White Paper to act as spoilers. Britain encouraged this when it refused to grant amnesty to the mufti or rebel leaders. In a threat to any leader who might abandon them, rebel commanders issued a statement that denounced the White Paper and warned that the Palestinian people were not subject to the Nashashibis, Husaynis, or Arab kings.[155] Rebels had proved their readiness to assassinate compatriots, and the mufti understood the danger in crossing them.[156] Furthermore, as long as the British refused to speak with Husayni, he was determined to prevent any other Palestinian Arab from speaking in his place.[157] The mufti believed the White Paper fell short of nationalist goals, but he also rejected it because he had no personal incentives to do otherwise. The White Paper initiative thus collapsed. Rebels attempted to resuscitate the rebellion but were too weak. The termination of the revolt by the summer of 1939 was hence markedly different from the termination of the strike in 1936. Whereas the more cohesive Palestinian movement had halted the strike by political decision, the latter died slowly under the weight of internal and external violence.

The fragmentation that splintered Palestinians during the Arab Rebellion stood in contrast to a deepening cohesion in the organizational structure of the Zionist movement. The rebellion made the Yishuv more economically self-sufficient as jobs vacated by Arab workers in Jewish enterprises became permanently filled by Jews and Jews developed footholds in sectors for which they had previously relied on Arabs. The Jewish community received permission to open their own port in Tel Aviv to compensate for the strike's closing of the port in Jaffa. In addition, the revolt inspired greater ideological and strategic unity among rival wings of the Zionist movement, closing the gap between advocates of "restraint" and of "frontal confrontation" in favor of the latter.[158] Finally, Arabs' attacks propelled the Yishuv's military consolidation and development. The rebellion fostered a shift from a loose, localized, and voluntary armed force toward the establishment of an autonomous military apparatus with regular recruits and under centralized control. The government's initiation of joint British–Jewish policing efforts, including Major-General Orde Charles Wingate's Special Night Squads, gave hundreds of Jewish men instruction in combat. Moving into the 1940s, the gap between the organizational structures of the Arab and Jewish nationalist movements presaged the outcome should the two face each other in a fight for Palestine.

FROM FRAGMENTATION TO CATASTROPHE

As international powers became engrossed in World War II, Palestinians shifted their attention from political activity to economic recovery. It was difficult to do otherwise, as most of their leaders had been killed, exiled, or detained. By 1943, however, the Istiqlal Party had regrouped and called for elections to establish a new national leadership. Haj Amin intervened from exile to stifle the initiative. Bitterly anti-British and famously pro-Nazi, he was determined to block any perceived challenge to his exclusive leadership of the Palestinian cause.[159] Such was the state of Palestinian politics in 1944, when Arab heads of state met to lay the groundwork for the creation of the Arab League. Palestinians could not agree on delegates to represent them, and Arab states appointed an observer on their behalf. When Palestinians' quarrels continued, the League itself selected a Palestinian executive body. Though this initially excluded the mufti, he maneuvered to acquire control and restructure it as a new AHC. This AHC would not recuperate the aura of national unity that its first incarnation had briefly obtained. It was desperately short of funds, and its offices were split between Jerusalem and Husayni's new base in Egypt. The AHC attempted to create a new network of National Committees throughout Palestine but chose members on the basis of loyalty to the mufti rather than skill or local legitimacy. The committees thus lacked the grassroots grounding of their 1936 predecessors and likewise their capacity to organize collective action.[160]

Meanwhile, Jewish forces initiated their own campaign of attacks and bombings against the British in Palestine. Exhausted, Britain finally relinquished its Mandate to the United Nations in 1947. That November the General Assembly approved Resolution 181 partitioning Palestine into Arab and Jewish states, with international control over the Jerusalem–Bethlehem area. The Yishuv accepted the plan. The AHC and Arab states rejected it, charging that Jews constituted a third of the population and owned less than 10 percent of the land, yet were awarded a state in 56 percent of Palestine. Jews responded that most of that state consisted of desert. Arabs retorted that Jews also obtained most of the coastline and that 45 percent of the population falling within the borders of the future Jewish state was Arab.

Violence between Arabs and Jews began almost immediately. Arab fighters took the offensive, but Jewish forces soon gained the upper hand. The AHC did not have a plan to prevent civilian panic and by March 1948 approximately 75,000 Palestinian Arabs had fled the country. Most were members of the urban middle class terrified by violence and chaos.[161] A new Jewish offensive got under way, and fear and rumors impelled entire Arab towns and villages to flee. The outflow accelerated following a massacre in the village of Deir Yasin. On May 14, 1948, Jewish leaders declared the establishment of the state of Israel. The armies of five Arab states mobilized against it, and conventional combat ensued. By June, when the first Arab–Israeli ceasefire went into effect, another 200,000–300,000 Palestinians had become refugees.[162]

Stronger leadership, institutions, and collective purpose might have given Palestinians greater resilience with which to preserve their collective existence in the face of war and uncertainty. However, the national movement's fragmentation rendered it brittle in the face of external pressure. Decades under colonial administration had left Arabs without autonomous institutions capable of providing security, governance, or services after the British withdrawal. By contrast, Israel inherited the proto-state institutions that had been developing since the start of the Mandate. These empowered it to plan, protect, and mobilize troops and supplies effectively. Martin van Creveld writes, "Man for man, the Jews were better armed, better led, and something that proved decisive, possessed countrywide organization, both political and military."[163] Palestinian Arabs, on the other hand, remained torn along familial, provincial, and other social lines. Disputes emerged between Arab volunteers, Palestinian fighters affiliated with the mufti, and Palestinian forces linked to other factions.[164] Jealous of its power, the Husayni-led AHC prevented the establishment of a more inclusive, capacities-based leadership capable of putting forth clear directives to the population. Communities were not integrated into organizations that might have coordinated and protected them. Had people had institutions to aid their steadfastness, they might have been less prone to take flight.

Cooperation among the Arab states was no greater than that among Palestinians.[165] Arab armies refused to submit to a central command or invasion plan. Arab leaders disagreed on nearly every aspect of strategy except for the need to weaken Amin al-Husayni, whom many disliked personally and feared would drag them into a military quagmire. In February 1948, the Arab League rejected the mufti's appeal to establish a provisional Palestinian government. It also prohibited him from attending key discussions on the League's Palestine policy. At the same time, Transjordan was conducting secret talks with British and Jewish leaders about annexing areas that the partition plan designated for an Arab state.[166] Hardly had Israel declared its independence when Abdullah announced his establishment of a military administration over central Palestine. This became known as the "West Bank" of the Jordan River.

The June 1948 ceasefire collapsed with an Egyptian attack that July. By October, Israeli expulsions had propelled the flight of another 100,000 Palestinians.[167] Husayni attempted to salvage the national movement by convening some 90 Palestinian figures in a meeting in Gaza. This assembly announced the formation of the All-Palestine government and proclaimed Palestine to be independent. Nonetheless, this effort came too late to forestall either Israel or King Abdullah. That very day, Abdullah gathered Palestinians opposed to the mufti in a counterconference in Amman, which called to unite both banks of the Jordan under the Hashemite throne. He assembled hundreds of others in similar meetings in the months that followed. Given the split between Palestinian Arabs aligned with Abdullah and those aligned with Haj Amin, the All-Palestine government was an empty shell. It would continue to exist until 1963, though in name only.[168]

Israeli offensives during the following months caused another 130,000 Palestinians to flee.[169] The war came to a close in 1949 when Israel signed four armistice agreements with Arab states. Israel had lost 1 percent of its population in the fighting but secured the establishment of the Jewish state. It extended over approximately 78 percent of Mandate Palestine, or 50 percent more territory than that allotted by the United Nations partition

plan. Approximately 600,000–760,000 Palestinian Arabs, some 60 percent
of their total population, had become refugees.[170] Egypt assumed control in
the Gaza Strip, the 5-by-28-mile swath of land on the southern Mediterranean
coast. Transjordan maintained control of East Jerusalem and the West Bank.
Renamed the Hashemite Kingdom of Jordan in 1949, it officially annexed the
West Bank the year after.

The fragmentation intensified by the Arab Rebellion contributed to
Palestinians' inability to prevent the dissolution of Arab Palestine in 1947–
1949. Palestinians would call the war *al-Nakba*, or "the Catastrophe." As
Khalidi writes, "Palestinians entered World War II in effect headless – without even the semblance of a unified leadership.... The crippling defeat they
had suffered in 1936–39 was among the main reasons they failed to overcome
it."[171] Fragmented in the face of the foreign powers sanctioned to decide the
future of Palestine, in the face of Arab states with disparate interests, and
in the face of a well-organized Zionist movement, the Palestinians' defeat in
1948 was all but a foregone conclusion.

CONCLUSION

During three decades under British rule, the Palestinian national movement
undertook protest to advance its political rights and prevent the establishment
of a national home for the Jewish people in Palestine. The movement's strategies evolved in accord with such circumstances as increasing Jewish immigration, land acquisition, and institutional strength, as well as Britain's continued
refusal to accommodate Arabs' entreaties. Nevertheless, these conditions did
not mechanically dictate the character of Palestinians' protest activity. Rather,
their impact was mediated by the organizational structure of the national
movement itself. The extent of movement cohesion or fragmentation critically
shaped whether Palestinians' will to oppose Zionism led a broad base of the
population to engage in unarmed protest or instead drove crowds or groups of
fighters to undertake lethal acts.

Palestinians' experience under the British Mandate illustrates the organizational mediation theory of protest and, in so doing, anchors three claims
regarding the relationship between movement cohesion and protest. The first
claim is that movements are politically cohesive to the degree that leadership,
institutions, and collective purpose bring their members together. They are
fragmented to the degree that they do not. Palestinian Arab society shared a
nearly universal opposition to Zionism and many made great sacrifices for the
cause of national independence. Nevertheless, the movement's organizational
structure was fragile due to endemic antagonism among traditional leaders
and those leaders' failure to build autonomous institutions. At the outset of
British rule, cooperation among elite families, combined with the absence
of internal challengers, gave the nationalist effort some top-down unity.
With time, however, socioeconomic transformations and Zionist expansion
brought a larger cross-section of the population to demand bolder politics

and greater participation. Leaders failed to adapt to these challenges, and the legitimacy of inherited patterns of political and social order waned. Political organizations emerged, but they were generally too limited, factionalized, or personalized to integrate country-wide collective action or manage multiple sources of fragmentation. Some of these fragmenting forces emerged from within Palestinian society. These included elite rivalries, class tensions, and a clan-based social structure in which groups resisted submission to another's command. Other fragmenting forces came from Palestinians' embeddedness in complex international and regional interests. The Mandate fed the contradiction between patriotic opposition to the Balfour Declaration, on the one hand, and dependence on government employment and services, on the other. Beyond this, British policies exacerbated divisions by positioning elite families against each other and emphasizing Palestinians' religious differences at the expense of their nationhood.

Another impediment to unity was the ambiguity of boundaries between the Palestinian nationalist movement and larger Arab and Muslim identities. This was evidenced by the easy penetration of foreign fighters during the Great Rebellion and the intervention of Arab and Muslim governments in Palestinians' internal and external affairs. Most critically, however, fragmentation was fed by the very fight against a stronger adversary. The Zionist movement had greater human, material, political, and international resources than those available to Palestine's indigenous Arab population. Furthermore, the colonial power formally endorsed Jews' national ambitions, but not those of Arabs. There was no obvious strategy for how Palestinians could best confront this challenge. It was thus little wonder that they differed in their views of what to do or that they jockeyed for personal advantage along the way. These endogenous and exogenous factors compounded each other in fragmenting the Palestinian national movement, notwithstanding moments of patriotic unity.

The second claim anchored by the history of Mandate Palestine is that cohesion increases a national movement's capacity to carry out nonviolent means of protest. During the first decade under British rule, the Arab political public cohered around the default leadership of urban notables. Inter-elite cooperation facilitated legal forms of protest, such as demonstrations, petitions, and diplomacy. Nevertheless, elite-led protest lacked the social grounding and institutional power to prevent or control outbreaks of grassroots violence, such as the riots of 1920, 1921, and 1929. As nationalist grievances intensified, leaders' ability to channel the population's anger and fear into nonviolent action hinged upon their capacity to build an organizational structure that integrated popular involvement and represented popular aspirations. The 1936 rebellion represented the zenith of such cohesion during the Mandate years, though it was incomplete and short-lived. Its onset witnessed a national leadership body in the AHC, an institutionalized network of National Committees, and strong collective purpose behind clearly articulated goals. This organizational structure was the context in which people of different social classes, religions, and regions participated in a six-month general strike, as well as mass demonstrations, boycotts, and acts of noncooperation. Palestinians did not use nonviolent tactics to the exclusion of violence. Nonetheless, movement cohesion helped them to channel some of the will to rebel into broad-based, unarmed activities and sustain those activities in the face of government repression. Relative unity also helped Palestinians to terminate the strike and shift to political–diplomatic action when leaders judged necessary.

The third claim illustrated in this chapter is that a movement's fragmentation increases the likelihood that protest activity will become violent. By the time the Arab Rebellion resumed in 1937, exhaustion had drained collective commitment and elite rivalries had splintered authority structures. Given this weak organizational structure, the movement proved brittle under intensifying pressure. The government deported national elites, arrested local leaders, outlawed committees, and increased collective punishment. In doing so, it gutted the popular, leadership, and institutional elements that generate cohesion in any self-determination movement. The resulting fragmentation left the Palestinian movement without the political tools to mobilize nonviolent forms of protest or impose constraints on the turn to force. In addition, divisions generated incentives for violence apart from opposition to Zionism. Elites and rebels took up arms in competition for power within Palestinian society. Neither public opinion nor the exiled leadership nor institutional bodies effectively restrained those with weapons and a will to use them for any motive, private or political. This fragmented organizational structure mediated the way that other factors, such as British repression, popular despair, and Arab state intervention, affected nationalist protest. Fragmentation also decreased the movement's capacity to transition to a political settlement when the opportunity emerged.

The substantiation of these claims highlights the limits of explanations of protest that do not take into account a movement's organizational structure. Some argue that Palestinians rationally escalated to radical strategies as moderate strategies failed to change British policy. However, strategic adaptation alone cannot account for how broad-based protest got off the ground in 1936 in a way that it had not previously. Nor can it explain why violence after 1937 had a particularly lethal character. Furthermore, it is ill-equipped to elucidate the descent into internecine violence or the rejection of the 1939 White Paper, both of which seemed to defy cost–benefit calculus. My emphasis on organizational structure sheds light on these puzzles. It also challenges the argument, widespread at the time and since, that Palestinian elites were the primary engine of protest violence. "Everybody knows that the terrorists have a well organized center in a neighboring country," the Hebrew daily *Ha'aretz* asserted in 1938, in a reference to the mufti and other exiled leaders. "These outbreaks are not incidental," the daily *Haboker* concurred. "There is a guiding hand."[172] Nevertheless, leaders' preferences were never the only factor that determined the character of protest. Before 1936, outbreaks of violence proceeded despite elites' preferences to the contrary. Even as Amin al-Husayni became more militant, he appears to have been more effective in thwarting the rise of an alternative leadership than in directing violence on the ground.

The organizational mediation theory of protest sheds light on these patterns in protest, as well as on the collapse of the Palestinian community in the 1948 war. The war left Palestinians geographically scattered, socially devastated, economically dislocated, and leaderless. Nevertheless, from disaster came forth the makings of a revitalized national unity.

3

Roots and Rise of the Palestine Liberation Organization, 1949–1987

The Nakba destroyed Palestinians' national life in nearly every respect. Villages were erased, homes and fields dispossessed, and families torn asunder. Decades of urban and commercial development were lost. The dispersion of refugees – 10 percent going to the East Bank of the Jordan, 39 percent to the West Bank, 26 percent to the Gaza Strip, 14 percent to Lebanon, 10 percent to Syria, and 1 percent to Egypt – left Palestinians a diasporic nation.[1] The exodus of hundreds of thousands of people on foot with only the clothes on their backs began their descent into a day-to-day battle for subsistence.

Palestinian refugees insisted that they had fled temporarily under duress. In December 1948, United Nations Resolution 194 affirmed their right to return to their homes inside the new state of Israel. Arguing that returned refugees would constitute a fifth column, Israel sealed the borders. It appropriated the lands of nearly four hundred villages emptied during the war and established 186 Jewish settlements in their place.[2] As years passed, refugees' emergency tents evolved into 59 concrete refugee camps administered by the United Nations Relief and Works Agency for Palestine Refugees in the Near East (UNRWA). Some refugees attempted to infiltrate Israel to return to their homes, harvest crops, or smuggle goods. Infiltrations gradually became more political, resulting in hundreds of violent incidents from 1951 to 1955.[3] Responding to these acts, Israeli forces carried out harsh reprisal raids causing deaths in the thousands.[4] In the succeeding decades, Palestinians formed political groups and expanded cross-border operations as a strategy to revitalize the national movement. Their efforts eventually became embodied in the Palestine Liberation Organization (PLO).

The PLO's strategies would continue to evolve with the tumult of regional and international politics. Yet they were never a simple derivative of that ferment. The PLO's strategic action was also mediated by its own fragmented organizational structure. That fragmentation stemmed from ideological disputes, power struggles, outside interference, and Israel's refusal to accommodate Palestinians' demands. This chapter employs the organizational mediation theory of protest to analyze the effects of this fragmentation. It differs from conventional examinations of PLO politics, which typically consider how factionalism affected the *success* of Palestinians' methods. By contrast, I consider how factionalism affected the very choice of methods.[5] My analysis likewise differs from Yezid Sayigh's seminal work, which concludes that armed struggle drove Palestinians' development of statelike institutions.[6] Taking the inverse of that argument, I propose that gaps in Palestinian statism – that is, the lack of a monopoly on the means of coercion and decision making in the national community – were themselves factors contributing to armed struggle. This relationship was interactive and complex. Fragmentation helped propel armed strategies, but armed strategies also created opportunities for both fragmentation and for managing fragmentation. As act and ideology, armed struggle mobilized people despite geographic dispersal and political differences. At the same time, it offered an arena in which groups competed. That competition itself shaped how, when, and by whom violence was undertaken.

This chapter has four sections. The first traces the historical events giving rise to the PLO. The second section analyzes how fragmentation in the PLO affected its use of violent strategies, particularly by encouraging escalatory outbidding among Palestinian factions, facilitating the formation of radical splinter groups, and obstructing the leadership's pursuit of a compromise settlement. The third section examines the PLO's paradoxical recovery of some elements of cohesion after its expulsion from Lebanon and how this cohesion aided the shift from military means. The fourth section concludes the discussion.

AFTER DISASTER

What Palestinians experienced in the aftermath of the Nakba was not fragmentation as much as the near disintegration of their national existence. Nonetheless, feelings of historical injustice, exile, and alienation became the basis for a renewed sense of collective purpose. "Every Palestinian was lost," Anis al-Qasim wrote in the 1950s. "It made no difference whether he left the homeland or remained in it, whether he was impoverished and lived in a tent or became rich and purchased gardens, or whether he carried a refugee certificate or a diplomatic passport."[7] Older refugees passed on the memory of Palestine as a paradise lost. Children found common ground in their experience of being legally distinguished, economically disadvantaged, socially stigmatized, and residentially segregated in host states. Illustrative are Fawaz Turki's pained recollections of growing up Palestinian in Beirut, where he watched a street performer's monkey imitate a Palestinian picking up his food rations and heard jokes that began with "Did you hear the one about the Palestinian who ... ?"[8]

Past tragedy and lived indignities both reinforced Palestinians' common consciousness and pinned it to the right of return. "Return is the rock on which our nation in exile is founded," Turki wrote. "It is as if the ultimate Palestinian question were: I want to Return, therefore I am."[9] The nationalist awakening of youth marked a transition from a resigned *jil al-nakba* (generation of the disaster) to the activist *jil al-thawra* (generation of revolution). Education, esteemed as a rare source of security and pride for a vulnerable nation, likewise contributed to this shift. Hundreds of thousands of Palestinian children attended UNRWA's free schools and then studied in universities throughout the Arab world.[10] Education contributed to the reconstruction of a middle class and fostered skills and opportunities for political engagement. With a similar effect, tens of thousands obtained employment in Arab oil-exporting states. This raised living standards for families back home and cultivated relationships among Palestinians from different parts of the diaspora.

Palestinians thus came together in a unifying sense of nationhood despite, if not due to, the fragmenting effects of 1948. Their identification as Palestinians increasingly transcended the religious, class, and clan cleavages that had been destructive in prior eras.[11] Nevertheless, various obstacles hampered the transformation of collective identity into collective action. In the "frontline" Arab states that were home to most refugees, governments viewed Palestinians as destabilizing and restricted their independent mobilization. Politically minded Palestinians thus typically joined, and were manipulated by, existing Arab political parties. They became among the most eager supporters of Egyptian President Gamal Abdel Nasser and Arab nationalism. At the American University of Beirut, George Habbash and others formed the Arab Nationalist Movement (ANM) in the early 1950s on the platform that Arab countries' liberation from imperialism was the key to the recovery of Palestine. The ANM later developed close relations with Nasser.

During the same era, many young refugees in Gaza joined the Muslim Brotherhood. Yet many became frustrated with the Brothers' aversion to armed activity. Among them, Yasir Arafat and Salah Khalaf (Abu Iyad) went on to rally students at the University of Cairo behind Arafat's stance that Palestinians must not wait for Arab unity to liberate their homeland. Insisting that Palestinians instead rely only on themselves, these "Palestine firsters" gained popularity after Israel's six-month occupation of Gaza during the Suez War. They were then joined by another young refugee from Gaza named Khalil Wazir (Abu Jihad). Arafat and his comrades later moved to Kuwait, where they formalized their group as the Palestinian National Liberation Movement, or Fateh.[12] Their clandestine organization grew into a network and began issuing a magazine, *Our Palestine*, which facilitated contacts with Palestinians in other countries.

Fateh's founders were deeply concerned about fragmentation in the national struggle and envisioned their group as a vehicle for overcoming it. Familial-based factions of the Mandate era had crumbled when their leaders were removed. Against that tendency, Fateh sought to build an authentically popular organization.[13] Eschewing partisanism, they presented Fateh as a revolution that transcended Left and Right, distanced itself from inter-Arab disputes, and welcomed financial support from any regime. The lynchpin of Fateh's strategy for achieving both unity and national liberation was armed struggle. Fateh argued that guerrilla activity could wear Israel down by attrition. It could also entangle Arab states in the conventional war that they preferred to postpone. Echoing Frantz Fanon, Fateh's founders urged refugees to take up arms in order to conquer their immobilizing despair and reclaim their honor. They hence saw violence against Israel as a meeting ground for all Palestinians regardless of political and territorial barriers, as well as a mechanism for linking vanguard leaders to the masses. As Khalaf wrote, "Only armed struggle would be capable of transcending ideological differences and thus become the catalyst of unity."[14] In this way, fragmentation among Palestinians impelled violent means of protest with the aim of overcoming that very fragmentation.

By the 1960s, Nasser was adamant that Arab armies avoid a war with Israel for which they were not ready. Yet he also recognized that Palestinians were restless for a resolution of their plight and saw that the status quo of Arab representation of the Palestinians was insufficient. In 1964 he led the first Arab League summit in authorizing Ahmed Shuqayri, the League's Palestinian delegate, to establish "foundations for organizing the Palestinian people."[15] While the League's intention was not to sanction a proto-state institution, that is what Shuqayri proceeded to build. Ambitious and outspoken, he assembled 422 notable Palestinian figures and declared their gathering the first session of the Palestinian National Council (PNC). The PNC approved a Palestinian National Charter and announced the formation of an overarching structure named the "Palestine Liberation Organization." The PNC, confirmed as the PLO's parliament and highest authority, elected an Executive Committee and Shuqayri as chairman. The second Arab summit recognized the PLO and its military branch, the Palestine Liberation Army (PLA).

The rebuilding of an organizational structure for the Palestinian struggle thus split along two tracks: guerrilla groups propelled from the bottom up and the PLO sanctioned from the top down. These tracks were mutually antagonistic. Fateh viewed the PLO as an "envelope" by which Arab states sought to contain Palestinian nationalism within their own interests. Shuqayri insisted upon the legitimacy of his exclusive leadership of the Palestinian people. The resulting fragmentation in the national movement mediated the turn to armed action. Before 1964, Fateh recruited and trained members but had not planned on commencing military operations. Arab recognition of the PLO and PLA, however, fueled a sense of competitive urgency. Arafat urged a swift start of guerrilla activity at least in part to preserve the political–military initiative and protect Fateh from being overshadowed by Shuqayri's PLO.[16] After internal debate, Fateh carried out its first sabotage attack against Israel on New Year's Day 1965, issuing a statement in the name of al-Asifa, which became known as its military wing.

Fateh fedayeen, or "freedom fighters," continued to execute attacks, including bombing pipelines, water pumps, warehouses, and power plants, as well as planting land mines on roads, highways, and railroad tracks. Their approximately one hundred attacks by the 1967 war left at least 11 Israelis dead and 62 injured.[17] Fateh accompanied its exploits with pronouncements that famously exaggerated their menace. Military activity garnered popular support, which pressured other Palestinian groups to prove their nationalist credentials by doing likewise. The ANM increased recruitment efforts and undertook preparations for guerrilla action, though it continued to obey Nasser's preference against irregular strikes on Israel.[18] Also engaging in military recruitment was the Palestine Liberation Front (PLF), formed by Syrian army officers of Palestinian origin, foremost among them Ahmed Jibril. Lest he fall behind, Shuqayri cooperated with the ANM and the PLF in establishing the PLO's own fedayeen squadrons. The squads, called the "Heroes of the Return," began reconnaissance missions and eventually guerrilla raids. Other ANM affiliates carried out military action under other names.

Divisions among Palestinian parties were aggravated by divisions among Arab states, themselves heightened by the "cold war" between the left- and right-leaning Arab regimes.[19] Fearful of Israeli retaliation, Jordan and Lebanon restricted fedayeen activities as much as they could, logistically and politically. Criticizing Jordan's King Husayn as a colonial puppet, Nasser asserted his superior commitment to Palestine through militant rhetoric. Yet he was no less hostile to Fateh, which he thwarted by arresting its activists, hampering its activities, and even accusing it of being an agent for the CIA.[20] The Ba'ath Party that took power in Syria after 1963 took a different track. It championed Fateh by offering it training, weaponry, and publicity. This support stemmed from the Syrian regime's ideology and its own internal political dynamics, as well as its aspiration to outstrip Egypt in the contest for leadership of the Arab "revolutionary" camp.[21] In the words of one Syrian official, the Ba'ath sought to "rub Nasser's nose in the mud of Palestine."[22]

These dynamics contributed to fragmentation in the struggle for Palestine, which mediated protest against Israel. Internal competition and outbidding pushed rival groups to undertake armed action more quickly, and perhaps more forcefully, than they would have otherwise. Guerrilla strikes against Israel doubled between 1966 and 1967,[23] with attacks by Fateh alone quadrupling from March to April 1967.[24] Attentive to Fateh's rising popularity, Shuqayri engaged in increasingly bellicose rhetoric, including his infamous pledge to throw Jews into the sea.[25] Escalation fed harsh retaliation on the part of Israel's army and profound fear in its society. Guerrilla activity also contributed to the realization of one of Fateh's goals: to entangle Arab states in conventional war. This came to fruition when, against a backdrop of ongoing border tension and a series of fateful steps by all parties, Israel launched a preemptive strike in June 1967. In six days it routed the armies of Egypt, Syria, and Jordan, annexed Arab East Jerusalem, and occupied the West Bank, the Gaza Strip, Egypt's Sinai Peninsula, and Syria's Golan Heights. In the course of the war, another 250,000–300,000 Palestinians became refugees.

NATIONALIST REVIVAL

In the Palestinian national movement's struggle for cohesion and self-determination, the 1967 war represented both calamity and opportunity.[26]

For many ordinary Palestinians, the defeat confirmed Fateh's claim that Palestinians could not depend upon others to liberate Palestine and must instead take their national struggle into their own hands. As state armies retreated, many regarded the Palestinian fedayeen to be the only force defending Arab honor by taking up arms against Israel. This perception redoubled in March 1968. Israel invaded a Fateh base near Karameh, Jordan, and Palestinian and Jordanian forces launched an ambush that inflicted heavy losses. Although Arab casualties were greater and Israel achieved its operational objective, the Arab world heralded the daylong "Battle of Karameh" as a mythic victory.

Against the backdrop of the 1967 rout, the Palestinian resistance movement rose "like a phoenix out of ashes" to reap "a harvest of hero-worship."[27] The word "Palestinian," for two decades synonymous with the downtrodden and displaced, came to conjure images of youth, intelligence, courage, and sacrifice.[28] These developments led to an auspicious shift in the structure of political opportunities for guerrilla mobilization. State leaders eased restrictions on the fedayeen to recover their credibility and divert criticism from their own public regarding the war. Egypt and Syria provided guerrillas with new military and logistical aid, and the fedayeen expanded their bases in Syria, Lebanon, and especially Jordan. The Arab press, once reluctant to acknowledge Fateh, published its communiqués with enthusiasm.[29]

The post-Karameh euphoria renewed Palestinians' optimism in their collective purpose. Many hailed the fedayeen for forcing the world to pay attention to Palestinians as a people. Young refugees testified that the Palestinian revolution "gave me the answer to who I am" and "was the most important event ... in all our lives."[30] Yet even as Palestinians came together in a reinvigorated patriotism, the authoritative institutions and leadership needed for organizational cohesion remained elusive. Riding the wave of enthusiasm, dozens of guerrilla groups formed – by some counts, 70 or 100.[31] Many existed in name only or did not endure. Nevertheless, their proliferation undermined command and control in the movement as a whole. For one Israeli journalist, the flurry of press conferences in which Palestinian groups repeated the slogan "Unity in Combat" was proof of their disunity. "Every new organization declares with absurd logic that it is the catalyst speeding up the reaction for unity, but none is prepared to make the concessions essential for any compromise," Ehud Ya'ari wrote.[32] Fateh tried to bring guerrilla groups together in a series of coordinating bodies. Still, factions continually resisted submission to a central authority.

The factors driving fragmentation among fedayeen were many. Ideological differences were critical in some cases, such as the ANM. Habbash's desire to distance himself from Nasserism and the ANM led him to focus on the armed Heroes of the Return. Advocating greater leftism, Nayef Hawatmeh led another ANM faction in carrying out raids under the name "the Vengeance Youth Organization." After 1967, Heroes of the Return and Vengeance Youth united with Jibril's PLF to form the Popular Front for the Liberation of Palestine (PFLP) under Habbash's leadership.[33] Still, disagreements continued, aggravated by personal, generational, and class tension between Habbash and Hawatmeh.[34] When the Hawatmeh faction launched a coup to bring the PFLP closer to Marxism-Leninism, the PFLP's non-Marxist military commanders departed and established their own group, the Popular Front for the Liberation of Palestine – General Command (PFLP-GC). Violent clashes between the Habbash and Hawatmeh blocs ensued. The latter, with encouragement from Syria and Fateh, established the Popular Democratic Front for the Liberation of Palestine (PDFLP; in 1974 changed to DFLP). Smaller groups continued to splinter from the PFLP and differences persisted among those who remained.

Whereas ideological debates within groups caused them to splinter, debates *between* groups impeded their coordination around common goals. This was a recurrent theme in the relations between the three largest factions. Fateh focused on Palestinian nationalism, avoided social questions, shunned intervention in Arab states' internal affairs, and publicly denounced military activity conducted outside the Middle East or aimed at civilians. By contrast, the PFLP called for Arab unity, social revolution, and the overthrow of conservative Arab governments. Its tactics included violent actions against civilians in Israel or abroad. The PDFLP shared the PFLP's opposition to "reactionary" Arab regimes, yet called for stricter adherence to Marxist principles. At least officially, it sided with Fateh in criticizing violence against civilians.

Beyond strategic differences, the very fluidity of the Palestinian revolution – lacking geographic limits, a single forum for decision making, or binding regulations – enabled ambiguous, redundant, or marginal factions to multiply. As activists faced minimal institutional barriers to creating new factions, they could do so on the basis of mere whim or ambition. For example, Issam Sartawi founded a group that he merged with Fateh. In a subsequent meeting of Fateh leaders, he found himself in an argument over what appeared to be a minor issue. Reportedly, he stood up and declared, "I came into this room as a member of Fateh, I'm leaving it as the secretary-general of the Action Organization for the Liberation of Palestine." With this, a new organization, AOLP, was born.[35]

Another source of fragmentation in the organizational structure of the fedayeen movement as a whole was weak command and control within each faction. In many political settings, power seekers attempt to form "minimum winning coalitions." They want a sufficient number of partners to gain power, but do not want more, as each will later claim its share of the spoils. In self-determination movements, by contrast, factions may compete to amass the largest possible team to demonstrate that *they* represent the will of the nation. Among Palestinians in the late 1960s and 1970s, this imperative of large numbers sometimes ran counter to the requirements of organizational cohesion. A competitive factional marketplace encouraged cadres' lack of discipline and side switching. Stories abounded of fighters who coerced higher pay or benefits from their organizations by threatening to move to a rival faction.[36] Competition for numbers also led some factions to obtain an institutional or ideological looseness. Fateh deliberately embraced doctrinal ambiguity in the spirit of a "catchall" party. This broadened its appeal, yet left it with marked differences of opinion within its ranks. In addition, Fateh came to absorb throngs of recruits before it built the infrastructural capacity to coordinate their participation. Before the Battle of Karameh, Fateh was a small, clandestine group in which members were trained on a personal basis. After Karameh, founding member Khaled al-Hassan recalled, "People started to join Fateh by thousands.... We were forced to make our mobilization and ideological education to the people ... by masses."[37] Fearful that factions would form within Fateh, leaders isolated its different sectors to prevent any from uniting to seize control. This reform was rational from the perspective of averting coups. However, it created long-term obstacles to cohesive collective action.[38]

Beyond ideological disagreements, personal rivalries, and weak institutions, one of the principal engines of fragmentation between and within fedayeen groups was their interpenetration by Arab states. The 1967 war shocked Arab leaders into granting space to the fedayeen. It was not long before they were again competing for influence over the Palestinian cause, but the terms of this competition changed. Before the war, Arab governments jockeyed with each other and with Palestinians with regard to whether and how to impose restrictions *on* the commandos. After the war, Arab states competed in offering funding and/or territorial bases *to* the commandos. As they regained the initiative, they found a new way of competing: by intervening *within* the Palestinian movement. Their main method was to create fedayeen squads to serve as proxies for their own interests.[39]

Thus, in the spring of 1968, the Syrian Ba'ath Party created Sa'iqa, which effectively became Syria's representative within the Palestinian national movement. Syria's rival, the Iraqi Ba'ath Party, created its own Palestinian proxy, the Arab Liberation Front (ALF). Egypt, meanwhile, lent support to smaller organizations. Some Gulf states gave funding to Fateh. Even domestic struggles within a state could drive fragmentation among Palestinian forces. In the power struggle that dominated Syrian politics in the late 1960s, Ba'ath Party Assistant Secretary-General Salah Jadid used his base in Sa'iqa to compete with Minister of Defense Hafez al-Assad. Assad in turn took advantage of his ties to PLA brigades based on Syrian soil.[40] Competition unrelated to Palestinian affairs thus pitted two nominally Palestinian forces against each other.

For Hassan, state intervention fundamentally distorted Palestinian pluralism. Before 1967, he explained, "Palestinians were forbidden to participate in any political activities related to their cause, the natural consequence being the creation of many clandestine organizations." After the war, however, organizations multiplied that were "Palestinian in name only, for in reality they were extensions of the Arab parties they represented."[41] These organizations exhibited the same contradictions and rivalries as their patrons. Interpenetration by the fragmented Arab state system thus fed fragmentation within the Palestinian struggle, which in turn opened space for further interference. Had Palestinians had a more cohesive organizational structure at the outset, they might have been less vulnerable to such dynamics. Fuad Jabber wrote, "The Palestinian national movement is likely to remain at the mercy of the dynamics of inter-Arab politics ... for as long as it lacks a substantial degree of structural unity and ideological cohesion."[42]

By the late 1960s, the organizational foundations of the resistance movement revealed the contours of the fragmentation that would shape the national struggle for decades to come. In one development, however, it produced a crucial element of unity. Having alienated too many, Shuqayri resigned from the PLO in December 1967. An interim chairman encouraged Fateh and other commando groups to join the PLO apparatus. Some suggested that Fateh assume complete command and invite other fedayeen to join as independents. Apprehensive of the new situation, Fateh proposed that each guerrilla group join the PLO with representation commensurate to its size. Other groups concurred. When the PNC convened in February 1969, Fateh members formed the largest bloc and elected their spokesman, Yasir Arafat, as PLO chairman. With this, two previously antagonistic institutional forms, the PLO and the fedayeen movement, came together under a single head. Nevertheless, all guerrilla factions retained their autonomy within the PLO umbrella. This was a temporary safeguard that became a long-lasting obstacle. The PLO leadership, in Helena Cobban's words, "could never thereafter exercise the degree of monopoly over the national struggle which the leaders of most other successful modern-day national liberation movements enjoyed."[43]

AN ORGANIZATIONAL BREAKTHROUGH AND ITS LIMITS

Restructured after 1969, the PLO represented an organizational milestone. It offered mechanisms for deliberating policy and electing a legitimate leadership, a clear set of symbols and slogans, and an institutional framework connecting Palestinians across state borders and ideological divides. In principle, the PLO's highest authority was its parliament-in-exile, the PNC. The PNC convened 21 sessions between 1964 and 1998, during which time its membership increased from 105 to more than 650. In addition to approving the PLO's budget and political program, the PNC elected the PLO Executive Committee (EC) through interfactional negotiations. The 15-member EC comprised representatives of commando groups and independents. In 1970, the PLO created a 40-member Central Council to act as a sounding board and intermediary between the EC and PNC. The EC chose its chairman: Yasir Arafat from 1969 until his death in 2004, when he was replaced by another founding member of Fateh, Mahmoud Abbas (Abu Mazen).

The PLO stood as a source of leadership and institutions, as well as a focal point for the collective purpose of the Palestinian people. Nevertheless, it remained fragmented. The PLO was not a political organization as much as a political system. It was the umbrella under which Palestinian organizations, as well as the states that stood behind them, bargained over least-common-denominator goals. For Fateh-PLO leaders, the most basic goal was preserving the PLO's existence as the source of independent Palestinian decision making, what they referred to as *al-qarrar al-filastini al-mustaqeel*. To validate its claim to represent all Palestinians, the PLO had to be sufficiently open to contain the full range of Palestinian opinion. Yet to convince all factions to subscribe to the PLO, the leadership had to grant their demands that they keep their own structures, programs, and alliances. The consequence, wrote Bard O'Neill, was a catch-22: "While [the PLO] desperately needed a single institution to provide cohesion, the viability of such an institution was dependent upon a meaningful political consensus which did not exist."[44]

The relationship between the PLO and its own army illustrated the limits of its command and control. The PLA consisted of infantry brigades based in Syria, Egypt, and Iraq, as well as battalions in Jordan and Lebanon. Each host state controlled the PLA units on its soil and used them in its rivalries with other states. Syria dominated the officer corps. The Fateh-PLO leadership had virtually no power over its nominally subordinate military branch. On the contrary, the two had opposing interests. The PLA was a conventional army that depended on Arab states for safe bases and heavy armaments. It tended to look negatively upon the fedayeen, whose irregular strikes put these states at risk of Israeli reprisals. In turn, leftist commandos criticized the PLA as a lackey force. These tensions drove competition, which produced organizational inefficiencies and contradictions. In 1968 the PLA created its own fedayeen wing to tap into the popularity of the guerrillas and prevent its recruits from leaving to join guerrilla groups instead. In 1971 Fateh established regular battalions and an air unit. This ensured that the PLO would have its own loyal army should it ever find itself in combat against the PLA.[45]

Lacking the sovereign authority of a state, the PLO could not enforce binding rules to compel its constituent parts to act in a unified way. Instead, leaders relied on a range of stratagems for managing fragmentation. One tactic was the convention of reaching decisions by consensus. To choose the PNC, for example, factional leaders conducted lengthy negotiations until all agreed upon a fair distribution of seats among various commando groups, military formations, and civic associations. Such informal give-and-take managed fragmentation in the PNC's program, as well as its membership. Factions engaged in laborious backdoor talks to produce the PNC's political platform. The PNC would then take a formal vote to confirm that which was already effectively accepted.[46] Further ensuring no major objections, platforms tended to be so vague that any party could see them as representing its preferences.

Consensus decision making helped hold together the PLO umbrella. Yet it also made every organized voice a potential veto. The leadership was constantly fearful that splintering in the PLO would spell the end of its claim to represent the Palestinian people. Small factions exploited this fear by implicitly or explicitly threatening to split the organization if policies were not to their liking. The norm of unanimity thus encouraged a tactic that some named the "blackmail of unity."[47] Consensus decision making impeded policy changes in general, and conciliatory measures in particular. A strategy for managing fragmentation thus had the perverse effect of giving minority groups disproportionate power. Fateh-PLO leaders compensated with yet another strategy. They paid deference to rhetoric about internal democracy but made most pressing decisions in consultation only with each other. In effect, many matters were decided in secret by a core leadership of Arafat, Wazir, Khalaf, and Farouk Qaddumi, supplemented by Khaled al-Hassan, Mahmoud Abbas, and Muhammad Ghunaym.[48] Fateh leaders also ensured that the majority of those holding seats on all PLO bodies were Fateh loyalists, as were many categorized as "independents."

Some PLO leaders favored more forceful management of fragmentation through the creation of a semibureaucratic structure with a hierarchical command. A minority advocated the physical elimination of dissident factions.[49] Yet most viewed this approach, referred to as the "Algerian solution," as a recipe for bloodshed. All fedayeen groups had their own military wings, and any effort to unify them by force could spark internecine violence. Invoking lessons from the past, Arafat argued that this was a "red line" that Palestinians must not cross:

> During the [1936–1939] revolt our Palestinian leadership was divided and the rival groups fought each other.... When our leaders turned to the gun to solve their internal problems, our enemies took advantage of the situation and launched a campaign of assassination to destroy our leadership.... [B]ecause we are not in our own land our enemies are all around us and inside us. If we begin seriously to fight with each other our enemies will take the opportunity to destroy us as they did in the 1930s.[50]

Through the mid-1970s, therefore, sources of division within the PLO were many and tools for managing fragmentation were weak. One of the most powerful resources for encouraging cooperation, the power of the purse, was as yet unavailable. The penetrated political economy of the Palestinian movement strengthened marginal groups at the expense of the political center. Arafat explained, "If I want to hold back financial aid from a small organization [i.e. to control its activities] this group might go to a certain Arab government and obtain help from there."[51] A PLO colleague agreed: "It was practically impossible to unify the commando organizations when each one of them was supported and subsidized by one or another Arab country whose causes and quarrels they espoused."[52]

This situation changed as the PLO enlarged its bureaucracy, military apparatus, mass mobilization organizations, and network of social services. It greatly expanded its institutions after 1978, when Arab states pledged $250 million per year to the PLO, in addition to $150 million for a joint PLO–Jordanian committee to distribute to the occupied territories. These monetary transfers rendered the PLO something of a rentier national liberation movement.[53] As in rentier states, the leadership's fiscal decisions did not concern how to produce wealth, but how to allocate it in politically beneficial ways.[54] The Fateh-PLO leadership used this new budget to undertake various neopatrimonial strategies to manage fragmentation. To curb interorganizational conflict, it solidified the domination of Fateh vis-à-vis other factions. By the 1980s, Fateh was absorbing more than three-quarters of Arab funding to the PLO and filling 80 percent of PLO military positions and 90 percent of political positions.[55]

Arafat also employed PLO monies to centralize power in his own person. He already dominated official Fateh and PLO institutions. Beyond this, politicized spending helped him render this formal political system subservient to an *informal* system built on personal loyalties and exchange. Across PLO factions, Arafat contained or co-opted dissenters by making access to jobs and benefits dependent on his discretion. Within Fateh, this tendency was even more pronounced. Officially, Fateh's pyramid configuration consisted of a broad-based General Assembly, intermediary Revolutionary Council, and executive Central Committee. Intertwined with this official organization, however, was an unofficial structure akin to a series of rings in which power and resources radiated outward from the "Old Man." Arafat was the nucleus of one circle formed by his deputies and advisers, each of whom was the nucleus of his own circle of assistants, who likewise served as nuclei for other circles, all the way down to the grass roots.[56] Palestinians thus spoke of "lines" through which money and directives flowed from Fateh power brokers to cadres. Other PLO leaders mobilized resources, alliances, and even violence to compete with Arafat. Nevertheless, his personal hegemony over the national movement became the rule.

Arafat's dominance, pursued with what Sayigh called an "obsessive drive for absolute control,"[57] was a strategy for managing fragmentation insofar as it consolidated decision-making power. The creation of ties of personal and patrimonial loyalty did likewise because it integrated a far-flung diaspora and gave hundreds of thousands of Palestinians a stake in the survival of the PLO under its perennial leadership. Nonetheless, neopatrimonialism also bred resentment and inefficiency. It subjected the national movement to the whims of particular personalities or outside benefactors with their own interests in the Palestinian cause. "Endemic and planned corruption"[58] was an unstable proxy for leadership, institutions, and collective purpose as sources of movement cohesion. As the organizational mediation theory of protest would predict, this had profound effects on Palestinians' strategies in the struggle for self-determination.

FRAGMENTATION AND VIOLENCE

From Fateh's launching of the Palestinian revolution in 1965 until the late 1980s, the national movement was generally committed to armed struggle against Israel. Like other movements, the PLO regarded armed force as an appropriate response to injustice and a necessary strategy for coercing a powerful adversary to make concessions. It also believed arms to be essential to protect its institutions and civilian constituents against violent threats. Even had these rationales not applied, the PLO's engagement in nonviolent rather than violent protest would have been unlikely. For Palestinians residing outside Israel's borders, civil disobedience and noncooperation hardly appeared a viable means to pressure the Jewish state.

In this sense, the PLO's employment of arms was overdetermined by the circumstances of the Arab–Israeli conflict. Yet these external circumstances alone do not explain patterns in how, when, and why the PLO used armed strategies. Rather, its internal organization also played a role. The organizational mediation theory demonstrates that movement fragmentation contributed to escalating, broadening, and perpetuating violent forms of protest. In addition, it disrupted the shift to diplomatic strategies. Weak command and control affected the path, timing, and character of the PLO's armed struggle in different ways over time. In the 1960s and early 1970s, it was factional competition for public support that most fueled violent strategies. The PLO's goal was a "democratic, secular state" in all of historic Palestine. The resistance movement was on the ascent, there was no realistic possibility of forcing Israel to negotiate or concede territory, and fedayeen strikes were cheered throughout the Arab world. In this context, the more groups claimed credit for attacks, the more they stood to improve their political standing within the national movement.

After 1974, the use of arms became less competitive and more instrumental. The incipient Middle East peace process presented factions with difficult questions on which they took different positions. As the PLO leadership came to endorse a Palestinian state in the occupied territories, groups used armed struggle to position themselves vis-à-vis such a settlement. In carrying out attacks, factions' intended audience was not only Israel and Palestinian public opinion, but also the other factions with which they bargained to determine the PLO's program. Violence against Israel remained an idiom for internal contestation, but its logic became not only outbidding (a struggle for popularity), but also spoiling (a struggle over political outcomes). The remainder of this chapter explores these dynamics. It offers both a condensed analytical history of the PLO in exile and an evaluation of mechanisms that anchor the organizational mediation theory of protest.

Fragmentation and the Jordan War

The roots of the conflict between Palestinian nationalism and the Hashemite Kingdom of Jordan stretched to mandatory times. Tension worsened with the emergence of the PLO and its claim to represent all Palestinians, given that the majority of King Husayn's subjects were Palestinian in origin. It worsened still when the fedayeen established an operational base in Jordan and emerged as a parallel political system with its own courts, militias, and media.

Nevertheless, a bloody showdown between Jordan and the PLO was not automatic. Rather, it was an outcome mediated by the Palestinian movement's organizational structure. Arafat repeatedly voiced his wish to concentrate on Israel and avoid problems with his Jordanian host. Yet he did not exercise full command and control over the fedayeen. Palestinian commandos goaded the monarchy and army by violating local laws, flaunting their arms, and conducting car searches and arrests. Leftists shouted Marxist slogans from mosques and called for the overthrow of the "reactionary" regime. In addition, fedayeen attacks from the East Bank to the Israeli-occupied West Bank provoked harsh reprisals for which Jordan paid a heavy price. Israel became increasingly intent on pursuing the fedayeen after the PFLP's first hijacking of an airplane in 1968. Jordan became decreasingly keen on hosting them. By June 1970, three major clashes between Jordanian and Palestinian forces ended in agreements in which Husayn bolstered the Fateh leadership in the hope that it would rein in smaller groups.[59] Believing it impossible to confront fragmentation by imposing central authority, Arafat instead sought to manage it by "harmonizing" with opposition factions. This proved insufficient, particularly in checking Fateh's main rival, the PFLP.

In September 1970, fragmentation and violent protest against Israel was the backdrop to a fateful collision between the PLO and Jordan. The PFLP hijacked four jetliners and landed them on a Jordanian land strip, which it declared liberated territory. King Husayn demanded their release. Fateh suspended the PFLP from the body that nominally coordinated all guerrillas but insisted that it lacked the power to do more.[60] When the PFLP ignited the planes, the Jordanian army responded with a 12-day assault on Palestinian bases. The onslaught resulted in more than three thousand casualties and became known as "Black September." Arafat ultimately reached a ceasefire with Husayn, against criticism from the PDFLP and Fateh leftists. In the weeks that followed, the PFLP continued to defy the PLO leadership by attacking the Jordanian army, and the army continued to hound Palestinian forces.[61] The army sustained its "creeping" offensive until it forced the last of the fedayeen from Jordanian territory in July 1971. Defeated, the PLO established a new political and military headquarters in Lebanon.

Most analysts attribute this Jordanian civil war to the fundamental contradiction between the sovereignty of the Hashemite state and the autonomy of the nonstate PLO on its soil.[62] However, exclusive focus on this clash erroneously suggests a correlation between the cohesion of the Palestinian movement and its conflict with the regime. It implies that the more the PLO consolidated in Jordan, the more the monarchy saw it as a danger. An organizational mediation approach invites a different interpretation. Husayn resented the PLO but resisted fighting it for fear that public opinion and the army rank and file might side with the fedayeen. As long as these concerns deterred confrontation, PLO–Jordan relations constituted an equilibrium. It was the PLO's fragmentation that eventually destabilized this equilibrium by increasing the costs of the movement's presence and leading the king to conclude that the potential benefit of a crackdown exceeded the risks.

Had the PLO leadership exercised greater control over the fedayeen, might it have averted this fate and sustained a modus vivendi with the regime? The question is open to debate. What an organizational mediation analysis predicts and evidence supports, however, is that fragmentation in the Palestinian movement mediated the actions that precipitated conflict. Institutional disarray increased the fedayeen's propensity toward indiscipline. This freed them to behave in ways that provoked the regime and gave the king a pretext to repress the movement as a whole. Internal fragmentation and competition were likewise the context in which opposition factions carried out spectacular operations. Each sought to distinguish itself as the vanguard of the revolution, and the central leadership lacked tools to restrain them. While such fragmentation plagued the movement from the start, it reached a climax in September 1970. Hisham Sharabi wrote shortly after, "On the eve of what was to be the Jordan civil war, the Palestine resistance was divided as never before."[63] In Khalaf's words, "We had twelve organizations which meant twelve leaderships, twelve different strategies and twelve different guns pointing in twelve different directions. From all that our ills grew."[64]

Just as fragmentation contributed to violence with Jordan, so did that violence contribute to greater fragmentation. Conventional wisdom holds that conflict with an out-group spurs unity in an in-group. The Palestinian case reveals how the opposite effect may be conditioned by the in-group's organizational structure. On the one hand, Black September increased Palestinians' feelings of solidarity. On the other, it fueled strategic disputes and organizational crises. Factions traded blame for the disaster and diverged on the appropriate response. Whereas Fateh leaders urged focus on Israel, the PFLP and PDFLP continued to call for the overthrow of King Husayn.[65] Within nearly every faction, young cadres criticized older leaders for mishandling events. In the PFLP, members forced a suspension of terror attacks and expelled their chief military planner, Wadi Haddad. Nevertheless, the PFLP went on to claim responsibility for nearly as many international attacks against civilians after the suspension as it did before.[66] Haddad continued hijackings and similar actions under the auspices of a new group, PFLP – International Operations. Other groups would break from or emerge within the PFLP in the years that followed.

Fateh likewise faced internal upheaval. The 1971 Fateh General Congress saw the emergence of two camps: a right wing amenable to reconciliation with Jordan and a left wing that called for the movement to return underground and intensify armed struggle. Among the latter were young, angry cadres who had barely survived Jordan's final offensive and accused Fateh leaders of having abandoned them.[67] When conservative Fateh representatives later engaged in reconciliation talks with Jordanian Prime Minister Wasfi Tal, a squad of these fighters shocked the movement by gunning him down. It claimed the assassination in the name of the Black September Organization (BSO). During the next two years, BSO became the principal Palestinian agent of transnational attacks on civilians. It gained notoriety for the 1972 kidnapping of Israeli athletes at the Munich Olympics, among dozens of other acts.

Had the Palestinian movement's unruly divisions not set it on a collision course in Jordan, perhaps there would have been no Black September or Black September Organization. BSO was motivated by despair, revenge, and commitment to armed struggle. As an organizational phenomenon, however, its emergence was mediated by movement fragmentation. It illustrated the tendency of a weakly unified movement to prove organizationally brittle rather than resilient in the face of repression. Its particular character was an outgrowth of fragmentation as well. Radicalized Fateh cadres opposed their leadership's conciliatory stance and opposition to terrorism. The official leadership lacked the tools to restrain them without precipitating a split or the exodus of discontented members to a rival faction. Rivalries among elites added to this internal tension. With Arafat's encouragement, the Fateh Congress censured Khalaf and his aides for their role in the Jordan debacle. According to Sayigh, it was a lieutenant embittered by this censure who became the main force behind BSO.[68]

These strategic disagreements and personal animosities, in the context of a loose organizational structure, gave rise to BSO as a semi-splinter group. As in the case of al-Aqsa Martyrs Brigade (AMB) after the year 2000 (see Chapter 6), many argued that the group was the product not of structural fragmentation, but of Arafat's desire to extract the benefits of violence without the cost of openly advocating it.[69] Whether these were Arafat's calculations, it does not explain the ambiguous relationship between Fateh and its offshoot. BSO was not *organizationally* independent of Fateh. Its members never left the movement and the leadership acquiesced to its existence. Nonetheless, BSO was *operationally* autonomous. Its tactics, secrecy, and temporary "phantom cells" represented a break from Fateh's tradition of mass mobilization.[70] Its first attack took the leadership by surprise. Its subsequent operations depended neither on Fateh's instructions nor on its direct approval, though it is unclear if they occurred with its knowledge. Far from obeying Arafat, BSO members were partly motivated by scorn for his concessions.[71]

In the absence of command and control, formation of a semi-splinter group was a strategy for managing fragmentation. It was a rational choice for mainstream leaders and hardline cadres alike. BSO was not a rupture in Fateh as much as a mechanism for avoiding one. It was an institutional contortion, a midway point between loyalty and exit, which both revealed the movement's fragmentation and contained it. BSO was a safety valve for Fateh radicals who might otherwise have directed their ire at their own leadership.[72] It prevented these cadres from abandoning Fateh, while giving the leadership a measure of influence over events that might occur regardless.[73]

Nevertheless, the risks associated with semi-splinter groups came to fruition in BSO. Given the autonomy of BSO's decision making and the secrecy of its operations, it took actions that jeopardized Fateh's interests. Its violence against civilians encouraged other factions to carry out international operations in defiance of Fateh policy and put Fateh's patron relationships in peril. This reached a climax when BSO seized the Saudi embassy in Khartoum. Furthermore, although BSO's leaderless structure helped evade surveillance, Israeli intelligence identified the group's ties and targeted its reprisals against

Fateh. In light of these liabilities, Arafat moved to terminate the group in 1973 by assigning its leading figures to new posts under his supervision.[74]

BSO was an experiment in managing fragmentation, and Fateh was able to eliminate the group when it judged necessary. Such was not the case with others who completely cut ties to the PLO. Muhammad Abd al-Ghafur broke from Fateh and began organizing violence from Libya. Sabri al-Banna (Abu Nidal) did likewise, forming the Abu Nidal Organization to carry out attacks against Israeli and foreign civilians. He also assassinated Palestinian figures deemed moderate, among them Salah Khalaf in 1991. As these individuals were bound by none of the national movement's institutions or collective understandings, Fateh sought discipline by other means. Abd al-Ghafur was gunned down on Arafat's orders, and al-Banna was sentenced to death in absentia by a Fateh tribunal. He evaded the sentence thanks to sanctuary and support from Iraq, Syria, and Libya. In return, these states used him as a Palestinian vehicle for their own interests.

International Violence

The Palestinian national movement's fragmentation into factions, splinters, and semi-splinters expanded its use of the most radical armed tactics in the national movement's repertoire: international attacks on civilians. For the period between 1968 and 1984, Ariel Merari and Shlomo Elad identify 435 acts of Palestinians' "terrorism outside of Israel," which they define as the systematic use of violence that pursues political aims, is directed at a wider population than the immediate victims, and is perpetrated by Palestinian groups beyond Israel's borders.[75] I use their data, displayed in Figure 3.1, to illustrate patterns in transnational attacks as a particularly high-profile form of violent protest.

A rationalist explanation of such violence suggests that it was a "weapon of the weak" by which the movement exerted a powerful impact with minimal resources. Those who hijacked international aircraft insisted that their tactics forced the world to pay attention to the Palestinian plight when it would have preferred to ignore it. It also offered a utilitarian alternative to cross-border guerrilla attacks when Jordan, Syria, and Lebanon increased restrictions on operations from their territory.

These rationales offer a general explanation, yet fall short. The strategic rationality of transnational attacks was debatable. They not only cost the Palestinian movement world sympathy, but also directly contributed to its expulsion from Jordan, where it had enjoyed freedom of maneuver along the longest border with Israel. The PLO leadership itself viewed transnational attacks as contrary to Palestinian interests and a diversion from its strategy of people's war. Fateh criticized external operations, and Arafat declared a moratorium on them in 1974. Nevertheless, by Merari and Elad's calculations, Palestinians registered nearly twice as many incidents during the six years after that moratorium as during the six years before it. What explains the persistence of this kind of violence despite its questionable utility and the leadership's preferences

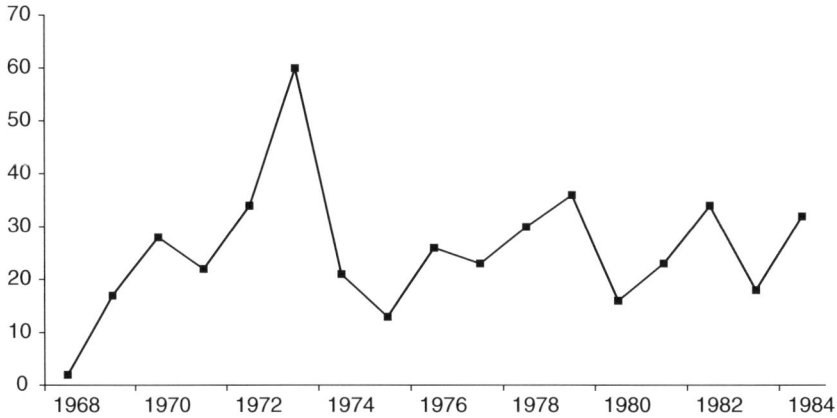

FIGURE 3.1. International attacks by Palestinian groups, 1968–1984.
Data source: Ariel Merari and Shlomo Elad, *The International Dimension of Palestinian Terrorism* (Jerusalem: Jaffee Center for Strategic Studies and Jerusalem Post Press, 1986).

to the contrary? The organizational mediation theory shows that these patterns cannot be understood independent of the role of fragmentation.

The Palestinian movement's fragmentation mediated its protest in several ways. First, the limits of central authority allowed groups to form and operate outside institutional constraints. Of the 435 attacks that Merari and Elad enumerate, only one-fourth were carried out by official PLO member groups. The groups perpetrating the remainder were not identified, not identifiable, or not PLO members at the time. They were thus not even nominally bound to the decisions of the PLO's chairman or political councils. Had they recognized the PLO as a source of authority, they might have been less likely to engage in strategies that it denounced. The PLO's structural inability to govern the behavior of all Palestinian factions was mirrored in factions' inability to govern their own members. Fragmentation within Fateh mediated the rise of BSO, which led to a spike in violent attacks in 1972–1973. The ultimate control that Fateh exercised over BSO could not be replicated over the Abu Nidal Organization, which became the single greatest Palestinian agent of transnational attacks on civilians. Nor was the PFLP able to put limits on Wadi Haddad, who continued to sponsor international operations after he was expelled from its ranks. Abu Nidal and Haddad committed 38 percent of attributable international attacks from their emergence as independent actors until 1984. Many lives might have been saved had Fateh been able to implement its sentence against al-Banna or had the PFLP's censure of Haddad curtailed his freedom of action.

Second, low institutional barriers to the formation of splinter groups enabled the proliferation of small groups with narrow agendas. Tiny squads, such as the Arab Nationalist Youth Organization and the Action Organization for the Liberation of Palestine, executed 25 international attacks. Given their size, such groups were often highly motivated to carry out extremist violence and well situated to avert foreign intelligence agencies. This kind of violence was a less fitting strategy for mass-based organizations, which had well-known leaders and fixed infrastructure. Nor was it in the institutional interests of the statist PLO, which sought international recognition and support from governments to secure subsidies, territorial bases, and inclusion in diplomacy. The Fateh-PLO leadership had much to lose by violating the international norm against terrorism. Undeterred by such concerns, small groups took advantage of fragmentation to act freely at the margins of the national movement.

Third, factional splintering not only decreased constraints on transnational violence, but also generated motivations for doing so. For minor factions, high-profile attacks offered a sensational way of gaining fame, recruits, and influence. Barry Rubin observed, "The smaller the faction, the more it needed to use terrorism to seize headlines in a grab for a share of power and glory."[76] For more established factions, such attacks provided a means of distinguishing themselves from Fateh, disrupting its diplomatic outreach, and claiming a reputation for superior nationalism. The PFLP, the second-place contender for power throughout this era, was thus the PLO member most engaged in transnational violence.

Finally, although it was not mainstream groups that committed most of the headline-grabbing acts of transnational violence, those acts acquired some mainstream legitimacy in the nationalist repertoire. Operations such as plane hijackings obtained a "logic of appropriateness" apart from a "logic of expected consequences."[77] Many came to be seen as rightful regardless of whether they helped Palestinians achieve statehood. Once such operations became an accepted tactic, groups competed for the public support that they yielded. Fragmentation rendered the Palestinian movement a highly competitive arena rather than a hierarchically ordered and internally consistent entity. In consequence, internal contests fed outbidding, which not only fueled violence but also pushed it to increasingly radical forms.

Impeding Diplomacy

During the first decade of the fedayeen movement, a fragmented organizational structure encouraged escalatory outbidding. While this dynamic persisted, the 1973 war ushered in a new development. Thereafter, fragmentation mediated factions' turn to violence to contest not only their relative standing, but also the very strategic objective of the national struggle. The war demonstrated both Israel's continued vulnerability and the limits of Arabs' military power. Seeing an opportunity to push for an end to the conflict, the United Nations hosted Egypt, Jordan, Syria, and Israel in a first-ever Arab–Israeli summit in Geneva. This was envisioned as a preliminary step in a multi-round process for reaching a comprehensive settlement in the region. Though Israel refused to allow the PLO to participate, the United States and Soviet Union indicated that they might consider its inclusion in subsequent rounds.[78] The PLO thus faced the difficult question of whether to embrace diplomacy and abandon its exclusive emphasis on armed struggle, the national program since 1969.

Most self-determination movements experience internal debate when faced with a transition from military to political strategies. Yet whereas a cohesive movement can maintain command and control, a fragmented movement risks being torn in various directions. In the Palestinian case, hardline factions denounced the incipient peace process because it implied acceptance of United Nations Security Council Resolution 242. This resolution called for Israel's withdrawal from territories occupied in 1967 in exchange for peace and security for all states in the region. The PLO rejected it because it signified acceptance of Israel and did not acknowledge Palestinians' national claims. Indeed, it mentioned Palestinians only as the "refugee problem." Though the PLO would not endorse UNSCR 242 until 1988, developments after the 1973 war sparked serious debate within its ranks. Many Arab and other heads of state were reluctant to back the PLO formally as long as it sought the elimination of Israel. In consequence, some PLO leaders argued that they needed to make concessions if they were to gain Arab recognition and the right to represent Palestinians in world diplomacy. If not, Jordan would play that role and use negotiations to advance its own claims to the West Bank.[79] This competition became all the more urgent after Husayn unveiled his 1972 "United Arab Kingdom" proposal to unify the occupied territories with Jordan.[80]

Under these circumstances, Fateh led the 1974 PNC in adopting the 10-Point Transitional Program. This called for the establishment of a national authority in any Palestinian areas liberated from or evacuated by Israel, as a "phased policy" en route to total liberation. It also endorsed "all means of struggle," thereby sanctioning diplomatic methods in addition to military ones. The leadership went to lengths to assure its base that it had not relinquished the goal of recovering all of Palestine or the right to return. It was lost on no Palestinian, however, that the transitional program represented a monumental turn toward de facto acceptance of partition and the principle of land for peace. Reinforcing this turn, PLO leaders articulated their desire to participate in the peace process.[81] In addition, Arafat reportedly sent private messages to U.S. officials indicating his willingness to accept the state of Israel.[82]

In one respect, increased inclusiveness in the organizational structure of the PLO contributed to this political landmark. A number of activists deported from the West Bank were included in the PNC and EC for the first time during the 1974 session. Like most Palestinians under Israeli occupation, they were more supportive of a two-state settlement than were refugees in exile, who longed to recover homes in what had become Israel. The growing role of West Bankers in PLO forums demonstrates that the more a movement's decision-making process is institutionalized to represent and integrate the opinions of the breadth of the population, rather than simply to set bounds on their competition, the more moderate its outcomes are likely to be. Nevertheless, to the degree that the PLO remained an umbrella for rival subgroups, the leadership could neither enforce its new political program on hardline factions nor block Arab state intrusion. Following the PNC vote, the PFLP, PFLP-GC, ALF, and the Palestinian Popular Struggle Front (PPSF) formed the Front of Palestinian Forces Rejecting Surrenderist Solutions, or Rejection Front. Iraq and Libya immediately pledged support.

Had the PLO leadership been able to impose its preferences, opposition factions might have been forced to choose between fighting PLO policy and enjoying the benefits of PLO membership. Given the national movement's loose organizational structure, however, factions could do both. Rejectionists suspended their membership in PLO executive councils to protest the new program. However, they did not completely withdraw from the PLO umbrella. The movement's organizational structure opened a middle ground between exit and loyalty. It allowed the opposition to take advantage of its freedom within the movement while averting the costs of tearing it apart. The clash between the Fateh leadership and the Rejection Front thus illustrated the tension between the PLO's status as an *actor* pursuing a political project and as a *system* configuring a political process.[83] This tension was suppressed as long as leaders managed fragmentation by upholding the consensus goal of liberating all of Palestine through armed struggle. Once they compromised on this goal, fragmentation intensified.

Arafat understood that the phased program might bring the national movement to the breaking point. In sanctioning the program, he gambled that his leadership would prevail. Yet opposition groups were not going to submit without a fight. In interviews, lectures, and publications, they denounced the program as treason. They also intensified military activity, including 13 attacks inside Israel in 1974. These claimed more Israeli lives than in any year until 2002. The PFLP-GC took the lead by carrying out a suicide mission in Kiryat Shemona that April, garnering broad public support and a wave of new recruits. The pressure to compete rippled throughout the Palestinian movement. The PDFLP had spearheaded the phased program even before Fateh adopted it. After 1974, however, some leaders advocated renewed attacks. As PDFLP commander Mamdouh Nofal expressed it, such operations were imperative in order "to deflect the accusations of treason." The PDFLP thus carried out a raid on a school in Ma'alot, Israel, leaving 23 children dead. In response, Libya rewarded the PDFLP a $1 million monthly stipend.[84] Those who viewed this violence only as conflict between Palestinians and Israel missed its logic as a conflict among Palestinian factions, mediated by the fragmented organizational structure of their national movement. In escalating attacks, rejectionists sought to force concessions on the part of Arafat and Fateh. Only secondarily did they seek to coerce Israel. In Sayigh's words, attacks were intended "not to revitalize the armed struggle, so much as to challenge the PLO leadership politically and demonstrate opposition to the peace process."[85]

Just as the Fateh leadership sought entry into the peace process to avoid being marginalized in regional and international politics, so did hardline factions challenge these efforts to avoid being marginalized in Palestinian politics.

Executing military operations lent rejectionist factions leverage over other factions that wanted to pursue diplomacy. Arms were a "force multiplier" giving small factions the influence that they lacked due to their minority presence in PLO decision-making bodies. Indeed, it allowed them to transfer political contestation from the realm of formal institutions, where Fateh dominated, to military realms in which all enjoyed freedom of maneuver. For some factions, this shift to armed action was a response to an existential threat. Some Arab leaders made statements that it was necessary to "change the structure of the [Palestinian Liberation] Organization from within and turn it into a moderate and acceptable organization."[86] For opposition factions, the existing organizational structure of the PLO was the guarantee of their political relevance and strategic autonomy. For those determined to preserve that organizational structure, military activity was a logical and justified response.

Like competition between factions, divisions within factions generated motivations for violent protest. Heads of rejectionist factions actually voted in favor of the phased program at the PNC meeting but retreated after they encountered resistance within their organizations. Khalaf recalled, "No sooner had the Palestinian Congress session ended than arguments and outbidding erupted within the various organizations, with the more radical elements in each accusing their comrades of having approved a 'liquidationist' text."[87] Intrafactional disputes contributed to spoiler attacks, as they did spoiler rhetoric. Sayigh argues that a radical wing of the PFLP-GC perpetrated a suicide mission against a kibbutz in northern Israel in June 1974 to protest the vote of their leader, Ahmed Jibril, in favor of the PNC resolution. In its aftermath, he retracted his vote.[88] Conflict was similarly intense in Fateh, where the rank and file was more militant than the leadership.[89] One motivation for Fateh leaders' sanction of the suicide attack in Nahariya in June 1974 was thus to appease hardline opposition within the faction.[90] Beyond this, Fateh participated in military activity to demonstrate its capacity to obstruct peace talks, should they exclude the PLO.[91] Just as radical factions had incentives to use violence against Israel to send a message to Fateh, Fateh had incentives to use violence to send a message to international and regional players. Against this backdrop, it carried out a terror attack in Israel on the eve of a visit by the U.S. secretary of state, who was coming with the purpose of promoting Israeli–Egyptian negotiations.

While war as politics by other means was not unusual, the organizational fragmentation of the Palestinian movement gave such warfare unusual forms. Rather than one nation using violence to signal and advance its preferences, multiple groups within the same nation used similar forms of violence to signal distinct and even contradictory preferences to others both within and outside their movement. Many observers failed to distinguish between the different political intents driving this multilevel game. Israeli leaders dismissed the PLO's peace overtures as "double talk" and argued that violence was the same, whether carried out by Fateh or rejectionists.[92] Yet this conclusion was untenable given the role of organizational structure in mediating protest.

Writing at the time, O'Neill appealed to Israel to recognize "the fact that the PLO and the Arab states do not constitute a monolithic grouping" and to "refrain from the tendency to treat all acts of terrorism as if they were sanctioned by the PLO."[93]

Strategic rationality in the overarching conflict might have dictated that the Palestinian national movement turn away from violent protest at this time. Nevertheless, fragmentation made that improbable. Even fear of fragmentation had this effect. In the absence of truly authoritative leadership and institutions, armed struggle remained one of the movement's primary unifying principles. Paradoxically, Fateh elites inched toward a negotiated settlement to advance the PLO's international standing but could not embrace negotiations unequivocally, because this risked destroying the national unity on which the PLO was based. According to Shaul Mishal, these dynamics kept Fateh's "diplomacy in chains."[94] The opposition, however, was no less "chained" to the Fateh leadership, at least for as long as the costs of exiting the PLO outweighed the benefits. The upshot was an intricate game in which both leadership and opposition tested the political constraints that they imposed on each other. Any shift from armed to unarmed strategies required that the leadership gain the upper hand in this game. It would do so either by marshaling new sources of movement cohesion or by wagering that it could manage the internal disputes that controversial policies inevitably provoked.

In 1974, the leadership wagered that it could move toward a two-state compromise without jeopardizing the status of the PLO as the unifying "address" for Palestinian nationalism. It tested the limits of the movement's fragmentation, and the gamble paid off. Ultimately, international diplomatic activity in the mid-1970s failed to produce a comprehensive peace process. Nevertheless, the PLO's overtures toward those negotiations successfully advanced its quest for recognition. In 1974 the Arab League declared the PLO to be the sole legitimate representative of the Palestinian people, and the United Nations granted it observer status. By the early 1980s, the PLO had offices in more than 130 countries around the world.[95] Fragmented or not, the Palestinian national movement had come very far from the disaster of 1948.

Entanglement

After its expulsion from Jordan in 1970–1971, the PLO established its headquarters in Lebanon, where it developed into something of a state within a state. During the decade that followed, the movement's organizational structure continued to mediate the turn to arms in multiple realms of conflict. Palestinians' complicated situation in Lebanon stretched back to 1947–1948, when the influx of a hundred thousand refugees tested the demographic balance between Maronite Catholics, Sunni, Shi'a, Druze, and other sects in Lebanon's system of confessional power sharing. While most Lebanese sympathized with the Palestinian cause, the presence of armed Palestinians alarmed those anxious to preserve Lebanon's status quo. At the same time, fedayeen found allies in many Lebanese Muslims and leftists, who resented a system in which Christians were guaranteed disproportionate power and elites neglected the country's poor periphery. As in Jordan, the fedayeen in Lebanon came into repeated conflict with authorities. In 1969 the government and PLO signed the Cairo Agreement, which authorized the PLO to maintain weapons and act as the governing authority in Palestinian refugee camps. It allowed guerrillas to carry out attacks on Israel from Lebanese soil, though only in coordination with the Lebanese army.

The Cairo Agreement granted the Palestinian national movement the greatest political independence that it would enjoy in any Arab state. Still, as in Jordan, the movement's fragmentation precipitated tension with its hosts. Weak command and control allowed fedayeen to behave in sometimes offensive, abusive, or criminal ways. Khalidi attributed such "excesses" (*tajawuzat*) to the PLO's "major structural problems of discipline, motivation, and organization."[96] In Wazir's words, "Part of our mistakes was a lack of strong control over our Palestinian organization.... Every organization was still free to do whatever they could."[97] The limits of PLO coordinating bodies rendered them unable to compel factions to coordinate with the army before launching attacks on Israel. These attacks triggered harsh Israeli retaliation. According to Lebanese sources, Israel's violations of Lebanese territory averaged 1.4 incidents per day from 1968 to 1974 and seven per day from 1974 to 1977.[98]

Against simplified correlations between out-group conflict and in-group unity, Israeli strikes did not automatically increase solidarity between Lebanese and Palestinians. Nor did it spur political unity within Lebanese society or within the Palestinian struggle. Rather, a pattern emerged wherein guerrillas attacked Israel, Israel shelled Lebanon, Lebanese critics denounced the fedayeen and the Cairo Agreement, and the PLO leadership pledged to restrain guerrilla activity. The pledge would hold until unruly factions violated it with another attack and the cycle began anew. In May 1973, a bombing believed to be the responsibility of the PFLP-GC, followed by a clash between the PDFLP and Lebanese troops, dragged the PLO into another bloody confrontation with its Lebanese hosts. This ended in the Melkart Protocol, whereby PLO leaders pledged to end attacks against Israel and observe restrictions on personnel and arms. Nonetheless, the weakness of leadership, institutions, and agreement on basic strategy continually limited the PLO's ability to deliver on that promise.

The relationship between fragmentation in the Palestinian movement and violence in Lebanon became more complex, as did conflict among Lebanese groups themselves. In April 1975, gunmen killed several figures in the Maronite Phalange Party. The Phalange retaliated by ambushing a bus and killing its Palestinian passengers. Muslim and leftist parties came together under the banner of Kamal Jumblatt's Lebanese National Movement (LNM) to demand political and social reform of the Lebanese state. Christian groups rallied with the Phalange to preserve the political system and reduce the PLO's presence in the country. All sides formed militias.

Arafat hoped to avoid entanglement in the emerging Lebanese civil war. Yet he could not prevent left-leaning Palestinian factions from partnering with the LNM. Instead, he took pains to reassure Christian leaders and to negotiate ceasefires.[99] Palestinian rejectionists and Christian militias engaged in street battles regardless. That December, the Phalange blockaded refugee camps and killed some two hundred in an event that would be called "Black Saturday." Under criticism of leftist factions and faced with the duty to defend its constituents, the PLO leadership finally announced its official alliance with the LNM. The new coalition was named the "Joint Forces."

Command and control remained elusive. The Joint Forces was made up of 30 distinct parties, and each maintained its own leadership, organization, and resource base. These groups did not defer to a central authority any more than did PLO factions or the familial blocs of Mandate Palestine. This fragmented organizational structure mediated the spiraling violence. In 1975, Syria intervened with a ceasefire that endorsed the Phalange position. It dispatched its army and Palestinian proxies to enforce it. PLO leaders condemned the intervention, but Sa'iqa protested that it could not be expected to oppose Syria. Neither could the PLA, 93 percent of whose troops came from refugee camps in Syria.[100] In Sara Bar-Haim's words, "The Lebanese civil war was thus for a short time transformed into a Palestinian civil war."[101] On one side, the PLA and a member of the PLO EC obeyed Syrian commands and defended the Lebanese Right. On the other, most PLO members defended the Left. Arafat repeatedly sought ceasefires, yet hardline Palestinian factions protested his concessions. Christian militias continued their offensive, regardless.

The PLO was figuratively torn between its obligation to the Lebanese Left and its desire to avoid conflict with Syria. Given its organizational structure, it could not avoid becoming literally torn as well. Palestinian and Lebanese leftists clashed with Sa'iqa. Sa'iqa, the Lebanese Ba'ath Party, and PLA forces attacked the Iraq-supported ALF. Fateh skirmished with Sa'iqa and Sa'iqa shelled PLO offices. Differences emerged even among PLO loyalists. Whereas Arafat sought an understanding with Syrian President Hafez al-Assad, PLO leftists sought military victory. The fighting overlapped with broader disputes over strategy in the conflict with Israel. Syria wanted to prevent Fateh from aligning with the increasingly conciliatory Egyptian president, Anwar Sadat, whereas the Fateh leadership continued to seek inclusion in the Middle East peace process. In this context, disputes within the Palestinian camp became the context for spoiler violence. The goal of obstructing Arafat's diplomacy gave oppositionists additional motivation to escalate fighting in Lebanon.[102]

A November 1976 ceasefire produced a brief calm that allowed Palestinians to refocus on Israel. The 1977 PNC clarified its 1974 endorsement of a national authority in any liberated Palestinian territory to mean acceptance of a state with those borders. The PLO leadership further signaled its readiness to coexist with Israel by holding meetings with Israeli peace activists, initiating indirect dialogue with the United States, moving to revive relations with Jordan, and agreeing to restrict fedayeen activity. Each of these measures met with

challenges from rejectionist forces. All PLO factions condemned Sadat's visit
to Jerusalem in 1977, though Arafat continued to communicate his wish that
the PLO be included in international diplomacy. Meanwhile, opposition factions continued to engage in violence on the Israel–Lebanon border. Israel
did likewise. In 1978, Israel launched its first large-scale invasion of southern
Lebanon, pushing PLO forces north of the Litani River. Arafat accepted the
subsequent ceasefire, as well as the deployment of a United Nations peace-
keeping force to the buffer zone declared in the south. The Rejection Front
denounced the ceasefire and Iraq instructed its proxies to sabotage it. Both
continued to launch guerrilla strikes against Israeli troops. These were simultaneously strikes against the Jewish state and against Arafat's diplomatic
efforts.[103] Knowing that hardliners would veto any ceasefire, Arafat did not
seek authorization from the requisite PLO councils and instead personally
promised the United Nations that Palestinians would end border strikes.
Rejectionists were incensed as he proceeded to impose his ceasefire by force.
Their dismay continued as Israel and Egypt signed the Camp David Accords in
1978 and a peace treaty in 1979. Neither recognized Palestinians' right to self-
determination. The PLO and Arab League denounced Egypt's separate peace,
but Arafat continued to send feelers to the United States. He also reached a
new agreement with Jordan.

PLO oppositionists condemned Arafat's political concessions. In making
that critique, they often denounced what they called "Fateh hegemony." Their
criticism exposed the fine line between democracy and fragmentation in the
national movement. Rejectionists called for greater accountability in the PLO,
at least in part with the goal of perpetuating armed struggle. The leadership acted autocratically, at least in part with the goal of advancing a diplomatic strategy. The PLO was beleaguered either by the problem of excessive
democracy (which allowed smaller factions to veto steps aimed at political
moderation) or by the problem of weak institutions (which allowed elites to
circumvent established procedures of consultative leadership). Had all activists complied with a single process of collective decision making, they might
have achieved the cooperation necessary to pursue a more coherent policy in
the conflict with Israel. Yet this did not come to pass because PLO members
disagreed on the process of strategy making, as they did on the content of that
strategy. The result was a situation in which the Palestinian movement neither
fully made war nor fully sought peace.

A flare-up of guerrilla attacks from southern Lebanon led Israel and the
PLO to negotiate a ceasefire through intermediaries in July 1981. At the same
time, Israel's new Likud government was preparing an offensive to drive the
PLO from its border once and for all. The gravity of the danger convinced
Palestinian mainstream and opposition forces alike that they must not give
Israel any pretext to invade Lebanon. This consensus empowered Arafat to
enforce the cessation of hostilities for almost a year. The United Nations
counted nearly two hundred Israeli violations of the ceasefire and not a single
Palestinian one.[104] Nevertheless, Israeli strikes eventually stretched the limits

of the PLO's command and control, as did the chaos of Lebanon's ongoing civil strife. Interfactional cooperation, a product of transitory circumstances rather than organizational structure, eventually broke down. That June, Abu Nidal shot the Israeli ambassador in London and Israel launched its invasion of Lebanon. Troops reached the edge of Beirut. After a three-month stand-off, the PLO agreed to leave Lebanon. The leadership relocated its headquarters to Tunis, while more than ten thousand fighters accepted refuge in eight countries. The United States assured the PLO that it would protect Palestinian civilians in its absence, yet removed its peacekeepers shortly after the evacuation. The Israeli army then entered Beirut. Under the shadow of its control, Phalangist forces attacked the Sabra and Shatilla camps and massacred an estimated 2,750 refugees.

The PLO's sanctuary in Lebanon may have been doomed from the outset. In Rex Brynen's view, it was "an indirect danger to the economic, political, and confessional privileges of the Lebanese elite by the very fact of its being."[105] Yet as in Jordan, the Palestinian movement's organizational structure mediated behaviors that made its presence more damaging for its host state than it might have been otherwise. The PLO leadership could not discipline the everyday behavior of their cadres. It ordered freezes on armed activity, yet factions continued to execute attacks that provoked Israeli reprisals. These tendencies increased discord between Palestinians and Lebanese, and within Lebanese society itself. Beyond this, the Palestinian movement's fragmentation was an enabling factor in nearly every step of the process of its entanglement in the Lebanese civil war. Given weak institutions and collective purpose, the PLO's experience in Lebanon was one in which it was easier for opposition groups to sustain military activity than it was for the leadership to enforce ceasefires or shift toward political strategies. This situation changed, however, when the PLO was forced far from the theater of battle with Israel.

EXPULSION AND ORGANIZATIONAL STRUCTURE

Most observers judge that the PLO's expulsion from Lebanon was a major blow to its already weak internal cohesion. As Emile Sahliyeh observed, "Destruction of the PLO's military structure in southern Lebanon and Beirut deprived [Arafat] of a significant tool, which in the pre–Lebanon War phase had enabled him to impose organizational discipline and unity upon his followers."[106] The organizational mediation theory of protest supports a different interpretation. The loss of the Lebanese sanctuary decreased cohesion in the national movement in the short term but paradoxically aided it in the long term. This, in turn, shaped strategy in the conflict with Israel.

This outcome is attributable to a fundamental distinction in the organizational barriers to entry for violent protest and for diplomacy. Whereas participation in diplomacy requires recognition of a certain political status, the requirements for participation in armed struggle are more logistical and material. Only the official PLO leadership could be a player in international diplomacy, because only it could claim the external and internal legitimacy to speak for the Palestinian people. In the military realm, by contrast, any group with minimal resources could launch an attack that commanded attention. As long as the PLO was based in Jordan and Lebanon, opposition factions had derived political leverage from their capacity to carry out attacks across the border into Israel. The loss of military capabilities and proximity to Israel in 1982 was thus especially devastating for them. It had a different impact on the Fateh leadership because it sought openings for diplomacy. In consequence, expulsion from Lebanon did not restrain all of its strategic options.

Hence, the termination of a military base in Lebanon weakened all Palestinian groups, yet the severity of its impact varied according to groups' organizational strength and strategic preferences. After 1982, hardline factions continued to denounce a political settlement, as well as initiatives to reconcile with Jordan and Egypt. However, they no longer had the same ability to challenge diplomacy by use of arms. This shift in the organizational balance of power between leadership and opposition reinforced the shift in the PLO's orientation from Lebanon to the occupied territories. Driven from its refugee base, the leadership increasingly moved toward the goal of a Palestinian state in the West Bank and Gaza Strip.

Still, hardline factions did not easily surrender their battle for political influence. Support from Arab states helped them compensate for their curtailed capacity for guerrilla warfare. Libya gave assistance to rejectionist groups, and Syria encouraged an anti-Arafat current among the thousands of bitter Fateh cadres who remained in Syria or Syria-controlled Lebanon. In 1983 PLO officer Sa'eed al-Muragha (Abu Musa) led these fighters in an armed uprising against Arafat that became known as the "Fateh Rebellion." He accused Arafat of corruption, abandoning armed struggle, and seeking a treasonous negotiated settlement. He also claimed that, given Arafat's disregard for the democratic councils of Fateh and the PLO, the grass roots had no alternative but to use force to seek a redress of grievances. The revolt illustrated familiar patterns in the relationship between fragmentation and protest. It was a form of spoiler violence insofar as rebels aimed to disrupt Arafat's diplomacy as well as contest his leadership. Internal divisions invited external intervention, which fed both divisions and violence. Syria gave military assistance to Fateh dissidents and Libya offered millions of dollars.[107] Had factional conflict and Arab state interference continued to reinforce each other, the split might have been irreparable. In that case, Khalidi warned, "We'll have Jordan's Palestinians and Syria's Palestinians. What was an independent actor will now become two appendices."[108]

Facing this crisis, Arafat found that standard tactics for managing fragmentation were of little value. He could not distribute monies to buy dissidents' loyalty, because they obtained resources elsewhere. Nor could he appeal to the customary give-and-take of PNC deliberative bodies to reach a compromise, because the dispute between the rebels and leadership had become unbridgeable. The PLO chairman thus resorted to his last tool: personal charisma. To join his loyalists in the trenches, he snuck back into Lebanon, narrowly dodging an ambush in Damascus and circumventing Israeli surveillance along the way. Once on the ground, he rallied popular support at refugee camps and raised loyalist fighters' morale. This strategy worked. Momentum turned in Arafat's favor and he compelled the rebels to accept a ceasefire that November.

With the termination of the Fateh Rebellion, the fragmented Palestinian movement coalesced into three camps. The PFLP, DFLP, and other factions announced their formation of the Democratic Alliance. They advocated cooperation with Syria but avowed commitment to PLO unity. The PFLP-GC, PPSF, Sa'iqa, and Fateh dissidents called their coalition the "National Alliance." They rejected the PLO as long as it remained under Arafat's leadership. The third camp consisted of Fateh's official leaders and their supporters. They convened the PNC in 1984 in the hope of obtaining legitimacy as the true representatives of the Palestinian movement. Opposition groups boycotted the meeting, but Arafat created a quorum by appointing loyalists to substitute for delegates who refused to attend. He also altered the PNC's decision-making procedure from one of consensus to one of majority rule.

Paradoxically, this change proved an effective strategy for managing fragmentation. For nearly 15 years, the criteria of unanimous decision making had given opposition groups disproportionate leverage. The institution of majority rule, however, rendered their voices commensurate with their small numbers. In freeing the leadership from the need to avoid alienating any party, it curtailed opportunities for obstructionism and centralized authority. It was thus only when national unity appeared to be near collapse that the Fateh leadership was forced to confront organizational fragmentation directly. Empowered with a new PNC endorsement, Arafat continued his diplomatic outreach and in 1985 reached the Amman Accord. The Jordan–PLO declaration of willingness offered Israel comprehensive peace in exchange for withdrawal from the occupied territories.

The Palestinian opposition was up in arms. At Syria's initiative, all opposition factions except the DFLP and West Bank–based Communist Party announced their establishment of an alternative to the PLO, which they called the "Palestinian National Salvation Front." After years of trying to dominate the Palestinian movement, Syria appeared to consecrate a split within its ranks. Yet it overstepped its bounds. The movement's fragmentation had been sustained by the fact that small factions exploited their autonomy *inside* the PLO. They had not exposed their organizational and political weakness by moving outside its framework. In siding with Syria over Arafat, however, they did precisely that. This came to the fore in 1985, when the Syria-backed Amal movement launched the War of the Camps, a three-year siege against Palestinian refugee camps in Lebanon. It justified the assault as an attempt to oust lingering pro-Arafat guerrillas. To Syria's surprise, the Palestinian National Salvation Front and the DFLP united with the Fateh to defend the camps. Other pro-Syria factions attempted to remain neutral. However, their cadres would not stay on the sidelines while Palestinian civilians were bombarded. Arafat understood that they were caught between their nationalism and their links to the Syrian regime. To force them to choose their loyalties, he escalated fighting.[109] This strategy for managing fragmentation bore fruit; all factions rallied around the PLO, even though doing so empowered a leader and diplomatic orientation that they opposed. The outcome contradicted the prediction put forth by Andrew Kydd and Barbara Walter, that radicals escalate violence to discredit moderates engaged in peacemaking.[110] In the War of the Camps, it was moderates who escalated violence with the objective of discrediting radicals.

The War of the Camps was the culmination of years of multifaceted struggle among the Fateh leadership, Palestinian opposition factions, Arab regimes, and Lebanese parties. It contributed to consolidating political authority and collective purpose in the national movement. Arafat established his domination over Fateh, Fateh asserted its domination over the PLO, and the PLO affirmed its independence. Renewed intra-Palestinian cooperation was confirmed in the national unity session of the PNC held in April 1987. The PFLP and DFLP came back into the PLO fold and the Communist Party obtained full membership. Arafat led reconciliation among Palestinian groups, and those who disagreed with him acted as a loyal opposition. The Palestinian national movement that began as a convergence of grassroots initiatives in the 1960s and underwent dramatic splits in the two decades that followed thus achieved a novel degree of cohesion by the late 1980s.

The Fateh leadership had succeeded in keeping the PLO together. Nevertheless, it was not able to prevent the waning of the PLO's influence in the world. The Iran–Iraq war absorbed the attention of the Arab states, and the decline of the Soviet Union drained a key source of the PLO's international support. In 1987 the Lebanese parliament voided the Cairo Agreement, and the Arab League summit largely ignored the Palestine question. Yet within this diplomatically frozen situation, the rumblings of an uprising against Israel began in the West Bank and Gaza Strip. The character of this rebellion would be mediated by the organizational structure of the national movement during that historical juncture. The Tunis-based PLO was arguably more cohesive than it had been. The territorial concentration of Palestinians in the occupied territories allowed them to be organizationally cohesive in a way that the diaspora could never be. If fragmentation had encouraged and enabled armed struggle during the first two decades of the Palestinian revolution, relative unity provided the grounds for a different kind of revolution in 1987.

CONCLUSION

Analysis of the roots and rise of the PLO and its experiences during two decades demonstrates how a movement's organizational structure affects its strategies. First, the case of the PLO illustrates the obstacles that impede a stateless nation's attempts to build leadership, institutions, and collective purpose. The forces creating divisions among Palestinians after 1948 included territorial dispersion, ideological diversity, and repression or manipulation by the different states under which they lived. Against these fragmenting factors, the strength of national identity and aspirations ultimately revitalized the self-determination struggle. The shared experience of exile became the basis for popular consensus on the need to recover Palestine. This unifying collective purpose spurred the formation of underground political-military groups, which in turn forged the PLO as a legitimate leadership.

The PLO developed an institutional framework for the Palestinian national movement to the degree that it acquired political status, bureaucratic complexity, and the allegiance of its constituents. PLO elites served as recognized spokesmen articulating a national program. Nonetheless, the PLO never consolidated a monopoly on decision-making authority as did many other self-determination movements. This was due to the enduring autonomy of its subsidiary factions, its penetration by Arab states with their own agendas, and its own battles over strategy, ideology, and personal ambitions. Arafat undertook various strategies to manage this fragmentation. He and other leaders dispersed patronage to co-opt would-be dissidents, engaged in long negotiations to devise compromise policies, threatened physical coercion, and inspired loyalty through personal charisma. Yet this leadership did not establish complete command and control. The PLO's fragmentation was fundamentally embedded in the context of Israel's refusal to negotiate or relinquish territory. Fateh leaders' inability to demonstrate progress toward a political settlement sustained the popularity of opposition factions that espoused unwavering commitment to armed struggle.

Second, the Palestinian experience illustrates the mechanisms by which a movement's organizational structure mediates its strategic action in general and its engagement in violence in particular. For some, armed struggle seemed inevitable given the ideologies of the era, dispossessed refugees' urge to assert dignity and courage, and the limits of alternative means for coercing a powerful state to concede land. Yet these factors did not alone dictate how and when armed struggle was used. Their influence on strategy was filtered through the configuration of cooperation and conflict among Palestinian forces. This opportunity structure fundamentally shaped incentives for and constraints upon the use of arms. To the degree that the PLO was divided into factions, factions were motivated to carry out military action not only to further their goals against Israel, but also to compete with each other. In claiming credit for increasingly bold attacks, rival groups sought to amass public support, claim the mantle of superior nationalist commitment, or win the backing of external patrons. Using military force to compensate for their political weakness, aspirant factions sought influence over the Fateh establishment just as the PLO sought influence over Arab governments. It had been the limits of state sovereignty and legitimacy that allowed the Palestinian national movement to assert its own autonomy from within the cracks of the Arab state system. The limits of centralized authority in the PLO had a similar effect. It allowed member factions to exploit those realms in which they could act without sanction from above. Foremost among these was the realm of armed force.

Apart from spurring escalatory competition, the PLO's organizational structure impeded its ability to shift from military to diplomatic strategies. Many factors appeared to support such a shift, including the start of a Middle East peace process and the PLO's need for international legitimacy to compete with Jordan's King Husayn. Nevertheless, fragmentation fed motives and opportunities for armed struggle in defiance of these factors. Factions used their autonomy under the PLO umbrella to carry out attacks aimed at derailing the leadership's political outreach. The leadership was ever fearful of the Palestinian movement's splintering, which discouraged it from unequivocally calling for a negotiated settlement.

Beyond this, the basic limits of command and control were the context in which factions drew the national movement into conflicts apart from the struggle against Israel, namely the Jordanian and Lebanese civil wars. They also created openings that facilitated intervention by states that had their own interests. By sponsoring proxy groups, outside actors increased hardliners' capacities for violence, if not directly ordering them to employ it. Finally, chronic divisions within factions, combined with weak institutions for enforcing decisions, reduced barriers to the formation of splinter groups. These groups were well positioned to use political violence because their small size enabled secret structures and narrow agendas. Splinters and semi-splinters such as the BSO and Abu Nidal Organization became agents of the most dramatic attacks of this era.

Some aspects of the national struggle during the four decades following 1948 were peculiar to the situation of exile and dispersion, Israel's formidability as an adversary, and Palestinians' centrality to the politics of a turbulent Middle East. However, the ways in which the movement's organizational structure mediated its behavior were not uniquely Palestinian. They illustrate how the character of protest does not follow automatically from the instrumental or noninstrumental motives that propel a movement's members. Nor does it derive exclusively from external opportunities and constraints. Rather, the effects of these pulls and pushes on a movement's actions are mediated by the structural framework that coordinates its members. A movement's use of violent or other strategies is systematically conditioned by its internal cohesion or lack thereof.

4

Occupation and the First Intifada, 1967–1993

The eruption of a popular uprising in the West Bank and Gaza Strip in 1987 surprised Israel, the PLO, and the world. No less astounding was the cohesion that the revolt made manifest. From Ramallah, Joost Hiltermann exclaimed that it was "remarkable ... that the entire population could be mobilized simultaneously, and that a support structure needed to sustain the uprising's momentum came into being and functioned efficiently, with a leadership that was promptly accepted as legitimate by the population."[1] Don Peretz similarly marveled that the unrest "within days ... developed into an organized movement; within weeks a coherent set of objectives was articulated."[2]

These and other scholars note the unity behind what became known as the *Intifada*, a grassroots effort to "shake off" the Israeli occupation. Yet none have systematically analyzed how this unity affected the processes or forms of protest. Most studies document the Intifada's causes and consequences and do not craft theory about why it had the character it did.[3] This chapter demonstrates how leadership and institutional networks, bolstered by society's sense of collective purpose, gave Palestinians an organizational structure that sustained an uprising based largely on nonviolent protest. The chapter proceeds in four sections. The first traces the organizational development of the Palestinian national movement in the West Bank and Gaza during the first two decades under occupation. The second section examines movement cohesion during the Intifada and the mechanisms through which it facilitated nonviolent protest. The third section considers how the toll of extended rebellion and repression increased both fragmentation and violent protest during the uprising's waning years. The fourth section concludes the discussion.

UNDER OCCUPATION

The principal challenges to cohesion in the Palestinian national movement during the British Mandate were colonial policies, elite rivalries, and weak institutions. During the ascendancy of the PLO, major obstacles were factional competition and external intervention. In the West Bank and Gaza Strip after 1948, the main hindrance arguably lay with outside actors. Their competing efforts to lure or suppress Palestinians thwarted their organization on a national basis.

Ruling the West Bank from 1949 to 1967, Jordan sought to win Palestinians' loyalty to the Hashemite Kingdom by offering citizenship and educational and economic opportunities. Simultaneously, it enticed local leaders to maintain social control in their communities.[4] It forbade the creation of specifically Palestinian political parties and in 1957 disbanded parties altogether. In the poor and overcrowded Gaza Strip, Egypt thwarted nationalist mobilization with less inclusion of the local population. It forestalled guerrilla activity by steering restive Gazans into a Palestinian adjunct to its own army.[5] Meanwhile, social divisions among Gazans undermined their commonality of interests. Indigenous residents of the Strip often resented the 1948 refugees, who outnumbered them three to one. Refugees felt similar resentment toward "residents," who often employed them for low wages.[6]

Israel's seizure of the West Bank and Gaza in 1967 and subsequent annexation of Jerusalem spurred many Palestinians to protest. In Jerusalem and the West Bank, prominent individuals issued manifestos condemning the occupation. Lawyers and teachers went on strike, and local elites formed committees to launch a campaign of civil disobedience.[7] Nevertheless, Israeli authorities suppressed this activity by deporting, imprisoning, or harassing those who spearheaded it.[8] Concurrently, Arafat smuggled fighters and weapons into the West Bank in an attempt to mobilize a popular liberation war. Guerrillas launched dozens of limited operations but met with little popular support. Israel infiltrated and destroyed the poorly organized network and imposed broad punishments to deter the population from engaging in further insurrection.[9] In Gaza, meanwhile, fighters initiated a guerrilla campaign to expel Israel. Underground forces carried out acts of sabotage, killed Palestinians accused of collaboration, and took control of many neighborhoods. Israel brought the rebellion to a halt in 1971 with a severe crackdown. Led by Ariel Sharon, this entailed a 24-hour-a-day curfew, mass roundups, and the transfer of more than twenty thousand residents from their homes.[10]

By the early 1970s, three powers competed for influence in the Palestinian territories. Jordan sought to retain loyalty by paying municipal salaries and calling for a return to the prewar status quo. The PLO worked to rally residents to its side using appeals to nationalist sentiment, and eventually economic inducements. At the same time, Israel upheld military rule through a combination of carrots and sticks. It denied Palestinians the rights of citizens but allowed them to work and travel in Israel. It co-opted traditional elites and new collaborators and prohibited nationalist expression. The army, and after 1981 the Civil Administration that it established to administer the territories, governed Palestinian life through some twelve hundred military orders that served as law under occupation. Israel punished political activism with such measures as house demolitions, imprisonment, curfew, travel restrictions, and "administrative detention" without charge or trial. From 1967 to 1978, it deported more than one thousand Palestinians.[11]

These policies obstructed the organizational cohesion of a national movement in the occupied territories. The movement's center of gravity solidified with the PLO in exile, referred to as the "outside." The outside in turn encouraged the "inside" to focus on *sumud*: remaining steadfast on Palestinian land until the fedayeen achieved liberation through armed struggle. Still, nationalist activity was never dormant. In the West Bank, a network of underground committees addressed local welfare issues and discussed strategies for resisting occupation without falling victim to state repression. The committees were composed of PLO activists, Ba'athists, Arab nationalists, independents, and, until 1970, Hashemite loyalists.[12] The Communist Party played a particularly dominant role. It benefited from years of experience with covert organizing under Jordanian rule. Israel also granted it greater freedom in recognition of its call for coexistence with the Jewish state.

Nationalist activism grew in accord with socioeconomic developments that, as under the Mandate or with the first generation raised as refugees, expanded political consciousness and capabilities. Labor in Israel, engaging at least one-third of the Palestinian workforce, raised living standards. Remittances from labor in the Persian Gulf did likewise. In consequence, real GNP increased by 119.5 percent in the West Bank and 86.4 percent in the Gaza Strip from 1967 to 1987.[13] As Glenn Robinson explains, these changes in the labor market hastened the demise of the peasantry and undercut conservative rural patron–client relationships.[14] At the same time, it sharpened and politicized a sense of injustice. Dire conditions in low-sector jobs, lack of legal protection, and subjection to high taxes and discriminatory fees made many Palestinians who worked in Israel ripe for political recruitment.[15]

Other developments had a similar effect. The initiation of pro-PLO newspapers and media spread nationalist awareness.[16] The establishment of Palestinian universities in the 1970s brought young people from different backgrounds together in an activist student movement.[17] Imprisonment on political and security grounds served as a "school" for a generation of Palestinians. In Israeli jails, Palestinians formed relationships with comrades from across the country, studied politics and philosophy, and redoubled their commitment to national liberation. Many of those detained were or became members of PLO factions. Factions in the territories mirrored the ideological disputes and competition of their parent organizations abroad. Nevertheless, their relative isolation from the vicissitudes of Arab politics limited the intensity of internal conflict. In addition, Israeli prohibitions forced mobilization underground, which paradoxically aided political cohesion by obstructing the proliferation of factions typical in the diaspora. Only four parties built enduring grassroots foundations: Fateh, the DFLP, the PFLP, and the Communist Party.

In 1973, the PNC called for a nationalist organ to unify all national and democratic forces in the occupied territories. Fulfilling this call and centralizing their own grassroots initiatives long under way, activists formed the semiclandestine Palestinian National Front (PNF). The PNF aspired to be a single organizational framework through which groups in the occupied territories could coordinate their efforts.[18] It gained cohesion from several elements. First, it was tightly linked to the PLO, yet not without losing its local grounding and flexibility. The Front was formed through lengthy consultations between grassroots activists and PLO elites. In addition, it adopted the PLO charter. Second, the PNF had an inclusive collective leadership. The PNF Central Committee brought together representatives from the PLO factions as well as other political parties and independents. It also included merchants, farmers, students, labor and association leaders, and religious figures. Third, the Front was firmly grounded in the grass roots. The Central Committee maintained communication with local committees in every town, each of which featured a membership as broad-based as its own. Local committees in turn worked with the range of civil society organizations in their communities. Finally, the PNF embodied a strong collective purpose. It seized upon Palestinians' optimism in the wake of the 1973 war and provided an organizational structure to channel it into collective action. Its formal political program articulated consensus objectives and outlined the principal concerns of Palestinians under Israeli occupation.

Both the organizational structure of the PNF and the mechanisms through which that structure mediated nonviolent protest foreshadowed the 1987 Intifada. The Front organized boycotts on labor in Israel, a strike by political prisoners in Israeli jails, a boycott of Jerusalem municipal elections, and a campaign of noncooperation with the army. In particular localities, affiliated local committees held demonstrations, built barricades, delivered protest notes to military governors, and read nationalist declarations from minarets. They also carried out a host of specific tasks designed to spread and sustain protest. These included issuing leaflets, distributing food during curfews, raising money for families of those who had been killed or imprisoned, and running messages between towns. Mobilization at this juncture was not strictly nonviolent, as protestors also threw stones and Molotov cocktails and burned tires. Still, the scope of popular and political mobilization far outweighed that of protest intended to cause physical harm.

The PNF Central Committee supported nonviolent protest by articulating its political goals. In manifestos, it called for an end to Israel's appropriation of Palestinian lands. It also condemned the various plans through which Israeli policy makers proposed some kind of Palestinian autonomy in lieu of full independence. The Front presented a petition to the Arab Summit, in which 180 dignitaries called for recognition of the PLO as the sole legitimate representative of the Palestinian people. It submitted a memorandum to the United Nations to the same effect. Finally, the PNF sent statements to the PLO in which it repeatedly urged the PLO to adopt diplomatic means and the goal of a Palestinian state in the West Bank and Gaza Strip.[19] In this way, the Front not only gave the national movement a stronger voice in the occupied territories, but also gave the occupied territories a stronger voice in the national movement.

Nevertheless, cohesion proved difficult to sustain. By 1977, the PNF had largely collapsed. This was the outcome of pressure from external actors as well as the gradual simmering of internal disputes. Israel deported the Front's leading figures and arrested hundreds of activists. Palestinian activists themselves disagreed on whether the PNF was the PLO's arm in the interior (as the Fateh-PLO leadership wished), an alternative to the PLO (as this leadership feared), or a partner to the PLO (as most PNF leaders and leftist factions hoped).[20] Fateh and the Communist Party accused each other of trying to dominate the PNF. The Communists urged nonhierarchical relations between the inside and outside wings of the national movement. The PFLP and DFLP agreed, not least because hierarchy inevitably put Fateh on top. These disagreements undermined the PNF's aspirations to be a central body for the resistance. The PNF was unable to generate strategies for managing such fragmentation, however, because its members were loyal primarily to their factions and only secondarily to the Front as a coalition.[21]

Repression and clashing visions thus eroded the PNF as an organizational structure. Nevertheless, Palestinians' sense of collective purpose continued to unify them. In 1976 Israel held municipal council elections in the West Bank in the belief that its favored candidates would win. To its surprise, pro-PLO candidates scored overwhelming victories. The outcome confirmed the eclipse of traditional, pro-Hashemite elites and legitimated a new generation of leaders who were better educated and more resolutely nationalist. Moshe Ma'oz described the far-reaching effect: "Under the mayors' leadership and the guidance of the PLO, there emerged a more cohesive national political community. Even though latent conflicts and occasional disagreements still existed ... the overall picture has been one of national unity and cohesion."[22]

According to one mayor elected in 1976, that unity had two sources.[23] Primarily, those who gained office were "part of the people." They arose from and lived in their communities, which kept them accountable. Proximity and shared interests helped them to know, consult, and cooperate with each other and the population at large. In addition, the everyday nature of the confrontation with Israel compelled a degree of unanimity. Whereas abstract ideological questions sometimes engaged factions in the diaspora, the occupation forced Palestinians to produce concrete plans to sustain their livelihoods, land, and collective dignity. Political conditions hence generated a pragmatic political agenda around which it "was very simple for people to unite."[24]

Legitimate local leaders and collective purpose gave national forces in the territories the capacity to respond to new challenges, such as Israel's election of the right-leaning Likud Party in 1977 and 1981. Menachem Begin's government increased the annual expenditure for Jewish settlements in the West Bank from an average of $5 million in 1977 to $36 million by 1983. It nearly tripled the number of settlements and increased the settler population fivefold.[25] Another challenge was the Camp David Accords, which proposed Palestinian autonomy rather than statehood. To mobilize protest against these developments, West Bank mayors and civil society activists formed a coalition called the "National Guidance Committee" (NGC). As activists revived the underground PNF to plan protest activities, the NGC served as its public face in implementing those plans.[26]

With this organizational framework, the NGC, West Bank mayors, and a regrouped PNF helped Palestinians hold mass demonstrations in the wake of Camp David.[27] As during the PNF's campaign, the nonviolent character of this protest was predictable given Palestinians' minimal access to weapons. Nonetheless, this does not explain how activists mobilized large crowds despite fears of repression or kept gatherings from becoming riotous. Such feats would not have been possible had organizational structure not played a mediating rule. The PNF provided a forum for cross-factional consensus, and mayors and other NGC members served as respected leaders rallying participation in each community. These institutions were grounded in local relationships, but were also linked country-wide into an effort of broad scope.

Though this protest was nonviolent, Israel's move to suppress it was swift. It banned the NGC and deported or dismissed some West Bank mayors. Settlers planted bombs that maimed other mayors. In 1981, Begin launched the Iron Fist, a series of policies that expanded curfew and restrictions on political activity, universities, and the press, as well as more forceful military repression. Israel also established the Civil Administration, an adjunct to military rule that Palestinians saw as a cover for creeping annexation of the territories. It then unveiled the Village Leagues: an attempt to formalize its network of Palestinian collaborators as an alternative leadership in the rural West Bank. That scheme met with public disdain and collapsed.

Israel was not alone in opposing the new Palestinian leadership and institution-building in the occupied territories. Jordan likewise intervened to bolster conservative leaders at the expense of pro-PLO mayors.[28] The Arab Gulf states, meanwhile, gave support to Islamic-oriented groups to counter the secular nationalist trend, if not the Communist Party specifically.[29] Apart from this, the NGC experienced internal divisions. When some NGC members questioned the PLO's monopoly over the national movement, Fateh leaders in Beirut took steps to subordinate the NGC to its control. The DFLP and PFLP sought to bolster the NGC in order to challenge that very control.[30] The struggle for position among Palestinians on the inside thus mirrored the dilemma of fragmentation outside. Opposition groups might have preferred to cooperate in a more cohesive movement if that movement had been responsive to their political ambitions and strategic preferences. As long as they saw cohesion as submission to Fateh domination, however, they preferred a national movement characterized by dispersed authority. The battle over the NGC, like the PNF, revealed the complex relationship between the inside and outside wings of the Palestinian struggle. On the one hand, the PLO offered a unifying source of national identity, leadership, and strategy. On the other, divisions among PLO groups in exile reverberated in the West Bank and Gaza Strip. Rival leaders in the diaspora attempted to mobilize loyalists in the territories as tools in their disputes.[31] These cross-pressures intensified after 1982, when the PLO shifted attention to the occupied territories and became increasingly active in asserting influence there.

With the demise of the NGC and removal of West Bank mayors, Palestinians under occupation were left without a visible leadership or an overarching structure for political organizing. Still, grassroots initiatives kept nationalist activity alive. Since the 1970s, Palestinians had been meeting in discussion circles to generate ideas about how to confront the occupation. Increasing numbers joined professional associations, student groups, and the Communist Party. These groups mobilized volunteers in self-help projects such as cleaning streets, constructing public playgrounds, and assisting farmers with harvests. Building on this foundation, activists established new mass organizations in the fields of health, agriculture, labor, and women's issues. These groups, many of them fronts for underground PLO factions, provided vital services that helped communities withstand the hardships of occupation.

The creation of civic organizations intensified after 1978, when the PLO began distributing funds from the millions of dollars that the Arab League pledged to the occupied territories. The result was what some labeled a "war of the institutions."[32] As PLO factions vied to recruit as many members as possible, tens of thousands of men, women, and youth became linked in political networks. This grassroots organizing represented a radical alternative to traditional, top-down patterns of politics. It schooled a new generation that was raised under occupation, was not afraid to challenge it, and viewed community-based political participation as a way of life. As one West Banker recalled, "We grew up on volunteer work. There was an extraordinary amount of mobilization and activity. It was part of the structure of our society."[33]

Outside the framework of the PLO, meanwhile, a distinctly Islamic political trend was developing, primarily in Gaza.[34] The Egyptian Muslim Brotherhood had founded branches in Palestine during the Mandate. After 1948, the West Bank Brotherhood was deferent to its Jordanian counterpart and to the monarchy. Its leaders were generally traditional and it gave minimal attention to grassroots organizing. By the 1970s, it was overshadowed by nationalist groups. In the Gaza Strip, by contrast, the Brotherhood's experience of operating independently and clandestinely under Egyptian rule gave it an organizational capacity to survive after 1967.[35] It grew with the regional ascent of political Islam and a Gulf-funded surge in mosque construction. In the early 1970s, Brotherhood member Shaykh Ahmed Yasin founded the Islamic Center, a network coordinating educational and charitable activities in poor communities. The Brotherhood also established civic affiliates that contested their PLO equivalents in university and syndicate elections, which were regarded as a barometer of factional strength. This brought the Brotherhood into conflict, and occasionally violent clashes, with Fateh and other groups. Israel granted Islamists greater freedom to encourage their development as a counterweight to the PLO.[36]

With time, some Islamists criticized their movement's emphasis on social outreach rather than armed struggle. They broke away and established a new group, Islamic Jihad, to carry out military operations. Against this backdrop,

Yasin and others became convinced that the Brotherhood should adopt a more confrontational stance. The impetus was both nationalist duty and organizational interest. After all, if they did not embrace militancy, more Brotherhood members might defect to Islamic Jihad.[37] Echoing the outbidding dynamics familiar within the PLO, competition in the Islamist camp thus escalated protest strategies. When riots erupted in December 1987, Yasin and colleagues announced the formation of a new group: the Islamic Resistance Movement, or Hamas. Initiated as an armed front for the Muslim Brotherhood, Hamas soon superseded and absorbed it.

By the mid-1980s, the trend toward militancy was sweeping the occupied territories as a whole. Palestinians' frustrations mounted as Israeli settlements expanded and the PLO became enmeshed in internal and external troubles. Yet there was no longer a leadership body in the territories that put forth a clear strategy of resistance. Without institutions to channel grievance, protest became more violent. Israel registered 656 "disturbances of public order" in the West Bank in 1977, 1,556 in 1981, and 2,663 in 1984.[38] Stone throwing and other illegal acts of protest rose from 953 in 1985 to 1,358 in 1986. Armed attacks rose from 351 in 1983 to 870 in 1986.[39] In 1985 Israeli Defense Minister Yitzhak Rabin revived the Iron Fist policy with such countermeasures as administrative detention, censorship, school closures, and deportation. That year also saw the start of a new trend: sporadic assaults on Israelis that were not attributable to any political faction.[40] In 1987 the occupation entered its 20th year with no end in sight. "People had a huge sense of frustration," a West Bank leader recalled. "They felt orphaned, like there was no father. They felt like they had nothing to lose and were very ready to make huge sacrifices."[41] An economic downturn compounded daily hardships.[42] Gaza in particular seemed to be a "pressure cooker ready to explode."[43] Would that explosion take the form of violence or would an organizational structure develop to enable more broad based and less lethal forms of protest?

In many ways, the former appeared to be more likely. The PLO professed armed struggle, and Israeli repression nourished calls for revenge. Yet while these motivations for militancy had existed for decades, the organizational structure through which they were filtered had transformed. People in the occupied territories were nearly unanimous in their espousing of nationalist goals. Lesch observed, "Palestinian residents of the West Bank and Gaza Strip articulate a clear consensus concerning their political aspirations. They demand the end to Israeli military occupation and ... assert their right to form an independent state."[44] In addition, a dense network of political and social associations brought together a broad stretch of the population. One activist noted, "There is hardly a single Palestinian household that does not have one member organized in one faction or another."[45] Furthermore, Palestinians voiced sweeping agreement on their national leadership. Polls revealed that more than 90 percent of Palestinians in the territories claimed the PLO as their sole representative.[46] After the PNC's national unity session in April 1987, reinvigorated cooperation among PLO leaders spurred cooperation among their factions under occupation. This in turn encouraged cooperation on the part of the Islamic movement.[47] Such was the situation moving toward the end of the year, when an unexpected spark set the occupied territories aflame.

A NEW KIND OF REVOLT

On December 8, 1987, an Israeli truck collided with laborers from Gaza, leaving four dead and seven injured. As an Israeli had been killed in Gaza two days earlier, many Palestinians viewed the crash as deliberate. Riots ensued in Gaza's Jabalya refugee camp and spread throughout Gaza and then the West Bank. The army responded to the demonstrations with gunfire, killing 26 Palestinians during the next month. Mounting injuries and funerals fanned the flames. Before long, Palestinians dubbed the unrest an "*intifada*," literally a "shaking off" of the occupation.

The Intifada was a popular uprising in which people of all walks of life sought "to create a daily series of acts of defiance"[48] that would assert their nationalist will, demonstrate the unsustainability of military rule, and compel Israel to reach an agreement with the PLO. Tactics spanned all of Sharp's categories of nonviolent protest, namely the expression of opposition, noncooperation with authorities, and concerted intervention.[49] Throughout the country, Palestinians took part in street demonstrations, the illegal display of nationalist symbols and political graffiti, and defiance of soldiers on the streets. Youths erected barricades behind which they declared their communities to be liberated zones. Merchants carried out a commercial strike by shutting their doors on designated days and times, thereby synchronizing the rhythm of life with the uprising. Nonviolent protest evolved to disengagement, including the boycott of Israeli goods and services and the expansion of local manufacturing and food production in the quest for self-sufficiency. Palestinians tried to minimize their dealings with the Civil Administration, even though it had come to govern all aspects of life. Public employees resigned en masse. Residents forwent applying for the licenses and permits required for an array of essential tasks, sometimes at tremendous personal and financial cost. Families withdrew deposits from Israeli banks and workers complied with periodic strikes on labor in Israel. Some refused to pay taxes and fines or to carry Israeli-issued identity cards. Participation was not universal and limited acts of force, most notably stone throwing, were frequent. Still, the hallmark of the Intifada, particularly during its euphoric first years, was nonviolent protest. This was made possible by relative cohesion in the organizational structure of the national movement.

Foundations of Cohesion

An institutional framework for the popular uprising developed from the bottom up. When the Israeli army imposed a curfew on refugee camps that were the initial nuclei of demonstrations, people from outside the camps created committees to collect donations of food and medicine on their behalf. Other committees formed inside the camps to distribute those donations and provide door-to-door medical assistance. As the uprising continued and Israel stiffened barriers to freedom of movement, the neighborhood became the basic unit of social and political organization. Neighborhood committees emerged throughout the occupied territories. With time, their tasks expanded from the provision of immediate services to the organization of protest activities and the meeting of communities' long-term needs as necessary to sustain that protest. According to some estimates, within months there were as many as 100 committees in each major town and 10 in each camp and village.[50]

Popular committees formed the institutional backbone of the Intifada.[51] They tapped into the preexisting networks of PLO factions and civil society groups to organize people horizontally on a geographic basis. They also organized people vertically along lines of profession, technical expertise, and interest.[52] Merchant committees managed strikes, food storage committees amassed dry goods for curfews, and health committees established makeshift clinics. Educational committees organized underground classes when Israel closed schools, and agricultural committees planted "victory gardens" to reduce dependence on Israeli foodstuffs. Strike forces of young men served as the Intifada's popular army by enforcing directives and taking the lead in stone throwing. In each community, a coordinating committee oversaw other committees and tended to problems and concerns as they arose. As foreign journalists and fact-finding missions arrived in the territories, other committees were formed to collect and analyze information, publish fact sheets, and address the media.

Linked to the institutional framework of popular committees was a single, legitimate leadership. This took shape when representatives of the DFLP, Fateh, the PFLP, and the Communist Party formed the United National Leadership of the Uprising (UNLU). The UNLU was an underground, anonymous, consensus-based body that determined the Intifada's goals, translated them into short-term objectives, and consolidated achievements before initiating activities that gradually escalated the pace of the uprising.[53] UNLU members communicated with each other clandestinely and issued directives to the public through communiqués, or *bayanat*. Activists secretly printed and distributed these leaflets throughout the West Bank and Gaza Strip. The first was released in January 1988. They were issued on a roughly bimonthly basis for the next two years and sporadically thereafter. Communiqués sought to inspire Palestinians by praising their efforts and urging continued commitment. They also set forth the national movement's position on political developments and outlined a calendar of protest actions by declaring the days on which strikes, demonstrations, and other actions would be held. For example, Bayan no. 11 called for teach-ins on March 24, 1988, Bayan no. 19 for the storage of food and medicine on June 16, 1988, Bayan no. 27 for sit-ins opposite UN offices on October 24, 1988, and Bayan no. 45 for the hanging of black flags on September 17–18, 1989.[54]

Nearly immediately, the UNLU obtained remarkable legitimacy. Witnesses observed that the population obeyed its directives as "the highest law of the land"[55] and received each communiqué as a "legislative-executive-judicial document with the force of a constitution."[56] In some respects, the UNLU was less an actor than an ongoing process of coordination among the major factions in the occupied territories and, through them, the PLO leadership.[57] In cultivating this coordination, UNLU members were aided by their common social profiles. Like the population at large, they tended to be young and pragmatic. Many were of humble origins and most had honed their political skills in prison, the student movement, or community organizing. The UNLU was effective in leading society because it was an authentic extension of society. Members were grounded in their respective factions, which continued to compete for popular support and maintain links to different leaders in Tunis.[58] Nevertheless, the UNLU offered a powerful mechanism through which factions negotiated their differences and determined a collective agenda for the uprising. This in turn increased the cooperation of their cadres in the field.[59]

The combination of the UNLU and popular committees engendered a new organizational structure for the national movement in the Palestinian territories. This both inspired and was inspired by an invigorated sense of collective purpose in society. "Palestinians have never been more at one in terms of their self-view," Khalidi noted. "There exists today a strong sense of national unity, of loyalty to a unified set of symbols and concepts, and of mutual interdependence."[60] To some, the Intifada not only embodied national unity, but also transformed it from a "mere alliance between PLO factions" to a more profound solidarity rooted in society.[61] "A new basis for cohesion emerged because cohesion acquired a social dimension," reflected a leader based in Tunis at the time. "Society could not split or splinter like factions could split and splinter. In one way or another, society had to reach a decision about how to do things."[62] Strong collective purpose was also rooted in an unprecedented ethic of egalitarianism. "The big success was that you didn't talk about people in terms of majority and minority," a Jerusalem-based analyst explained. "In the first Intifada everybody was equal. It was not about who had more or less. It was not about leadership or contacts or money. This was a revolution in the movement."[63]

There is no doubt that ideological, class, and generational tensions remained in the national movement. As in the 1930s, the Intifada gained revolutionary zeal from the desire of protestors to overturn social and economic hierarchies. Thus, the uprising witnessed youths directing their elders, the poor setting an agenda for the well-to-do, the occupied territories moving ahead of the PLO in Tunis, and political aspirants shunting the traditional elite to the sidelines.[64] What prevented social tensions from becoming an engine of strife as during the Arab Rebellion, however, was the Palestinian movement's more cohesive organizational structure. It is thus through analysis of the role of organizations in mediating protest, not the Intifada's own rhetoric or subsequent nostalgia, that evidence of national unity becomes manifest.

EXPLAINING PROTEST

Crystallizing in 1987–1988, the leadership, institutional, and popular elements of movement cohesion generated a capacity for unified action that facilitated and increased Palestinians' use of nonviolent protest strategies. It did so through several mechanisms, examined here in turn.

Nonuse of Arms

The Intifada was not without shows of physical force. Protestors confronted soldiers by throwing stones and Molotov cocktails, and also burned tires and attacked accused collaborators. For most Palestinians, however, these activities were not intended to harm or kill, as is basic to the definition of violence. Rather, they saw them as nearly symbolic forms of defiance against a well-equipped military. They also justified them as self-defense measures intended to deter the army from patrolling residential areas, where it carried out arrests, searches, and beatings. Beyond this, participation in street clashes became a rite of bravery, particularly for boys and young men.[65] The physical force mustered by unarmed civilians in the Intifada was thus categorically distinct from the military operations that Palestinians had championed in prior decades. The Israeli army confirmed this distinction by construing its mission in the Intifada as one of policing rather than combat.[66] Palestinians also carried out sporadic stabbings, but these were individual incidents and not a nationalist strategy adopted by the movement at large.

UNLU leaflets periodically encouraged stone throwing or other acts involving limited force. However, they eschewed the use of firearms and the deliberate killing or injuring of Israelis. At the same time, the UNLU instructed Palestinians to take part in hundreds of specific protest activities that involved no physical force whatsoever. During the Intifada's prime years, the public complied with overwhelming discipline. Although protest acts occurred daily throughout the territories, the number of incidents involving weapons was tiny (see Table 4.1). By the end of 1988, the Intifada had claimed only 12 Israeli lives, in comparison with 332 Palestinians ones (see Figure 4.1).

Against the backdrop of intense repression and decades of exaltation of armed struggle, Palestinians' extensive use of nonviolent protest, and limited use of violent protest, is puzzling. Explaining these patterns, many insist that Palestinians did not use firearms simply because they did not have them. There is no doubt that there was less access to weapons in the occupied territories in the 1980s than during other junctures in the national movement. Nevertheless, as Brigadier-General Aryeh Shalev noted, Palestinians possessed "light arms in the thousands."[67] Journalists Ze'ev Schiff and Ehud Ya'ari agreed that there were enough weapons in the territories to "have wreaked havoc among unsuspecting Israelis."[68] Palestinian sources likewise reported that "hand grenades and guns have always been available to Palestinians, albeit in limited quantities."[69]

TABLE 4.1. *Palestinian Disturbances in the West Bank and Gaza Strip, 1988–1992*

	Unarmed Protest Incidents	Shooting Incidents	Percentage of All Incidents Involving Shooting
1988	23,053	38	0.16
1989	42,608	102	0.24
1990	65,944	158	0.24
1991	30,948	262	0.84
1992	24,882	344	1.36

Data source: Israel Defense Forces Spokesman's Unit, *Incidents in Judea, Samaria, and the Gaza District since the Beginning of the Uprising* (Jerusalem, December 1992), 7.

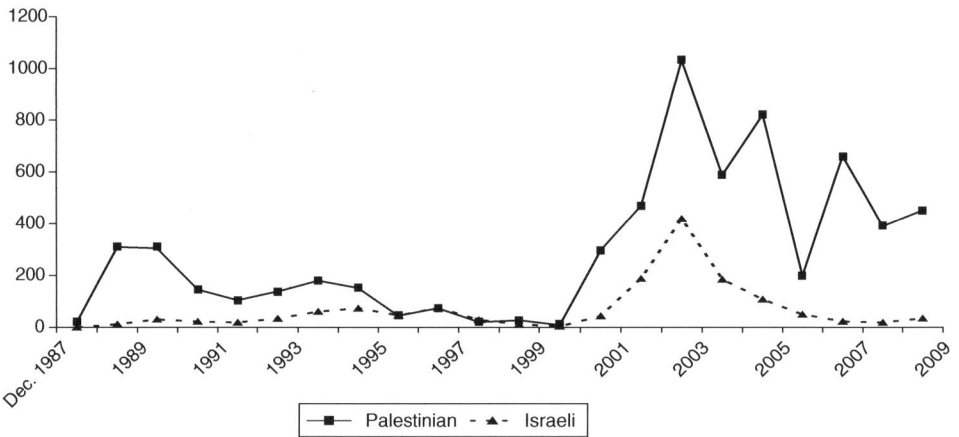

FIGURE 4.1. Israeli and Palestinian fatalities, start of the first Intifada through 2009. *Data source*: B'Tselem: The Israeli Information Center for Human Rights in the Occupied Territories.

Beyond firearms, protestors could have made more extensive use of knifings, the deliberate crashing of cars, improvised explosives, or other operations that required only the resources at their disposal. That they did not suggests that lethal violence was averted as a matter of collective commitment, not material constraints. "Palestinians insist that if they wanted to actually kill Israelis, they would have used lethal weapons," Souad Dajani wrote upon touring the territories. "What amazed this writer … was the interesting departure from the norms of the past. Palestinians in the Occupied Territories were continuously insisting that they would not resort to arms. Any escalation in the use of violence on their part would be as a last resort, for defensive purposes only."[70]

Others attribute the low levels of violence to protestors' rational calculation that nonlethal strategies had a better chance of success. In Shalev's view,

Palestinians understood that any use of arms would invite Israel to create a bloodbath, jeopardize international support, and undermine the sympathy of liberal Israelis. "It is primarily a 'street-smart' attitude ... that accounts for the nonuse of firearms," he concluded.[71] This logic is compelling yet inadequate. It ignores the basic clash between public goods and private interests that defines the collective action problem. What is rational for a group is not always rational for each of its members. It is unlikely that the 1.3 million residents of the occupied territories spontaneously arrived at the same belief in the efficacy of nonviolent protest and seamlessly committed themselves to it. Indeed, the increasing rate of lethal attacks in the years preceding the uprising demonstrates that they did not. Given violence in the mid-1980s, one might have expected the riots that erupted in 1987 to escalate into more killing and destruction.

The organizational mediation theory of protest accounts for these anomalies. It shows that strategic or material factors did not solely or directly determine collective action. Rather their effects were filtered through the movement's internal structure, which mediated the actions that were possible and probable. A legitimate leadership generated a norm of mass nonviolent protest, and committees in every neighborhood put it into practice. A unifying sense of collective purpose inspired people to believe in popular protest or to conform even if they did not. This cohesion gave Palestinians a powerful alternative to armed resistance and aided restraint even when state repression aroused the desire for revenge. Traveling in the occupied territories, Joe Stork reported, "Perhaps the most impressive evidence of the authority of the Unified Leadership has been the widespread unity and discipline around methods and tactics, and in particular the decision not to take up arms."[72] Organizational cohesion made this unity and discipline possible. Without it the Palestinian movement could not have launched and sustained nonviolent protest or kept violent protest to the minimum it did.

Mass Participation

Apart from aiding restraint on physical force, a cohesive organizational structure supported nonviolent protest by recruiting huge numbers to take part in it.[73] Some social sectors certainly played more prominent roles than others.[74] Nevertheless, the Intifada was distinguished by the involvement of people who had not typically participated in protest. UNLU communiqués and popular committees recruited people of all walks of life, regardless of gender, age, class, and profession. As testimony to the Intifada's breadth, Palestinian citizens of Israel held mass demonstrations in solidarity as well.

The movement's organizational structure was crucial in bringing about such sweeping participation. The national leadership and local committees encouraged universal involvement, and an overarching sense of collective purpose rendered participation an exercise in self-empowerment. "People believed that they were taking the future into their own hands ... in the willful act of

building society," a participant recalled.[75] A decentralized organizational character, building on personal relationships and focusing on needs close to home,
also helped increase participation. Organizing at the community level broke
down barriers of fear. Another participant explained, "For the first time, people who were reluctant to join illegal organizations came to participate in
neighborhood committees. There was a big role for all sorts of people."[76]

The organizational structure of the national movement in the territories
helped preempt the problem of free riding. Unanimity with respect to goals
both inspired people to contribute and generated social expectations that they
do so. One activist analyzed the population's motives for participating as a
formula: "Seventy percent came from the commitment that people had inside
[themselves], 15 percent came from people's fear of public pressure, and the
other 15 percent from people who just follow, no matter what."[77] Beyond this,
the uprising's organizational infrastructure gave activists the means to take
specific measures to expand its participatory base. Some popular committees carried out censuses to register community residents' skills and assign
residents appropriate roles in the collective effort.[78] The UNLU called on different social sectors to contribute in defined ways. For example, Bayan no. 3
encouraged academics to write poems, songs, and slogans; Bayan no. 27 urged
lawyers to organize press conferences; Bayan no. 36 appealed to accountants
to refrain from preparing tax reports; and Bayan no. 48 asked students to do
their patriotic duty by behaving responsibly during exams.[79] Women played
a particularly key role in nonviolent protest. A massive demonstration on
International Women's Day in March 1988 marked the pinnacle of an average
of 115 weekly demonstrations by women since the start of the uprising.[80]

Beyond generating participation, organizational structure helped integrate
participation to ensure that the Intifada spoke with one voice. In January
1988, several intellectuals and public figures independently issued the Fourteen
Points, a document outlining the uprising's short-term demands. Palestinian
public opinion was skeptical. These individuals lacked a popular base and
were perceived as Israel's preferred interlocutors.[81] Nevertheless, the UNLU
eventually adopted the Fourteen Points as a consensus document. It thus
managed potential fragmentation by linking an autonomous effort with its
own and preserving the national movement's united front.[82] The public figures created a pool of spokespeople to represent the Intifada before the media
and foreign delegations. They thereby filled a role that the UNLU's clandestine nature prevented it from assuming.[83] Plural initiatives might have become
divisive. Guided by a popular sense of collective purpose, they were instead
complementary. Some sectors of the polity organized nonviolent protest, and
others articulated its message to the world.

Israel deliberately sought to quell the uprising by weakening this participatory base. Countermeasures aimed to divide those who were willing to pay the
high price of rebellion from those who were not.[84] On this basis, the army sur-
rounded refugee camps and closed universities. Had the Intifada been limited
to those who typically spearheaded protest in the past, this might have stifled

the uprising. Given the much broader participation, it did not.[85] As another countermeasure, Israel declared popular committees to be illegal and made membership punishable by up to 10 years in prison. Nonetheless, the organizational structure of the uprising had become too entrenched to eradicate. F. Robert Hunter wrote, "At the most basic level of society, the leadership had become the mass, and the mass, the leadership. A fusion had occurred."[86]

Sustaining Protest

To sustain nonviolent protest, Palestinians had to adapt to changing circumstances and cope with the exhausting toll of rebellion and repression. It would have been difficult to meet these challenges had the national movement been less cohesive. Interfactional coordination created a system that ensured the continuity of the UNLU despite Israel's efforts to eliminate it. For some two years, every time authorities identified and arrested UNLU members, their factions replaced them with new representatives. The leadership's authority thus did not depend upon particular individuals. Instead, it became institutionalized in cooperative relationships among social forces. Reinforcing this cooperation was mutual consultation between the UNLU and society as a whole. The national leadership was organically linked to popular committees, which implemented communiqués and filtered back information through factional representatives. These linkages helped the UNLU tailor its schedule of protest actions according to an understanding of local needs and capabilities. Its directives were not imposed on society as much as they "arose from and were received by, the people, themselves."[87]

These mechanisms of communication and coordination helped keep the protest effort resilient, as opposed to brittle, under pressure. On the one hand, leaders managed potential sources of fragmentation by rallying the population. On the other, they heeded its limits. "The masses must first be convinced through their daily struggle that these tactics are beneficial to them," an activist observed. "We should not be adventurous and declare a boycott while we are not ready to enforce it. This would betray weakness, not strength."[88] In this spirit, the UNLU deliberately varied the location and pace of protest to preserve the initiative while giving communities a chance to rest.[89] A total boycott on labor in Israel would have been a dramatic step. The leadership did not call for one, however, because it appreciated that families could not go without that income. As a more sustainable option, it asked those who could stop working in Israel to do so and instructed others to strike once a week.[90] Similarly, it praised East Jerusalem shop owners when they maintained a strike for 40 days. Yet it then urged them to return to business on a part-time basis lest their savings run out and residents shop at Israeli stores instead.[91] When Israel ordered the closure of Palestinian universities and high schools, the UNLU encouraged popular committees to organize an alternative system of underground education. At the same time, it called on Israel to reopen the schools and encouraged students and teachers to return when it did.[92]

The flow of information between the grass roots and the UNLU served a similar function. It enabled the latter to avert fragmentation and sustain nonviolent protest by revoking decisions when appropriate. In 1989, Israel declared that male Gazans could enter Israel only with a magnetized identity card that they could obtain upon demonstrating a flawless security and tax record. Intifada leaders in Gaza forbade Palestinians to acquire cards and confiscated those they found. After several weeks, however, the UNLU recognized that blocking work in Israel was creating excessive hardship. It thereupon returned the cards and ceased to mention the issue.[93] On the flip side, when the leadership deemed that people were ready to intensify protest, committees stepped in to guide the process. After an initial phase focusing on street protests, the leadership decided that the time was right to shift from demonstrations to disengagement. Committees made this possible by organizing banking, mail, and other services as alternatives to Israeli ones. When Palestinian police officers resigned from the Civil Administration, committees assumed some of their functions in mediating disputes, patrolling neighborhoods, and preventing crime.

A cohesive organizational structure also helped sustain protest by keeping the UNLU abreast of quotidian complaints so that it could address them in communiqués. Leaflets showed particular sensitivity to economic hardships. They responded by urging acts of solidarity intended to ward off problems that might otherwise derail the protest campaign. Bayan no. 16 asked lawyers to reduce their fees, Bayan no. 26 urged merchants not to partake in price gouging, and Bayan no. 27 suggested a maximum cost for doctors' appointments.[94] Beyond this, the leadership was creative in continually developing new forms of resistance that would express defiance while minimizing the burden on society. Thus, in 1989 it declared that the occupied territories would not adopt daylight saving time in sync with Israel, but two weeks earlier.[95] On these and myriad other issues, the organizational structure that linked the leadership to the population helped the national movement coordinate expectations and behavior. This prevented the excesses that had undermined unity and contributed to unruly violence during the 1936–1939 Arab Rebellion.

The role of organizational structure in mediating leaders' ability to manage potential fragmentation was crucial because fragmentation was the aim of many state countermeasures. Dajani observed, "Israel is quite aware of how crucial unity and coordination is in sustaining the strength of the Intifada and has spared no effort to try to cause splits, dissension, and confusion in the Palestinian camp."[96] For example, the army tried to sow confusion by printing false communiqués that presented a timetable of protest activities different from that set forth by the UNLU. Palestinians' cohesiveness helped prevent them from being fooled. Whereas real leaflets contained instructions that would be met by consensus, the imposters were identifiable because they articulated views that were likely to cause dissension.[97]

Organizational cohesion was thus both the Intifada's distinguishing characteristic and its source of strength. Communities that were not placed under curfew mobilized to send food to communities that were. Wealthier families sometimes bought bags of flour and rice to leave anonymously at the doors of others who had fewer means.[98] The leadership specifically designed activities to generate and manifest camaraderie, such as strikes in solidarity with prisoners or volunteer work to help farmers. Social solidarity was essential for sustaining nonviolent protest because repression created situations in which individuals could not manage alone. For example, in what some referred to as the "Shopkeepers' War," store owners closed their stores in observance of strike hours. Soldiers would use crowbars to break the locks on their iron shutters. At night, volunteer locksmiths secretly repaired the locks, enabling the strike to carry on the next day. Even street clashes manifested such complementary divisions of labor. When troops entered a neighborhood, youths sometimes divided into teams. Lookouts on rooftops signaled when the army approached, stone throwers went into action to forestall the troops, and a defensive squad covered the offense as it retreated.[99]

The Intifada became a battle of wills in which Palestinians and Israelis each strove to demonstrate that they controlled the West Bank and Gaza Strip. A unified organizational structure helped the Palestinian national movement gain the upper hand in this contest. Since 1967, labor and detention in Israel had brought many Palestinians to learn Hebrew and develop an understanding of Israeli society. During the Intifada, activists followed the Israeli press. They recognized that their use of nonlethal strategies fueled disagreements among Israelis regarding whether to remain in the territories.[100] In some respects, therefore, Palestinians' political cohesion contributed to Israelis' political fragmentation. Some Palestinians had long advocated nonviolent protest on those very grounds.[101] It was only when the national movement developed an interconnected leadership, institutional framework, and collective purpose, however, that it acquired the means to make mass nonviolence a reality. The strategic rationale for unarmed resistance may have existed before the Intifada; the organizational structure to carry it out took shape uniquely during its course.

Opposition Contained

Another way in which organizational structure aided nonviolent protest was by controlling internal divisions. The most acrimonious political divide in the territories was between Islamist and secular forces. Islamist groups remained outside the PLO, and their call for an Islamic state in all of historic Palestine contradicted its goals. The Islamic Jihad movement coordinated with the UNLU at the beginning of the uprising but later operated independently. The newly established Hamas movement did not join the UNLU and coordinated with it to only a limited degree, when at all.[102]

This split could have easily precipitated fragmentation and thereby threatened the command and control on which nonviolent protest depended. The highly politicized atmosphere might have encouraged factions to compete with each other by carrying out increasingly militant acts. This seemed particularly likely for Hamas, which was formed just three days into the uprising and was eager to prove itself. Nonetheless, Islamist forces were attentive to the popular stress on unity. During the height of the uprising's cohesion, they understood that unity demanded that they work within the basic parameters that the Intifada leadership set forth. Thus, with the exception of the stabbing of a soldier in October 1988 and the detonation of two roadside explosives to no effect, neither Hamas nor Islamic Jihad carried out armed attacks during the Intifada's first year.[103] Hamas issued its own leaflets, called for its own strike days, and sponsored its own demonstrations. Yet it did not stray far from the consensus on popular, unarmed means of resistance. To do otherwise would have jeopardized its quest for popularity.

The UNLU, in turn, was astute in managing this source of potential fragmentation. It understood that it could best guard the cohesion of the national movement by giving Hamas space to distinguish itself. Thus, if Hamas declared a strike on a particular day, the UNLU would take care not to do likewise.[104] Beyond this, the population's sense of collective purpose was powerful enough to compel Islamist and nationalist forces to observe implicit limits on their competition. "For the most part it was possible to contain disputes and keep them from getting out of hand," a UNLU member recalled. "In those cases when we could not reach an effective understanding, the public became the lever of pressure."[105] Just as rival groups respected public opinion, so did public opinion respect rival groups. Local committees tended to comply with directives from both the UNLU and Hamas.[106] Most Palestinians believed that the Islamists did not challenge the uprising's unity as much as contribute to it by augmenting overall participation.[107] This was Hamas's view as well.[108]

From Protest to Diplomacy

One outcome of this cohesive organizational structure was a new political complementarity between the national movement in the occupied territories and the PLO in Tunis. The long-standing differences between the movement's two wings did not disappear during the uprising. Arafat in particular remained fearful that insiders might gain recognition as an alternative leadership and shunt him to the margins. Nonetheless, most see the period from 1988 to 1990 as the height of cooperation between the inside and outside.[109]

Most Palestinians under occupation professed an organic link to the PLO and admired its leaders. Indeed, they aimed their efforts at empowering them to conduct diplomacy on their behalf. The UNLU solidified this link by referring to itself as the "struggle" or "political" arm of the PLO and by adding the PLO's name to its communiqués. Khalil Wazir, the PLO figure responsible for the occupied territories, monitored and guided events through personal contacts with a network of local activists. Links between faction heads in Tunis and their cadres under occupation enabled exchanges of information and consultation, as well as an inflow of money to support the Intifada.[110] Faysal

Husayni, perhaps the most prominent inside leader, reputedly described the partnership as one of people standing in quicksand. In proverbial terms, the PLO let insiders climb on its shoulders to scale a wall, trusting that that they would rescue it upon reaching the top.[111]

Inside–outside cooperation was itself a powerful tool of nonviolent protest. Under the pressure of sweeping popular support for the PLO, Jordan severed the last of its administrative and financial ties with the West Bank in July 1988. It thereby relinquished all claims to the territory. Given Palestinians' long struggle with the Hashemite regime, this decision marked a significant victory for Palestinian nationalism. Yet it also created political uncertainty. Factional heads in Tunis feared that Jordan's disengagement could lead Israel to annex the occupied territories. Leaders initially took contradictory stances on how best to respond to the new circumstances but gradually found common ground.[112] Their agreement revealed how enhanced cohesion between the territories and the PLO contributed to cohesion in the PLO itself.

The PLO newspaper gave voice to the emergent consensus. It explained that Palestinian leaders in 1948 had been unable to "build themselves" in order to take independent initiative. "In 1988, however, the Palestinian situation in national, political, leadership, and unity terms is one million times better," it wrote.[113] Empowered by the national movement's growing cohesion, Arafat issued a declaration of Palestinian independence at the November 1988 session of the PNC. The Council announced the establishment of the state of Palestine, officially endorsed the 1947 United Nations partition plan, and accepted UNSCR 242. It thereby did what the leadership never before believed it could do without tearing the movement apart: it effectively recognized Israel.

Hardliners who opposed this decision conceded to majority rule. Had they instead withdrawn from PLO bodies as they had in the past, they would have sabotaged this landmark event. Unity in the occupied territories fortified the PLO mainstream vis-à-vis its opposition. PFLP chairman George Habbash said, "The intifada has forced us – and I'm glad it has forced us – to stay inside the PLO Executive Committee even with the differences we still have."[114] The PLO extended its declaration by launching the "Palestinian peace initiative." In this worldwide diplomatic campaign, more than a hundred countries pledged full or qualified recognition of the new Palestinian state.[115] Arafat spoke before the United Nations General Assembly and held a press conference in which he explicitly recognized Israel and condemned terrorism. In response, the United States opened official dialogue with the PLO.

The PLO's diplomatic momentum stalled in the absence of Israeli reciprocity. In January 1991, the American-led invasion of Iraq unsettled the stalemate. Arafat decided to support Sadam Husayn. As a result, Gulf states cut financial support and the PLO found itself isolated. In Israel, meanwhile, bombardment by Iraqi missiles convinced decision makers that they needed to shift their focus from policing the territories to graver threats. Against this backdrop, the United States and the USSR sponsored the Madrid peace conference in

October 1991. It brought together representatives of Israel, Syria, Lebanon, Jordan, and the Palestinians. Israel insisted that Palestinian representatives come from the territories and attend under the auspices of a joint Palestinian–Jordanian delegation. They did so, but attended only with PLO sanction. They also communicated with the Tunis leadership throughout the conference, as other delegations were well aware.

Polls showed that 87 percent of Palestinians in the occupied territories supported participation in the Madrid conference. Some even celebrated it by handing flowers to Israeli soldiers.[116] This show of collective purpose reduced incentives for obstructionism. Factions that opposed negotiations did not try to sabotage them as in more fragmented eras. Hence, spoilers of peace talks were not a given. Their activity varied with the structure of political opportunities in the national movement, which was in turn a product of the movement's relative cohesion or fragmentation.[117]

In the two years following Madrid, Palestinian representatives from the West Bank and Gaza negotiated with Israel in 12 rounds of bilateral meetings in Washington. Palestinian negotiators would report ongoing frustration in their dealings with a Tunis leadership relentlessly afraid of being marginalized. Nevertheless, the incipient peace process stood as the crowning achievement of coordination and restraint among the various components of the Palestinian national movement. As a UNLU member reflected, the occupied territories launched a grassroots initiative and the PLO transformed it into a political initiative.[118] The result, mediated by organizational structure, was a milestone in the turn from violent to nonviolent means as the strategic choice of the Palestinian national movement.

REPRESSION, FRAGMENTATION, AND VIOLENCE

No sooner had riots begun in 1987 than Israel resolved to restore order. To that end, it deployed some seventy thousand soldiers in the occupied territories in 1988 alone. When the United Nations Security Council condemned Israel's use of live ammunition against civilians, the army outfitted soldiers with clubs. In the words of Minister of Defense Yitzhak Rabin, they could then "break Palestinians' bones." In the assessment of leading Israeli journalists, soldiers' beatings of unarmed protesters became systematic.[119] The army introduced plastic and rubber-coated metal bullets to limit harm to protestors, yet casualties mounted. Save the Children estimated that 7 percent of all Palestinians under the age of 18 were injured due to shootings, beatings, or tear gas during the first two years of the Intifada.[120] Gradually, Israel concentrated on targeting the "hard core" of Intifada activists by dispatching undercover squads and deploying sniper units on rooftops.[121] It also carried out a legal crackdown, arresting or imprisoning some fifty thousand Palestinians.[122] These sometimes occurred in mass roundups aimed at preempting anticipated protests. By the end of 1988, about ten thousand Palestinians were held without charge or trial in administrative detention, a six-month incarceration eligible for renewal.[123]

Investigations found that detainees routinely met with harsh interrogation and ill-treatment falling within accepted definitions of torture.[124] Israel also deported 32 Palestinians during the Intifada's first year and delivered expulsion orders to another 27.[125]

Some means of punishing Palestinians for the uprising were collective in nature. Israel closed Palestinian universities for most years of the Intifada and West Bank schools for a total of 12 months.[126] The army imposed round-the-clock curfews some sixteen hundred times at various locations during the first year of the uprising. On any given day, at least twenty-five thousand Palestinians were confined to their homes.[127] Soldiers also searched homes and offices without warrant and occasionally cut entire communities off from electricity, water, or fuel.[128] Israel struck at the rural population by destroying trees and inhibiting the transport and sale of agricultural products. It also placed villages under curfew during harvest time, leaving crops to spoil in the fields.[129] It demolished or sealed the homes of more than a thousand Palestinians in 1988 alone.[130] Israeli settlers added to the impact of army operations by carrying out their own acts of violence against Palestinian persons and property.[131]

Other measures were specifically economic. By July 1988, the Intifada's tax revolt had decreased payments by 40 percent.[132] Israel responded by confiscating property and licenses, imposing a new vehicle tax, setting up roadblocks to check tax receipts, and making a range of essential bureaucratic procedures contingent upon tax payment. Families whose children were accused of throwing stones faced financial penalties, such as fines or stiff bails to release the youths from custody. In addition, Israel sought to sever the political and financial link between the occupied territories and the PLO by cutting international phone lines, restricting the entry of money into the West Bank, banning Fateh's youth movement, and censoring pro-PLO newspapers. Most critically, it assassinated Wazir in April 1988.

During the first two years of the Intifada, Palestinians' unity empowered them to withstand these measures. Nonetheless, cracks emerged with time. The organizational structure attained during the Intifada was more cohesive that that attained before or since. Yet Palestinians neither completely surmounted factionalism nor transformed committees and networks into a durable institutional apparatus.[133] Society remained segmented, and the organizational structure for unity was thus stronger in some places than others. This had a direct effect on the use of nonviolent protest. A small village like Beit Sahour – where nearly everyone was related in some way – was able to lead the country in civil disobedience. Organizational cohesion in the village even gave it the capacity to combine nonviolent protest with outreach to Israelis. A local leader explained:

> Shortly after the Intifada started, a group of intellectuals in Beit Sahour decided to open a dialogue session with Israeli groups. This was very embarrassing for the Israeli government, which was saying that Palestinians are terrorists. In the middle of the Intifada we brought 25 Israeli families to spend

a week in Beit Sahour in our houses. It was planned that they would come
by the back roads so they would not be caught by the army. The night they
arrived was like a festival – all Beit Sahourians were here.

Now here comes the role of consensus. It was enough for one child to throw
one stone to disturb the whole thing. That did not happen because of the
general consensus. This general consensus was not only among people. It
was also among political factions. Far left political factions like the PFLP and
DFLP were also a part of this decision.[134]

Nonviolent protest reached its greatest heights in tightly knit and relatively
affluent Beit Sahour. Yet this was difficult to achieve in more complex and
splintered settings. The West Bank's largest town, Nablus, was characterized by long-standing familial rivalries and tensions between rich and poor.[135]
These divisions obstructed the development of a single organizational structure for community cooperation, command, and control. Laetitia Bucaille
found that Nablus's militant activists acted on a "repressed desire for social
vengeance, insofar as compelling the bourgeoisie to adopt the behavior of
ordinary conservative working people was a triumph and a vindication in
itself."[136] Factional competition compounded socioeconomic resentment. The
town's strike forces were divided between the Fateh-affiliated Black Panthers
and the PFLP-affiliated Red Eagles. Eventually, these groups defied UNLU
directives and carried out violent acts as they wished.[137]

By 1991, the pace of popular demonstrations had declined and the uprising reached a stalemate. It became apparent that the Intifada would not rev-
olutionize society, achieve total civil disobedience, or force Israel to end the
occupation.[138] The mood in the occupied territories deteriorated from a unifying collective purpose toward directionlessness. Some with means left the
country or sent their children abroad. Threatening to confiscate businesses,
Israel gradually coerced merchants to pay taxes. Such defections weakened
the Intifada's united front and nourished bitterness among those who had no
escape from the revolt's high social, economic, and educational costs.[139]

The crumbling of the Intifada leadership was a critical component of this
loss of cohesion. During the Arab Rebellion, Britain's targeting of leaders
decapitated the national movement. This paved the way for protest that was
less focused, less disciplined, more vulnerable to internal power struggles,
and ultimately more violent. The arrest, killing, and deportation of activists
during the Intifada had a similar effect. As Israel removed experienced leaders, younger militants assumed a greater role in the uprising. They tended to
lack the prudence of those who had gained political training in universities
or prison. They were therefore quicker to resort to arms.[140] Israel's arrest of
Palestinian figures known for advocating coexistence, such as the editor of a
binational Hebrew-language magazine, compounded the radicalizing effect of
repression. An Israeli journal reflected, "Having removed the moderates, the
authorities are left face to face with extremist elements and then claim 'there is
nobody on the other side to talk to.'"[141] This commentary echoed the remarks
of exiled leaders of the 1936 strike, as it foresaw future trends.

The UNLU managed to be resilient in the face of repression during the Intifada's height. Again and again, Israel arrested UNLU members, and factions replaced them. Yet this process of renewal could not be sustained indefinitely. By March 1990, Israel's imprisonment of consecutive UNLU coalitions had ended its operation as a coherent entity.[142] With the waning of a united leadership, each faction acted more independently and competitively. Factions also increased their struggles for control over popular committees, with the effect of undermining committees' standing as a framework for unifying community action.[143] This breakdown of the cohesive organizational structure changed the relationship between the occupied territories and the PLO leadership. Insiders' cohesion had forced Tunis to respect their political voice. As the Intifada splintered, however, the outside was able to deal with the inside through domination more than through partnership.[144] During the last two years of the Intifada, Tunis dictated the UNLU's communiqués.[145]

Israel's assassination of Wazir hastened this fragmentation. Though a stalwart member of Fateh, Wazir had played a crucial role in building national institutions that benefited all factions. Insider activists noted that he "listened" to them and integrated them with the PLO on the basis of respect for their unique political culture and skills.[146] His assassination was a devastating blow that spurred Israel and Arafat to compete for control over the uprising. Wazir had distributed funds to the occupied territories sparingly and with the goal of bolstering the PLO. By contrast, Arafat used them extensively to the effect of increasing loyalty to him personally. In consequence, Sayigh explains, "The reasonably unified clandestine organization and the more centralized youth movements and semi-public associations that Wazir had painstakingly constructed in the shadow of the Israeli occupation fragmented rapidly into competing factions and cliques under the impact of Arafat's patronage."[147]

In what resembled a tactic of divide and rule, Arafat allowed second-tier leaders to vie for dominance by creating and funding their own groups of adherents in the occupied territories. An activist from Bethlehem recalled the emergence of "channels," or lines of influence connecting figures in Tunis with cliques who answered to them. "There was a channel called the *Samidun* and a channel called the '*Aidun*," he explained. "All of these different channels implemented orders coming from many different sources of authority. This gave rise to contradictions and conflicts."[148] Under the PLO's control, the Intifada shifted from a process of social transformation to a resource to be invested for diplomatic gain.[149] One activist, speaking for many disillusioned insiders, argued that the PLO "hijacked" the uprising:

> At first, everyone participated in demonstrations together. Then members of different factions started appearing in demonstrations wearing something that represented their particular factions. Then each faction started sponsoring its own demonstrations. Then Arafat started sending money to the occupied territories and this wrecked everything. If one person had money, he could use it to gather a group of people around him to use against another

group. Money broke society into different groups, rather than having all people be equal and in solidarity with each other.

The first Intifada was good when people were going forward with their own momentum. Then Arafat took over. At one point, Arafat said, "I have the next *bayan* in my pocket." This was the signal that the Intifada was over.[150]

Diverging interests, loss of vision, and factional power struggles were signs that the movement's organizational structure was crumbling. Disintegration of command and control both increased the motivation for violent protest and reduced constraints on its use. As the masses withdrew from active participation, masked men appeared on the streets and knife attacks on Israelis multiplied. Armed strike forces acquired a greater presence. A UNLU member recalled:

In the beginning, there was no serious effort to use arms. The power of the daily demonstrations, their large size, and the mass public participation left no need to search for other methods.... As time wore on and Israeli aggression intensified, the popular aspects of the Intifada began to diminish and some armed incidents occurred.... The more the situation inside weakened, the more that things shifted to the outside and the more armed activity increased.[151]

The ratio of unarmed general disturbance events to shooting incidents dropped from 607 to 1 in 1988 to 72 to 1 in 1992 (see Table 4.1). Hamas in particular increased its use of lethal force. The movement carried out 11 attacks from 1987 through 1991 but increased attacks fourfold to 46 during the two years that followed.[152] These trends reflected not only the increasing militancy of the Islamist movement, but also the end of the previously unifying optimism regarding nonviolent protest and diplomacy. As long as a critical mass of the public and political forces came together behind the nonviolent Intifada and negotiations, Hamas would put its popularity in peril if it acted as an obstructionist force. Hamas had denounced the 1988 PNC endorsement of a two-state solution and the subsequent Madrid conference. Yet it silenced its guns because the Palestinian population and PLO supported them.[153] As the Washington talks dragged on, many Palestinians became convinced that Israel was using negotiations to forestall an agreement rather than reach one. Consensus collapsed into divergent views on whether to continue or suspend negotiations and what either meant for the Intifada.[154] These cracks in the national movement opened political space for Hamas to intensify violent protest. Ziad Abu-Amr, a leading scholar of Palestinian Islamism, wrote:

Lack of alternatives on the part of Hamas and its awareness of the Palestinian internal balance of power ... [served to] mitigate its opposition to the negotiations. As it became evident that the peace negotiations were not yielding any tangible results more than a year after their initiation, the Palestinians have become more disillusioned.... Being aware of this disillusionment, Hamas was emboldened and became more aggressive in its opposition to the PLO and its tactics against Israel.[155]

When Palestinians cohered around the mainstream, groups at the margins tempered their militancy. As internal cooperation broke down, opposition groups faced fewer costs in pushing political boundaries. In December 1992, Hamas and Islamic Jihad carried out five attacks that claimed the lives of six Israeli security force members. Israel responded by banning Hamas, arresting Shaykh Yasin and some 1,600 Palestinians suspected of Islamist ties, and expelling 415 of them to southern Lebanon. There they obtained training from Hezbollah, which would later prove useful in carrying out more lethal violence. Meanwhile, Hamas–Fateh tensions, contained during the cohesive early years of the Intifada, worsened. Hamas positioned itself as a main foe of the peace process and Fateh stood as its main backer. Arafat sought to manage this fragmentation by inviting Hamas to integrate into the PLO, but the initiative collapsed when Hamas demanded 40 percent of seats in all PLO bodies. By 1992 the two movements were exchanging harsh rhetoric and their cadres engaging in gun battles.[156] This fragmentation facilitated and encouraged outbidding in the confrontation with Israel. On a West Bank highway in April 1993, Hamas executed its first suicide bombing.

Yet the majority of Palestinians' acts of lethal violence were attacks on neither Israelis nor factional rivals. They were attacks on Palestinian civilians accused of collaborating with Israel. Government co-optation had long challenged unity in the Palestinian struggle, as in other self-determination movements.[157] At the outset of the Intifada, cohesion helped Palestinians forge nonviolent strategies for coping with this problem. The UNLU condemned informants, and popular committees organized opportunities for public "repentance" whereby collaborators renounced their actions and relinquished Israel-issued weapons to their communities. Under the pressure of strike forces and social sanction, hundreds of collaborators repented. Countless others were dissuaded from becoming new collaborators.[158] An organizational structure strengthened by leadership, institutions, and collective purpose thus helped the national movement to devise unarmed means of confronting one of the occupation's most important tools of control.

By the end of 1988 Israel had rebuilt its collaborator network by redoubling traditional pressures as well as entrapping some of the tens of thousands of Palestinians filtering through Israeli prisons.[159] UNLU communiqués justified a strident response. As local and national leaders' control over the Intifada waned, however, the counteroffensive exhibited unruly dynamics characteristic of the Arab Rebellion. Some denounced collaborators on the basis of scarce evidence or personal vendetta. Others labeled as collaborators those involved in such activities as crime, prostitution, drug dealing, or adultery.[160] Israeli sources claimed that only 35–40 percent of Palestinians killed for collaboration actually worked for the Israeli authorities.[161] By 1990 the annual tally of Palestinians killed by Palestinians superseded the number killed by Israel.[162]

As in the Arab Rebellion, Intifada violence against collaborators was difficult to classify as internal bloodletting or protest against the occupying power.

On the one hand, the targets were Palestinian. On the other, collaborators were no less vital for upholding the occupation than were soldiers in uniform. Palestinians thus saw strikes against them as self-defense. Regardless, collaborator killings were a form of violence directly mediated by increasing fragmentation in the national movement. Like attacks on Israel, violence against collaborators represented a switch from mass-based mobilization to individualized lethal acts. They thus stood in contrast to the earlier nonviolent protest campaign, which had both demanded and inspired popular participation. Collaborator killings reflected the gutting of the grassroots leadership. Many of those attacking suspected informants were the less disciplined youth who assumed a larger role in the Intifada after more mature leaders were imprisoned. It was also an outcome of the waning of national authority structures. The UNLU, Arafat, and prominent individuals repeatedly condemned collaborator killings, but their appeals had little effect.[163]

As the organizational structure for nonviolent protest deteriorated, so did the Intifada's initially effective strategies for managing fragmentation. Society showed signs of unraveling. "Under the hammer-blows of various misfortunes," one journalist observed, "the rock of Palestinian resistance has fissured."[164] Far from the ethos of consensus, some groups forcibly imposed their views on others. Threats and harassment brought nearly every woman in the Gaza Strip to don a headscarf, irrespective of personal choice.[165] The waning of mechanisms for community law enforcement unleashed rising crime. One activist called the Intifada a "phantom starting to eat its children." A Palestinian daily published his lament:

> Frightening nightmares haunt us all: writers, farmers, laborers, clerks, and the educated ... the elderly, women, and even cripples. We are frightened for ourselves, of ourselves, of a dream that became a nightmare.... A friend of mine was arrested four times, and each time soldiers broke into his house, but today he is more afraid of break-ins by masked individuals who have no address or name or color.... There are merchants who pay protection money under the guise of making a donation for nameless people.[166]

Internal violence and turmoil created dynamics that another witness described as civic disintegration:

> The goals of the Intifada ... are now considered unattainable in the short term and, many believe, in the long term as well. The psychological effect is best characterized as a kind of collective self-withdrawal.... Political factions in Gaza have begun to fight over control of those few remaining resources that are perceived to exist.... Virulent factional rivalries are replacing directed collective action.... In the absence of an effective leadership and authority structure, one group is pitted against another, disorder increasingly prevails, and political interests are being pursued at the cost of some of the Intifada's greatest achievements.[167]

Meanwhile, unbeknownst even to Palestinians engrossed in negotiations in Washington, a different track of negotiations was reaching a climax.

Arafat confidants were secretly meeting in Norway with Israelis authorized by Yitzhak Rabin, elected prime minister in 1992. The political and financial decline of the PLO after the Gulf War, as well as the specter of an ascendant Hamas, lent urgency to these talks. In September 1993, the PLO and Israel made the stunning announcement that they had reached an agreement. For Arafat and his inner circle, it was a dramatic wager that they could leap over all obstacles and achieve Palestinian national aspirations.[168] For many activists who had formed the backbone of the Intifada, it was an ignoble end for their sacrifices. One would later mourn, "The revolution is started by the courageous, exploited by opportunists, and its fruits are harvested by cowards."[169] The signing of the Declaration of Principles on the White House lawn, followed by Arafat's call on all Palestinians to "return to ordinary life," was the symbolic end to an uprising whose dream of unity had already died.

CONCLUSION

Analysis of the first Intifada substantiates three claims stemming from the organizational mediation theory of protest. First, the stronger a self-determination movement's cohesion before the onset of heightened conflict with the state, the more likely it is that conflict will cause adherents to unify rather than splinter. For the national movement in the occupied territories, developments during the two decades following 1967 laid the foundation for this cohesion. In the early years, Palestinians were pulled between loyalty to Jordan, submission to Israel, and support for the PLO. By the 1980s, they had come to identify overwhelmingly with the national movement, an ethic of civic volunteerism, and the goal of statehood in the West Bank and Gaza Strip. When riots erupted in 1987, the population's sense of collective purpose developed into the consensus that all Palestinians should contribute to a popular insurrection for independence. A unified leadership translated collective purpose into collective action. A network of hundreds of neighborhood committees generated a cross-class, cross-regional infrastructure for activism.

A cohesive organizational structure facilitated both containment of the Islamist opposition and a new partnership with the PLO in exile. This combination of leadership, institutions, and collective purpose helped make Palestinians resilient in the face of Israeli countermeasures. Factions agreed to a system of rotating representatives to sustain the united leadership when members were imprisoned. Popular committees mobilized volunteers to help communities manage curfews, economic hardship, and disengagement from Israeli institutions. Popular consensus sustained commitment despite mass arrests, house searches, deaths, and injuries. Had the national movement been less cohesive, repression would have dampened participation and sparked infighting more quickly than it did, and to more detrimental effects. At the height of the Intifada, however, repression was met by the most extensive example of cooperation and unified political action in Palestinian history.

Second, the Intifada demonstrates how movement cohesion increases the possibility of nonviolent protest. In the uprising, organizational unity generated the cooperation necessary to channel initial riots into such unarmed actions as commercial strikes and boycotts, unarmed street demonstrations, and disengagement from occupation institutions. It is doubtful that Palestinians could have sustained this strategy without an authoritative leadership's dissemination of a timetable for protest actions, committees' coordination of these actions at the local level, and the population's far-reaching commitment to participation. In addition, cohesion aided collective restraint on the use of force, even when repression intensified and emotions ran high. Throwing stones and igniting Molotov cocktails were prominent in Palestinians' protest repertoire. Lethal violence, however, was not an Intifada strategy. Finally, the national movement's organizational structure facilitated the extension of nonviolent strategies from protest to diplomacy. It consolidated the mainstream of the PLO, enabling it to declare its willingness to coexist with Israel, begin dialogue with the United States, and shepherd Palestinian inclusion in the Middle East peace process. Factions that opposed these concessions were tempered by majority sentiment. They did not try to sabotage negotiations or withdraw from PLO bodies as they had in eras characterized by greater fragmentation.

Palestinians' cohesive organizational structure nonetheless weakened over time. Their mobilization of nonviolent protest did likewise. The Intifada's later years thus illustrate a third generalizable relationship: as movements fragment, their protest is increasingly likely to become violent. Palestinian civilian protestors faced a powerful adversary. Repression took a heavy toll and the goal of ending the occupation remained elusive. Setbacks chipped away at Palestinians' sense of purpose and resolve. The arrest, killing, and deportation of Intifada leaders eliminated those most capable of managing divisions and drained the institutional networks that they had built. In result, the inside leadership became factionalized, popular participation waned, the Tunis leadership wrested control, and the use of physical force increased. Groups that opposed negotiations became emboldened to carry out spoiler attacks. As some ignored the leadership's pleas and killed accused collaborators, the final stages of the Intifada took on characteristics familiar from the 1936–1939 Arab Rebellion.

Popular grievances, elite interests, material resources, and straightforward strategic calculations also shaped Intifada protest. Yet arguments emphasizing these variables leave many patterns unexplained. They should thus be qualified to consider how their effects on protest are filtered through a movement's organizational structure, and specifically the degree to which it is cohesive or fragmented. Few would contest that deprivation and political despair fueled the eruption and spread of the Intifada. Without leadership and grassroots organizations, however, this mass outpouring might have propelled lethal violence rather than such activities as a commercial strike, resignations, nonpayment of taxes, and the administration of underground schools. Palestinians would not have supported nonviolent protest had they not believed it to be an effective strategy. Yet this begs the question of how they managed to launch and sustain such a strategy and why they used civil resistance as the "weapon of the weak" during this historic juncture and not others. Strategic rationality cannot alone explain how communities disciplined the emotive forces fueling escalation. Facing military occupation, many Palestinians wished to take up arms. Under such circumstances, only ideological and institutional discipline could contain the will to rebel within the realm of mass nonviolent protest.

The first Intifada achieved this discipline because the bulk of society was integrated into political and social institutions that were in turn integrated into a united leadership. This organizational structure created and enforced a popular consensus against armed violence. When leadership, institutions, and collective purpose began to crumble, commitment to this strategy did likewise. The story of the rise and fall of the first Intifada is hence a story about the rise and fall of movement cohesion. In its fall, an entirely new chapter in the Palestinian struggle began.

5

The Oslo Peace Process, 1993–2000

On September 13, 1993, the PLO and Israel signed the Declaration of Principles (Oslo I) and committed themselves to a phased framework for negotiations. The following May, negotiators finalized the Cairo Agreement. According to its terms, the Israeli army withdrew from Gaza and Jericho and transferred control over those areas to a new Palestinian self-governing apparatus, the Palestinian Authority (PA). In September 1995, the Taba Agreement (Oslo II) mandated Israel's redeployment from Palestinian towns and villages in the West Bank. It divided that territory into Areas A, under full PA oversight; Areas B, in which security matters were under joint Palestinian–Israeli control; and Areas C, where security matters were under full Israeli control. Israel and the PLO pledged to commence permanent status talks on the issues of Jerusalem, refugees, settlements, water, and borders no later than May 1996. Talks were to conclude in a final peace settlement by May 1999.

These deadlines were missed, as were dozens of others from September 1993 to September 2000. Rather than delivering a resolution of the Israeli–Palestinian conflict, the Oslo process produced both historic breakthroughs and acts of bad faith. Israel transferred about 60 percent of the Gaza Strip and 17 percent of the West Bank to Palestinian self-rule.[1] Yet it also imposed new restrictions on Palestinian freedom of movement, confiscated tens of thousands of acres for settlement expansion, doubled its settler population by the year 2000, and paved approximately 250 miles of bypass roads for exclusive Israeli use in the territories.[2] It carried out interim withdrawals in a limited and unilateral way, continuously fueling Palestinian fears that Oslo was a vehicle for denying them sovereignty more than granting it. The PLO recognized Israel and coordinated security, economic, and other matters with its former enemy on a nearly daily basis. Yet Palestinians also carried out acts of violence that claimed more Israeli lives during the six-year period after the Oslo Agreement than before it.[3] The number of Palestinians killed by Israelis was greater. Never since 1948, however, had the death tolls of the two communities so closely approximated each other (see Figure 4.1).

What accounts for Palestinians' engagement in both negotiations and violence? Some observers understand violent protest in this era to be Islamists' attempts to derail peace with the Jewish state. Others attribute it to the inherent defects of the Oslo process, which pushed Palestinian opposition outside the realm of acceptable politics without resolving its underlying grievances. Still others view violence as tit-for-tat. In February 1994, Jewish settler Baruch Goldstein killed 29 Palestinians praying in Hebron's Ibrahimi Mosque. In revenge, Hamas carried out its first suicide bombing inside Israel 40 days later. Israel retaliated with various measures, including the assassination of Hamas and Islamic Jihad leaders. These organizations then responded with more bombings.

All of these explanations carry validity. What they overlook, however, is the role of a movement's organizational structure in mediating its strategic action. This relationship comes to the fore in the case of the Palestinian national movement from 1993 to 2000. Definitively shifting its focus to the West Bank and Gaza Strip, the Palestinian struggle consolidated itself in a national territory and society. Still, multiple sources of fragmentation remained. Arafat pursued familiar strategies for managing fragmentation, but these bred resentment even when they produced compliance. At the outset of the peace process, a measure of collective purpose and centralized leadership made it possible for Palestinians to commit to negotiations. Nevertheless, this cohesion was weakly institutionalized and ultimately dependent on expectations that went unfulfilled. In this context, opposition took violent forms. Palestinians' unity depended on Israeli concessions. These became less attainable as the fragmented Palestinian movement failed to deliver the complete termination of attacks that Israel demanded. The organizational structure of the Palestinian movement was thus part of a vicious cycle that contributed to eroding prospects for peace. Given the conflict's fundamental asymmetry, Israel's obstinacy and missteps did likewise.

This chapter analyzes these developments in three sections. The first examines how the mixed character of leadership, institutions, and collective purpose in the Palestinian movement generated both new forms of fragmentation and new strategies for managing it. The second traces how this organizational structure shaped incentives and opportunities for protest violence. The third section concludes the discussion.

HOLDING TOGETHER

Collective Purpose

The announcement of the Oslo Agreement shocked Palestinians. Some cheered the advent of statehood. Others accused the PLO of legitimating a reconfiguration of the occupation in order to save itself from isolation and bankruptcy.[4] Critics charged that Oslo guaranteed neither Palestinian statehood nor a settlement freeze. In this view, it instead gave the more powerful party opportunities to create "facts on the ground" that would prejudice any eventual

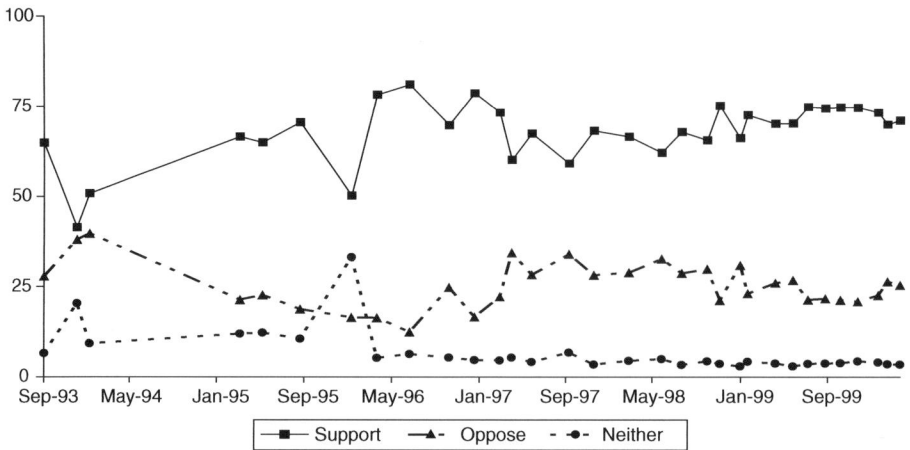

FIGURE 5.1. Percentage of public supporting or opposed to continuation of the peace process.
Data source: Center for Palestine Research and Studies (CPRS) and Palestine Center for Survey Research (PSR), Public Opinion Polls, September 1993–April 2000.

agreement in its favor. Arafat's supporters responded that the accord was the best available option. They insisted that Israeli–Palestinian cooperation could build confidence between the two former adversaries. This, they asserted, was Palestinians' best hope to convince Israel to relinquish land and accept Palestinian sovereignty in the West Bank and Gaza Strip.

With time, Mouin Rabbani explains, Palestinian opinion settled into four camps: enthusiastic supporters consisting mostly of Arafat and his inner circle, intellectuals and prominent individuals who supported peace but criticized Oslo's flaws, a rejectionist camp that saw Oslo as high treason, and the bulk of the population, which gave the agreement conditional support.[5] Opinion coalesced as the PA apparatus took shape and Arafat returned to Palestinian soil in July 1994. The gap then gradually narrowed between Oslo's champions, who no longer spoke of impending independence, and the opposition, which pragmatically abandoned aims to annul the agreement.[6] In the words of national poet Mahmoud Darwish, who resigned from the PLO EC in protest against Oslo, "The accord has become a fact and one does not deny facts."[7] Few Palestinians believed that Oslo gave them their due. Nevertheless, opinion polls showed that a majority supported it as the strategic choice of the national movement. Illustrative are trends across more than 30 surveys conducted by Palestinian pollsters on a semi-regular basis from the fall of 1993 through the spring of 2000. During this period, an average of 70 percent of Palestinians in the West Bank and Gaza endorsed the continuation of negotiations (see Figure 5.1).

Other surveys confirmed these trends. Twelve polls from May 1995 to April 2000 found that Palestinians were on average twice as likely to say that they were optimistic about the future as opposed to pessimistic.[8] During the same time period, a plurality consistently reported that they expected the peace process to lead to a Palestinian state.[9] Thus, whereas previous eras saw Palestinians divided on strategy, the 1990s witnessed convergence on goals and means. As long as public opinion favored negotiations, those who opposed Oslo had to reconcile themselves to the new reality or alienate themselves from the political mainstream. Nevertheless, skepticism remained. In a July 1995 survey, 81 percent of Palestinians said that they did not trust the intentions of the Israeli government regarding a peace settlement. This figure would not drop below 57 percent in polls over the next five years.[10]

Given such reservations, popular support for the peace process appeared to be built on two pillars. The first was exhaustion. Sayigh calculated that 350,000–450,000 Palestinians had been subjected to Israeli interrogation and 100,000 received prison sentences between 1967 and 1987. During the Intifada, 1,200 were killed, more than 100,000 wounded, and 80,000–90,000 detained.[11] In this context, many welcomed Oslo because they saw it as an end to decades of suffering. They accepted it even though they did not believe that it gave them their due. As a refugee in Gaza remarked, "I feel like a man who has lost a million dollars and been given ten ... but you see, I lost the million dollars a long time ago. So I will keep the ten.... After so much bloodshed, I accept. But, please, don't ask me how I feel."[12] Another Gazan remarked, "In supporting the agreement, people were not supporting a political solution but were trying to find a way out of their social and personal quagmire.... We want to get rid of the army so we can become human beings again."[13]

The second pillar of Palestinians' support for Oslo was the hope that it would deliver political and economic gains. Jamil Hilal and Mushtaq Husain Khan explained that support for the leadership was a precarious gamble. The wager was that Arafat's system would yield independence and prosperity more rapidly than Islamist forces could rally opposition against it.[14] Rabbani spoke for many when he warned that, just as popular support made the peace process viable, so would it vanish if Oslo failed to deliver:

> If Palestinian children can safely walk on streets leading to open schools, if their parents can find meaningful employment and decent housing, and their grandparents live out their days free of open sewers, curfews and arbitrary humiliation, this will be a large and pivotal constituency.

> If, however, Palestinians remain or are again subject to lawless violence by Israeli soldiers and/or settlers, economic development fails to materialize, limited autonomy is not transcended, and the Palestinian authority proves a good imitation of other Arab regimes, the group will gradually vanish and in its absence play an equally pivotal role.[15]

The latter is what came to pass. Israel only partially implemented prisoner releases and redeployments. It postponed permission for a Palestinian airport and seaport and delayed transfer of tax monies to the PA.[16] Israeli settlements and roads divided Palestinian land into noncontiguous areas that Israel could cut off from one another. Furthermore, Israel imposed severe new restrictions on freedom of movement. Having instituted a policy of open borders between Israel and the occupied territories in the early 1970s, Israel initiated restrictions during the Intifada and in March 1993 began requiring Palestinians to obtain permits to enter Jerusalem. After Oslo, Israel stiffened restrictions on the movement of people and goods into, out of, and between the West Bank, Gaza Strip, and East Jerusalem.[17] In the Palestinian public perception, therefore, the peace process and closure took effect at the same time. Restrictions on movement were to be ameliorated through a Palestinian-controlled "safe passage" connecting the West Bank and Gaza Strip, but Israel did not allow it to become operative. Israel argued that closure was necessary to stop terrorists, but it affected all Palestinians in myriad ways. It is difficult to exaggerate its deleterious impact on people's daily lives.[18]

Like expectations for sovereignty over land and movement, Palestinians' longing for economic recovery met with disappointment. Economic straits by the end of the Intifada were dire.[19] Polls thus found that people's most immediate hopes for the peace process were economic.[20] By the year 2000, however, per capita income levels were about 10 percent below what they had been before the Oslo Agreement. The World Bank estimated that 21 percent of residents of the Palestinian territories lived below the poverty line.[21] For the previous quarter century, the Palestinian economy had been built around open markets and employment in Israel. Before 1993, unemployment in the Palestinian territories was 7 percent. Thereafter, it ranged between 20 percent when the border with Israel was open to 30 percent when it was closed. It soared to 60 percent when Israel imposed total closure.[22] The average number of Palestinian laborers in Israel dropped from 116,000 in 1992 to 33,000 by 1999. From 1993 to 1996, closure and the requirement of Israeli permits for the transport of goods cost the Palestinian economy an estimated $2.8 billion. This was equivalent to 80 percent of one year's GDP.[23] The easing of closure led to economic recovery after 1998, yet remained insufficient for the burgeoning Palestinian population. This was especially the case in the Gaza Strip.

Economic and political disappointments, combined with frustration with corruption in the PA (discussed later), generated a demoralization that was palpable in commentaries throughout the 1990s.[24] The collective purpose that had empowered the Intifada seemed to be replaced by generalized depoliticization. This shift was reflected in the changing face of civil society. The uprising exhausted Palestinians' ethos of volunteerism and dense network of civic associations. Once a Palestinian government was established, many people judged that they no longer had to participate in the grassroots provision of social services. In addition, many mass organizations had difficulty crafting new and relevant agendas. Traditionally fronts for illegal PLO factions, some were rudderless in the changed circumstances of self-rule. Other community groups lacked sufficient resources after outside donors shifted funds from local initiatives to the PA.[25] In consequence, many of the activists who had coordinated the vibrant popular mobilization of the 1980s withdrew from political life. Others filtered into nongovernmental organizations aligned with foreign patrons or disconnected from the grass roots.[26] The number of registered organizations swelled, but many succumbed to pressure to ally with Arafat's regime. They thereby became part of a system of nondemocratic and clientelistic relationships more than genuine vehicles for civic engagement.[27]

Meanwhile, other fault lines were sharpening. The negotiation process solidified the political rift between Fateh and its allies on one side and those who swore opposition to Oslo on the other. New social divisions emerged as PA-granted monopolies and Israel-awarded passage through checkpoints increased the gap between haves and have-nots. The ostentation of the few who profited from Oslo created, in the words of a Hamas spokesman, "a crack in the Palestinian society which had been accustomed, during all the occupation years, to common support and solidarity."[28] Many of those raised under occupation felt alienated by the culture of PLO figures returning to the territories.[29] The returnees were popularly derided as "Tunisians." Telling are the reflections of an activist from Jerusalem:

> The collective vision had become blurred. There began to be internal squabbles over positions and influence that we never even knew existed.... For the generation that was 12 and 14 years old during the first intifada, our leaders outside were like gods. When a leaflet was published, we looked at it as if it were coming from heaven and we followed it word-for-word. If there was a strike, then everyone went on strike. There was no doubt that the call would be observed. When the political organizations gave instructions to write slogans on the walls, we did it. When there were instructions to hold a march in the streets, we participated. We never questioned why or how. But when our leadership came back, we saw many practices that we didn't like.... That's why a lot of us decided to keep our distance from politics.[30]

The norms that had unified Palestinians in the past were deteriorating. In the words of one Jerusalemite, "We are [now] a nation without values: everything has been fragmented in the Intifada and there is nothing new to set in place of what we have lost."[31] As another in Gaza said, "There is nothing left inside us. We are only shapes."[32] Palestinians' sense of collective purpose after Oslo was thus not the confident, inspiring consensus it had once been. Nevertheless, mainstream opinion continued to support negotiations due to a combination of hope and the absence of alternatives. A 1997 press article noted, "Through all the political wrangling and delays, the economic woes of the Palestinian territories, and acts of violence: an overwhelming majority of the Palestinians in the West Bank and Gaza Strip support the peace process ... the real crisis will be when they withdraw their support."[33]

Leadership and Institutions

The Oslo process gave rise to a new institutional framework for the Palestinian national movement. Palestinians validated their political leadership in fair elections in 1996. Voter turnout rates topped 90 percent in Gaza and 68 percent in the West Bank.[34] Arafat's election as PA president by 88 percent of the electorate codified his political supremacy. The elected Palestinian Legislative Council (PLC) worked diligently to unify a body of law from the existing medley of Israeli, Jordanian, Egyptian, British, and Ottoman regulations.[35] New ministries began offering critical services, particularly in the realms of health and education. This institution building set forth a Palestinian apparatus governing Palestinians on Palestinian soil and thus made the long-pursued national entity a reality on the ground. An academic explained, "The diasporic project was a fictive entity because it was based on a virtual society.... The brilliance of Arafat was that he saw that such a society cannot exist *infinitum* unless it grounds itself in a territorial unit." In this sense, the PA helped forge a "national society" integrating people from the West Bank, Gaza Strip, and Jerusalem, as well as those whom Israel allowed to return from the diaspora or prior deportation.[36]

These developments solidified a new organizational structure for Palestinian politics. Nonetheless, the cohesion attained under the PA was ultimately attributable more to the centralization of power than to the institutionalization of authority. The pluralist national movement was transformed into something akin to a one-party regime. The PLO created the PA as a subsidiary to govern territories ceded by Israel. Nonetheless, the PA effectively superseded the PLO as the interlocutor most recognized by the international community. Concurrently, PLO institutions that had united and represented Palestinians since 1969 atrophied. Arafat embarked on the Oslo process without proper authorization from PLO councils. He convened the PNC just twice after 1988. Those sessions were called only in deference to Israeli and American demands to annul certain clauses of the Palestinian National Covenant.

The decline of the Palestinian Left sealed the deterioration of PLO pluralism. Weakened after the fall of the Soviet Bloc, leftist parties split over the peace process. On one side, the PFLP and DFLP opposed Oslo. On the other, the Palestine People's Party (formerly the Communist Party) and Fida (a new party that split from the DFLP) supported it. In the immediate wake of the agreement, Damascus-based leaders of leftist and Islamist groups established the anti-Oslo Alliance of Palestinian Forces. Power struggles and ideological incompatibilities soon caused its collapse.[37] Thereafter, leftist parties neither offered a coherent alternative to the peace process nor established an effective presence in the new political system.[38] PFLP and DFLP leaders insisted that they were holding steadfast to the principles of the PLO in opposition to Arafat's PA.[39] Critics accused them of clamoring for a PLO that no longer existed.[40] The leftist opposition joined Hamas in boycotting the 1996 PA elections. The result was that 68 of the 88 members of the PLC were Fateh members or affiliates. The remainder represented a broad range of views, from Islamist to Marxist. They did not cohere as a bloc.

While Fateh consolidated its power over the political system, Arafat consolidated his power over Fateh. Assassinations of Arafat's main contenders for authority – Wazir in 1988 and Khalaf in 1991 – aided this process. By the first Oslo Accord, in Sayigh's estimation, Arafat's "political control was so personalized that Palestinian politics had become almost wholly subservient to his sense of timing, temperament, and choice of priorities and methods."[41] Oslo gave Arafat vital international support, which offered both political and financial resources. He employed these resources in strategies to manage fragmentation in the Palestinian movement. One strategy was the assertion of the presidency over other branches of government. At the outset of the peace process, public figures vociferously called for checks and balances.[42] Surveys showed that 88 percent of Palestinians in the territories wanted greater democracy in national decision making.[43] Against this public pressure, the PA acquired authoritarian traits typical elsewhere in the region. The president established control over the PA judiciary and employed it to quell critics. Human rights groups decried grossly unfair trials, torture of political and other detainees, deaths in custody, and rushed executions by the president's own State Security Court.[44]

Arafat's domination of the PLC was no less pronounced. Oslo stipulated that the government be overseen by parliament. Nonetheless, Arafat set up PA ministries and began directing agencies 18 months before legislative elections were held.[45] Once elected, the PLC approved hundreds of resolutions and laws that the president did not ratify or implement.[46] The president circumvented the parliament by issuing his own primary legislation through eight hundred presidential decrees and orders.[47] Legislators criticized the executive branch's noncooperation, queried its ministers, and wrote reports exposing its corruption, but to little effect. A lawyer from Hebron elaborated:

> Arafat refused to sign the Basic Law [the PA's interim constitution] because he saw that would strengthen the legislature. Arafat refused to sign the Judiciary Law because he did not want a strong, independent judiciary. Arafat refused to sign the Civil Service Law because that would mean that control over hiring would no longer be in his control. Arafat was afraid that the PA would slip from his hands. So he strengthened himself at the expense of the PA.[48]

Arafat's control of the formal political system centralized power in his person. His control of the underlying informal political system served a similar function. As in the PLO in exile, real power in the PA flowed through noncodified channels based on personal persuasion, coercion, and exchange. This underlying network was composed of horizontal links, through which similarly ranked individuals formed their own alliances and competed for influence. It was also composed of vertical links, through which power and resources flowed from Arafat to layers of deputies and ultimately to the grass roots. Positioned atop the formal and informal networks, Arafat engaged in what had long been his primary strategy for managing fragmentation: the neopatrimonial distribution of jobs and benefits.

Although most international aid never passed through his office, the president disbursed tax and custom revenues with virtually no oversight.[49] Arafat's own lifestyle was sparse. However, he used corruption and toleration of subordinates' corruption as a political tool. "Arafat is practical," one West Bank commentator noted. "The reward of having people on board is greater than resorting to repression."[50] In the words of another, "He could co-opt even the devil."[51] With this rationale, Arafat granted jobs in an inflated PA to ensure the loyalty of a broad section of society, including those who disagreed with Oslo. He created superfluous senior posts so that he could bestow important titles on key individuals.[52] In many of these appointments, Arafat counterbalanced potential challengers by intentionally setting them against each other. He also made alliances with traditional elites and clans, even instituting an Office for Tribal Affairs.[53] This revived their power, which had waned with the rise of a new generation of activists before and during the Intifada.

Rates of bribe taking were much lower in the Palestinian territories than many places in the developing world. What distinguished corruption in the PA, however, was the degree to which it operated as a substitute for institutional development.[54] Israel was aware of these trends; it controlled the spigot for a large portion of PA funds and arguably designed their diversion to Arafat so that he could use them as necessary to control violence and marginalize Hamas.[55] Rabin had famously remarked that Arafat would be more effective than Israel in fighting terrorism because he would be unburdened, as the Israeli government was, by a supreme court or human rights groups. Nor would he be burdened by an independent comptroller. Prioritizing security over democracy and good governance, Israel contributed to the creation of an organizational structure for Palestinian politics in which Arafat had a free hand to deal with internal affairs as he deemed fit.

These strategies for managing fragmentation came to the fore in the PA security forces. This allowed Arafat to confront two potential challenges. The first was powerful second-tier Fateh leaders who could potentially mobilize against him. Preempting this threat, Arafat created some 11 separate, ambiguously defined police and intelligence forces. He appointed rival elites as commanders. This was a perilous game of containing political divisions by encouraging them but subordinating them to Arafat as their sole arbiter. The second threat to Arafat's dominance came from the PLO rank and file who had been the Intifada's foot soldiers. Thousands of young men expected some share of the PA, which they viewed as an achievement won by their sacrifices. At the same time, many of these activists had spent their youth in prison or street battles. They had suspended their educations and often lacked the technical skills that the new administration and economy needed. As a solution to this political conundrum, Arafat gave these cadres jobs as security officers. The outcome was an estimated 35,000 officers by 1997. Palestinians had a 50-to-1 ratio of police per capita, one of the highest in the world.[56] The corollary of this bloated sector was a deluge of weapons in PA areas.

As a strategy for managing fragmentation, neopatrimonialism was useful for getting the negotiation process off the ground. In the short term, it won the loyalty of tens of thousands of bureaucrats and potentially restless cadres by tying their interests to the PA and Oslo. This not only prevented them from defecting to the opposition. It also enlisted them to suppress that oppo-sition. Nevertheless, such strategies did not build a cohesive organizational structure. It was not grounded in autonomous institutions, a compelling sense of collective purpose, and leadership that people followed due to legitimacy rather than contingent private benefit. Divide-and-conquer tactics gave rise to a chronically weak PA. It was characterized by infighting at all levels and a personalized centralization of power at the top. Many honest and hard-working people offered their talents to build what they hoped would be a Palestinian state-in-the-making. Widespread hiring on the basis of political criteria, however, introduced incompetence into the civil service. Indeed, it nourished a system in which nervous elites sometimes saw competent subor-dinates as a threat. It also made the PA the largest employer in the territories and bred resentment among those who did not have connections.

The Fateh movement represented a microcosm of these dynamics. Repression during the Intifada had ravaged Fateh's coherence as a political movement.[57] In addition, division took root between an "old guard" of returnee elites and a "young guard," raised in the occupied territories.[58] The former held a monop-oly over the machinery of the national movement but little connection to the grass roots. The latter had street credibility but were largely excluded from formal decision making. The top leadership viewed Fateh as the power base of the PA. Young guard leaders, by contrast, called for its transformation into a political party distinct from the government.[59] Led by West Bank General Secretary Marwan Barghouti, they appealed for reform and democracy. They insisted that time was overdue for the convening of the Fateh General Congress, the membership-wide plenary that elects the movement's top leadership coun-cils. Arafat and Fateh elites refused, perhaps out of fear that accountabil-ity would result in their ouster. They also blocked internal Fateh elections at other levels.[60]

Facing such obstacles, Barghouti acted independently to promote his polit-ical orientation. He established the Fateh Higher Committee as a forum to give institutional voice to his cohort. He also maintained relationships with the rank and file through what was called *Tanzim* (literally "organization"). Tanzim was a loose network of activists who spearheaded activism in the 1980s and remained Fateh's grassroots expression after Oslo.[61] Many of these cadres criticized the corruption of Fateh "fat cats." Barghouti, however, was one of the few who articulated disapproval of the president himself. "Yasir Arafat has become the one and only political reference point for the Palestinian people," he remarked. "It is not true that Fateh, through its framework and leadership councils, currently leads the Palestinian people. Neither is it true that it is Fateh that leads the Palestinian Authority. Arafat does."[62]

Despite its internal troubles, Fateh remained preeminent among Palestinian factions. Surveys confirmed that Palestinians supported it more than any other faction. In this context, Figure 5.2 outlines the contours of a Palestinian move-ment between organizational fragmentation and cohesion. On the one hand, fragmentation was limited by Fateh's domination of the political landscape.

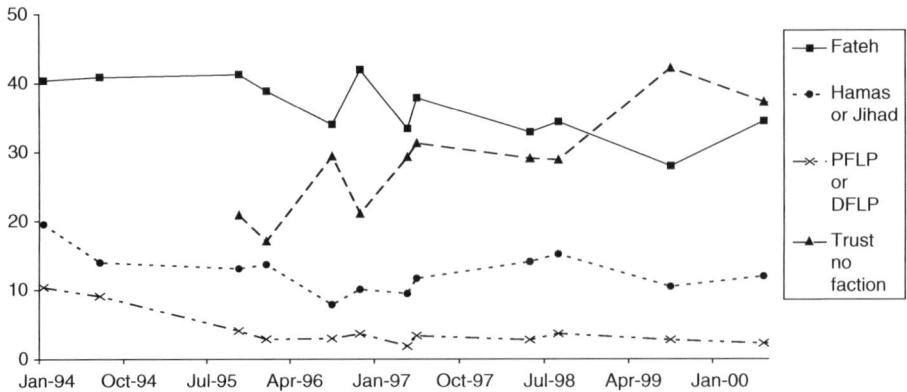

FIGURE 5.2. Trust in and support for Palestinian factions, 1994–2000.
Data source: JMCC, Public Opinion Polls, January 1994–June 2000.

Its prominence was the legacy of its historic leadership of the national struggle and the mainstream appeal of its political program. No less, it was aided by its unmatched material resources and access to the levers of the PA. Fateh's traditional opposition, PLO leftist groups, ceased to represent a challenge. Nonetheless, two sources of division in the Palestinian movement were significant. The first was general social disillusionment. This was manifest in Palestinians' fastest-growing political current: lack of confidence in all political forces. The second was the Islamist opposition. Hamas stood aloof from the system that Arafat built, maintained its reputation for clean administration, delivered needed social services, and did not compromise on its criticism of Oslo. Defying Arafat's strategies for managing fragmentation, it represented a tenacious fissure in the organizational structure of the national movement. This had important consequences for strategies of protest in the conflict with Israel.

CROSS-STRATEGIES

Negotiations

Any movement seeking a negotiated resolution of protracted conflict is liable to experience internal opposition from those who are ideologically opposed to concessions or who have a vested interest in the continuation of hostilities. A movement must be organizationally cohesive if it is to enforce an agreement in the face of such splits. The threat of domestic challengers may motivate leaders to initiate a peace settlement.[63] However, a settlement is unlikely to stick if they cannot force critics to submit. An authoritative leadership, backed by institutions and popular support, must marginalize oppositionists. Otherwise, spoiler violence is likely.

   This emphasis on the role of a movement's organizational structure in mediating peacemaking offers a new perspective on the Oslo process. It differs from explanations that attribute Israeli–Palestinian negotiations to exogenous shocks such as the Gulf War.[64] It likewise differs from arguments that Israelis and Palestinians had simply fallen into a "hurting" stalemate,[65] that the Oslo backchannel succeeded due to its secrecy,[66] or that some unique combination of macro- and microlevel forces produced a breakthrough.[67] Moreover, this interpretation is distinct from those focusing on changes within Israel that made it more amenable to peacemaking.[68] In contrast to these other analyses, I contend that Palestinian engagement in the Oslo process was critically enabled by movement cohesion. It would have been impossible if not for the increased power of the PLO-Fateh mainstream vis-à-vis its rivals. Given that the PLO began to move toward a two-state solution as early as 1974, Oslo did not reflect a radical shift in strategy. What changed in the early 1990s was Israel's responsiveness and the decline of internal Palestinian opposition.[69]

   Chapter 3 demonstrates how fragmentation in the PLO in the mid-1970s allowed leftist factions to obstruct diplomatic initiatives. By the late 1980s, PLO bureaucratization had increased Arafat's control over institutions. The expulsion of the fedayeen from Lebanon had decreased rival groups' freedom to carry out military activity. Furthering these trends, the Intifada enhanced popular consensus behind a negotiated settlement. The PA gave this consensus an organizational structure grounded in society and territory. The coalescence of these factors was crucial for the peace process. A Palestinian academic observed:

> The political system that Arafat founded worked very effectively in the sense that it allowed the PLO under his leadership to negotiate on behalf of all the Palestinians. He was able to appropriate consent and create consensus on the parameters of the transitional arrangements. He was able to do this because he really believed that it was a transitional arrangement that would end with final status negotiations. Had people felt that this was going to be a dead-end, I think people would have voted against it. Even most of the opposition groups that came from the outside agreed to it – if not by word, then by the lack of opposition.[70]

   To the degree that the new organizational structure upheld leadership, institutions, and collective purpose, Arafat was able to sustain negotiations and promise to end violence. To the degree that major detractors remained, however, the potential for opposition violence did likewise.

Opposition Violence

From the Declaration of Principles until the start of the second Intifada, Palestinians carried out 149 lethal and nonlethal armed acts against Israel. Of these, 67 were perpetrated by unidentified suspects and 66 by Hamas or Islamic Jihad. About one-third of the latter were suicide attacks (see Table 5.1).

TABLE 5.1. *Suicide Attacks, September 13, 1993, to September 29, 2000*

Year	No. of Attacks in Israel (No. in West Bank/Gaza Strip)	No. Killed (No. Injured)	Group Responsible
Sept. 13–Dec. 31, 1993	0 (3)	0 (1)	Hamas (2); Islamic Jihad (1)
1994	4 (1)	38 (145)	Hamas (4); Islamic Jihad (1)
1995	3 (2)	37 (153)	Hamas (2); Islamic Jihad (2); unidentified (1)
1996	4 (0)	57 (216)	Hamas (3); Islamic Jihad (1)
1997	3 (0)	24 (410)	Hamas (2); unknown (1)
1998	1 (1)	3 (28)	Islamic Jihad (1); unknown (1)
1999	0 (0)	0	–
Jan. 1–Sept. 29, 2000	0 (0)	0	–

Source: Palestinian Violent Events Database, assembled by Mohammed Hafez, Naval Post-graduate School.

Islamist groups opposed recognizing Israel or renouncing armed struggle on ideology. Yet their actual use of violence did not follow from doctrine alone. It was also mediated by the organizational structure of the national movement. When the peace process began, violence was a tool by which the opposition tried to influence the terms of the new domestic political order. Hamas was a large and popular social movement with commensurate political ambitions. The political system authorized by Oslo, however, was premised upon Islamist groups' marginalization, if not elimination. Indeed, one reason that the PLO leadership embraced Oslo was to maintain dominance over internal challengers. So too did rivals use opposition to Oslo to challenge that dominance. Jeroen Gunning explains, "Oslo provided a golden opportunity to salvage [Arafat's] dreams of statehood, stay in power, and keep Hamas and other contenders (including Fateh's local cadres) out.... Each subsequent attack on the peace process, by Hamas or other contenders, must therefore be seen as, at least in part, an attack on this elite arrangement."[71] Hamas believed the Oslo Accords to be not only a treasonous surrender, but also a threat to its political existence. Violence against Israel was one means by which it fought back.

Competition for internal political power hence created an incentive for violent protest apart from motivations strictly tied to the conflict with Israel. In signaling that they retained the power to disrupt, Islamists warned Arafat to give them a "seat at the table" of Palestinian decision making, or at least not to destroy them.[72] Arafat staked his international credibility on the pledge that he would deliver an end to Palestinian violence and his domestic credibility on the pledge that Oslo would deliver statehood. Attacks on Israel threatened both. They were thus a considerable form of leverage. In communiqués issued after bombings, Hamas and Islamic Jihad frequently warned the PA not to "collaborate" with Israel by arresting their cadres and attacking their institutions. Hamas could afford to be militant in challenging Arafat and his peace strategy. Unlike leftist anti-Oslo groups, Hamas's funding and base of popular support lay outside Arafat's PLO.

To the degree that the Palestinian movement was fragmented into competing groups, anti-Israel violence was one domain through which groups struggled with each other. To the degree that majority opinion crystallized in favor of giving Oslo a chance, however, groups engaged in violence with caution. Political opportunities for violent protest thus vacillated in accord with the national movement's unity behind the peace process and the PA. In 1993 polls showed that some 80 percent of Palestinians believed that the opposition should express its views through democratic dialogue, not violence.[73] In the years that followed, a plurality consistently opposed armed attacks on Israeli targets.[74] As long as Palestinians were relatively united in favor of negotiations, Hamas was loath to be seen as defying that unity.[75] In the words of Hamas leader Ismael Haniyeh, "The scale of the attacks will be determined by the level of popular support for such a strategy."[76] Attentive to the public mood, Hamas leaders asserted that they sought neither to engage in conflict with the PA nor to defeat its agreements by force.[77] They also suggested various terms for an extended ceasefire if Israel withdrew to its 1967 borders.[78] Skeptics countered that Hamas was not sincere, as it never revoked its 1988 charter calling for the eradication of Israel. Students of the movement replied that the charter was a historical relic without practical influence.[79] They insisted that, even though Hamas fiercely resisted explicit acceptance of Israel, indications of its willingness to respect a de facto peace ought not to be dismissed.

Nevertheless, Palestinians' pro-Oslo unity was fragile and contingent. Arafat faced considerable political costs if, in fighting opposition groups, he appeared to be a lackey doing Israel's security work. "This is a real dilemma," one PA elite explained. "If we adhere strictly to the agreement and even just round up suspects, we are jeopardizing our legitimacy among our people."[80] These costs of suppressing the opposition rose as popular confidence in the peace process faltered. This occurred repeatedly in reaction to Israeli actions such as violent raids, arrests, delays in withdrawals, and settlement building. In this regard, the Goldstein massacre was a turning point. When Hamas responded by carrying out its first bus bombing, it did so in the expectation that it would meet with broad popular backing. It did.[81] That bombing took place half a year before Arafat returned to Palestinian soil and made the PA effective on the ground.

The national movement's organizational structure thus mediated this attack due to both the ambivalence of popular preferences and the incomplete institutionalization of political authority. In addition, Hamas's own organizational structure mediated its military tactics. Shaykh Ahmed Yasin had founded Hamas as a clandestine, decentralized movement.[82] After the arrest of senior members in September 1988, Yasin instituted reforms to protect the movement against infiltration and decapitation. He increased horizontal compartmentalization between local activists, as well as vertical linkages connecting them to Hamas leaders abroad. Nevertheless, Israel continued to arrest senior figures, including Yasin himself. In response, Hamas figures in exile intervened to restructure the movement. They instituted strict hierarchies in which subdistricts inside the West Bank and Gaza Strip were linked to operationally specific headquarters abroad. Inside leaders remained a vital source of political and logistical guidance on the ground. However, the outside leadership thereafter held ultimate influence over financial resources, essential decision making, and propaganda. It also controlled the Izz al-Din al-Qassam military brigades.

This division between the inside and outside had an important effect on Hamas's tactics. After Oslo, the Gaza leadership was living under the PA. Aware of society's longing for calm, it became increasingly convinced that Hamas had to accommodate itself to the reality of Oslo. Leaders based in Jordan and Syria did not face the direct consequences of confrontation with the PA or Israel. They therefore tended to favor a more hawkish line. These differences of opinion came to the fore after five suicide bombings between October 1994 and August 1995, when the PA invited Gaza-based leaders to high-level talks.[83] The dialogue produced a new reconciliation. Hamas spokesmen indicated that they would support an enduring ceasefire if the PA stopped detaining their cadres. Arafat and Israeli Prime Minister Shimon Peres responded positively. Yet just as a Hamas–PA truce seemed possible, Hamas's Amman-based Political Bureau effectively vetoed it.[84]

Outside leaders might have been under pressure from Arab states. Alternatively, they might have worried that the PA was using Hamas's inside wing to isolate the outside wing in a tactic of divide and conquer. Under such circumstances, Gunning observed, "Militancy ... became a tool to prevent marginalization."[85] In the end, the PA–Hamas dialogue closed without Hamas renouncing its freedom to carry out attacks against Israel. A few months later, Israel assassinated Hamas explosives expert Yehiya Ayyash, and the Islamist opposition launched its most lethal campaign to date. Hamas carried out three revenge suicide bombings in Israeli cities between February 25 and March 3. A fourth bombing by Islamic Jihad brought the toll to 58 dead and more than 200 injured in eight days.

The mediating role of organizational structure was again apparent in these attacks. Outside leaders' funding and oversight of the military wing allowed them to direct operations without approval from the political leadership in Gaza. Moreover, decentralization enabled Hamas's armed brigades to carry out attacks even without authorization from the external leadership. Hamas had deliberately designed the military wing as a network of autonomous cells in order to avert Israeli intelligence. The consequence was an organizational structure in which cells faced few obstacles to acting on their own initiative. Such had occurred during the first Intifada.[86] It appeared to occur again in February 1996. Those bombings were claimed by Hamas's previously unknown Yehiya Ayyash units. Izz al-Din al-Qassam leaders denied involvement. Political figures in Gaza quickly appealed for a halt to operations, and some even called them a mistake.[87] According to senior member Ghazi Hamad, the movement's "political wing began to pay the price for military operations it was not aware of." He elaborated:

> [Hamas's] dilemma was whether to continue its armed struggle which meant inevitable confrontation with the PA, something that would exhaust the movement's energies and get her involved in continuous confrontation, or stop her military operations at least temporarily. However, the political leadership's inability to control the military organ made it difficult, and even impossible, to give an answer to these hard questions.[88]

In the absence of centralized command and control, it was difficult to identify who had instigated the 1996 attacks and for what purpose and audience. The outside leadership might have ordered the bombings to assert its authority over the Gaza leadership. Or perhaps the military wing was demonstrating its own right to determine Hamas's strategy. A Jerusalem-based weekly reported, "A series of leaflets, denials, and accusations left observers ... shocked at the apparent state of chaos within the Islamist resistance. It remains unclear whether the bombers were acting on their own initiative as part of a radical cell, were carrying out the orders of the leadership in exile, or were acting on behalf of the internal organization, which feared political marginalization."[89]

It is important not to exaggerate the cleavage between the Hamas leadership in the Palestinian territories and that in exile. Other differences existed, such as that between the movement's political and military wings, the West Bank and the Gaza Strip, and leaders inside and outside prison. More or less hardline members could be found in any of these subgroups. Furthermore, Hamas was generally more successful than other factions in managing fragmentation and preventing internal disagreements from undermining strategic coherence. Nonetheless, the preponderance of evidence suggests that the inside–outside split mediated the spike in violence in 1996.

That very violence, however, served as a turning point in the management of fragmentation in the national movement as a whole. Israel responded to the bombings by imposing the most severe closure on and within the territories in the history of the occupation. Closure resulted in losses estimated to be 40–60 percent of Palestinians' income and output.[90] It likewise affected public opinion. Some 70 percent of Palestinians said that they did not support the attacks inside Israel, and 59 percent approved the PA's taking measures to prevent them.[91] Majority sentiment propelled a shift in the balance of power among political forces. Support for Hamas dropped by nearly half between the February opinion poll taken before the suicide bombings and the August survey conducted in their wake.[92]

These developments emboldened the PA to confront its opposition in ways that it had until then resisted. External pressure did likewise. Faced with the possibility that the Likud would triumph in Israel's upcoming elections, the incumbent Labor government and the United States leaned on Arafat to take action. In response, Arafat ordered PA security forces to execute a sweeping campaign against the Islamist movement in March 1996. The PA struck at Hamas's membership base by arresting approximately 1,200 individuals. Some would later charge that PA officers abused them as they themselves had been abused in Israeli prisons. The PA also assailed the Islamists' institutional base by raiding universities, taking control of 59 mosques in the Gaza Strip, and storming 30 Hamas civic institutions. The outcome, a former Israeli intelligence officer explained, was dramatic:

> Between 1996 and 1999, Hamas was cut down. It became almost nonexistent on the Palestinian scene. Everyone was in prison. The Palestinian people agreed to the PA's policy against Hamas and they gave the PA the opportunity to carry it out. And many people in Hamas recognized that they had been mistaken.... Statements from a number of their leaders showed that they recognized that the era of struggling against the PA had ended.[93]

These new circumstances transformed Islamists' calculations about the utility of attacks. Before 1996, the PA was averse to an internal crackdown for fear it would undermine national unity. After 1996, the same fear encouraged Hamas to submit to the PA. Shaykh Yasin explained:

> We have two options. We can decide to prevent internal conflict with the Palestinian Authority, preserve national unity, and spare the Palestinians from fratricide. Another option is that we start fighting against the Palestinian Authority. That is what the Israelis and the Americans want. If the conflict broke out among the Palestinians the effectiveness of the resistance to the occupation would decrease.... We opted for the first, very bitter option to avoid the second, which is worse still. Hamas will remain the opposition to the Palestinian Authority in a peaceful and democratic way.[94]

Paradoxically, the PA's prior reluctance to suppress Hamas, justified as preserving national cohesion, was the context in which fragmentation had persisted. It was when the PA assumed the risks of employing force against the opposition that it came closest to subduing it. Throughout the 1970s and 1980s, Arafat had dared to push diplomacy only when he gauged that doing so would not cause irreparable splits. In the early 1990s, fears of fragmentation continued to constrain him. They thereby opened spaces for violent protest. In the spring of 1996, however, a shift occurred. The Palestinian leadership reached a new calculation of the risks and benefits of confronting spoiler groups. The PA apparatus gave it an unprecedented institutional capacity to take such action. Collective purpose in society gave it a popular mandate and thus political capacity.

The result was the exception to the rule in the Palestinian movement: not management of fragmentation, but employment of violence to defeat fragmentation. The show of force altered the political opportunity structures for opposition attacks. "As the PA continues to strengthen," an Israeli analyst observed, "Hamas's role as a channel of protest has diminished."[95] The secretary-general of Islamic Jihad also admitted as much. "The decision to continue military action exists ... but the opportunity does not," Ramadan Shallah told interviewers. "Martyrdom operations are governed primarily by favorable conditions on the ground."[96] The outcome was a dramatic drop in lethal violence against Israelis (see Figure 4.1). Isolated attacks continued, yet generally by lesser splinter groups. In March 1997, a Hamas cell carried out a suicide bombing, apparently without the knowledge or sanction of the leadership.[97] Leaflets in the name of the Qassam Brigades claimed responsibility for a July 1997 bombing, but many believed them to be forgeries. Neither the identity of the bombers nor the political rationale for the attack was conclusively established.[98] Its capacity for violent protest constrained, the Islamist movement refocused on social activism and the provision of services.[99] This allowed Hamas to maintain a subdued presence. It thus bided its time until cracks reemerged in the organizational cohesion that had developed in the national movement at its expense.

Controlled Rebellion

Both Israeli and Palestinian fatalities declined in the late 1990s, yet it was too late to reverse the impact of violence. An Israeli extremist's assassination of Yitzhak Rabin in 1994 was devastating for both Israelis and the peace process. In May 1996, Israelis elected the Likud's Binyamin Netanyahu on an anti-Oslo platform. The Netanyahu government refused to meet with Arafat, canceled restrictions on settlement development, demolished dozens of Palestinian buildings in East Jerusalem, and froze the already delayed Israeli withdrawal from Hebron.[100] By the summer of 1996, the optimism with which Palestinians had greeted Oslo was giving way to what activist Mustafa Barghouti identified as "posteuphoria." Pervading the territories was "a deep sense of frustration and discouragement, pessimism, and even alienation."[101]

In September 1996, Israel began excavating a tunnel alongside the Temple Mount/al-Aqsa Mosque compound. The government explained that it was a new entrance facilitating access to a valuable archaeological site. Palestinians decried it as assertion of Israeli sovereignty and a threat to the shrine's structure. Arafat and the Arabic media condemned the tunnel, the PA called a general strike, and PLC members led protest marches. Palestinian civilians clashed with the Israeli army at the checkpoints separating parts of the West Bank and Gaza Strip under Palestinian control from settlements and bypass roads under Israeli control. Protestors threw stones and Molotov cocktails, and soldiers fired tear gas and rubber bullets. PA police eventually returned fire. This realized the major Israeli fear that Palestinian police, trained and equipped for the purpose of stopping violent protest, would someday turn their weapons against Israel. Unarmed and armed protest activity spread across the Palestinian territories, and Israel retaliated by dispatching snipers, tanks, and helicopter gunships. Fighting came to a climax after Friday prayers at al-Aqsa. Muslim youths threw stones and Israeli police stormed the compound.[102] On the fifth day of clashes, U.S. President Bill Clinton called Arafat and Netanyahu to Washington for their first face-to-face meeting. Both leaders reined in their forces, leaving a toll of some 55 Palestinians killed and more than 1,000 wounded and 14 Israeli soldiers killed and 50 wounded.

Palestinian commentators attributed the tunnel riots to grassroots anger at the perceived threat to Jerusalem and Muslim holy sites. This anger became explosive due to cumulative frustration with the stalemated peace process. By contrast, many Israeli commentators accused Arafat of deliberately inciting violence. Andrea Levin charged that the riots were a "direct result of a determined campaign by the Palestinian Authority to bring out the masses and arouse public fury."[103] She cited evidence that the PA had sponsored busses to transport university students to checkpoint demonstrations. She also referenced Palestinian media announcements intended to "whip up fears and exhort violence." Arafat aide Mamdouh Nofal agreed that the Palestinian leadership played a decisive role in the unrest. He argued that Netanyahu's refusal to meet with the PA president delivered Arafat the one indignity that he would not tolerate: being treated as irrelevant. Arafat thus "gave the green light" to Fateh militias, security apparatuses, and demonstrators. He swiftly terminated the clashes once Netanyahu agreed to resume talks.[104]

A focus on the organizational structure challenges these interpretations. It suggests why the clashes cannot be attributed to either popular rage or elite interests alone. Instead, these impetuses were filtered through the structure of leadership, institutions, and collective purpose in the national movement. This in turn mediated protest as a distinctly *controlled* rebellion. Numerous observers report that PA policemen initially attempted to stop protestors from confronting the Israeli army and returned fire only when they were "shamed" into doing so.[105] Once gun battles ensued, however, many officers ignored orders to cease fire. Rabbani writes that the commander of the West Bank police "almost ignited civil war when he arrived to threaten punishment for those who continued firing." At that point, a security force branch composed of "hardened Fatah militants" joined the clashes on their own initiative. According to Rabbani, their "participation was imposed upon, rather than ordered by, Arafat." It was only then that he gave "tacit authorization" to their engagement by not ordering otherwise.[106] A roundtable of Palestinian academics concurred with Rabbani's assessment that the popular momentum spurring protest "had an element beyond Arafat's control." They also recognized that the president did not hesitate to exploit the crisis for political gain and hastened to stop it when that advantage was achieved.[107]

The result was a controlled rebellion. In Rabbani's words, the events were "neither an organized uprising nor an entirely spontaneous revolt."[108] On the one hand, Oslo's shortcomings exposed the limits of Arafat's strategies for managing fragmentation. He could not halt the widening gulf between the public's dissatisfaction with the peace process and his own obligation to uphold it. Indeed, in the months preceding the tunnel opening, some Palestinians claimed that the public was on the verge of explosion.[109] On the other hand,

Arafat retained sufficient authority to stimulate and/or curb popular unrest, depending on his assessment of the rewards for doing so. In consequence, popular dissatisfaction with the leadership's peace program gave the riots intensity. The lack of institutional limits and clear procedures among security forces contributed to their uneven escalation. The president's personal power ultimately set limits on the duration of protest. A still largely deferent Fateh movement was the tool for making his will effective on the ground.

Had Palestinians been more united behind the negotiation process, the Jerusalem excavation might not have triggered violence. Yet had they been more fragmented, the leadership might not have steered the rebellion as it did. The riots may have taken on a life of their own, with opposition factions or other disaffected parties vying to use the outpouring to their own advantage. Unleashed from the leadership's control, the violence might have escalated to the point of jeopardizing the negotiations rather than boosting them. Yet this did not occur. Instead, the leadership retained both the incentive and ability to maintain command and control. This served to keep the tunnel revolt subservient to a strategy based on negotiations with Israel. In the end, the events enhanced Arafat's popularity as well as that of the security forces.[110] The PA's demonstration of militancy also rallied a new unity among political groups, culminating in interfactional dialogue sessions that included Hamas and Islamic Jihad. Israel recommenced talks and committed to withdrawal from 80 percent of Hebron. Some young Fateh leaders pointed to this concession as proof that Israel yielded only in the face of violence.[111] Many in the Israeli army, meanwhile, saw the riots as evidence that Arafat had not given up violence. They began making contingency plans should Palestinians again take up firearms against Israel.[112]

Moving into the late 1990s, Arafat continued to manage fragmentation to the degree that his and Fateh's domination kept opposition in check. Yet popular frustration suggested the unsustainability of the status quo. These tensions in the organizational structure of the Palestinian movement mediated protest in a subsequent incident of controlled rebellion. In March 1997, Israel began constructing a settlement on the Har Homa/Abu Ghneim Mountain at the southern edge of territory annexed to Jerusalem in 1967. There was no issue that united Palestinians more than opposition to Israeli settlements. This unity helped channel popular outrage over Har Homa into nonviolent forms of protest, such as demonstrations and diplomatic appeals. The PA leadership raised the issue before United Nations councils and convened an international meeting on the topic. It refused to attend talks with Israel until settlement construction subsided. A new National Islamic Committee Confronting Settlements joined forces with the PA to create regional committees and coordinate protest throughout the West Bank.[113] The nongovernmental Land Defense Committee pitched tents near the Har Homa construction site. There, Faysal Husayni and other prominent figures led a round-the-clock vigil.

Despite Palestinian and international remonstrations, Israel broke ground on the settlement. Protests ensued in the West Bank and lasted two weeks.

Israeli forces killed three Palestinians and injured five hundred, yet demonstrators did not escalate their actions to armed violence. This restraint was attributable to the authority of senior leaders made effective through command, control, and interorganizational cooperation. Arafat's aim in encouraging protest was apparently a state of "controlled disorder" that would spur international intervention against settlements. At the same time, it would demonstrate Fateh's leadership of a popular issue, thereby preventing "the street" from turning to Hamas.[114] Fateh activists led confrontations with the Israeli army. They permitted crowds to throw stones and Molotov cocktails but prevented the use of guns. PA security officers enforced these limits, and formed human barriers to prevent demonstrators from reaching Israeli positions.[115] As a result, the Har Homa protests were both intense and unarmed. Like the tunnel events, they reflected a controlled rebellion.

Meanwhile, polls showed that Palestinians' confidence in the peace process continued to decline,[116] if not linger "between non-collapse and non-success."[117] Apart from Netanyahu's policies, Palestinians' disappointment with the PA negatively affected attitudes toward Oslo.[118] Surveys revealed that a majority believed there was corruption in the PA. An average of 30 percent disapproved of the PA's respect for democracy and human rights.[119] At the start of Oslo, Palestinians preferred Arafat to any other PA presidential contender by a ratio of 4 to 1. In later years, the percentage of respondents who would reelect Arafat as president was nearly matched by those who preferred no one, had no opinion, or would\not participate in presidential elections.[120]

In this context, the tunnel events, Har Homa demonstrations, and other protests during the last four years of negotiations demonstrated what Toufic Haddad called a "cycle of manipulation."[121] In each incident, popular discontent boiled. PA leaders allowed demonstrations in the interests of both defusing tension and using them for diplomatic ends. At the same time, they restrained the character and duration of protest to ensure that it would not jeopardize negotiations or the PA's political control. The organizational structure of the national movement was vital for mediating the character of this protest because it hinged upon Arafat's ability to steer, limit, and ultimately terminate unrest. Such command and control was organizationally feasible. With Hamas isolated and the PA dominating the political field, the leadership faced few significant challenges when it coordinated strategic action according to its own calculations.[122] Still, popular demonstrations warned of the limits of these strategies. As Marwan Barghouti recognized, "We are aware such protests could easily get out of control."[123]

Fateh was the lynchpin of this equilibrium of managed fragmentation. Despite its internal disputes and weak institutions, Fateh remained paramount on the Palestinian political scene. It continued to draw strength from its membership of hundreds of thousands, its mainstream ideology, and its claim to historical legitimacy as founder of the Palestinian revolution. It bridged the grass roots and leadership, rallying popular support for the peace strategy, on the one hand, and constituting the backbone of the PA's bureaucratic and coercive organs, on the other. The movement was thus one of the leadership's main instruments in managing fragmentation. As Oslo became mired in crises, however, Fateh experienced increasing fragmentation of its own. Cadres' calls for a General Congress came to naught. There had thus been no turnover in the Fateh leadership since 1989. Many voiced concern that Arafat's personal domination of Fateh, the PA, the PLO, and the negotiation strategy had caused these elements to blur in the eyes of the public. Some believed that Fateh needed to distance itself from Oslo to avoid losing more popular credibility.[124] Barghouti and his stratum of young, insider leaders had once been decisive supporters of the peace process. However, they increasingly questioned the continuation of negotiations under the existing formula. A Barghouti confidant recalled:

> Years of negotiations between the PLO and Israel had failed to produce any genuine advance in the Palestinian people's pursuit of their goals.... I was the head of the committee that met with Israel with regard to Areas C [Palestinian communities under complete Israeli control]. I spent two and a half years negotiating with the Israelis about extending a water pipe three meters so that water could reach between Area C and Area B [Palestinian communities in the West Bank under mixed PA and Israeli control].
>
> For Israel, partnership meant how to make your partner lose.... If we agreed that 800 prisoners would be released, they would release 500. If we agreed on people with high sentences, they would release car thieves!
>
> We were active in the first Intifada and we know how an Intifada erupts. The environment was heading toward an explosion. It just needed a spark.[125]

Hamas similarly concluded that a new uprising could be on the horizon. Asked why it had yet to call for one, a spokesman responded, "We are waiting for Fateh."[126] Hamas understood that Fateh's commitment to the peace process was the pillar of the organizational structure of the national movement in the West Bank and Gaza Strip. It was glue holding together leadership, institutions, and collective purpose after Oslo. "Fateh is what safeguards the PA," Fateh young guard leader Sufiyan Abu Zayda said. "It is what protected the PA when circumstances demanded it. It has the capacity to defend the PA and the PA cannot defend itself without Fateh."[127] Arafat managed fragmentation through Oslo's ups and downs as long as critical sectors within Fateh pledged their loyalty to Oslo or muted their voices. If they chose exit, however, the Palestinians' organizational structure might unravel. The result would most likely be violence.

THE END OF THE OSLO PROCESS

The election of Labor's Ehud Barak as prime minister of Israel in May 1999 revived hope for the peace process, but only temporarily. Barak concentrated on negotiations with Syria. He did not fulfill obligations toward the Palestinians, such as scheduled redeployments and prisoner releases. From

Barak's perspective, these interim steps threatened the stability of his coalition government without advancing a final settlement.[128] For Palestinians, nonfulfillment reduced trust in Israel's credible commitments and stood to prejudice eventual talks regarding permanent status. Furthermore, it reflected Palestinians' worst fears that Oslo would lead not to statehood, but to the kind of curtailed autonomy that they had rejected for decades.

Declining confidence created a situation ripe for protest. In May 2000, demonstrations on the issue of Palestinian prisoners and the general impasse spurred clashes with Israeli troops. Six Palestinians were killed and more than a thousand wounded. Later that month, Israel unilaterally left southern Lebanon after more than 18 years of occupation. Cheering Hezbollah, some Palestinians cited the withdrawal as proof that Israel relinquished territory only under fire. No less critically, it led many Israelis to assume that Palestinians would act upon this conclusion. Military planners argued that Israel must reassert deterrence to show Palestinians that they would pay a high cost if they attempted to emulate Hezbollah's armed example.[129]

In July 2000, the United States convened Israeli and Palestinian negotiators at the Camp David II Summit with the purpose of reaching a final settlement. Arafat agreed to attend only with Clinton's assurance that he would not blame Palestinians if it failed.[130] When the summit ended without an agreement, however, Clinton publicly praised Barak for his courageous steps and criticized the PA president for being unforthcoming. Subsequent media coverage solidified the image that Barak "left no stone unturned for peace," while Arafat refused to surrender the dream of all of Palestine.[131] Various participants at Camp David later contested this interpretation, arguing that Israeli and American mistakes contributed substantially to the summit's failure.[132] They credited Barak with having proposed staged withdrawals that would eventually lead to a Palestinian state in some 92 percent of the West Bank, with a capital in East Jerusalem, and shared control of the holy sites. Still, Israel had not guaranteed Palestinian territorial contiguity in the West Bank, full sovereignty over East Jerusalem, or a solution to the issue of refugees' right of return.[133]

Some suggested that the Palestinian delegation opened itself to criticism because it did not match Israeli proposals with counterproposals of its own. Palestinian negotiators claimed that their counterproposal was implementation of UNSCR 242 and 338.[134] That they did not develop a more effective strategy for pressing this vision, however, was predictable given the national movement's disunity by that stage. Arafat could not afford to reject Clinton's invitation to attend the summit. Once there, he faced enormous pressure to settle. Yet Fateh and the public were dubious, if not critical. Caught between contradictory demands, the PA was not able to coordinate a coherent negotiation strategy. Husayn Agha and Robert Malley recalled:

> Unlike the situation during and after Oslo, there was *no coalition of powerful Palestinian constituencies* committed to the success of Camp David. Groups whose support was necessary to sell any agreement had become disbelievers.... Domestic hostility toward the summit also exacerbated *tensions among the*

dozen or so Palestinian negotiators.... Appearing to act disparately and *without a central purpose,* each Palestinian negotiator gave preeminence to a particular issue.... Barak the democrat had far more individual leeway than Arafat the supposed autocrat. *Lacking internal cohesion,* Palestinian negotiators were unable to treat Camp David as a decisive, let alone a historic, gathering. (Emphasis added)[135]

Disunity was no less significant in the Israeli and U.S. teams at Camp David.[136] Israeli and Palestinian negotiators continued to meet after the summit's failure, though many believed that Oslo had hit a wall. The measure of cohesion that made the Palestinian national movement's commitment to the peace process possible was giving way to a fragmentation that made its continuation unlikely. For decades, Arafat had managed internal opposition in an effort to stitch together unity around the goal of an independent state in the West Bank and Gaza Strip. After Camp David, the path ahead was uncertain. An Israeli scholar of Palestinian affairs explained: "Arafat succeeded in leading the Palestinians into a quite integrative framework based upon [the objective of] Palestinian sovereignty on part of Palestine. This notion failed in deed, not in vision. When it failed to materialize, it created a void."[137]

Hardly had Camp David ended when the Israeli army began preparing for a resurgence of Palestinian protest by carrying out "large-scale exercises covering various scenarios of unrest – up to and including 'limited-scale war.' "[138] In mid-September, the Israeli chief of staff stated that it was only a matter of time before protest erupted in the territories. When it did, he remarked, "Palestinians would lose control of any street demonstrations."[139] By the end of the month, Israel considered canceling joint Israeli–Palestinian police patrols for the first time. "The Israelis and Palestinians are in constant friction and often one word can inflame the situation," *Ma'ariv* explained. "In disturbances of the peace that follow shooting incidents, the Palestinian policemen feel a commitment to their own people and join them instead of solving the problem."[140] These words would prove accurate a few days later, when a new Intifada began.

CONCLUSION

The experience of the Palestinian national movement in the West Bank and Gaza Strip during the Oslo process illustrates two general patterns in the relationship between a movement's organizational structure and protest. First, it brings into relief obstacles complicating leaders' strategies for managing fragmentation. During the Oslo years, Arafat sought to mitigate political divisions through policies that appealed to people's hopes for statehood, as well as their immediate interests in jobs and relief from the most direct forms of occupation. He centralized power by consolidating his control over the PA's executive branch and the executive branch's supremacy over the political system. From 1993 to 2000, these strategies for managing fragmentation helped generate a critical mass of Palestinian commitment to negotiations, despite significant reservations about the Oslo Accords. Nevertheless, these very strategies for managing fragmentation contained the seeds of their undoing. Popular support for Oslo was based less on an ideologically grounded sense of collective purpose than on expectations of future gains. As those expectations went unfulfilled, political divisions sharpened and demoralization became the norm. Leadership came to rely on coercion and co-optation as much as legitimacy. Personalization of power helped the president bind together key constituencies, but corruption fed resentment. The organizational structure of politics under Oslo was bolstered by exchanges of resources for loyalty more than independent institutions and robust civil society. This was inherently unstable. Should the president not want or be able to maintain his grip on the political arena, the system would fall to pieces.

Second, events during this era show that, to the degree that a movement can manage its internal fragmentation, engagement in a peace process is possible. To the degree that its strategies for doing so remain partial or ineffective, however, the peace process will be vulnerable to violent protest. During Oslo, the strength of Arafat's personal leadership was vital in his launching of a historic diplomatic initiative. It helped him employ various tactics to thwart opponents and to contain, or even exploit, popular discontent. The development of the PA as an institutional framework extended and enforced this leadership. Nevertheless, cohesion under the PA was not fully institutionalized, and the centralized authority unique to state sovereignty remained lacking. The injunction against violence thus relied on leaders' ability to suppress semiautonomous actors or persuade them to lay down their arms. Rival groups attempted to renegotiate the domestic balance of power ensconced in the post-Oslo organizational structure, and this contestation mediated action in the conflict with Israel. When Hamas carried out suicide bombings, therefore, it did not act only in opposition to the peace process. It was also driven by its competition with the PLO, desire to retain influence within Palestinian politics, and own internal divisions.

This analysis of the role of a movement's organizational structure in mediating protest reveals the insufficiency of conventional explanations of Palestinians' mixed engagement in both peace negotiations and violence during the Oslo years. This conflict behavior was not due strictly to rational calculations vis-à-vis Israel. Indeed, the simultaneous use of negotiations and violence arguably undermined the utility of either. Nor was the mix of armed and unarmed strategies determined by material resources. Violence varied notably during periods in which funds and weapons arsenals were constant. Finally, patterns of strategic action did not stem exclusively from elite strategy. Critics charged that Arafat encouraged violence even as he carried out negotiations.[141] This view of Arafat may or may not be correct, but it falls short as an explanation of violent protest. It ignores how a movement's organizational structure stands between leaders' interests and collective action outcomes. Suicide bombings in the 1990s challenged Arafat directly and deliberately. It was predictable that Arafat balked at forcibly crushing his opposition, however, given the precariousness of the balance of domestic political forces. Hamas had genuinely popular roots and the public abhorred internal violence. Moreover, Arafat had long demonstrated his belief that, due to the fluid and penetrated character of the Palestinian struggle, co-optation was better than repression. In this organizational context, the PA president had incentives to promote unity through strategies that sought to manage fragmentation, not obliterate opponents.

Palestinians' participation in the Oslo process illustrates how formidable obstacles to the settlement of asymmetric conflict can emerge from the organizational structure internal to any single party to the conflict. At the same time, these dynamics are not independent of the overarching struggle between the state and its nonstate challenger. A movement's capacity for command and control is continually conditioned by state policies and progress toward achieving the goal of self-determination. Leaders may unify their populations behind peace talks for some time. However, they cannot keep their constituents unified indefinitely when talks fail to bear fruit.

6

The Second Intifada, 2000

On September 28, 2000, Likud Party chairman Ariel Sharon, guarded by hundreds of Israeli soldiers, visited the al-Aqsa Mosque compound. What Israelis viewed as a domestic political challenge to Prime Minister Barak, Palestinians saw as an affront by the right-wing leader found to bear personal responsibility for the Sabra and Shatilla massacres. The following afternoon, Palestinians leaving prayers threw stones at Israeli police and worshipers at the Western Wall. Police charged the area. The subsequent confrontation left 70 police officers injured by Palestinian rock throwing, 6 Palestinians killed by Israeli gunfire, and more than 220 Palestinians wounded.

The next day, thousands demonstrated in areas where PA-controlled territory bordered Israeli military deployments throughout the West Bank and Gaza Strip. Palestinians threw rocks and Molotov cocktails at Israeli soldiers, who responded with tear gas, rubber bullets, and live ammunition. On the second day of the uprising, 12 Palestinians were killed and 500 injured; on the third day, 12 more Palestinians, 1 Palestinian citizen of Israel, and the first Israeli soldier were killed. It would later be reported that Israeli troops fired 1 million shots in those initial days, what a security official recognized as "a bullet for every child."[1] Palestinian casualties during the first three months nearly totaled those of the entire first year of the first Intifada. Beyond the numbers, some events became focal points, such as the killing of eight-year-old Muhammad al-Durrah in Gaza, which was caught on camera footage and viewed around the world.

Palestinian gunfire was confirmed on the fourth day, when PA policemen stationed at demonstrations entered the fray.[2] In the weeks that followed, Palestinian activists shot at Israeli military installations, settlements, and roads in the West Bank and Gaza. Israel shelled Palestinian neighborhoods, bulldozed homes and fields, and blocked movement with hundreds of new checkpoints. By February 21, 2001, 311 Palestinians and 47 Israelis had been killed and 11,575 Palestinians and 466 Israelis injured. Some 27 percent of Palestinian fatalities and 43 percent of injuries were those of children.[3] Palestinian protest became less broad based and more lethal over time.

A suicide bombing on New Year's Day opened the year 2001. By year's end, Palestinians had carried out more such bombings than they had during the previous seven years combined. Israel's reoccupation of most West Bank cities in 2002, followed by its construction of a separation wall/barrier, led to a marked deceleration of Palestinian attacks. Still, violence ceased on neither side (see Figure 4.1).

What became known as the second, or al-Aqsa, Intifada presents analytical puzzles. The Oslo process was marked by incendiary developments that did not trigger protest, protests that did not trigger the use of arms, and armed attacks that did not trigger protracted conflagrations. The contention erupting in September 2000, by contrast, ushered in one of the bloodiest periods in the history of the Israeli–Palestinian conflict. Why was the second Intifada more violent and less participatory than the first? Why did it become a prolonged violent conflict while earlier flare-ups did not? Why did protest endure despite enormous costs? Why did the violence defy repeated attempts to end it?

Familiar approaches to the study of conflict and social movements suggest competing answers. Emphasizing grievances and repression, some charge that Sharon's visit ignited Palestinians' pent-up frustration, and Israel's subsequent reprisals radicalized what began as unarmed demonstrations. While the sequence of events supports this mainstream Palestinian narrative, it is more helpful in accounting for the uprising's initial momentum than for why it was sustained and how it evolved over time. Grievances alone do not specify the agents, incentives, and interactions that mobilized violence. Nor do they explain the limitations of organized nonviolent protest when support for such a course existed.

Others, underscoring the role of elites in instigating violence, claim that Arafat engineered a revolt to win what he failed to achieve at the negotiating table. This mainstream Israeli narrative suggests that Arafat was "talking and shooting" to escape the costs of overt sponsorship of attacks while reaping any benefits they might harvest.[4] This interpretation offers a strong challenge to the organizational mediation theory of protest. It suggests that any seeming contradiction in Palestinians' actions were a deliberate strategy, not an unintended consequence of structural fragmentation. There is certainly evidence that Arafat did not take all possible steps to stop violence. Nevertheless, even senior Israeli intelligence officers disagreed on whether he instigated the uprising. Indeed, it was later reported that the head of Israel's military intelligence research division personally persuaded the government of the view that Arafat was to blame, despite minimal evidence.[5] Furthermore, many Palestinians who took up arms were deeply critical of Arafat. A satisfactory account of the Intifada must illuminate the sources of their motivations and freedom of maneuver.

Still other observers of the second Intifada emphasize resource availability. They argue that Palestinians employed arms simply because they had them. PA security forces accumulated tens of thousands of guns during the 1990s, while others appear to have purchased arms from Israelis on the illicit market.

Nevertheless, the leap from weapons endowment as fact to weapons endowment as causal explanation is insufficient. It neglects the politics of political violence. It does not explain why Palestinians made full use of the weapons they had during the second Intifada but did not during the first Intifada or Oslo years. Moreover, the gravest attacks, namely suicide bombings and rocket launchings, relied on improvised, homemade explosives. To explain these patterns, analysts must look beyond material factors and clarify why groups had the incentives and opportunity to take up arms how and when they did.

A last explanation of Intifada violence focuses on instrumental rationality. According to this view, Palestinians turned to arms after the fall of 2000 because they judged it to be the best way to obtain concessions from Israel. Many Israeli commentators warned that Palestinians looked to the lessons of the first Intifada, as well as those of Hezbollah in Lebanon, and concluded that Israel surrenders only under force. Indeed, in 14 polls from 2001 to 2005, a consistent majority of Palestinian respondents would say that they believed that armed confrontations achieved national rights in a way that negotiations could not.[6] Nevertheless, interviews and ethnographic work find that many Palestinians viewed armed activity as just and appropriate, regardless of strategic effectiveness.[7] Others criticized violent means as strategically disastrous. For example, in 2002 prominent Palestinians published an "urgent appeal to stop suicide bombings." They asserted that military means must be "assessed based on whether they fulfill political ends" and concluded that there was neither a logical nor a humane justification for willful targeting of civilians.[8] Birzeit University professor Salah Abdel Jawad expressed it more frankly. "The use of arms in popular confrontations is political and military suicide," he wrote during the Intifada's first weeks.

All of these explanations shed some light on protest during the second Intifada. Nevertheless, they fall short because they exaggerate the degree to which the Palestinian national movement behaved as a unity actor, be it one that reflexively responds to grievance, elite manipulation, resource availability, or self-evident strategic utility. Attention to organizational structure rectifies this analytical misperception. It demonstrates how the very nonunitary character of the national movement after 2000 limited nonviolent protest and heightened violent protest. Illustrating this argument, this chapter's first section examines the sources and character of Palestinians' fragmentation. The second section analyzes mechanisms through which fragmentation facilitated, intensified, and sustained violent protest. The third section traces the waning of the Intifada, and the fourth concludes the discussion.

DIMENSIONS OF FRAGMENTATION

In the first days of the new uprising, Palestinian commentators hailed "a unifying political event"[9] that showed that "the entire Palestinian people are now in the same trench."[10] Others spoke of "blurring" ideological divisions[11] and "dissolving factional loyalties."[12] Yet below the surface of solidarity were deep fractures. Heightened confrontation with Israel inspired patriotism, but did not transform this movement's fragmented organizational structure. As Coser argues, conflict with an out-group tends to unite an in-group. Whether it also results in centralization, however, depends on the nature of the conflict and the group's degree of preexisting cohesion.[13]

In the second Intifada, both factors worked against centralization. The nature of the conflict with Israel was inherently ambiguous. Whereas conflict before a peace process is typically aimed at attaining a satisfactory settlement, the objective of violence is much less certain after a settlement has proved unsatisfactory. Under such circumstances, is the goal to influence negotiations or end them, to enforce the agreement or abandon it? Different groups are likely to answer these questions differently, obstructing the achievement of a clear collective purpose once hostilities recommence. Movement members hence may find it easier to forge a unified purpose before a peace process than after one. Likewise, the Palestinian movement's lack of preexisting organizational cohesion rendered it brittle rather than resilient under the weight of violent conflict. The Intifada brought to light lingering strategic divisions and the fragility of the PA as a political order. In Sayigh's words, "All the flaws and weaknesses that had been built and reinforced and made a part of the system over the previous six years became immediately apparent when faced under pressure."[14] A review of the three dimensions of organizational fragmentation highlights these weaknesses.

Leadership and Institutions

Arafat was the paramount Palestinian leader when the second Intifada erupted. Nonetheless, the Intifada never developed authoritative leadership, defined as guidance toward the pursuit of known goals. As Graham Usher reflected on the Intifada's first anniversary, "It would be wrong to say the Intifada has realized none of its objectives. The Palestinian leadership never set it any objectives."[15] The uprising did not direct coherent collective action. Rather, it opened space for the fragments constituting the national movement to respond to fluctuating circumstances in their own way.

The first to step forward were the young Fateh activists identified with the Tanzim grassroots network. With Marwan Barghouti emerging as spokesman, these first Intifada veterans spearheaded street demonstrations. They could not definitively speak for the national movement as a whole, however, because they did not possess formal authority in the hierarchies of the PA, PLO, or even Fateh. Official PA or PLO leaders did have this authority but did not use it to offer leadership. During the first months of the Intifada, no major PLO or PA decision-making body convened, much less issued directives to the public.[16] Instead, Fateh elites made conflicting declarations. "They are against the intifada; at the same time, they are with the intifada. They are against the terror, and they are with the terror," commented Muhammad Dahlan.[17] PA institutions exerted little influence as events unfolded. Sara Roy observed, "The

PA has virtually become a nonpresence, having failed to articulate any leadership, political, or organizational role for itself."[18] A refrain heard throughout the Palestinian territories captured it all: "There is no leadership."[19]

Some Palestinians beseeched Arafat to fill the leadership vacuum by addressing domestic and international audiences with an unambiguous statement of what Palestinians were fighting for and what means they were prepared to use.[20] Yet contradictions built into the organizational structure of the Palestinian movement gave him no incentive to do so. Oslo obligated the PA to suppress militancy while producing disappointing outcomes that fueled militancy. When the Intifada began, these competing imperatives immobilized PA elites. Arafat, caught between a duty to uphold Oslo and the popular pressure to oppose it, did neither.[21] Rather, he allowed fragmentation to take its course. This choice was individually rational given the gap that Camp David had revealed between what Israel was willing to offer and Palestinians to accept. Collectively, however, it would have devastating consequences for the achievement of Palestinian self-determination.

If the PA's institutionalized contradictions prevented it from offering leadership to the Intifada, Fateh's weaknesses kept Tanzim from doing so in their place. Young guard leaders did not wield an effective framework for mobilization because their movement had undergone an ambiguous fusion with the PA. Nor were they able to articulate a concrete program, because Fateh's official strategy remained one of negotiating with Israel. To circumvent these constraints, Barghouti developed a new approach for leading the Intifada. One of his colleagues explained:

> There was an organizational crisis inside Fateh after ten years in which the movement's members had been drained and scattered. After the [first] Intifada, some members went to the security forces. Some went to this ministry or that ministry. We did not have a complete structure.
>
> There are two kinds of leadership: leadership based on a particular structure and leadership based on a particular project or plan. We created something new and completely different: "leadership of climate." We saw that we needed leaders with charisma, a strong ability to address the public, a proper political vision. So we started with four or five people and we started appearing on all the satellite channels in Arabic, English, and Hebrew.... And we produced a climate of confrontation.[22]

Barghouti's "leadership of climate" helped rally participation in demonstrations. Yet it could not inspire cohesion around a unifying vision of goals and means because it did not speak for all political currents. To rectify this, Fateh leaders helped establish the National and Islamic Forces Higher Committee (NIFHC), a coalition of 14 factions that sought to coordinate protest activity and speak before the media.[23] Still, the NIFHC did not determine a single Palestinian strategy as much as offer a forum for dialogue. It did not become an authoritative, consensus leadership for the second Intifada as the UNLU had been for the first. The difference between their names made this distinction stark.[24] The NIFHC did not bring factions to relinquish their autonomy, and factions had no incentives to do so voluntarily. The new Intifada gave competing organizations a chance to circumvent the PA's monopoly on representation and increase their political clout. They could accomplish this more by undertaking independent initiatives that distinguished their respective movements than by succumbing to a collective body. Furthermore, though Arafat approved the creation of the NIFHC, he did not grant it real political power. By comparison, the UNLU had enjoyed some genuine autonomy due to its distance from Tunis. The PLO, in turn, had an interest in bolstering an effective, if subordinate, UNLU because it was its default representative under occupation. Given the relatively cohesive relationship between the UNLU and PLO, the strength of the former was a signal of the strength of the latter.[25]

The limits of the NIFHC were most evident in relationship to Hamas. Although Hamas allowed its activists to participate in demonstrations, it hardly became involved as an organization during the Intifada's first months. Many Hamas leaders suspected that Fateh was using the uprising as a ploy to boost the peace process. Their doubts increased when the PA released Hamas members from PA prisons, only to re-arrest them under Israeli pressure.[26] One Fateh grassroots leader claims that he and his colleagues met with Hamas representatives early in the uprising and invited them to join in leading it. He recalls that they refused, saying, "This is your guys' Intifada and God only knows what you want from it. Tomorrow you might end it and make an agreement with the Israelis. Then, you'll come and put us in jail."[27]

Hamas's skepticism diminished as Palestinian casualties mounted, the PA weakened, public support for militancy intensified, and the Intifada became entrenched. Judging that the damage to Oslo was irreversible, Hamas entered the Intifada more formally. At that point, the Fateh activist explains, the two factions met again:

> We requested another meeting and they agreed to participate in the NIFHC. They began to come out into the streets with us.... With that, the climate that we had created got politically muddled. Whereas before there had been just one message, there began to be two. The first message was national liberation and national independence. But they injected other messages, like "Islam is the solution."
>
> We realized that this would move the Intifada away from its goals and we opened a dialogue to unify the Intifada's program.... We spent more than 15 months and we could not reach agreement. The [NIFHC] was able to agree to a certain extent on the program of daily activities. A demonstration here, a demonstration there, a strike ... but there was no united political program.[28]

Factions had incongruent strategies and clashing organizational ambitions. They were therefore unable to develop an organizational structure that coordinated all political groups. Haydar Abd al-Shafi blamed Arafat for permitting fragmentation and his rivals for exploiting it. "The chairman insists on remaining the sole decision maker," he said. "And since he is unable to force his decisions on others, Hamas and the others continue to do as they wish."[29] In numerous publications and symposia, Palestinian analysts bemoaned the fragmentation beleaguering the national struggle. "The political movement has lost a unified and unifying center," Jamil Hilal wrote. "From the smallest organization or group to the largest organization and institution, everyone has come to speak in the name of the Palestinian people ... without the majority of people knowing or being consulted."[30] Hani al-Masri warned that "Palestinians must crystallize a single national strategy that defines goals, means of struggle, tools, plans, stages, coalitions, and possibilities, and integrate under a single resistance, single policy, and single decision. If they do not, chaos will spread and grow. And chaos is the shortest path to defeat and disaster."[31]

Collective Purpose

Compounding impediments to an authoritative leadership and institutional framework for the Intifada, Palestinians in the occupied territories faced difficulties in unifying behind a clear sense of collective purpose. Nearly all Palestinians believed that they should not continue negotiations under the terms that had governed the preceding seven years. They also shared a will not to surrender to military pressure. Beyond this, there was no consensus on what the national movement should do or what the pragmatic objective should be. "Oslo reached a wall and there was a spontaneous reaction to escape," a West Bank lawyer explained. "When people search for an exit, it is not always clear to them where they're heading. It was like being in a burning house; you just want to get out."[32]

Averaged over six surveys from June 2001 to October 2003, the percentage of Palestinians who believed that the final goal of the Intifada should be an end to the occupation (46 percent) was nearly equivalent to that believing that the goal should be liberation of all of Palestine (45 percent). The former objective was associated with the Fateh grass roots and the latter with Hamas. Only 6 percent on average believed that the Intifada's final aim was the improvement of Palestinians' negotiating position, which most analysts believed to be the preference of the PA leadership. Qadura Fares observed, "The main obstacle we face in our struggle is that we have no one strategy or vision. We have different factions and fractions within factions pursuing different strategies."[33] Jamal Zaqout feared that Palestinians were bound "to become the cog in the wheel of Sharon's grand design ... because that is what happens when your entire strategy is based on anger and emotion."[34] For those who had experienced the first Intifada, the contrast with the 1980s was painful. "There's no unified command, no program, no real coordination between the different political forces," one first Intifada veteran said of the second Intifada. "The 1987 Intifada was a complete system which ruled our lives. And the objective was clear. Today nobody knows what we want."[35]

EXPLAINING VIOLENCE

Militarization

The Fateh activists who were initially at the forefront of the second Intifada sought both to advance Palestinians' national goals vis-à-vis Israel and to advance their political interests vis-à-vis rivals. The peace process had created a situation in which, to quote Agha and Malley, "[t]he PA was doing the governing; Hamas and other radical groups were doing the fighting; Fateh was left with only remnants of each."[36] Dissatisfaction with Oslo and the PA undermined Fateh's standing, and many Tanzim members hoped a return to the streets could save their movement. They therefore embraced the uprising as an opportunity both to pressure Israel and to reestablish Fateh's role in the national struggle. They also welcomed it as an avenue to attain greater political, economic, and institutional power within Fateh itself. Fateh elites were wary of the popular Barghouti and grassroots mobilization in general. Yet, as in the 1936 Arab Rebellion, they understood the political risks of contesting the wave rising from below. After all, frustration with the national leadership was part of what had brought protest to the boiling point.

Competition between Fateh's young guard and old guard contributed to both camps' adoption of positions that fueled the uprising. Aspirants' desire to challenge the establishment reinforced their motivation to rally crowds against Oslo. The establishment's need to weather this challenge motivated it to allow protest rather than suppress it. Fragmentation in the Palestinian movement thus generated incentives that propelled escalation from above and from below. It also weakened constraints on that escalation. Given Fateh's loose organizational structure, members needed neither formal authorization nor majority approval before acting on their own vision of confrontation with Israel. A Fateh activist explained:

> You can't speak of anything in Fateh called "strategy." Fateh is a situation more than it is an organization where members meet to discuss details and take decisions.... Fateh is based on initiatives and orientations. A strong, active person or few people can decide that they want to gather a group. They decide that they want to confront the occupation, and then they do so. Or another group of people can issue a declaration that they want to talk with Israel and then go ahead and meet with members of the Knesset [the Israeli parliament].... When the institutional dimension is missing, individuals come to play a large role. What the Fateh movement gives you is legitimacy to take an initiative.[37]

Fateh's organizational structure gave members opportunities to spearhead protest. However, it did not give them tools to contain protest within non-violent bounds. As Israeli troops shot demonstrators, shocked Palestinians called for self-defense and revenge. PA police officers, themselves members of society, experienced this hardening public mood. Their action in response was mediated by the conflicting political imperatives that governed the security forces as an apparatus. The 1996 tunnel riots had demonstrated that officers were caught in the contradictions of Oslo no less than was the PA leadership. A Fateh leader explained:

> The basic role of the Palestinian police was to prevent people from starting confrontations. But they were not able to prevent large crowds from gathering. Demonstrators would face the Israeli army and security force officers stood behind the demonstrators.
>
> If Israel had reacted with tear gas, no one would think of shooting. But the army started opening fire. The police were trapped between the order to stop people from gathering and what was happening on the ground in front of them. People started pressuring them to do something. They would say, "Why are you just standing there?" These police officers found themselves in a real moral dilemma.[38]

Palestinians' use of weapons began when security force officers shot from their side of checkpoints at Israeli soldiers on the other side. Israeli investigators found that PA officers neither initiated fire nor withheld it when Israel fired.[39] Palestinian casualties quickly mounted, and impromptu armed cells emerged. In the West Bank, these were initiated by Tanzim activists and security force officers. In Gaza, activists affiliated with both Fateh and other factions formed armed Popular Resistance Committees (PRCs).[40] Cells engaged in shooting and igniting explosives against Israeli military and civilian targets inside the territories occupied in 1967. Their activity revealed the limitations of the "leadership of climate" that Barghouti had developed. His colleague explained:

> One of the negative aspects of "leadership of climate" is that the message that you put forward is not understood by all people in the same way. "Climate" means that you shape the general framework for action. You delineate the scope of popular activities. Leadership of climate is work with the public, not work with cells. But if, as a result of that climate, cells begin to emerge, it becomes very difficult to control them.[41]

Protest underwent a disorderly militarization in this context characterized by the absence of definitive leadership, institutions to govern interfactional coordination, or popular consensus. When Palestinian shooting began, it was less disciplined, less answerable to political decision, and more subject to emotional and reactive escalation than it would have been otherwise. As Ali Jarbawi described it, Palestinian use of arms coalesced "spontaneously, haphazardly, and procedurally" rather than due to a unified design.[42] Sayigh argued that the Intifada was a "dysfunctional revolt" driven by the "chaotic and counter-productive" launching of "uncoordinated, 'freelance' attacks."[43] Abdel Jawad forcefully argued that Palestinians' unsystematic shootings against a vastly better equipped army were a recipe for disaster:

> [S]hootings take place from a distance, and frankly speaking, are fruitless. While these people do not lack faith or the willingness to sacrifice, they do

suffer from a lack of appropriate weapons, a shortage of ammunition and more importantly, a severe lack of experience, training and knowledge. They also lack discipline and a central leadership.... It is understandable that young men publicly carry arms as a recognizable symbol of a brave resistance for a people subject to the ugliest kinds of oppression. In our present circumstance, however, this hands Israel the excuse for crushing this resistance on a silver platter.[44]

Evidence indicates that Israeli military leaders believed that swift and overwhelming force was necessary to reassert deterrence and nip the uprising before it grew larger.[45] They responded to the Intifada by loosening open-fire regulations and deploying snipers at demonstrations.[46] They retaliated against Palestinian gunfire with greater shows of force. An Israeli journalist described this escalation with an anecdote:

[Palestinian negotiator] Nabil Sha'th was touring the Gaza Strip ... with a European visitor. He wished to demonstrate the degree of the IDF [Israel Defense Forces] aggression to his guest. He asked his bodyguard to stick out his head and fire a single shot from his handgun. The bodyguard fired once. Upon hearing the shot, the entire sector came to life. The IDF fired from dozens of weapons, including tanks, for two hours non-stop. Hell fire came from guns, machine guns, heavy guns, anti-tank rifles, and what not. Heavy, constant, never ending fire was the response to a single shot in the air.... Similar incidents were logged over time and in every sector.[47]

Israel also targeted the broader spaces that Palestinian gunmen used for cover. On this basis, it bulldozed millions of dollars' worth of Palestinian houses, fields, and trees,[48] and used tanks, helicopter gunships, and warplanes to shell civilian neighborhoods.[49] These attacks caused civilian casualties, property damage, and trauma, particularly for children.[50] After two Israelis drove into Ramallah and were beaten to death by an angry crowd, Israel expanded its reprisals to include bombing of PA security installations. To deter suspect travel, it also instituted hundreds of new roadblocks, effectively severing the Gaza Strip into three enclaves and the West Bank into hundreds of territorial clusters.[51] Severe closure into, out of, and within the Palestinian territories accentuated the restrictions already in place. It resulted in millions of dollars in economic losses per day[52] and contributed to a surge in Palestinian unemployment from 10 percent in September 2000 to 28 percent in December 2000. During the same period, the percentage of Palestinians below the poverty line increased from 21 to 35.[53] Checkpoints affected nearly every aspect of daily life. "The theft of time and of any semblance of normal activity has reached undreamed of proportions," Amira Hass reported. "The best minds in Palestinian offices ... are taken up day and night with the simple task of retrieving a travel permit."[54]

Israeli authorities asserted that, given the gravity of the assault against their people, its response was defensive and restrained.[55] Dozens of international and local investigations charged that it was excessive.[56] Facing this military reaction, the participation of Palestinian civilians in unarmed demonstrations receded. At the same time, armed incidents multiplied. Under these rapidly shifting conditions, competing Palestinian groups asserted themselves by utilizing whatever advantage they had relative to other groups. For Fateh aspirants, this was mobilization of the grass roots. For the Fateh establishment, it was mobilization of the security forces. PA elites and security force commanders wielded personalized authority over tens of thousands of armed officers who relied on them for their livelihoods. According to the analysis of a former UNLU member, establishment figures used this resource to impose control over an uprising that began as a popular initiative:

> In the first Intifada, the young generation both launched and led the uprising. But in the second Intifada, there were two heads: one that launched the Intifada and another that interfered.
>
> We in the young generation learned from the first Intifada that a civilian uprising is better and that an armed Intifada will reap negative results. For the first weeks, this Intifada remained civilian. It stayed that way until people from the old generation interfered and militarized it. It did so by way of the security forces.... The old generation does not come from this idea of a civilian uprising. It was raised among military training camps and battles.
>
> After the outsiders started militarizing this Intifada, it became a reality imposed on us. Some voices called for an end [to military activity], but it was too late. By the second or third month the situation was out of control. [57]

Whether or not PA elites encouraged violence, neither they nor others defined a clear strategy to guide it or built a structure for command and control. By the end of 2000, Palestinian groups had conducted three attacks against civilians inside Israel. Israel had carried out assassinations of nine Palestinian activists. On January 1, 2001, Hamas executed its first bombing inside Israel since 1998. The following month, Sharon was elected prime minister of Israel on a pledge to crush the Intifada. With minimal possibility of a return to negotiations in the short term, both Palestinians and Israelis toughened their reliance on military force.

The organizational structure of the Palestinian national movement facilitated the militarization of what began as an unarmed uprising. Competition within Fateh increased aspirants' motivations to organize protest in contradiction to their leaders' obligations under Oslo. Competition within Fateh simultaneously reduced those leaders' incentives to oppose protest, lest they find themselves in a contest for popular legitimacy that they might lose. Fragmentation mediated strategic constraints as it did motivations. Given the fragility of PA and PLO institutions, those who wished to take up arms faced few impediments. Violent protest invited reprisals that led to further fragmentation and violence. In the face of this pressure, the national movement was brittle rather than resilient. Had the post-Oslo political system bolstered leadership, institutions, and collective purpose as forces coordinating collective action, Palestinians might have generated a new unity as hostilities escalated.

In comparative terms, they had done so at the outset of the first Intifada. In the fall of 2000, by contrast, those who championed protest were unable to reconcile divergent interests. Prior organizational divisions and weaknesses left them with minimal means to enforce discipline. Convergence on the need to oppose Israel was not a proxy for a cohesive organizational structure. Fragmentation thus mediated the initial militarization of protest. It would likewise sustain it as the Intifada evolved.

Inhibiting Nonviolent Mobilization

In addition to facilitating the militarization of protest, fragmentation in the Palestinian national movement constricted alternative avenues for *nonmilitarized* protest. The shift from mass-based nonviolent resistance to lethal attacks was not attributable to public preferences alone. An August 2002 survey found that 80 percent of respondents in the West Bank and Gaza approved of "a large-scale Palestinian movement committed to nonviolent action against Israeli occupation using such methods as demonstrations, boycotts, and civil disobedience." Fifty-six percent said that they would be willing to participate in such a movement.[58]

Nevertheless, during most of the second Intifada, nonviolent protest remained localized and overshadowed by the use of force. Most Palestinians attributed this to the escalatory effect of Israeli repression. The political geography generated by Oslo also played a role. Although Israel retained ultimate control over land, borders, water, and movement, Palestinian civilians had fewer encounters with Israeli functionaries or soldiers than in prior eras. During the first Intifada, everyday friction with occupation authorities had created sites conducive to unarmed defiance and civil disobedience. During the second Intifada, by contrast, Palestinians and Israelis came into contact primarily at checkpoints. This arrangement encouraged militarized clashes over protest strategies such as noncooperation and disengagement. Palestinians could hold demonstrations in downtown Ramallah or Gaza City, but there were no longer representatives of the Israeli state or army there to witness them.

The factors of repression and geography are important. Yet they focus on the relationship between Palestinians and Israelis and neglect the organization of relationships among Palestinians themselves. Since the 1980s, Palestinian society had changed in ways that inhibited civic mobilization. The post-Oslo system increased political corruption and socioeconomic inequalities, both of which undermined social solidarity and trust. It hastened the dispersion of intellectuals and civil society activists from mass-based organizations to a professionalized sector of foreign-funded nongovernmental organizations. This weakened their connection to the grass roots and led many people to resent them as "armchair revolutionaries."[59] The leftist and Communist groups that had been a principal force behind popular organizing for decades had all but vanished from the political landscape. Similarly, the polarization of national politics between the two largest factions marginalized the political independents who had traditionally been vital at the community level. "[Now] there are only two blocs on the Palestinian scene: Fateh and Hamas," one of the few unaffiliated members of the PLC explained. "The presence of all other forces has become symbolic and unimportant."⁶⁰

Many Palestinians called on their compatriots to try to rekindle the mass nonviolent protest of the first Intifada, arguing that this would be the most effective strategy for achieving national rights. An activist who was imprisoned for the 1988 Beit Sahour tax revolt urged Palestinians to "bring the masses back to the battlefield and directly confront the structures of occupation ... through massive, nonviolent resistance."⁶¹ Abdel Jawad encouraged people to remember the first Intifada and "learn from its strengths such as popular committees, popular and societal forms of struggle, social solidarity, economic boycotting and an emphasis on public opinion."⁶² A West Bank journalist argued that the lessons of the past proved that nonviolence was the rational choice. "We tried popular activity in the first Intifada and it was excellent," he explained. "We needed to benefit from our prior experience. That is what we are suffering today."⁶³

What was ignored in these pleas, like analogous ones from outside Palestinian society, was that the Palestinian national movement no longer possessed the organizational structure necessary for nonviolent protest on a national scope. The social ties, norms, strategic clarity, and dense network of civic groups that generated cohesion and facilitated broad-based nonviolent protest in 1987 were scarce in 2000. Another leader in Beit Sahour's civil disobedience campaign lamented:

> Changes have occurred which had a very devastating effect on Palestinian society, including but not limited to the destruction of all of the values that we had built during the previous 35 years of occupation.... These were the values that had tied everyone together.... The loss of values from one side and introduction of corruption into the society from the other side; these two elements caused the total breakdown of the internal front.
>
> *Was it possible to re-create this social structure in the course of the second Intifada?*
>
> No, it was impossible. The damage to the social structure was too severe.... I see no chance that 1988 could have been repeated. We are talking about different preparations, different societies, and different leadership.⁶⁴

Nonetheless, throughout the Palestinian territories, people demonstrated a will to participate in civic protest. A community activist in the Dheisheh refugee camp elaborated:

> It wasn't as easy to mobilize people as during the first Intifada. In the first Intifada people were in popular committees. They were members in different groups and took part in popular education. Everyone could be busy and connected to each other. But in the second Intifada these roles were very limited. The PA, the security forces, and some fighters – they dealt with everything.

Everyone else just watched. There was a gap between [them] and the people who were waiting to contribute but didn't know how....

I remember in 2002 when Israel invaded the camp. The PA did not exist anymore and children had no milk. It was almost a disaster. [Our community center] used part of our budget to buy milk. Then the army came and people got scared. They fled and left the center open. The army left and some other people entered the center and stole the milk.

Someone went to the mosque and announced, "This milk is for the children, please bring it back." And 80 percent of the milk was returned to the center. So here you can see how much readiness the people had to contribute.[65]

Despite organizational limitations, the second Intifada was not without nonviolent protest. The early months in particular saw frequent demonstrations and other shows of solidarity. Yet no authentically grassroots leadership set forth a compelling vision of how protest could be made safe, broad-based, and effective. Nor did the uprising develop overtones of social and political transformation, which had helped inspire sweeping participation in the 1980s.[66] The absence of a clear collective purpose, or even some "achievable endgame," led to feelings of paralysis.[67] One estimate suggested that only 5 percent of the population was actively involved in the second Intifada.[68] Another conspicuous indicator of the change from the first Intifada was the relative absence of women from the frontlines.[69] For most Palestinians, "participation" in the uprising meant suffering through checkpoints and repression, and pledging to continue doing so until independence was achieved. Many charged that the word "Intifada" was not even appropriate to refer to the events that began in the fall of 2000.

Important exceptions came to the fore in 2003 as Israel began constructing a system of concrete, metal, and barbed wire in the West Bank that Israelis called a separation fence and Palestinians called "the Wall." Apart from unilaterally imposing a new border, the barrier severed Palestinian communities, bulldozed homes and fields, and blocked people from traveling to family, work, and school. It also threatened to confiscate an estimated 8–10 percent of the West Bank and East Jerusalem.[70] Several villages in the Wall's route launched unarmed demonstrations to fight it. In order to do so, they developed elements of organizational cohesion atypical of the fragmentation characterizing the national movement as a whole. Residents of Budrus created a popular committee to rally cross-cutting participation in protest. The result was ongoing demonstrations that involved men, women, and children, representatives of different political factions, and also sympathetic Israelis and foreigners.

Residents of Bil'in expanded this model. A group of core coordinators gathered representatives of all factions and social institutions in the village and on that basis formed the Committee of Popular Resistance against the Wall and Settlements.[71] This inclusive initiative laid the foundations for a cohesive organizational structure to direct a village-wide campaign. It set forth a leadership and institutional framework, both of which met with sweeping popular support and the endorsement of all political forces. This organizational structure mediated the character of protest. Starting in February 2005, the coordinating committee led the village in carrying out daily, unarmed demonstrations at the barrier. As protests continued for several months, the leadership closely monitored the public mood. It eventually judged that daily demonstrations were becoming too taxing and that it could best preserve villagers' energies by channeling them into a weekly demonstration instead.[72] Bil'in thus began organizing a protest every Friday. It would continue to do so, practically without exception, for more than five years. To sustain the interest of both participants and the media, campaign coordinators planned a unique theme for each protest. They created props and costumes and sometimes mounted elaborate performances. Most residents took part in the weekly ritual, as did dozens of international and Israeli activists.

The cohesion of the movement in Bil'in helped institutionalize nonviolent protest and sustain it, despite people's fatigue and Israel's retaliation with tear gas, beatings, shootings, and the killing of unarmed protestors in 2009 and 2011. Cohesion also helped campaign coordinators gain the authority to overcome such obstacles as false rumors about the indiscretions of foreign volunteers and the committee's misuse of funds. The village could not have rallied mass participation week after week without an organizational structure that enforced and renewed a spirit of unity. The Bil'in campaign was thus, according to one of its leaders, "like a piece of the first Intifada inside the second Intifada."[73]

Interfactional Competition

From the outset of the second Intifada, some in Fateh-Tanzim believed that it was imperative that they lead protest lest Hamas do so first. In taking to the streets, however, Fateh encouraged Hamas to do the same. When Fateh signaled that it was not fully behind the Oslo process, it changed the system of incentives and constraints under which all other factions jockeyed for standing. A security force officer noted:

> Everyone understood that Fateh was the key to the game. If Fateh did not participate in armed activity, then Hamas would consider itself a target for Israel and the PA. The same applied to the PFLP and Islamic Jihad. But if Fateh marched with armed men in the street, after that everyone else would march. If Fateh opened fire, then others would do so. If Fateh carried out a bombing, then others would do so. All that was needed was the first step, and then others would finish.[74]

Fateh aspirants' early leadership of confrontation with Israel indicated splits within the Fateh bloc that had previously undergirded the PA and Oslo status quo. It signaled instability in the alignment of political elites, a factor that social movement scholars regard as a primary dimension of the opening of political opportunity structures in ways that encourage mobilization.[75] Given Fateh's domination of the political system, its actions communicated a shift in the costs and benefits that other factions could expect if they challenged the peace process. As the political field changed, rival groups picked up arms to ensure their relevance. This ushered in a *militarization of political competition.* As that competition came to provide an additional impetus for attacks, it in turn drove the *politicization of military activity.*

Islamic Jihad was the first to up the ante by detonating explosives in three incidents by the end of 2000. It proceeded to execute eight suicide bombings in Israel in 2001, more than it had carried out during its entire history until that time. The PFLP likewise revitalized its political presence in the national movement by launching attacks. It executed or attempted 10 car bombings in Israel between February and July 2001. Israel responded by assassinating the group's secretary-general. The PFLP claimed revenge by carrying out Palestinians' first assassination of an Israeli cabinet member. Meanwhile, Tanzim activists announced their formation of al-Aqsa Martyrs Brigade (AMB), which became the militia through which Fateh participated in armed activity. The need to compete domestically was an important impetus for its creation. A founding member of AMB explained, "Without AMB, other factions will rise up and take Fateh's place. If guys want to get involved and they see that there is no place for them in Fateh, they will go to another faction."[76]

Once some factions claimed responsibility for attacks on Israel, others followed or risked being left behind.[77] Shedding its initial skepticism, Hamas fully embraced the Intifada as an opportunity to end the Oslo process and advance its leadership of the Palestinian struggle. It intensified suicide bombings against Israeli targets, carrying out more bombings in 2001 alone (17) than it had during the entire peace process (16). Hamas's attacks met with the general approval of the Palestinian public, narrowing the popularity gap between Hamas and Fateh as never before (see Figure 6.1). Support for Fateh generally declined during this period, recovering only somewhat in November 2004 due to emotional solidarity after Arafat's death.

Under pressure of waning popularity, AMB carried out Fateh's first suicide bombing after Israel assassinated one of it field leaders in January 2002. In the three years that followed, it claimed sole responsibility for more suicide bombings than did Hamas. The PFLP also began suicide bombings, thereby marking the Marxist group's adoption of a tactic that much of the world associated with Islamic militancy. Under Oslo, Fateh's condemnation of suicide attacks had imposed basic limits on violent protest. From 1994 to 1999, Palestinian groups carried out 23 suicide bombings. Thereafter, an unmoored balance of power gave all factions incentives to demonstrate superior nationalism through violence. In consequence, Palestinians carried out 123 suicide bombings from 2000 to 2005. Of these, 30 percent were carried out by Fateh and the PFLP. Both groups had eschewed suicide attacks during the peace process years.

The decision of major factions to engage in suicide attacks did not reflect the enactment of a new policy in the national movement as much as a free-for-all in the context of Israeli repression and movement fragmentation. The Palestinian struggle had become, in the words of a local leader, "like a body

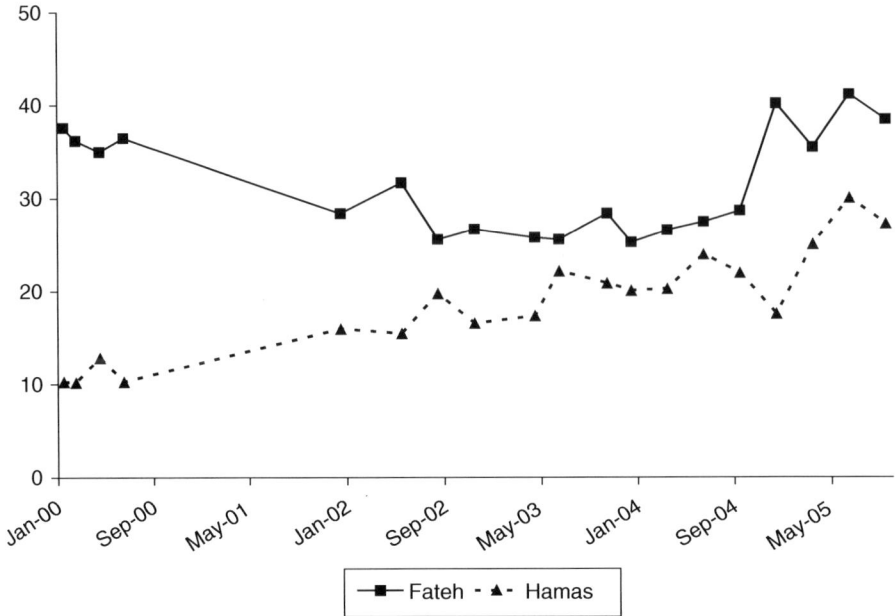

FIGURE 6.1. Support for Fateh and Hamas, 2000–2005.
Data source: CPRS and PSR, *Public Opinion Polls*, January 2000–September 2005.

that has brain failure and no longer controls its own organs and movements."[78] An AMB member explained:

> In the beginning, we believed that we needed to strike at Israel, but to do it in a way that could also win international sympathy. Then the suicide bombings began and this strategy descended into chaos.... From there, the situation developed without commitment to the clear strategy of limiting resistance to Israeli targets inside the 1967 borders. Very unfortunately, al-Aqsa Martyrs Brigade and all of the other factions went astray.[79]

As Israel further tightened restrictions on movement from the Gaza Strip, Hamas distinguished itself with another tactical innovation: unguided home-made projectiles filled with explosives, which were fired from Gaza into Israeli communities. Not long after Hamas debuted these Qassam rockets, Islamic Jihad and AMB began to launch them as well. With competitive pressure running high, the number of rockets fired at Israel increased from 60 in 2001 to 861 in 2006.[80] These killed more than a dozen Israelis and traumatized towns in southern Israel. In retaliation, Israel carried out air strikes and raids into the Gaza Strip. These reprisals flattened homes and fields, destroyed property, and left hundreds dead. In December 2008, rocket fire was the spark for a brutal war in the Gaza Strip.

The primary engines for the development of rockets were Israeli policies and general Palestinian popular support for armed resistance. The effect of these pressures on the actual use of rockets, however, was mediated by the organizational structure of the Palestinian movement. Unregulated by a central leadership or institutional framework, competition spurred factions to produce both more and stronger projectiles. Factions gave rockets names specific to their organizations and claimed launches in bold media statements. Some accused them of risking public safety for narrow political gain.[81] "Those who [fire rockets] are a certain group that does not represent the people and nation, doing it without thinking about the general interest," the PA interior minister declared in 2004. "There is no vision or purpose to the missiles."[82] The PA security apparatus and PLC condemned rocket fire, but the PA lacked the institutional capacity to stop militants from acting autonomously. "The Authority has allowed each faction to form its own armed militias, whose mission now is not only to resist the occupation but to attempt to impose their own set of values," Ashraf Ajrami wrote.[83] Unruliness was not only the distinguishing political characteristic of rocket fire, but also part of its menace. "The problem does not lie in the fact that the Palestinians have Qassam rockets," an Israeli military correspondent observed, "but in the motivation and the lack of restraint of those who launch them."[84]

Intrafactional Competition

Like interfactional competition, *intra*factional competition was a mechanism by which a fragmented organizational structure mediated violence. Fateh offers a telling case because it set the tone for the national movement at large. In the words of Birzeit University professor Hisham Ahmed, "What happens in Palestinian society is mirrored by Fateh and vice versa."[85]

Divisions within Fateh facilitated and encouraged violent protest in various ways. Differently situated individuals engaged in militancy against Israel as a means of bargaining with each other for status, resources, and turf within the faction. The Barghouti cohort sought to establish their political influence vis-à-vis the PA establishment, as well as advance its preferred strategy toward Israel. Such was also the case for the younger Tanzim members who formed AMB. These young men had been street activists during the first Intifada but tended to feel shut out of meaningful political participation after Oslo. Taking up arms gave them the political voice that they lacked. It made them a force with which to be reckoned and pressured Fateh elites to take them seriously. In other words, violent protest signaled to those who benefited from Oslo that they could not assume the indefinite acquiescence of those who did not.

The political gap between Fateh elites and cadres was exacerbated by socioeconomic tensions. AMB cadres often hailed from refugee camps and poor city neighborhoods. Apart from nationalist motives, some were drawn to militancy as a vehicle to social power and prestige. It allowed them to walk the streets with weapons, claim the mantle of nationalist lore, and flaunt a status to be admired or feared. That a sense of social and economic exclusion can impel young men to take up arms finds evidence in cases from militias in sub-Saharan Africa to street gangs in Los Angeles. What is new in this analysis is its emphasis on how organizational structure mediates the activity in which these sensibilities result. In the Palestinian case, internal competition and weak institutions created an open playing field in which those drawn to militancy could take individual initiatives based on any rationale, be it strategic, social, or personal. A contrasting case is Lebanon's Hezbollah. In mobilizing the traditionally underprivileged Shi'i community, Hezbollah also tapped into its constituents' sense of marginalization. It was effective in preventing indiscipline, criminality, and the misuse of weapons, however, due to the cohesiveness of its organizational structure. A tight hierarchical framework, charismatic leader, and inspiring ideology formed the institutional setting in which the movement trained recruits and channeled their energies into clearly defined strategies. Social exclusion can hence fuel protest in any context. The character of that protest, however, depends on the degree to which an organizational structure instructs, coordinates, and restrains it.

The second Intifada illustrates these patterns. It was disenfranchised young men in Nablus's old city and camps who took the lead in founding AMB. For them, despair with the peace process was mixed with resentment against corrupt leaders and the wealthy families who dominated their town.[86] Given Fateh's fragmented organizational structure, these young activists faced few barriers to initiating their own militia force. A founding AMB member from Nablus recalled:

> When the Intifada began, young guys in Fateh started meeting. In different regions and cities, those who wanted to get involved would come together and discuss what they wanted to do: plant a roadside bomb here, have an exchange of fire there, etc. And that's how it began. As time passed, we became more and more active. We arrived at the point where we wanted to issue a statement about these activities. We were going to issue the statement in the name of Fateh, but that was problematic. We needed to identify ourselves more precisely. People suggested different options for a suitable name, and we finally decided on the "al-Aqsa Martyrs Brigade."[87]

Arafat had ultimate sway over AMB, but according to one senior Fateh official, he was more the "shepherd" who held the purse strings of a fluid network than a mastermind setting forth goals and means.[88] In this sense, AMB, like BSO in the 1970s, was part Fateh militia and part semi-splinter group. It gave Fateh a safety valve for its restive younger members. Once set in motion, however, AMB was not under strict control from above. According to the International Crisis Group, AMB "never formed a coherent, disciplined military organization led by a unified command implementing guidelines and decisions of a political leadership."[89] Human Rights Watch agreed that AMB fighters operated "under loose, personality-driven local command structures, with a degree of autonomy and improvisation."[90] Israel's pursuit of Intifada activists drove AMB cells underground, and barriers to movement within the West Bank and Gaza inhibited their communication and coordination.[91] Even within a single town, several cells often functioned separately, sometimes competing for turf. For example, Ramallah was said to contain five distinct AMB cells.[92] Some large families formed militias that became identified as AMB, yet were loyal primarily to clan interests. Until 2002, for instance, the core of Tanzim-AMB in Bethlehem was practically synonymous with the Abayat family.[93]

Fateh's fragmentation fueled conflict among Fateh elites as much as between elites and the grass roots. This conflict likewise mediated Intifada violence. Sponsoring militant groups was a way in which rivals in the upper echelons of the PA could vie with each other. By trading patronage for loyalty, they were able to use militants as proxies in their contest to establish who "controlled the street." Many of these elites were security force commanders. They wrested control over Intifada fighters because those fighters were often former subordinates. Some 80 percent of AMB cadres were security force personnel, as were perhaps half the Gaza-based PRCs.[94] AMB thus reflected the problem of incomplete institutionalization in the PA, namely the lack of regulation of its multiple, unwieldy security branches, infighting among commanders, and the use of public resources and personnel to create private fiefdoms. In AMB, the personalized politics long characterizing Fateh became militarized. Power struggles and even petty feuds ensured a continued flow of resources for insurgency, which in turn ensured a continued flow of recruits. This was particularly the case as closure and restrictions on labor in Israel brought unemployment to record levels. For many young men, joining a militant cell under the patronage of a Fateh power broker was not only a way to fight Israel. It was also one of the few available ways of obtaining an income to make ends meet. The upshot, as a Palestinian daily put it, was that "privileges provided by Fateh have created an entire class of mercenaries."[95]

Overlapping horizontal and vertical cleavages in Fateh exposed the perverse consequences of strategies employed to manage fragmentation in earlier eras. After Oslo, Arafat mollified Fateh cadres' discontent by granting them jobs in a bloated security sector. He kept elites' ambitions in check by setting them against each other. The president thus found a short-term fix to Fateh's problems without having to engage in longer-term reform of its organizational structure. Such patrimonial exchanges kept fragmentation in check as long as opinion in Fateh and in society voiced confidence in the peace process. When those conditions failed to hold, Fateh collapsed into its antagonistic components. Strategies for managing fragmentation that were rational at one point were thus deleterious when conditions transformed.

Divided from the start, AMB further disintegrated due to Israeli repression. The arrest of some 9,000 Intifada fighters and extrajudicial executions of another 166 by the end of 2004 removed field leaders.[96] As second-tier activists vied to fill the vacuum, AMB cells experienced internal strife or ruptured into smaller splinters.[97] Those who assumed influence, rising "quite literally by a process of elimination,"[98] tended to be less disciplined than their predecessors. Echoing patterns familiar from earlier rebellions, killed activists' replacements were typically younger and less experienced. They were often more loyal to clans, cliques, or localities than to any central leadership. "The result," Usher concluded, "was a movement dissolute and in disarray, with a widening gulf between its political and military wings."[99] This fragmentation at the grass roots created opportunities for rivalries at the political top. Fighters' lack of commitment to a clear national strategy rendered them vulnerable before the sway of senior patrons. They were more prone to be manipulated than were the assassinated leaders whose places they assumed, a susceptibility that competing elites well understood.[100]

The proliferation of power centers in Fateh as an organization, and hence throughout the Intifada as a campaign, allowed local circumstances and particularistic agendas to multiply incentives for violent protest. It also impeded efforts to bring violence to a halt. Testing ceasefires, no less than funding groups of fighters, was a realm in which elites vied to demonstrate influence. A West Bank resident noted:

> There was very strong competition between the heads of the different security forces over who controlled the street. For example, some might negotiate with the Israelis and say, "We in Preventative Security can make things quiet." But then groups connected to the Military Intelligence service would go out and shoot.[101]

Hamas was more internally cohesive than Fateh. Nevertheless, it also had organizational vulnerabilities and divisions that affected its use of violent protest. Israeli policies of closure, incursions, arrests, and killings accentuated these difficulties. This was particularly the case in the West Bank, where Israel maneuvered more freely than in Gaza. A Hamas member in Ramallah explained:

> The second Intifada weakened the organizational framework of Hamas completely.... There were constant arrests in the organizational and administrative body of the movement, which continue until today. For that reason, we can't say that Hamas has a clear organizational framework with a top leadership and a pyramid below it.[102]

A major source of fragmentation in Hamas remained its political wing's lack of full command and control over the military wing. As during the Oslo years, Qassam Brigade cells occasionally executed attacks without sanction and sometimes against the leadership's wishes. For example, whereas the Hamas leadership was committed to a unilateral Palestinian ceasefire in June 2003, a rogue cell sealed its collapse by carrying out a suicide bombing. Neither inside nor outside leaders authorized the bombing, and both were reportedly dismayed by its occurrence.[103] In addition, the split between Hamas's Damascus- and Gaza-based political leaderships sometimes infused militancy with motives beyond that of striking Israel. According to Israeli sources, the movement's dispatch of its first female suicide bomber in January 2003 was a tactical escalation prompted by the pending selection of a new head of the Hamas political bureau. Shaykh Yasin reputedly wanted a role in the selection process, but leaders in Damascus viewed him as too moderate. Yasin hence had "to prove to the external Hamas that he's just as tough as they are."[104] Against this backdrop, he apparently retreated from earlier support for a ceasefire and authorized the unprecedented recruitment of a woman for a suicide operation.

Collapsing Authority

The essence of fragmentation in any national movement, in the words of a Gaza-based analyst, "is not only that there are multiple strategies and decision-makers, but that these are not governed by law or mechanisms agreed upon by society."[105] Had the Palestinian national movement had stronger mechanisms of law and governance, overlapping spheres of internal competition might not have played such a role in escalating protest. However, the already weak institutions of the PA became more debilitated as the Intifada wore on. Israel's refusal to transfer customs monies collected on the PA's behalf caused an acute budget crisis, and closure prevented public employees from reaching work. This hastened the disintegration of the PA's capacity for service provision. It left international agencies and the Islamist movement to play greater roles in meeting the population's basic needs.

Israel's targeting of security force installations and personnel likewise contributed to the dismantling of law enforcement. Although it was opposition factions that perpetrated the most extreme violence during the first year and a half of the Intifada, Israel concentrated reprisals against the PA on the claim that it was failing to fight terror. Had it struck a more cohesive movement, this pressure might have compelled the national leadership to impose an end to violent protest. Mediated by a fragmented organizational structure, however, strikes had the contrary effect. Retaliation against the PA redoubled Hamas's incentives to use violence against Israel; by doing so, it both attacked its external rival and brought on reprisals that destroyed the institutional apparatus of its internal rival. Moreover, it attained these benefits without causing harm to its own organization.[106]

Israeli strikes on the PA also encouraged violent protest in a second paradoxical way. As security forces came under fire, officers took their arms and fled to safety in underground militia cells. The disintegration of the security establishment thus served as a conduit of fighters and weapons for the Intifada.[107] In the process, the PA's capacity and legitimacy gradually collapsed. A telling incident occurred during the Intifada's second year, when Arafat ordered PA police to detain Hamas's two top leaders in Gaza. Residents of their neighborhood came into the streets to block the arrests, and the police had no recourse but to run away. No longer a suprafactional power, the PA came to focus less on governance than on protecting Fateh from its rivals. The result, an analyst in Gaza explained, was that "the PA has stopped being the arbiter of domestic political struggles, and instead has become a party to these struggles."[108]

The decisive blow to the PA came in the spring of 2002. Whereas no Israelis were killed in suicide bombings in 2000, 87 were killed in 2001 and

78 were killed in the month of March 2002 alone. The deadliest was a suicide attack that killed 30 Israeli civilians, mostly senior citizens, as they celebrated Passover. Two days later, on March 29, Israel launched Operation Defensive Shield, whereby it reoccupied all West Bank cities except Jericho. When Israel withdrew 45 days later, it left a toll of 497 Palestinians dead, 1,447 injured, and more than 8,500 arrested, in addition to 1 million civilians subjected to curfew, and hundreds of millions of dollars in property destroyed.[109] Israel also arrested Marwan Barghouti, besieged Bethlehem's Church of the Nativity, and demolished parts of Nablus's old city and the Jenin refugee camp. By the summer of 2002, the PA was an empty shell. The presence of Israeli tanks in West Bank towns shattered what remained of the Oslo stipulation that those areas be under PA control. It also undid much of the state-building process undertaken in the 1990s. Hass described the army's raiding of governmental and nongovernmental offices where computers were smashed and files burned, and dubbed it a campaign to "destroy Palestinian civil institutions ... sending all of Palestinian society backward."[110]

Beyond damage to PA institutions was the immobilizing of the PA president. Israeli troops confined Arafat to his Ramallah compound, and Prime Minister Sharon and U.S. President George Bush declared him to be irrelevant. This further discouraged the PA leader from fulfilling the functions of leadership. Some Palestinians judged that Arafat reasoned that his political salvation would come not in rebuilding a cohesive organizational structure for the national movement, but in encouraging greater lawlessness and violence. Through fragmentation, he indirectly communicated to the international community that he was the only one who could bring order. This carried the warning that, should world powers insist on circumventing him, the result would be chaos.[111] A leader who knew Arafat well explained:

> The behavior of a leader who is in prison is different from one who is free.... Arafat saw himself as a world leader.... So to lock him in two rooms had an enormous effect on him. He had the kind of personality that if you came to him and spoke to him with respect, he would give you anything. But if you attacked, he would fight back....
>
> Arafat had the military, moral, and political capacity to bring the Intifada to an end, but that would have taken a strong decision and would have sparked confrontations with armed groups like Jihad and Hamas. But when Israel and the world began to say that Arafat was irrelevant, he had no incentive to end it. Regardless, he would not stop it unless there was some reason for political hope ... unless he could say that he had an alternative.[112]

Israel and the United States called for Palestinian "reform," meaning a change in leadership. In May 2003, Arafat bowed to this pressure and signed the Basic Law, the interim constitution that he had ignored since it was passed by the PLC in 1997. He also accepted amendments that transferred some of his authority to the new post of PA prime minister. To this post he appointed Fateh veteran Mahmoud Abbas (Abu Mazen), the favored candidate of Israel and the United States. Abbas was soft spoken and without a popular following; he had long been an advocate of negotiations and was the most high-ranking PLO figure to denounce military activity in the second Intifada. Abbas pledged adherence to the Road Map, a staged peace plan drafted by the Quartet of the United States, European Union, United Nations, and Russia. In principle, Abbas's assumption of leadership was a chance for the national movement to rebuild cohesion. In practice, fragmentation between his authority and that retained by Arafat impeded his mission at every turn. Belittling Abbas as a quisling, Arafat maneuvered his loyalist base among Fateh cadres and security force branches to block Abbas's attempts to dismantle militant groups. Israel might have boosted Abbas's credibility by releasing prisoners, dismantling settlements, or lifting closure. In the absence of such concessions, however, the exasperated prime minister resigned after six months.

Arafat was determined not to be marginalized and hence to prevent any other Palestinian from exercising political power at his expense. Nevertheless, he could not guarantee his own effective power on the ground. As domestic governance crumbled, it was not clear if Arafat lacked only the will to restore order or also the capacity to do so. By June 2004, as many Palestinians said that they did not feel the presence of the PA as said that they did. The percentage that believed that Arafat exercised total or some control over domestic affairs (48) was less than the percentage that believed that he controlled little or nothing (49).[113] Arafat's personalized power had long been the glue holding Fateh and the PA together and its waning unraveled them. "Accustomed to divide and conquer, [Arafat] can still divide, but he conquers less decisively than before," the International Crisis Group wrote. "Competition among leaders, never far from the surface, has reached exceptional levels."[114]

With the disintegration of central authority, political power devolved to the local level. There, anyone with a weapon or group of followers could attempt to dictate affairs. In 2004 a struggle among PA security commanders for personal domination of the Gaza Strip was the backdrop for riotous demonstrations, the burning of buildings, kidnappings, assassination attempts, and the bombing of an American convoy.[115] In the West Bank, PA security forces repeatedly arrested Intifada fighters, only to see their armed comrades storm prisons or courtrooms and set them free. In other instances, security forces anticipated such troubles and did not even attempt to make arrests. With the breakdown of the organizational structure of Palestinian political life, violence became privatized. The influence that violence procured did as well. While some armed men used this influence to act as welcome community mediators, others turned their guns against compatriots in a situation that became known as the "chaos of weapons" (*fawda as-silah*) or "security lapse" (*al-infilat al-amini*).[116] Reminiscent of the Arab Rebellion after 1937, internal strife was difficult to avoid in a society under siege and increasingly unmoored by economic, social, and physical insecurity. Reports chronicled increases in murders and suicides, drug use, violence against women, and a 60 percent rise in crime from pre-Intifada levels.[117]

Still, given the state of political and social fragmentation, it was surprising that Palestinians did not witness *more* internal violence. Cut off from each other, communities largely managed to govern themselves. According to an independent PLC member, their capacity to do so was attributable to the cumulative development of civil society during decades under occupation, the strength of the family unit, and individuals' sense of personal responsibility.[118] A Nablus resident put it more bluntly. When asked what ruled his town in the virtual absence of formal law or government, he replied, "What is left of our morals."[119]

Foiled Ceasefires

During the first three years of the Intifada alone, more than a dozen ceasefires collapsed or broke down before taking effect. Many Israelis charged that ceasefires failed because Arafat did not want them to succeed.[120] Many Palestinians retorted that it was Sharon who wished to avoid returning to the negotiating table and that he carried out assassinations and raids to that end.[121] Both arguments have merit but cannot completely account for the phenomenon. On the Palestinian side of the equation, the organizational structure of the national movement also mediated this outcome. In particular, the dispersion of decision-making autonomy generated obstacles to terminating the violent protest that the Intifada unleashed.

In the first five weeks of the uprising, Israeli and Palestinian representatives negotiated three ceasefires. Arafat refused to sign one, and two others did not take hold despite his official consent. During this early phase, a ceasefire might have been welcome to the few who viewed the Intifada as a temporary bargaining tactic. For the majority who called for a decisive break from the stalemated Oslo process, however, ceasefires threatened a premature end to the uprising. Tanzim and opposition factions denounced the leadership's willingness to make a deal with Israel at a time of daily Palestinian funerals.[122] When Arafat exercised greater control over the Palestinian arena, such as during the waning of the first Intifada in 1993 and the tunnel riots in 1996, he had effectively terminated protest when he judged it auspicious for the achievement of national goals. It is possible that he did not believe the fall of 2000 to be opportune in this sense. However, he also faced a movement that was less cohesive under his leadership. Any declaration of a hasty end to the uprising would have met with internal resistance, which Arafat preferred to avoid.

In these early weeks, Fateh was leading the uprising. Arafat thus did not need to bargain with other factions to reach a workable cessation of hostilities. Rather, he had to bargain primarily with Israel in order to obtain concessions that would satisfy Palestinian public opinion. This situation changed as Fateh's competitors became emboldened. On November 1, 2000, Arafat and former Israeli Prime Minister Shimon Peres agreed to a ceasefire, but Islamic Jihad detonated a bomb in Jerusalem the next day. The ascent of elements beyond the PA president's immediate control reduced his ability to enforce a ceasefire single-handedly. This was complicated by Israel's insistence, repeated throughout the Intifada, that Palestinians sustain a certain number of days without an attack before Israel halt its military operations. One West Banker observed, "When Israel said 'there will be no ceasefire until Palestinians stop using violence,' it gave any group the power to wreck it."[123]

Under those circumstances, the challenge of reaching a cessation of violence came to require negotiations among Palestinian political forces in addition to negotiations between the PA and Israel. This reflected the fragmentation trap that had vexed the PLO throughout the 1970s. The weakness of central authority invited the proliferation of armed groups, yet the containment of armed groups demanded central authority. In April 2001, Arafat ordered Gaza PRCs to dissolve and the security force officers among them to return to duty. They ignored the command, as West Bank AMB cells did at later points.[124] That fall, Arafat declared his willingness to accept Israeli and American ceasefire demands, but popular demonstrations protested against them.[125] When the PA forcibly repressed a demonstration in Gaza, riots erupted that left two dead and several PA institutions burned and looted. The upheaval, Charmaine Seitz observed, "was an abrupt summation of Palestinian Authority attempts to choreograph a ceasefire."[126]

The fragmented organizational structure of Palestinian politics hence impeded ceasefires in two initial ways. At the outset, it created a situation in which Arafat could impose a ceasefire only to the degree that he defied public opinion. Later, it gave rise to conditions in which a ceasefire also demanded that he forcibly constrain forces that did not defer to his command. Fragmentation came into play in a third way with Israel's extrajudicial executions of Intifada activists and political leaders. Assassinations typically incited organizations to seek revenge. In doing so, they acted on factional calculations rather than national ones. This trend was particularly detrimental when the timing of an assassination and revenge attack coincided with the negotiation of a ceasefire. "If there is no central leadership, there is no one to say if a time is opportune or not," an activist explained. "Everyone within Fateh and Hamas chose his own timing. And sometimes the timing that is right for a particular political group is different than the timing that is right for the nation as a whole."[127]

The triangular relationship between assassinations, factional imperatives, and foiled ceasefires recurred throughout the second Intifada. Israel's assassination of PFLP Secretary-General Abu Ali Mustafa in August 2001, followed by the PFLP's assassination of Israeli Minister Rehavem Ze'evi, doomed the shaky truce that Arafat declared after September 11. The following month, a U.S. envoy was en route to discuss a ceasefire when Israel assassinated Hamas military leader Mahmoud Abu Hannud. Hamas responded with two suicide bombings that brought those discussions to an end. That December, Arafat's declaration of a ceasefire led to four weeks without attacks inside Israel. However, the assassination of AMB leader Raed al-Karmi provoked the group to execute its first suicide attack. In July 2002, Fateh called for a ceasefire and Hamas indicated its conditional support. The next day, Israel killed Hamas leader Salah Shehadeh and 14 others with a one-ton bomb on a Gaza apartment building. Hamas declared the ceasefire plan defunct with two suicide bombings. In June 2003, the PA called for interfactional talks on a ceasefire and Hamas replied that it would consider the invitation. The next day, Israel fired missiles at Abdel Aziz al-Rantisi and the movement canceled all talks. Later that month, following Prime Minister Abbas's acceptance of the Road Map, Fateh, Hamas, and Islamic Jihad declared a three-month temporary ceasefire, or *hudnah*. Hamas did not break the truce, even as Israel arrested sympathizers and killed three field activists. When Israel assassinated Ismael Abu Shanab, however, Hamas resumed suicide attacks and the ceasefire collapsed. In each of these instances, the effect of an Israeli extrajudicial killing on the prospects for reaching a cessation of hostilities was not automatic. It was filtered through the organizational structure of the Palestinian movement. The fragmented relations between factions rendered each attack not simply a strike on Israel, but also a defection in the game of intra-Palestinian cooperation. No central leadership or authoritative rules of national decision making enforced bounds on how and when factions acted. Had such existed, external pressures might not have led ceasefires to collapse.

A fourth way in which fragmentation complicated ceasefires emerged as Fateh's supremacy waned and Hamas's power grew. Thereafter, the task of reaching an end to armed hostilities intersected with that of building cohesion in the national movement itself. A ceasefire would succeed only if Islamist factions accepted it, and they would accept it only if offered the power sharing that they and their constituents believed their due. To reach some consensus on goals and means, therefore, the national movement needed to craft an organizational structure that reflected the changed balance of domestic forces. "The time in which one political party can dominate the Palestinian arena is past," Beverly Milton-Edwards and Alastair Crooke wrote. "The PLO has neither the capacity nor the will to enter into war with the Islamists, and vice versa."[128]

In this context, Israel's 2002 reoccupation of the West Bank was a turning point because it demonstrated that Israel could go far in immobilizing protest without having to strike a bargain with the Palestinians. This convinced some Fateh activists that Palestinians needed a period of calm to rebuild and reassess. The only way to obtain such calm, some reasoned, would be to declare a ceasefire unilaterally. Fateh had the most to gain from such a respite, as it was invested in saving the PA from further ruin. Hamas and other opposition groups had more to lose, particularly because they feared that an end to the Intifada and renewal of Israeli–PA security coordination would target them with a fresh wave of arrests. Within Hamas, Gaza-based leaders were more sympathetic to Fateh's perspective. They sensed the public's weariness and faced the constant danger of Israel's extrajudicial killings. By contrast, the Damascus bureau feared that a unilateral ceasefire might strip it of its greatest source of influence within Palestinian politics: the power to dispatch military brigades as it saw fit.[129] Hamas's exiled leadership thus had little incentive to relinquish its freedom to attack – unless Fateh were to compensate it with concessions in domestic politics.

In July 2002, Fateh leaders put forth a unity proposal to this end. It called upon factions to form a single leadership body that would determine the form and timing of resistance activity. It implicitly restricted armed operations to the territories occupied in 1967. Factions engaged in dialogue on and off for the next two and a half years but reached no enduring ceasefire. The absence of Israeli reciprocity was a crucial factor in this outcome, yet not the only one. Even a unilateral Palestinian ceasefire required credible commitments from autonomous actors with divergent preferences on internal and external matters. "Everybody is bargaining with a very different set of expectations," a senior negotiator commented during the June 2003 talks.[130] Beyond this, fragmentation raised the possibility that agreements negotiated by the upper echelons might not hold at the grass roots. For one Palestinian academic, the January 2003 dialogue sessions failed because "factions have lost control on the ground. Most of the military operations [against Israel] are being carried out by gunmen who don't report to their political leaders. Even if the factions had reached an agreement, this wouldn't have meant a complete end to the violence."[131]

Compounding these mechanisms through which the Palestinian movement's organizational structure mediated efforts to terminate hostilities was the generally uninstitutionalized character of national decision making. This gave the process of agreeing on a ceasefire a stochastic element, which the Intifada environment of uncertainty and intensified competition accentuated. Under swiftly shifting circumstances, caprice could determine whether a ceasefire went into effect. To illustrate such serendipity, it is worth citing the recollections of one Fateh leader at length:

> America was going to attack Iraq and we needed a safe boat to put the Palestinian people in a better place. Marwan [Barghouti] sent a letter to a colleague and me [to deliver to the Hamas leadership in Syria]. We went and met with Hamas and after four days of discussion, we agreed on a ceasefire.
>
> But there was an internal issue. I knew that if we reached a ceasefire and Abu Ammar [Yasir Arafat] didn't accept it, he'd throw it in the garbage.... Abu Ammar was surrounded and under siege. No ceasefire document could come from him. We thought we could put this card in his hand and he could also benefit from it. But he understood that there were others in Syria who might benefit as well. He wanted the card to belong only to him. Also, maybe he didn't want this to hurt relations with the Egyptians, which would be the case if we stopped the Cairo dialogue and went to Damascus instead. The president had many things to think about.
>
> We returned from Damascus with the ceasefire agreement. I went to Arafat and said, "Israel and America won't let you go from one room to another. God willing, I can do so.... I won't conspire against you. We believe that this agreement is a tool in your hand, that it will serve you and the Palestinian people. But we're not the ones who decide. You are. If you don't want this agreement, you can throw it away."

I left his room at five in the evening. Later I was called to a meeting on the issue of a ceasefire. The president was there. So were Fateh Central Committee members and others. They began the discussion [about how to reach a ceasefire] from zero, as if the agreement we'd just reached with Hamas in Damascus didn't exist. They formed a Fateh committee that would try to start a dialogue with Hamas in Gaza from scratch. Then they began to talk about making a ceasefire declaration that would include references to the Road Map, UNSCR 242 and 338, the Beirut decision, the Arab Summit decision and so on. All of these were decisions that Hamas did not accept. It would be impossible to make a declaration like that and issue it in the names of both Fateh and Hamas.

I understood from all of this that Abu Ammar didn't want an agreement. So I said that I would like to speak. But Abu Ammar kept skipping over me and giving other people a chance to talk.... Finally he gave me my turn and I spoke. I said, "What do we want from Hamas? We want just one sentence: a ceasefire for such and such duration. What is all this stuff about 242 and 338 and the Arab Summit? That won't lead to an agreement." But everyone else just kept talking about 242, 338 and so on.

I realized then that this issue called for a confrontation, even if the price was high. So I spoke again, saying, "Abu Ammar, it's nine o'clock. The check-point is going to close and I have to get back home to Jerusalem. Please excuse me to leave." He said, "OK. Take care, goodbye."

I left the room and I immediately called Agence France Presse. Without mentioning President Arafat, I said that the Fateh Central Committee was currently meeting in Ramallah and it wanted to interject into the *hudnah* declaration political matters that would destroy it. I told the press agency everything and they distributed the statement to all of the TV channels....

I had an interview on al-Jazeera at ten o'clock. Again I said, "There is a Central Committee meeting that is discussing political matters which threaten the *hudnah*. This means that there will be no *hudnah*." I finished with al-Jazeera and received a call from Khaled Mishal [head of the Hamas Political Bureau in Damascus]. He asked, "What is happening?" I said, "We reached an agreement with you and we are committed to that. But there is an internal attempt on the part of some members of the movement to put pressure on Abu Ammar. Everything might go back to zero. Understand from this whatever you wish."

Ten minutes later, Hamas announced a unilateral ceasefire. I talked to Khaled Mishal and said, "Congratulations, you are deciding between war and peace. Those others gave you the opportunity to take an initiative." Abu Ammar heard that Khaled Mishal had declared a ceasefire unilaterally for a period of three months. After one hour, Abu Ammar declared a ceasefire for a period of one year.

So, after all, we did end up producing a *hudnah*.[132]

The *hudnah* held for 52 days despite various provocations. It collapsed when a rogue Hamas cell carried out a suicide bombing and Israel responded by assassinating a top Hamas leader. With that, the cycle of arduous ceasefire negotiations and breakdowns, mediated by the organizational structure of the Palestinian movement, began again.

External Involvement

Echoing the dynamics of the PLO's experience in exile, organizational fragmentation during the second Intifada generated opportunities for external intervention. Palestinians' political divisions invited outside actors to attempt to use Palestinian activists to advance their own agendas. The nature of the exchange between local militants and foreign patrons was similar to that between local militants and PA elites. Its effect on violent protest was likewise. Local gunmen had incentives to carry out attacks against Israel in order to attain material support from outside parties. Outside parties had incentives to fund attacks in order to use local groups in the contest for power over and within the Palestinian national struggle.

In this context, Israel, and even many in the PA, claimed that Hezbollah and possibly the Iranian Islamic Revolutionary Guard were sponsoring AMB and Islamic Jihad cells, especially in the northern West Bank.[133] According to Israeli intelligence, these foreign patrons recruited Fateh operatives to form a new splinter group. Called the "Return Brigades," it carried out a number of attacks against Israeli and PA targets.[134] An intelligence report claimed that the group's goals were both to undermine the PA's negotiation project and to infiltrate its apparatus so that it could assume power should the Arafat regime collapse.[135]

A main force behind this mission was reputedly a dissident Fateh member in Lebanon who obtained funds from Syria and Iran and channeled them to the Return Brigades. His objective was apparently to weaken the Fateh leadership and establish his own base in Palestinian territory. His interests converged with those of disillusioned Tanzim-AMB affiliates who accused Fateh leaders of abandoning them.[136] As AMB did not integrate fighters into a disciplined framework, it was not difficult for it to circumvent the Fateh hierarchy and form direct relationships with external parties. The fact that it could independently obtain funding from outside sources, and thus fall under their orbit, was a threat to Arafat. It pressured him to continue funding AMB, lest others do so and wrest it from his control. Competition for influence over the Palestinian "street" thus fueled patrons' motives to continue funding fighters, sustaining capabilities for violence that would otherwise be weaker.

External intervention also impeded ceasefires. As mentioned, Arafat was hesitant to accept the *hudnah* reached between Fateh envoys and Damascus-based Hamas leaders at least in part because he suspected that Syria, Iran, and other parties were involved. Arafat's complicated history with the Syrian regime colored these calculations. He may have reasoned that if Syria had something to gain by a ceasefire, he had something to lose. Similar rationales came into play at Palestinian unity talks in January 2003, when Hamas and Islamic Jihad demanded that Syrian-sponsored PLO factions Sa'iqa and

PFLP-GC be allowed to participate.[137] Islamist parties knew that Arafat saw these groups as foreign agents bent on his ouster. The debate about their inclusion thus became another sticking point in what proved a fruitless attempt to reach a ceasefire.

Nonetheless, the ups and downs of Intifada ceasefire initiatives demonstrated that external intervention does not always sustain violent protest at the expense of conflict resolution. American, European, and Egyptian diplomats worked to terminate Israeli–Palestinian hostilities. The diplomacy with the best prospects for success was that built on the understanding that an end to violence required both Israeli concessions and Palestinian political cohesion. On this basis, Egypt acted as host and mediator for repeated rounds of Palestinian unity talks. It also offered to train and unify Gaza's armed groups into a reformed security apparatus under a single PA chain of command.[138] Such renewed cohesion in the Palestinian movement would mediate the likelihood of political violence. Still, cohesion would not alone determine it. Foreign involvement to end Palestinians' armed strategies could not accomplish much in the absence of viable negotiations with Israel. "Third party interventions are not the remedy to all the flaws of the [negotiation] process," said a European diplomat who knew this from experience. "The answer is to address some of those failings directly."[139]

THE WANING OF THE INTIFADA

Before and after Yasir Arafat's death in November 2004, many analysts debated whether his succession would be tumultuous or smooth.[140] Arguably, it was both. In January 2005, Palestinians chose Mahmoud Abbas to be the second president of the PA in free, fair, and peaceful elections. Nonetheless, Abbas inherited a situation characterized by weak institutions, intense factional competition, strategic directionlessness, and economic crisis. This was to say nothing of a society traumatized by years of violence.

Abbas's agenda was to end the militarized uprising, restart negotiations, and bring all Palestinian forces under, as he expressed it, "one authority, one law, and one gun." That March in Cairo, he convened negotiations with representatives of 13 Palestinian factions and announced a *tahdiyah*, or open-ended period of calm. Hamas agreed to halt attacks against Israel in exchange for Abbas's promise to hold new PLC elections and expand the PLO to include previously unincorporated groups. The Cairo Agreement was a milestone in the move toward cohesion because it gave all parties incentives to cooperate under the auspices of a single political system. In Usher's assessment, it represented "the greatest organizational harmony that has ever existed between the PA and Hamas."[141] This incipient cohesion helped discipline those who wished to carry out violence against Israel. Factions abided by the unilateral ceasefire more than any other ceasefire during the previous five years. The result was a substantial decline in Israeli casualties (see Figure 4.1).

To sustain these trends, Palestinians needed to transform a convergence of interests into a new organizational structure for the national movement. Only popular elections could give that structure the credibility it required to become durable. Khalil Shikaki commented, "Elections are the only means through which the PA can regain popular legitimacy, Hamas can be integrated into Palestinian politics, and Fateh can be united behind a single political will."[142] Abbas supported elections in the belief that they could pressure Hamas to moderate its militancy and thereby help the temporary *tahdiyah* become a permanent end to the armed Intifada. Hamas, eager for legitimacy, calculated that the time was right to transition to becoming a political party.[143] In the wake of September 11, international powers placed Hamas on the list of terrorist organizations and blocked its receipt of monetary transfers. It thus faced increasing difficulties in sustaining its charitable services. In addition, Israel's assassinations of Hamas's top leaders eliminated its paramount strategists and forced surviving leaders to fear for their lives. Hamas had boycotted the 1996 PLC elections because they were held under the auspices of the Oslo process. It also may have reckoned that it would perform poorly. Neither condition applied by 2005. Hamas could assert that Oslo was finished. Furthermore, after Israel's unilateral withdrawal from Gaza in July 2005, it could claim to seek to govern territory liberated by force of arms, not negotiations. Elections would enable Hamas to capitalize on the popularity that it had amassed during the Intifada while also attracting the many Palestinians who, fed up with decades of corruption and incompetence, were keen to vote against Fateh.

If Abbas and Hamas stood to gain from this reconfigured organizational structure, various actors within Fateh stood to lose. The PA top echelon risked losing the posts that they monopolized by virtue of blocking fair competition. Barghouti-inspired reformers risked losing to the degree that voters would punish all Fateh affiliates alike. AMB and other activists risked losing because their influence on "the street" sprang from the very lawlessness that the reinvigorated parliamentary and executive branches would remedy. Wary of competing with Hamas at the ballot box, Fateh members pressured Abbas to postpone parliamentary elections. Fateh primaries sparked infractions, from the burning of ballot boxes to gunmen's storming of election commission offices.[144]

As the general elections approached, Fateh proved unable to unite around a coherent electoral strategy. It nominated multiple candidates for each district seat, apart from its affiliates who added their names to the ballot as independents. Hamas, on the other hand, planned expediently and put forth one candidate per position. The outcome was that all votes for Hamas were channeled toward seats, while votes for Fateh were dispersed among many competitors. When elections were held in January 2006, the popular vote was a close split between 45 percent for Hamas and 41 percent for Fateh. Due to its careful navigation of the electoral system, however, Hamas and its affiliated independents won 78 of 132 seats. For the first time since the 1960s, Fateh found itself in the opposition.

The 2006 elections could have ushered in a new cohesion in the Palestinian national movement. All major political groups agreed to subordinate their wills to a single institution and a single set of rules. Sweeping voter turnout in fair elections represented a strong sense of collective purpose that granted legitimacy to this new organizational structure. Nonetheless, the unexpected Hamas victory revealed that neither all Palestinian parties nor the international actors that supported the elections fully consented to democratic contestation as the mechanism to govern Palestinian politics. Accepting the electoral outcome as the basis for a new organizational structure required that political forces submit not only to law and institutions, but also to a balance of power that many disliked. Those who disagreed with the terms of this new political cohesion, therefore, sought to challenge it by sowing familiar seeds of fragmentation. Israel refused to deal with the Hamas-led government or transfer the PA's custom revenues. The United States and the European Union cut off aid until Hamas recognized Israel, denounced terrorism, and complied with all previous agreements. Fateh officially accepted its defeat but unofficially avenged it by creating havoc in the streets. It defied orders from Hamas ministers, and even stripped PA offices of their supplies before ceding them to the new government.

Refusing to capitulate, the Hamas government was unable to pay the public employees' salaries on which more than a third of the Palestinian workforce depended. By September 2006, GDP per capita in the Palestinian territories dropped 27 percent while the real poverty rate rose to 67 percent.[145] Palestinians' divisions created opportunities for external actors to intervene, which in turn intensified their divisions. An elected Hamas legislator explained:

> The world is withholding salaries from us, although it is known that the majority of those salaries go to Fateh members. They want to incite Fateh members from within the ministries and administration to rebel against the Hamas government and cause it to fail....
>
> What Fateh is waging now is a conflict of interests and positions.... Outside forces are able to take advantage of the internal conflict. If America saw that the Palestinian people were fully united and against the blockade, it and other countries would not be able to boycott us like this. But when they see that there is an internal opposition that wants to change the system, it encourages them to interfere in the internal affairs of our society.[146]

Palestinian forces faced off in a struggle to determine the organizational structure of the post-Arafat political system. "A new government was created, but has not received recognition and the old government has not submitted," an independent lawmaker observed. "The head is Hamas and the muscles are Fateh. The head cannot make the muscles move. So the situation remains blocked under siege."[147] An Israeli analyst agreed, saying, "In the absence of any political process, it is all pure power politics."[148] A parliamentarian from the PFLP elaborated:

> The struggle between Fateh and Hamas today is not a struggle over political programs. The PA has become the goal, not the means. If you are debating

political programs, you can reach some resolution through dialogue. But the essence of the debate today, over control and power, can only lead to infighting.... During the first Intifada, there was popular authority built through participation. You couldn't fight over that kind of authority; it could only be shared by everyone. But the nature of authority has changed and the struggle over authority has changed with it.[149]

The potential transition to a newly cohesive organizational structure evaporated. After a year of tension, the Saudi-brokered Mecca Agreement brought Fateh and Hamas together in a unity government. Yet Israel refused to recognize it, and the United States reportedly funded and armed Fateh to defeat the Islamists.[150] Prodded by external intervention, the long-boiling confrontation between Fateh and Hamas exploded in June 2007. Hamas fighters ousted Fateh-affiliated security forces and took control of the PA in the Gaza Strip in a few bloody days. Hamas insisted that it was defending its right to govern against an impending Fateh coup. Fateh denounced its rivals as killers. Thereafter, Israel and the United States helped Abbas's PA consolidate power in the West Bank. Israel isolated Hamas by sealing Gaza's borders, leaving 1.5 million civilians unable to meet their needs for consumer goods, medicine, fuel, and raw materials for industry and construction. Gaza's economy collapsed into humanitarian crisis.

The internecine violence was shocking, yet predictable given fragmentation in the national movement. With no agreement on procedures for adjudicating competing interests, it was simply a matter of time before factions turned to violence to assert their wills. In the wake of events, Palestinians stood geographically divided and politically immobilized as never before. Some referred to the stalemate as *al-Wakseh*, or a "self-inflicted ruin." "The Wakseh took us back 50 years," a political figure said. "National hope has been lost."[151] Polls found that 85 percent of Palestinians supported negotiations between Fateh and Hamas.[152] Yet even as the public called for unity, Israel and other countries took measures that entrenched divisions. They supported Fateh and assisted the West Bank through various measures, from selectively releasing Fateh prisoners to channeling money to Abbas. At the same time, they fought Hamas and put pressure on Gaza. Insistent on preventing Hamas from entering the ranks of legitimate political actors, outside actors also frowned upon interfactional dialogue. In the words of a leading Israeli analyst, "An internal Palestinian reconciliation process does not jibe with Israeli interests."[153]

As the organizational mediation theory of protest would predict, fragmentation was conducive to Hamas's escalation of attacks. With both its political position and Gaza's civilians under siege, Hamas led factions in launching Qassam rockets. The monthly tally of rockets fired toward Israel increased from 30 in January 2007 to 120 in November 2007 to 310 in February 2008.[154] Attrition persisted until June 2008, when Israel and Hamas concluded a ceasefire via Egyptian mediators. Nevertheless, the two parties had different understandings of the unwritten terms. Hamas accused Israel of failing to open Gaza's border crossings, and the United Nations confirmed that Gaza's economic and humanitarian situation continued to worsen.[155] Israeli officials accused Hamas of smuggling weapons through tunnels from Egypt. Still, they did admit that the ceasefire had resulted in "a significant drop in Hamas terror activity."[156] Only 32 rockets were launched during the first four and a half months of the ceasefire. Many of these were fired by Fateh and other rival organizations with the aim of defying Hamas.[157]

The lull ended when Israel killed seven Hamas fighters whom they accused of digging a tunnel in a plan to abduct an Israeli soldier, as Hamas had abducted Corporal Gilad Shalit in 2006. Hamas and other groups retaliated with a barrage of rockets. When the ceasefire's six-month term expired, Hamas leaders announced that they would extend the truce only if Israel ended the blockade. Israel refused. It would later be reported that Hamas leaders in Gaza favored extending the ceasefire nonetheless and were "furious" when the Damascus-based political bureau made the "rash" decision to let it end.[158] Within 10 days, Israel launched an air and land war on the Gaza Strip. The 22-day assault left more than 1,300 Palestinians killed, 5,300 injured, and 100,000 homeless, in addition to nearly $2 billion in property destroyed.[159]

As Gazans recovered from lives torn asunder, Fateh and Hamas continued to struggle over whatever power remained in Palestinian politics, even if only recognition as Palestinians' legitimate representative. In the wake of the Gaza War, factions clashed on the question of who had the right to patrol the Gaza–Egypt border or distribute reconstruction funds, as well as the terms under which they would enter into dialogue or join a unity government. In the West Bank, the PA suppressed shows of solidarity with Gaza. In Gaza, Hamas suppressed shows of loyalty to Fateh. Israel and U.S. President Barack Obama continued to refuse to speak with Hamas. In doing so, they encouraged Fateh to sustain the hope of eventually reconquering Gaza and discouraged Hamas from seeking a modus vivendi with its rival. They thereby fed Palestinians' fragmentation without reducing incentives for militancy against Israel.

CONCLUSION

The second Intifada substantiates several dimensions of the relationship between a movement's organizational structure and its use of violent protest. First, intensification of conflict with an out-group does not necessarily increase unity in an in-group, particularly when that in-group lacks strong leadership, institutions, and collective purpose. When Palestinians launched protests in September 2000, Israel reacted with overwhelming force. The ensuing crisis exposed and exacerbated the national movement's preexisting fragmentation. It brought to the fore latent rivalries and the difficulty of finding a formula for collective decision making that was acceptable to all factions and factions within factions. Given the uncertainty of violence after a peace process, Palestinians did not develop a popular consensus on the goals of the new uprising. Rather, opinions diverged on whether it should be a tactic for bolstering negotiations, a strategy for ending occupation, or a return to armed struggle. These differences impeded the sense of collective purpose that had unified people across society in earlier eras.

Heightened conflict with Israel similarly revealed the weaknesses in Palestinian institutions and leadership. Ambiguous boundaries between the governance-oriented PA and resistance-oriented factions exposed the insufficiency of the PLO or any other framework for national decision making. Meanwhile, Arafat was caught between irreconcilable demands. In response, he did not set forth the authoritative vision that might have brought rivals together behind a clear definition of ends and means. Given this fragmented organizational structure, Palestinians were not able to forge unity in the face of Israeli countermeasures. Rather, military siege generated new pressures that increased competition among and within political groups while simultaneously undermining national instruments of law and governance. As Coser would predict, battle with Israel spurred feelings of solidarity but did not result in movement centralization. The outcome was a fractured movement whose capacity for command and control only weakened as conflict continued.

Second, the second Intifada illustrates the multiple mechanisms through which a movement's organizational structure mediates protest. Most critically, movement fragmentation inhibited the mobilization of nonviolent alternatives to violent means of struggle. During the first Intifada, a robust civil society and intrafactional cooperation facilitated broad-based, unarmed protest and civil disobedience. Yet the social networks, institutions, and norms of volunteerism that distinguished the 1980s had diminished considerably by the year 2000. In consequence, civic forms of resistance remained limited and localized. Many Palestinians had the will to participate in nonviolent protest, but the organizational structure of the national movement impeded the coordination of such a path on a large scale.

Apart from reducing opportunities for nonviolent protest, the movement's organizational structure encouraged violence by generating motivations for militancy apart from the goal of self-determination. Israel's repression spurred Palestinians' demands for revenge, which in turn spurred a race among Palestinian groups to claim responsibility for attacks. The result was escalatory outbidding that accelerated tactics from shootings to suicide bombings to the launching of rockets. Like competition among factions, bargaining for power within factions also fueled violence. For poorer, younger Fateh activists who lacked other forms of political influence, participating in military activity offered a way to advance their status and interests. In taking up arms, they seized a measure of influence within their communities and over their leadership's negotiation project. No less, military activity opened opportunities for PA power brokers vying with each other for turf. They found that sponsoring militant groups created pools of men dependent on their patronage and answerable to their orders. Funding insurgency hence offered a way in which they could jockey with each other for control of "the street."

Apart from these channels by which fragmentation multiplied motives for violence, the organizational structure of the Palestinian movement decreased constraints on its use. In the absence of central leadership or binding institutions, each faction pursued its own strategy according to its own timing. Local cells acted independently of their parent organizations. As the PA apparatus collapsed and its president withdrew, those with weapons were free to use them for a host of public or private reasons. Beyond this, cracks in the national movement invited outside actors to intervene and use Palestinian cells to carry out their own violent agendas. This introduced new incentives and funds for violent protest that would have been weaker had Palestinians been limited to the resources within their own community. Finally, fragmentation augmented obstacles to bringing hostilities to an end. Individuals and groups who advocated violent means were not necessarily bound by majority opinion or national dialogue. One party's ability to threaten violence became a source of leverage over other parties that wanted violence to end. Factions' bargaining over ceasefires thus came to hinge on the establishment of a new formula for domestic power sharing. The task of reaching a cessation of hostilities merged with that of rebuilding cohesion itself.

Fragmentation was by no means the only factor fueling violent protest in the second Intifada. Nevertheless, it played an important role in facilitating, intensifying, and sustaining it. Prominent accounts of the second Intifada attribute Palestinians' turn to military strategies to the availability of weapons, intense popular grievances, a leadership not fully committed to peace, learning from other experiences, or strategic interaction with an Israeli adversary that used intense violence of its own. All of these factors may have contributed to the militarization of the uprising. Yet they do not alone explain the timing and character of its escalation or its persistence over time. Rather, the effect of these variables was mediated by the national movement's fragmented organizational structure. The organizational mediation theory of protest accounts for anomalies that other explanations do not. It also illuminates the paradoxical consequences of counterinsurgency that exacerbates divisions in a nonstate challenger. If such policies seek to prevent a movement from uniting behind a strategy that can force the state to make concessions, then they largely achieve their goal. If they aspire to foster a partner with the capacity to make peace, however, they may be self-defeating.

7

Comparisons: South Africa and Northern Ireland

A full test of the generalizability of the organizational mediation theory of protest is beyond the scope of this book. However, preliminary analysis of the South Africa antiapartheid struggle and the Northern Ireland republican movement demonstrates the promise of its broad application. These cases differ from the Palestinian national movement with regard to the culture and social structure of the populations involved and the international and regional contexts in which they were embedded. Nevertheless, important commonalities indicate a sound basis for comparison. All three are self-determination movements that developed through various stages over the greater part of the 20th century. Each viewed its struggle as that of an indigenous population against dispossession that occurred when another people, facilitated by imperial power, settled their homeland. Conflicting claims to political power over a single territory spawned protracted conflicts in which insurgent national movements fought a state, as well as another ethnic, sectarian, or national group. In this context, the South African, Northern Irish, and Palestinian movements employed a mixture of armed and unarmed strategies. They ultimately engaged in peace negotiations as well. Along the way, each movement struggled with the challenge of unifying its ranks, asserting command and control, and instituting legitimate rules for the resolution of internal disputes over strategy, ideology, and external alliances. Each movement's success in doing so depended on the extent to which its organizational structure was made cohesive through leadership, institutions, and collective purpose. In turn, this organizational cohesion or fragmentation systematically mediated the movements' abilities to engage in nonviolent protest, as well as their propensities toward violence.

SOUTH AFRICA

European penetration of what became South Africa began in the 17th century with Dutch and other settlers from northwest Europe, who came to be known as Afrikaners. Colonists from Great Britain arrived later. In 1910 the

Union of South Africa combined these British colonies, Afrikaner republics, and neighboring African kingdoms as a dominion of the British Empire. The country's white minority proceeded to establish its domination over the 75 percent of the population that was not white. It did so through a series of informal and formal rules, such as those confining the right to vote to whites, restricting Africans' landownership to reserves, requiring nonwhites to carry passes at all times, and barring them from skilled trades. By the time South Africa attained independence in 1931, racial segregation and discrimination pervaded all areas of politics, economics, and society.

Resistance to white domination faced various obstacles. Those relegated to inferior status included the indigenous African majority, as well as sizable communities of people with Indian or Asian backgrounds, and mixed persons known as "Coloreds." Coloreds formed a political organization to represent their interests in 1902 and Indians did likewise in 1923. Nevertheless, the country's nonwhite populations had little in common with each other. Furthermore, each was disunited internally along ethnic, class, or other lines.[1] Among Africans, the bulk of society was traditional, impoverished, and rural. It tended to identify with tribes under the leadership of chiefs who wielded customary authority and often acted as intermediaries between their communities and the white state. A small black elite emerged thanks to education in Western or missionary schools. Some enjoyed salaried positions and saw themselves as harbingers of liberal civilization. Others became disillusioned when they failed to find employment commensurate to their preparation.[2]

In 1912 a cohort of African elites established a national organization that they hoped would rise above tribal cleavages and unify Africans. They called it the "South African Natives' National Congress," later changing its name to the "African National Congress" (ANC). The ANC brought together educated, middle-class "gentlemen" and rural "chiefs of royal blood."[3] ANC leaders were motivated by conservative values such as liberalism and constitutionality. Their goal was to attain equality and integration in middle-class white society, in the hope that they could then extend its benefits to the African population at large. Their "respectable" tactics, namely signing petitions, sending telegrams, forming delegations, and issuing press statements, proved their confidence in the possibility of reforming the system from within.

Other groups embraced more radical ends or means. The Industrial and Commercial Workers' Union galvanized a membership of some 150,000 mostly rural and poor Africans around calls for national liberation. However, it faced state repression from without and was weakened by corruption and divisions from within. This, in addition to the absence of a sustainable, pragmatic program, caused its collapse by the 1930s.[4] In the years that followed, African trade unionism grew in step with transformations in South Africa's political economy. Wartime production, industrialization, and the expansion of manufacturing caused a sweeping migration of Africans to the cities.[5] In this context, the Council of Non-European Trade Unions built a national membership that came to include some 40 percent of all African workers in commerce and manufacturing.[6] African unions organized tens of thousands of workers to participate in dozens of strikes, outstripping the union militancy of white workers.

The ANC did not develop links to unions. In consequence, Mona Younis explains, the efforts of the various parties opposed to white supremacy "did not translate into a coherent and cohesive national challenge."[7] The ANC did, however, forge a significant alliance with the Communist Party. The partnership began tensely and haltingly. Many ANC members were deeply suspicious of communist ideology and the Party's primarily white leadership. Nonetheless, the two groups developed unity through their common opposition to racialism. As Nelson Mandela later expressed it, "Theoretical differences amongst those fighting against oppression is a luxury we cannot afford at this stage."[8] As years passed, shared memberships and personal relationships further cemented the alliance. From 1960 to 1990, the need to survive underground brought mutual reliance to new heights. In the words of a leading account, the two groups eventually became "Siamese twins, inseparable without causing the death of one or both."[9]

Still, the ANC's attempts to persuade the government and white electorate of its concerns came to little avail. In 1943 the ANC adopted a more radical call for the abolition of discrimination. Distancing itself from tribal chiefs, it began to build an organizational structure based on a centralized leadership and local branches stretching to the grass roots.[10] Nelson Mandela, Oliver Tambo, Walter Sisulu, and other young activists established the Youth League as a pressure group within the ANC. They criticized the "old guard" ANC leadership for being too cautious and conciliatory. Advocating a greater shift to mass mobilization, they proposed their own Program of Action, which called for strategic escalation to strikes and boycotts.

Labor militancy likewise continued. It culminated in 1946, when the African Mine Workers' Union organized a strike by more than sixty thousand workers in one of the country's largest gold mines. Other unions joined the effort by calling a general strike of all black workers, and the ANC and Indian Passive Resistance Councils pledged support. The strike lasted a week before police forcibly suppressed it, leaving 12 dead and more than 1,200 injured. This watershed protest pushed the movement for racial justice toward a more radical nationalist ideology emphasizing direct action and class alliances.[11] The ANC, divided between the old guard, Communists, moderates, and the Youth League, shifted toward the latter.[12] In 1949 the Youth League won internal elections and assumed control of the organization.

Meanwhile, state racialism hardened. In 1948 the National Party triumphed in South Africa's parliamentary elections. Founded by Afrikaner nationalists, it would remain the ruling party until 1994. Under its guidance, the government codified white domination in a system known as "apartheid." Apartheid legally classified the population as white, black, colored, and Indian. The right to vote was reserved for the 20 percent of the population classified as white. Successive legislation assigned blacks to live in one of 10 territorial homelands known as "Bantustans," to which millions were forcibly resettled. Blacks needed passes to travel to white areas, where they could work only with the status of migrant laborers. Laws enforced strict segregation in public spaces, including beaches, parks, transport facilities, hospitals, schools, universities, and cemeteries. Marriage between persons of different races was prohibited, and discrimination in employment was the norm. State spending, services, wages, health, and overall conditions for blacks were below those for Indians and Coloreds, and far inferior to those enjoyed by whites.

Under these conditions, the movement against apartheid continued moving toward direct action. In 1952, the ANC and Indian Congress launched the Defiance Campaign. This was a coordinated protest in which people were directed to violate curfew and segregation laws. The objective was to force the state to make so many arrests that its capacity to enforce apartheid would be overwhelmed. The organizational structure of the young antiapartheid movement aided this nonviolent civil disobedience in several ways. Preparations had begun nearly one year earlier when the ANC and Indian Congress formed a Joint Planning Council. This was the first time they had acted "under a common leadership."[13] These leaders articulated the campaign's ultimate goal, equality, as well as the immediate objective of forcing repeal of six particular laws. They set forth a three-stage strategy. To begin, a select group of "trained and disciplined persons" would disobey specific laws. Organizers would subsequently increase the number of volunteers and sites of action. Finally, they would broaden the campaign to include the masses at large. In the leadership's words, protest would become sustainable because it would "gradually embrace larger groups of people ... and make possible for us to organize, discipline, and lead the people in a planned manner."[14]

The Defiance Campaign began that June when small "batches" of volunteers went into action in select localities and faced arrest. From there, it spread to numerous other localities and involved greater numbers of recruits. By mid-December, some eight thousand people had been arrested. The organizational structure proved effective in maintaining the nonviolent character of protest for nearly four months. The state responded by cracking down and arresting key national leaders and local organizers. While they were in detention, rioting erupted in various localities. The ANC swiftly condemned violence, issuing statements that urged protestors to be "peaceful, disciplined, nonviolent," even in the face of police shootings.[15] Leaders recognized the limits of their capacity to enforce the prohibition on violence that they preferred, and the campaign was brought to an end.

The Defiance Campaign inspired a surge of unity behind the ANC and its leadership of the movement against apartheid. In its wake, membership grew from less than seven thousand to a hundred thousand. An ANC circular letter credited the protest with bringing Africans of various stations together in "one stream" and producing a "mighty national organization."[16] In the years that followed, activists organized boycotts, demonstrations, and protests against high rents and bus fares. They also continued to work to build a cohesive and

encompassing organizational structure. In 1955, the ANC led the establishment of the Congress Alliance, a multiracial coalition that included the Indian
Congress, the Colored People's Organization, the nonracial South African
Congress of Trade Unions, and the mostly white Congress of Democrats.
Groups representing diverse constituencies thus came together under a single institutional umbrella. This provided an organizational framework within
which to define clear, common objectives. To this end, the ANC made use
of its own organizational reach by dispatching thousands of volunteers to
townships and rural communities across the country, where they asked people
what they wanted for South Africa. Political leaders then synthesized these
demands in a document titled the "Freedom Charter."

The Freedom Charter called upon South Africans of every color to unite
behind the goal of genuine democracy and equal rights without distinction
of race, sex, or belief. It also called for restoration of the national wealth of
the country to its people through state control of industry and trade, aid to
peasants, free education and medical care, lowering of rents and prices, and
protection for the rights of workers. The declaration of goals thus appealed to
adherents of national and class-based views of liberation alike. It concluded
with the words, "These freedoms we will fight for, side by side, throughout
our lives, until we have won our liberty." The Congress Alliance adopted the
Charter in a summit of several thousand of delegates from around the country,
dubbed the "Congress of the People." Activists read the Charter in full and the
crowd shouted its approval of each section. This grassroots process confirmed
the popular legitimacy of the Freedom Charter as a consensus statement of the
collective purpose of the antiapartheid movement. The Congress then selected
a National Coordinating Council to continue leading work toward the realization of those goals.

The Congress of the People embodied the new cohesion of the antiapartheid movement. However, it immediately faced challenges. State repression
was swift. Deploying security forces en masse, the government implemented
a crackdown that involved measures ranging from sweeping arrests to the
destruction of Sophiatown, a thriving black community on the outskirts of
Johannesburg. Apart from this counter-offensive on the part of the state, the
movement faced new tension from inside its ranks. The Freedom Charter confirmed the cross-cleavage unity of the antiapartheid struggle in its declaration
that "South Africa belongs to all who live in it, black and white." Yet in doing
so, it exacerbated latent tensions between those upholding nonracialism and
those advocating Africanism. Within the ANC, some young members urged
a more exclusive black nationalism. They criticized the leadership for being
excessively cautious and for falling under the control of white Communists.
For the second time in a decade, a cohort of youthful militants accused the
established ANC leadership of compromising on the struggle.[17] Reciprocal
hostile accusations spawned a violent clash, and in 1959 the radical wing of
the movement announced that it was splitting to form a new group: the Pan-
Africanist Congress (PAC).

Rivalry ensued as many younger members joined the new organization, and the PAC and ANC found themselves in a zero-sum competition for the same limited constituency. As in the Palestinian case, such competition provoked increasingly militant protest. The PAC's recruits were eager for action. In order to maintain their membership, leaders had no time to waste in proving that their group offered the better path.[18] Under such organizational pressures, the PAC decided to launch a campaign against the laws requiring blacks to carry passes. Several accounts confirm that the ANC was planning to launch its own anti-pass drive in March 1960, and the PAC deliberately seized the initiative by launching its drive first.[19]

The PAC's plan, reminiscent of the Defiance Campaign eight years earlier, was for people to leave home without their passes, to surrender to arrest at the nearest police station, and to accept imprisonment. They were to repeat this strategy until the large number of detentions choked the state's repressive apparatus. The PAC intended that the protest remain nonviolent, as the Defiance Campaign had been for several months. However, the limits of organizational cohesion mediated important differences in the conduct of protest. The 1952 campaign was led by an ANC that was fortified by four decades of institutional development. The ANC had planned for nearly a year in formal partnership with other groups, and trained volunteers to follow a carefully staged strategy. In 1960, by contrast, the PAC had barely existed for a year as an organization. In Gail Gerhart's estimation, it had had "no time to develop an organizational structure and train recruits."[20] Rather than instructing a small team, the PAC called on all South Africans to participate and articulated increasingly lofty demands. The hallmarks of movement fragmentation – domestic political competition, weak institutions, and lack of command and control – thus motivated the escalation of protest. Gerhart elaborates:

> With more time and the development of a disciplined organization, the PAC might perhaps have succeeded in training its initial recruits.... Why did the PAC rush into a campaign of confrontation with the government when its forces were still undisciplined and its organizational structure feeble? Pressure from an action-hungry following was clearly an important force in PAC decision-making; so was the strong sense of rivalry with the ANC and the desire to woo away its following.[21]

Leaping forward with a daring challenge, the PAC set a pace for accelerated protest. This stirred pressures within the ANC. Some ANC leaders urged caution, warning that it was unwise to undertake strategies that had little chance of success. They insisted that prior planning and organization was insufficient for a protest of such scope. Against these pleas, a restive rank and file sought to impose a bolder course of action. "Let us force our leaders into a tight corner," one such ANC member reportedly said. "If they think in terms of strategy, we think in terms of action."[22]

The PAC campaign launched its campaign, and the response was greatest in the Sharpeville township. There a crowd, estimated to range anywhere from

3,000 to 20,000, marched on the local police station. Watching throngs move toward them, the police panicked and opened fire. Some 69 protestors were killed and 186 injured, many shot from behind as they fled. Accounts differ on whether the crowd was unarmed.[23] Regardless, the organizational structure of the movement rendered highly unlikely the PAC's hopes for strictly non-violent civil disobedience. Thomas Karis and Gwendolen Carter note that few people "felt bound by PAC instructions" and a large number of youths were "itching to strike out." It was therefore predictable that the "violence-prone element became uncontrollable."[24]

The Sharpeville massacre sparked mass demonstrations, after which the government passed new measures prohibiting public gatherings, extending the use of torture, and authorizing detention without trial. It also declared a state of emergency, banned the ANC and PAC, and arrested thousands of their leaders and supporters. This assault further ravaged the organizational cohesion of the antiapartheid movement. It intimidated its membership base and forced its leaders into hiding. The antiapartheid movement's institutional capacity for nonviolent protest was left greatly reduced. In parallel, its commitment to exclusively unarmed means came to an end.

In 1961 the ANC established an armed wing called Umkhonto we Sizwe (Spear of the Nation, popularly known as "MK") and launched a sabotage campaign. MK was under a joint ANC–Communist Party leadership and Mandela was its first commander. In its first 18 months, it carried out some two hundred attacks, mostly on power plants and other facilities.[25] From the start, MK leaders' aim was "properly controlled violence" entailing a concerted effort to avoid loss of life.[26] The PAC also formed an armed wing. Although attacks by both groups resulted in no deaths and only minor damage, the government pursued the groups relentlessly. At the 1964 Rivonia trial, authorities sentenced Mandela and other ANC leaders to life imprisonment. Others activists fled South Africa and proceeded to build clandestine networks and guerrilla camps in neighboring countries.

The imprisonment and dispersal of the leadership imposed an enormous challenge on the existent organizational structure of the liberation struggle. It also generated new impetuses for fragmentation. Survival in exile required diplomatic, economic, and military support, and the scramble for state patrons was a boon to factional rivalry. Elisabeth Woods explains, "Competition between the ANC and the PAC for resources and alliances ... undermined any thoughts of a 'united front' in exile."[27] At the same time, this very competition eventually fortified the ANC as an organization while marginalizing the PAC as a formidable source of opposition.

This was the case because the ANC's multiracialism helped it attract aid from European states. Its alliance with the Communist Party garnered support from the Soviet Union. The PAC's black exclusivity, by contrast, impeded its attraction of funding from white-majority countries. It was thus forced to rely on much more limited support from African states and China. Under the latter's influence, it eventually declared itself Maoist.[28] In these circumstances, the limits of the PAC's collective purpose came to the fore. From the start, it had arguably been more unified around what it was against than what it aimed to achieve.²⁹ Thus, while it continued to vilify the ANC and Communist Party, it could not forestall its own organizational decline. The PAC experienced irreconcilable strategic disputes, successive coups by one faction against another, an internal assassination, and subsequent assassination attempts. By the 1980s, in the words of three scholars, it was "split into well-armed warring factions." Rife with "gangsterism and indiscipline," the PAC showed "no signs of an effective presence in South Africa."³⁰

The pressures of prolonged exile tested the ANC's organizational cohesion as well. Especially from the late 1970s, the ANC security department would be implicated in torture, ill-treatment, and executions of prisoners in its military and prison camps. These prisoners were typically MK members accused of being agents of the apartheid regime, although many appear to have been loyal fighters punished for voicing criticism.³¹ When MK soldiers in Angola mutinied in 1984, MK leaders violently repressed them. Mutineers were captured and subjected to even graver maltreatment during years of subsequent detention. Although Amnesty International later accused the ANC of bearing organizational responsibility for human rights abuse, victims and constituents alike usually absolved it. They distinguished the ANC as the embodiment of heroic nationalism from the particular "individuals" who committed crimes. Telling was the testimony of one former prisoner who recounted being tortured yet insisted, "I love the ANC because the ANC is the people."³² Even accusations of horrible abuses therefore did not mar the ANC's growing status as the leader of the antiapartheid movement and the backbone of its unity.

Apart from its troubles in exile, the banned ANC also faced difficulties sustaining itself inside South Africa. Criminalized and hunted, the ANC might have vanished as a source of leadership, institutions, and collective purpose had it not built underground networks.³³ In this it gained vital know-how from its main ally. The Communist Party had operated covertly since it was banned in 1950. Many of its leaders became leaders of the ANC underground such that the two organizations, as well as the MK forces that they had formed collectively, effectively merged.³⁴ In clandestinity, the ANC disseminated leaflets and publications, arranged aid to members, and generally preserved the ANC's presence in South Africans' lives. In sustaining an organizational structure, it managed to link the tradition of an older generation of ANC activists to newly politicized youth. At the same time, it developed connections to above-ground organizations, through which the ANC continued to influence events.

Though the ANC carried on clandestinely, its banning created a vacuum that new legal groups emerged to fill. In this context, the tension between nonracialism and African nationalism again came front and center. In the mid-1970s, a new movement called for black unity and psychological liberation. Known as the "Black Consciousness Movement," it gained particular popularity among school and university students. Its chief spokesperson, Steve Biko, accused predominantly white liberal groups of paternalism and hypocrisy. He formed an alternative organization exclusively for black students and quickly attracted a large number of recruits. While some saw Biko's movement and the ANC as rivals, others embraced them as complementary faces of the same struggle.[35] Initially distant from the both the ANC and PAC, Biko at one time explored the possibility of unifying all three groups into a single front. His efforts failed, apparently because each wanted leadership.[36]

Inspired by Biko's call for black pride, in June 1976 thousands of school-children in the Soweto township organized a march against the imposition of the Afrikaans language in schools. Police fired on the crowd and panicked rioting ensued. A swelling number of protestors threw stones, and a massive deployment of security forces fired indiscriminately. The confrontations, a general explosion of grievances with the apartheid system, left two hundred people killed and over a thousand injured. The following year, Biko was arrested and died in custody. Major Black Consciousness organizations were banned. In their criminalization, a new group emerged: the Azanian People's Organization. Even though it did not develop a strong presence, it was not immune from the pressure to compete with other organizations. As in other national liberation struggles, it kept up by establishing an armed wing.

The Soweto uprising provoked public outrage. This gave momentum to a new era of mass mobilization. It also set in motion developments that aided the cohesion of the antiapartheid movement under the unparalleled leadership of the ANC. State repression after Soweto eliminated nearly every institution that had espoused Black Consciousness.[37] With this collapse of the movement's structural base, thousands of its adherents fled to exile. There only the ANC had the infrastructural capacity to absorb them. As a result, the ranks of ANC cadres in exile increased from one thousand in 1975 to nine thousand in 1980.[38] ANC ranks likewise grew among black activists in prison, where ANC detainees carried out political education and recruitment. Many activists who had not initially joined the ANC were won over during the course of their sentences.[39] Meanwhile, in black communities throughout South Africa, the ANC dedicated an increasing share of its efforts and resources to popular mobilization. It showed its strength in popular campaigns to celebrate the 25th anniversary of the Freedom Charter and to demand freedom for Mandela, whose iconic stature had made him a focal point for the movement. More and more people thus pledged their loyalty to the ANC.[40] Before Soweto, the ANC was one of several antiapartheid organizations. In its aftermath, it emerged as "hegemonic."[41] Public gatherings increasingly sang its songs, displayed its colors, and hailed its exploits.

By the mid-1980s, the ANC was the clear leader of the struggle for racial equality and democracy in South Africa. Nonetheless, the ANC remained banned. As in earlier junctures, new groups again formed to fill the vacuum in legal organizing. Their character and orientation reflected socioeconomic changes that, as in the occupied territories during the 1970s and 1980s, facilitated a wave of grassroots engagement. Sweeping urbanization gave rise to close, built-up communities conducive to neighborhood-based action. An expansion of urban schooling and employment encouraged student and worker movements.[42] Against this backdrop, activists in the townships formed civic associations representing youth, women, workers, and churches. These local "civics" organized protests against high bus fares and rents, as well as consumer boycotts and other demonstrations that linked local issues to the larger fight against racial oppression. Protests gradually became larger in scope. A country-wide school boycott in 1980 mobilized not only students, but parents and teachers as well.

Nonetheless, civics lacked an organizational structure that rose above the local level. "What was absent," Gregory Houston notes, "was a national organization to provide coordination to the various struggles ... and to mobilize and sustain resistance to apartheid."[43] This organization took shape in 1983, when activists came together to oppose the government's proposal of a tricameral legislature that would offer racially segregated representation to whites, Coloreds, and Indians. Spurred to action, 565 local civics, representing some 1.65 million members from throughout the country, formed the United Democratic Front (UDF). The UDF was a federation of regionally based fronts of affiliated groups. From its very launching during a rally of ten thousand people, it sought to be a broad-based framework. Its embrace of all regions, sectors, and races was embodied in its slogan, "The UDF Unites, Apartheid Divides." The UDF adopted a structure that respected the autonomy of all groups, yet offered means to coordinate them. It did so by fulfilling such supra-local functions as organizing events, aiding communication among groups, producing media, channeling funds, and continually building the network to embrace a larger popular base. This organizational structure made the UDF, in the words of its leaders, "more than the sum of its parts."[44]

Like civic associations, labor and trade unions emerged as a major component of the organizational structure of the antiapartheid struggle. While unionism had a long history in South Africa, many trade unions had declined with the banning of the ANC. The late 1960s witnessed the revival of some of these older unions as well as the formation of new ones.[45] A particular boost to union agitation came in 1973, when strikes by sixty thousand workers in Durban spread across the country.[46] In 1979, trade unions forged a major federation, but it focused on workers' unity and shunned larger political questions. In the years that followed, however, labor organizers took note of the political mobilization sweeping the country. In 1985, they responded with an effort to bring workers together in a new "political unionism."[47] After extended unity talks, unions opposed to apartheid founded the Congress of South African Trade Unions (COSATU). Just as the UDF served as a broad umbrella movement for civic groups, COSATU became an umbrella for trade unions.

COSATU and the UDF, as well as the powerful National Union of Mineworkers, formally endorsed the ANC and the Freedom Charter. They thereby came to constitute an organizational structure that gave the antiapartheid struggle strong elements of leadership, institutions, and collective purpose. This cohesion enabled an exponential increase in nonviolent protest in the middle and late 1980s. UDF groups organized mass demonstrations, hunger strikes, and school and work stay-aways. They also sponsored boycotts of elections, services, government institutions, businesses, and rent payment.[48] In sweeping consumer boycotts, entire townships acted as one in withholding their purchasing power from designated retailers.[49] Groups distributed literature, organized huge mass meetings, and transformed funerals into political rallies displaying the illegal ANC flag. The UDF dispatched activists to gather 1 million signatures in opposition to apartheid; though only one-third of the target number of signatories pledged support, the very organization and implementation of the campaign served to increase the UDF's institutional capacity and personnel.[50] Meanwhile, COSATU unions took the protest campaign into major economic sectors. They led work stoppages that, at their peak, kept more than 11 percent of nonagricultural workers on strike.[51]

The cohesion of the antiapartheid struggle made possible this expression of "people's power." The UDF, COSATU, and ANC unambiguously declared their commitment to the goal of replacing apartheid with nonracial democracy. The fact that each group was its own independent umbrella gave their combination greater institutional power than had they constituted a single organization. Their different focuses appealed to different constituents and priorities, giving each a role in the liberation struggle. Moreover, each organization's independence allowed it to complement that of its allies and offer a security net when those allies faced government repression. The UDF thus served as a legal and open coalition at a time when the ANC was banned, and COSATU in turn played that role when the UDF was banned in 1988. To be sure, this organizational structure was not without internal friction. Tension continued between the ideological emphasis on class and that on political liberation, or between the prioritization of local goals and commitment to national goals. Civic associations also engaged in "chronic debate" over strategies and tactics.[52] As was the case with the PLO in Tunis and popular committees during the first Palestinian Intifada, different political cultures distanced the hierarchical, secretive, elite-centered ANC abroad from the younger, more participatory UDF groups in the homeland.[53] Yet also as in the occupied territories, activists in South Africa pledged loyalty to and reverence for their exiled leadership. Their political goals were one.

ANC leaders called upon townships to make themselves "ungovernable" and disrupt both the institutions of apartheid and the profits of enterprises that collaborated with it. At the same time, the antiapartheid movement mustered the organizational structure to give this protest a measure of discipline. The UDF called on people not simply to protest in the streets, but also to build structures to sustain long-term struggle.[54] Like the first Intifada under way at the same time, many South African communities declared themselves to be liberated from the regime whose legitimacy they denied. They organized street by street to assume the administrative, judicial, policing, educational, and welfare functions of collapsed state institutions.[55] The organization of alternative political structures was a dramatic break from the apartheid system. It both facilitated nonviolent protest and was a form of nonviolent protest in its own right.[56]

Popular revolt in the South African townships was never completely nonviolent. It spawned more violence as police repression fanned the flames of militancy. The banning of organizations and meetings obstructed planning, curfews prevented people from gathering in the streets, and strict restrictions on movement cut townships off from each other. As elsewhere, sweeping arrests had a devastating impact. In words that applied no less to Palestine at various stages of its history, Houston observed, "Removal of experienced and respected leaders from the political scene ... created a leadership vacuum."[57] Young men engaged in stone throwing, arson, looting, and brutal killings – dubbed "necklacings" – of accused collaborators. Vigilantism showed that, just as the organizational structure of the antiapartheid struggle enabled a tremendous expansion of nonviolent protest, so did the limits of that structure constrain its ability to restrain violence. The UDF adopted the slogan "From Mobilization to Organization" in order to rally people for sustained civic resistance. As the uprising continued, however, UDF internal documents admitted that mobilization had reached astounding proportions and organization had failed to keep pace.[58]

Meanwhile, the ANC matched protest activity in South Africa with an escalation of armed operations. Its guerrilla attacks inside South Africa increased from 40 in 1984 to 136 in 1985, and then to 228 in 1987.[59] Yet in contrast to earlier episodes of escalatory outbidding, this action bore the stamp of movement cohesion. On the one hand, the ANC saw this activity as "armed propaganda" intended to support the mass uprising by giving people pride and demonstrating the government's inability to provide security. On the other hand, the conduct of violence was itself an exercise in the management of fragmentation. Seeking to keep both more and less militant constituencies on board, the ANC "charted a middle path" by carrying out military operations but limiting them to prevent civilian casualties.[60] It later explained that it purposely avoided loss of life even though it possessed the "capacity to kill many thousands of civilians." Compared with other national liberation movements, the ANC argued, its "degree of restraint ... is extraordinary."[61]

The insurrection moved international parties to stiffen sanctions on South Africa. Exhausted by unrest and financial losses, more white citizens turned away from apartheid. Grassroots mobilization destabilized the economic and political foundations of the existing order, but only the ANC could offer a legitimate political strategy and act as an interlocutor for a political transition. During the late 1980s, various white South Africans held meetings with ANC leaders. As they gained confidence that their interests would be safeguarded in a postapartheid state, they moved to endorse formal talks. In this spirit, President F. W. de Klerk lifted the ban on the ANC and other groups and released Mandela from prison in February 1990. During the next three years, the ANC and the government engaged in negotiations that dismantled apartheid and culminated in multiracial elections in 1994. The ANC won more than 60 percent of the vote, more than three times that of its nearest contender. Mandela was declared the first president of a democratic South Africa.

The antiapartheid struggle's extensive use of nonviolent protest and relatively curtailed use of violent protest presents a puzzle. Jeff Goodwin argues that conventional theories would predict terrorism in this case because antiapartheid forces were weak and desperate to redress their grievances. They experienced extreme social polarization from the ruling minority and could claim that their use of terror was a response to state terrorism. In this context, Goodwin attributes the ANC's deliberate limiting of violence to its belief in multiracialism and its alliance with the Communist Party. It rejected violence against white civilians because this was the population that it was trying to reach as potential supporters.[62] Offering a different view, Stephen Zunes attributes the antiapartheid movement's limited use of violence to objective calculations of utility. Armed tactics would have been self-defeating due to the military superiority of the South African state, the small chance of military intervention by external allies, and the unsuitability of the terrain for guerrilla warfare. "The shift to a largely non-violent strategy ... was not the result of an ethical transformation," he concludes, "but was born out of necessity."[63]

These explanations shed some light on the strategy of the antiapartheid struggle. They are insufficient, however, because they focus only on the ideological or instrumental motivations of the movement's mainstream. They thus do not address the challenge presented by those factions that advocated greater militancy. Nor do they explain how nonviolent protest was actually mobilized and sustained, particularly when state repression provoked a radical response. To address these questions, an explanatory approach must shift focus from a movement's motivations to the system of relationships and rules that mediates the behavior in which such motivations result. Regardless of the reasons for limiting violence and engaging in nonviolent protest, the antiapartheid movement would not have been able to do so had it not developed a cohesive organizational structure. Indeed, a counterfactual question is worth considering: Had the PAC and other groups been more serious competitors, might the ANC have been impelled toward greater violence, perhaps even eclipsing engagement in civic direct action?

In the Palestinian case, small groups used violent attacks at least in part to challenge the mainstream leadership. This pushed that mainstream to carry out attacks of its own, lest it be left behind. The popular esteem for militancy that drove outbidding dynamics among Palestinian factions existed no less in South Africa.[64] Where the antiapartheid movement differed, however, was in the leadership, institutions, and collective purpose that consolidated its political center. The ANC's competitors did not have the material resources, operational opportunities, or moral clout to present a viable alternative. By the late 1980s, they jeopardized their popular support to the degree that they defied the black population's strong identification with the ANC and admiration for

Mandela. Given its overwhelming authority and the strength of its alliances, the ANC maintained an official endorsement of armed struggle with minimal risk that provocations from rival factions would escalate violence beyond its control.

When the time came to negotiate, the ANC was able to declare and enforce a ceasefire and marginalize groups that did otherwise. Though the Azanian People's Liberation Army carried out some attacks, disaffected whites perpetrated more violence against black South Africans during the peace process than vice versa. That spoiling actions by black dissenters were limited was, in John Darby's analysis, "a reflection of the dominance of Nelson Mandela and the ANC."[65] At the same time, violence *within* black communities intensified significantly during the negotiations. Bloody clashes between the ANC and the Zulu nationalist Inkatha Freedom Party resulted in two thousand deaths in 1992 alone. Various factions used violence out of both a defensive fear of loss of position and an offensive interest in gaining advantage. This violence was the outcome of a political struggle over power and turf at a time of uncertainty between the demise of apartheid and the codification of a new order.[66]

The announcement of elections sparked the opposition of Zulu nationalists and the PAC. Nonetheless, Mandela brokered deals that convinced his rivals to participate rather than disrupt the balloting. The transition from protest to politics was hence guided by a leader with exceptional prestige and an encompassing institutional framework under his direction. Sweeping support for the goal that Mandela embodied, a stable and prosperous multiracial South Africa, helped protect that process through inevitable trials and difficulties. The South African transition to democracy might have had a different end had the strategic behavior of the antiapartheid movement been mediated by a different organizational structure.

NORTHERN IRELAND

That internal fragmentation long beleaguered the Irish republican movement is captured in a joke: the first agenda item of any republican meeting is "the split."[67] The roots of the republican struggle in Northern Ireland stretch back to the 17th century, when the English monarchy took control of Ireland, established a plantation in the northern province of Ulster, and peopled it with Protestant settlers from England and Scotland. Subsequent centuries saw the displacement of native Irish, communal tension, rebellions, and wars. Britain maintained its rule and formally united with Ireland in 1800. Eventually, conflict deepened between Irish unionists, who supported continued union with Britain, and nationalists, who called for Irish autonomy. The former were predominantly Protestant and the latter predominantly Catholic. Still, the conflict did not fall strictly along religious lines.

Nationalist sentiment was exacerbated by agrarian conflict, both of which grew during the late 19th century. Britain eventually granted Ireland home rule, which Protestants opposed through organizations such as the Orange

Order fraternity and the Ulster Unionist Council. They also formed a powerful paramilitary group, the Ulster Volunteer Force. Most Irish nationalists, such as the Sinn Féin party, advocated constitutional means. A small minority advocated violence to expel the British from Ireland. This minority formed the secret Irish Republic Brotherhood, which was then superseded by the Irish Volunteers. In 1916 Volunteers led a seven-day insurrection against British rule and declared the independence of an Irish Republic. Popular support for this Easter Rising was minimal but surged when Britain executed the rebels. In its aftermath, Sinn Féin announced its support for independence. Becoming the focal point for republicans, it swept Irish seats in the 1918 general elections. Elected representatives gathered in Dublin in January 1919 and declared their assembly to be the parliament of the Irish Republic. The armed forces of the Republic, the Irish Republican Army (IRA), initiated guerrilla strikes against British forces in a war for Irish Independence.

In 1920 the British Parliament passed the Government of Ireland Act, which outlined separate home-rule institutions for the partition of Ireland into a northern and a southern area. Fighting continued for another year, when representatives of the United Kingdom and the Irish Republic signed the Anglo-Irish Treaty. The treaty granted limited autonomy to a 26-county Irish Free State, which in 1949 became the Republic of Ireland. It gave the six northeastern counties of Ulster, whose population was two-thirds Protestant, the right to opt out. Ulster's unionist and loyalist majority immediately voted to do so. They thereby established Northern Ireland as a state with devolved self-government within the United Kingdom. The IRA split over the treaty, and civil war ensued. Fighting continued for 11 bloody months until pro-treaty forces declared victory.

In the years that followed, two political currents offered competing visions for Northern Ireland's Catholic minority. Constitutional nationalists advocated political participation and called for an internal settlement that reconciled Ireland's unionist and nationalist traditions. Physical force republicans advocated armed struggle to defeat unionism and expel the British, whom they viewed as a colonial force. Republicans were committed to abstentionism; they would stand for elections but refuse to take office in the Irish Republic, the United Kingdom, or the parliament of Northern Ireland. The latter, commonly referred to by the name of its location in the Stormont area of Belfast, was rejected as illegitimate. In the decades that followed, both of these trends gave rise to activists and organizations that competed among themselves for leadership of nationalism or republicanism respectively, while also contesting each other for antiunionist constituents. In this they faced other cleavages among the Catholic population, such as that between city and countryside and between east and west in Northern Ireland. They also faced a tense relationship with the Republic of Ireland, which became decreasingly attentive to struggles in the North.

The main embodiment of physical force republicanism would remain the IRA. Sinn Féin played a secondary role as its political wing. In the first

decades after partition, the IRA's woe was less organizational fragmentation than organizational survival. It managed to carry out periodic attacks,
including bombing campaigns in England in 1939 and 1940, but met with
little public enthusiasm or military success. By 1945 most IRA members
had been killed or interned. Ed Moloney notes that the IRA's "structures
and leadership had evaporated," and the organization "effectively ceased
to exist."[68]

The IRA eventually rebuilt itself but remained institutionally unable to
assert an institutional monopoly over republican efforts. It experienced internal divisions, and those divisions increased motivations and opportunities for
the use of violence. In some instances, minor groups emerged outside the auspices of the IRA and pursued armed struggle on their own.[69] In other cases, it
was IRA members themselves who displayed "excessive zeal." Some initiated
military operations without authorization and were then punished by expulsion from IRA ranks. These renegades frequently formed splinter groups,
which became their vehicles for executing still more attacks.[70] Liam Kelly,
one such restive fighter ousted from the IRA, formed his own paramilitary.
Seizing upon his popularity in his hometown, he convinced local IRA units to
defect to his group. He and his recruits then proceeded to carry out a number
of dramatic operations.[71]

While Kelly's significance should not be exaggerated, his role is emblem-
atic of the mechanisms by which a movement's weak organizational structure
encourages lack of discipline, splintering, and factional competition, which
in turn mediate escalation in violent protest. On the one hand, some suggest that Kelly was provoked to undertake violent acts by the IRA's "sneers"
against him.[72] On the other, some propose that it was Kelly who provoked
the IRA to engage in violence. Indeed, some argue that he "single-handedly"
forced the IRA leadership into its most extensive military onslaught during
this era.[73] The IRA had vacillated in its planning of the operation for a year,
and it was arguably that hesitation that prompted members to opt for "solo
runs" or splinter groups in the first place.[74] Goaded by outbidding, the IRA
launched the 1956–1962 Border Campaign, a series of guerrilla attacks on
military and infrastructural targets that caused £1 million in damage.[75] The
campaign succeeded neither militarily nor in terms of mobilizing popular support. By the end, nearly all IRA Army Council members were interned and
elections showed a sharp decline in votes for Sinn Féin. Demoralized by the
lack of support, the IRA dumped its arms. In a formal statement it announced
that "foremost among the factors motivating this course of action has been the
attitude of the general public."[76]

Meanwhile, constitutional nationalists grappled with organizational problems of their own. Weak institutions and a lack of common vision likewise
mediated their behavior. In their case, fragmentation inhibited the capacity to
coordinate and sustain nonviolent protest. Mainstream nationalism in Northern
Ireland built "no structure or coherent party organization" before the 1960s.[77]
The inheritor of political agitation before partition, the Nationalist Party was

Catholics' main representative in the Stormont parliament. However, the party was little more than a collection of members of parliament engaged in patronage politics. It had no institutional apparatus or clear program.[78] Successive pressure groups emerged, including the National League of the North, the National Unity Organizing Committee, and the Irish Union Association. Yet each initiative experienced internal disagreements, failed to establish a mass base, failed to establish a mass base, and eventually collapsed. Declaring a mission to unite all nationalists, nearly five hundred persons assembled and launched the Anti-Petition League in 1945. They established an organizational structure that included a standing committee and dozens of local branches on both sides of the Irish border. With this organizational structure, the League held conventions, carried out a publicity and propaganda campaign, and held peaceable marches.[79] By 1951, however, it suffered from divisions over abstentionism and other matters, and was "visibly fragmenting."[80]

Neither the Nationalist Party nor the IRA offered Northern Ireland's Catholics legitimate leadership or institutions for effective mobilization. No single collective purpose or vision united the population. Indeed, a 1968 survey found Catholics equally divided among those who accepted, rejected, or did not know their opinion regarding the legitimacy of the existing constitutional order in the North.[81] Nonetheless, the population's ambivalence toward politics did not belie cumulating grievances. Northern Ireland's first leaders had replaced proportional representation with a winner-takes-all electoral system that maximized unionists' control. It also gerrymandered districts, further ensuring unionist victories even in areas with large nationalist populations. The result was one-party rule in Stormont, with the Ulster Unionist Party forming every Northern Irish government until 1972. Catholic disenfranchisement was reinforced at the level of local councils by laws that restricted voting to property owners and allotted multiple votes to businesses. Most assessments concurred that nationalists faced discrimination in housing, employment, appointments, and the selection of locations for major industries. Catholics were more likely than Protestants to fill the ranks of the urban unemployed and unskilled, or to be farmers barely extracting a livelihood from small plots of land.[82]

Loyalists contested charges of discrimination. They attributed Catholics' poverty to their lower levels of education and larger families.[83] They also claimed to be defending their state from a disloyal minority bent on destroying it. On these grounds, unionist governments extended the 1922 Special Powers Act from an emergency procedure to permanent authorization of search, arrest, and detention. The severe law also banned meetings, parades, publications, organizations, and other forms of political expression. Enforcing these measures was an official police force, the Royal Ulster Constabulary, as well as a reserve force, the Ulster Special Constabulary, or B-Specials. Nationalists accused these forces of sectarianism, mistreatment, and turning a blind eye to vigilante violence by Protestant gangs, if not joining them while out of uniform.

By the 1960s, social and sectarian tensions were palpable. Reforms by British Labour governments had increased access to education, fostering the growth of a Catholic middle class that enjoyed social mobility but found its aspirations for political equality blocked. At the same time, the least privileged of the Catholic population were experiencing economic decline.[84] These socio-economic developments created a constituency for protest, as similar trends in the 1980s did among Palestinians in the occupied territories and blacks in South Africa. Reasoning that improvement of conditions for the minority was necessary to preserve the union, a new Northern Irish prime minister instituted moderate reforms. Yet these both disappointed nationalists and spurred backlash among loyalists. In this context, the outspoken Ian Paisley formed a new unionist paramilitary.

Against this backdrop, new antiunionist organizations pressed for social and political change. The Homeless Citizens' League was formed in 1963 to protest discriminatory housing policies. The following year, some members created the Campaign for Social Justice to draw attention to a broader range of unjust practices through booklets, pamphlets, letters, and meetings. Three years later, the Northern Ireland Civil Rights Association (NICRA) took shape. NICRA was an umbrella organization whose leadership included representatives of trade unions and political parties as well as community activists. It identified a list of specific goals, namely an end to gerrymandering, discrimination, and voting restrictions, and abolition of the B-Specials. Under slogans such as "One Man, One Vote," NICRA used pressure politics to call for equal rights. It averted the issue of the partition of Ireland and sought support from Catholics and Protestants alike.

Other groups, inspired by the American civil rights movement, moved toward direct action. In 1968 the Derry Housing Action Committee organized several protest events. A nationalist member of parliament attracted media attention when he illegally occupied a house that he accused public authorities of allocating discriminatorily. Meanwhile, NICRA concentrated its efforts on lobbying and submitting complaints to the government. After the government ignored its entreaties for a year and a half, however, the association decided to engage in mass nonviolent protest. In August 1968, it joined other groups in organizing Northern Ireland's first civil rights march. Loyalists staged a counterdemonstration and authorities banned the march, but organizers effectively steered the crowd and protest remained peaceful.[85] That October, more militant activists held a second march in the expectation that the state would repress it and that repression would galvanize popular outrage.[86] As anticipated, police charged the crowd and beat participants with batons. Images of the bloodied demonstrators were televised, stunning international opinion and sparking two days of rioting.

The event is regarded as the start of the Troubles, a situation of unrest and episodic violence that enveloped Northern Ireland for the next three decades. In the aftermath of the riots, the pace of protest quickly escalated and new groups with different agendas took to the streets.[87] Radicalized students and socialists founded People's Democracy and, against NICRA's advice, held a four-day march on New Year's Day, 1969. Marchers were ambushed by Paisley supporters and brutally attacked. They later accused the police of doing little to protect them. As during the previous fall, bloodshed triggered riots. Then in August 1969, a loyalist parade passed near the Bogside, a Catholic area of Derry, and likewise sparked violent clashes between nationalists and police. Violence spread across Northern Ireland, deteriorated into sectarian clashes between Catholics and Protestants, and ended in deaths, injuries, property damage, and sweeping population flight. As the situation took on the character of civil war, Britain deployed troops in Northern Ireland for the first time since partition.

This Battle of the Bogside demonstrated civil rights activists' difficulties in institutionalizing the command and control requisite for strictly peaceable protest, especially in the face of counterviolence. The official investigation into events found that no demonstrators under NICRA's auspices carried weapons. Nevertheless, it criticized the association's open organizational structure, which welcomed supporters of all political persuasions without distinction. The investigation's report concluded that this structure undermined NICRA's ability to discipline the action carried out in its name:

> It is apparent that here is an organization of some substance, with a formal constitutional structure, means of co-operation with affiliated local associations with identical objects, and with a definite program of reforms.... The Association so far has been able to maintain its avowed policy of non-violent protest and agitation within the limits of the law.... But here is an instrument, already constituted and organized, which could without any excessive difficulty be successfully infiltrated by those whose intentions are far other than peaceful.[88]

The start of the Troubles exposed problems of organizational structure not only in the nonviolent civil rights movement, but also in the IRA. After the termination of the Border Campaign in 1962, IRA Chief of Staff Cathal Goulding had increasingly adopted a Marxist orientation. He called for the IRA to commit itself to anti-imperialism and to unifying workers regardless of sect. Shifting focus from armed struggle to economic and social agitation, he led the IRA in forming rural cooperatives and campaigns on issues such as housing and foreign ownership. He also advocated an end to the IRA's long-standing principle of abstentionism. These changes alienated much of the IRA's rank and file, who tended to be conservative, religious, lower class, and steeped in the traditional ideology of physical force republicanism. Ideological divisions, compounded by generational and personality gaps, simmered until the street violence of 1969 brought them to a breaking point. Angry members blamed Goulding for neglecting the IRA and even downgrading its arsenal. They claimed that his policies had rendered them unable to fulfill their most basic duty to protect Catholic civilians from attack.

The IRA appeared to be heading toward another split. Nonetheless, what sealed that outcome was arguably not the ideological dispute per se, but

Goulding's inability to manage fragmentation and prevent it from tearing the organization apart.[89] Rather than slowly building internal support and isolating opponents, he – "stupidly," in Gerry Adams's telling – moved too early and too quickly to push through his agenda.[90] When members opposed his reforms, Goulding confronted them directly and forced a vote. The result of the leader's inability to mollify or marginalize challengers was a historic divorce within republican ranks. Dissidents left and formed a new group: the Provisional IRA. Those who remained with Goulding became known as the Official IRA. Attracting old IRA units and new recruits, the Provos soon became the largest republican force. They pledged commitment to armed struggle and escalated military operations. Pushed by rivalry, the Officials likewise increased attacks. Against this backdrop, the number of deaths resulting from attacks by republican groups increased from 3 in 1969 to 18 in 1970 to 98 in 1971.[91]

In this context of escalating violence, Britain introduced internment without trial in August 1971. Sweeping arrest raids sparked more violence and population flight. Killing and destruction might have continued to the exclusion of unarmed protest. Against this tendency, however, an organizational structure emerged to steer the groundswell of popular outrage into civil disobedience. The development of a mass-based anti-internment campaign illustrates how cohesion enables and fortifies nonviolent protest. NICRA took the lead in urging nonunionists to forgo paying all rents and rates.[92] Other groups quickly voiced their support, including the newly formed Social Democratic and Labour Party (SDLP). Unlike its constitutional nationalist precursors, the SDLP developed a modern party structure.[93] SDLP members of parliament endorsed the rent strike, issuing a public statement that "[w]e expect one hundred percent support from all opponents of internment." Answering the call, some 160 local councillors and public figures resigned in protest. Approximately 200 Catholic officers in a British army regiment did likewise.[94] Meanwhile, opposition members of parliament declared an alternative to Stormont that they called the "Assembly of the Northern Irish People." Though meeting only twice, it succeeded in attracting media attention to the protest campaign. Other parliamentarians staged a 48-hour hunger strike near the British prime minister's residence in London.

Prominent personalities thus offered Northern Ireland–wide leadership to the nonviolent campaign against internment. At the same time, foreshadowing the first Palestinian Intifada and the South African insurrection, a grassroots infrastructure arose to make the campaign effective on the ground. According to John McGuffin, numerous communities in Northern Ireland formed defense, welfare, and other committees to mobilize participation in the strike. They also set up barricades and managed their own clubs and newspapers.[95] The glue of this campaign against internment was collective purpose. A 1972 survey of Catholic political activists found that 90 percent supported the rent and rates strike.[96] In McGuffin's words, "Internment has brought the people together and made them see the need for organizing from the grassroots up." As in the Intifada and South Africa's "semiliberated" townships, unifying popular consensus was fueled by a sense of empowerment. McGuffin observed that participation in civil resistance "gave many people, for the first time in their lives, the chance to ... exercise a very real measure of control over their jobs, their streets, their areas."

This organizational cohesion made possible a nonviolent protest of tremendous scope. Some labor stay-aways accompanied the civil disobedience campaign, notably the participation of eight thousand workers in a one-day industrial strike.[97] Tens of thousands of households withheld payment of rents and rates.[98] Some also extended the strike to utility bills, car taxes, television licenses, and court fines. The combination of strikes and resignations brought numerous local councils to a standstill, forcing the government to assume their functions. Illustrating the strike's impact, the government issued an Emergency Powers Act. This authorized the state to collect debts owed by nonpayers by deducting them directly from their public entitlements, such as unemployment benefits, pensions, or even death grants.

Throughout this period of heightened tension, NICRA complied with the authorities' ban on street protests. After several months passed and the internment policy remained in force, however, it decided to call another mass civil rights march. It held the march in Derry in January 1972 on what would become known as "Bloody Sunday." Estimates of the number of marchers range from three thousand to twenty thousand. The demonstration began as planned, with most participants following the organizers along the designated procession path. Some youths then diverged and marched toward the barricade of British paratroopers who had been deployed for the event. Protestors threw stones and paratroopers opened fire, killing 13. Soldiers claimed to have come under gunfire, a controversy that remained open until an official 12-year investigation concluded in 2010 that all of those shot had been unarmed. The killings stunned the population. In Bob Purdie's words, it served as the "execution squad for the civil rights movement."[99] In its wake, nonviolent protest waned and both the initiative and a surge of recruits moved to the IRA. Within months, Britain dissolved the Stormont parliament and assumed direct rule of Northern Ireland.

The year 1972 would be the bloodiest in the conflict, registering 470 lives lost, 10,000 shootings, and 2,000 bomb explosions.[100] Over the next quarter-century, the pattern of violence would shift from gun battles between the IRA and British army, to reciprocal sectarian assaults by Northern Irish paramilitaries, to a long stalemate dotted by sporadic attacks. Some 3,630 people would be killed, approximately 30 percent by loyalists, 10 percent by security forces, and 60 percent by republican groups.[101] The IRA was the foremost agent of violence perpetrated in the name of the republican cause. It shot British soldiers and unionist police officers, and bombed buildings, pubs, train stations, cars, and the Westminster Parliament. It also carried out kidnappings, beatings, torturous interrogations, and killings of Northern Irish Catholics suspected of disloyalty. These forms of violence developed over the course of the 1970s, when the IRA moved from optimism about a quick victory to a strategy of "long war." During these years, it also took its military campaign to the British mainland.

The IRA's organizational structure evolved, as did its use of violence. A Sinn Féin leader named Gerry Adams led a cohort of other young republicans from the North. They initiated a restructuring of the IRA along cellular lines. This re-formed the older framework, in which local units exercised great autonomy, into one that centralized control in a permanent leadership. As leadership came increasingly under Adams's sway,[102] the consolidation of authority enhanced the IRA's institutional capacity to direct the use of violence and better fight infiltration. It also gave leaders the means to guide the republican movement toward a political strategy, which the Adams camp eventually became convinced was necessary. That strategic shift received an unexpected boost from the hunger strike by republican prisoners in 1981, during which strike leader Bobby Sands was elected to the British Parliament. The deaths of Sands and other strikers unleashed enormous nationalist sentiment in Northern Ireland. A network of popular committees had formed to support the strike and, upon its termination, Sinn Féin absorbed them as an apparatus for grassroots mobilization. Seizing this structure and the political momentum, Adams led adoption of the "Armalite and Ballot Box" strategy. Sinn Féin then contested elections for the Northern Ireland Assembly, followed by elections for local authorities and the European Parliament.

These developments aided a shift in the relationship between the IRA and Sinn Féin from dominance by the former to parity and eventually to the latter's preeminence.[103] Also solidifying this change was the personal ascendance of Adams, Martin McGuinness, and their allies. Adams successfully inched aside Sinn Féin's traditionalist leaders hailing from the Republic of Ireland to become president of the party in 1983. This put Adams in a position to pursue a radical change in republican strategy, which he did by advocating taking seats in the parliament of the Republic of Ireland. Internal opposition was formidable. Nevertheless, Adams triumphed by skillfully managing potential fragmentation. He divided and discredited his rivals and stacked councils with loyal supporters. He began by introducing less controversial, interim changes and only afterward tabled more divisive ones.[104] Along the way, he placated the republican base by continually asserting his commitment to armed struggle. Thanks to these strategies for managing fragmentation, Adams succeeded in maneuvering Sinn Féin to formal approval of the decision to abandon the principle of abstentionism. A small group dissented by forming the splinter group Republican Sinn Féin and its military wing, Continuity IRA. However, the groups presented no serious challenge to the movement cohesion that Adams solidifyed under his command.

Adams then inched toward a policy that most republicans viewed as treason: negotiation of a settlement that accepted that Northern Ireland's constitutional status would change only with the consent of the majority of its inhabitants. Given the Protestant majority, this effectively meant sanctioning union with Great Britain. Adams continued to employ various techniques to manage fragmentation and thus achieve this goal without provoking a devastating split within republican ranks.[105] He moved gradually, engaging in secret talks for years and revealing them to the public only when he had built a base of support. He employed "chameleonic" rhetoric, ambiguous to the point of being deceptive, to reassure militant members even as he turned away from militancy.[106] He also made the most of IRA and Sinn Féin institutions, bending them to reach decisions in his favor but also preserving them to enforce those decisions once made. To reassure the IRA grass roots, Adams loyalists hosted "family meetings" around Northern Ireland in which they addressed fighters' concerns about the peace process. Finally, the Sinn Féin president forged a pan-nationalist alliance with the government of Ireland and his electoral rival, the SDLP. This helped bridge the ideological divide between republicanism and constitutional nationalism. It contributed to crafting a unified understanding of self-determination that inspired collective purpose among all Irish nationalists.

The Provisionals' path to peace was by no means completely cohesive or completely nonviolent. In balancing the pursuit of a political settlement with the management of fragmentation, one of Adams's strategies was to retreat as he deemed necessary. In August 1994, he led the IRA in declaring a cessation of military operations. The ceasefire bore little fruit, however. To the IRA's dismay, Britain continued to insist on IRA decommissioning as a condition for its inclusion in talks. After 15 months, republican discontent was "ominous."[107] The leadership took note of warning signs of grassroots restlessness, such as an increasing number of killings of accused drug dealers by IRA cover groups. Against this backdrop, the IRA executive made the decision to convene a general army convention that was sure to vote to terminate the ceasefire. Adams feared that it might vote to end his tenure as well. Preempting that risk, Adams joined the IRA Army Council in nullifying the ceasefire and authorizing a massive blast at London's Canary Wharf. The IRA would carry out more than a dozen other operations, including its largest bombing in Great Britain, before endorsing a new ceasefire in July 1997. For two seasoned observers, the violence perpetuated by the IRA between those two ceasefires was distinct from that of prior eras. It was a tactic not to inflict harm and coerce state concessions, but to win a seat at the negotiating table.[108] Beyond this, it was a tactic by the leadership to avert a devastating rift in Provisional ranks. Had such a rift occurred, negotiations would have had little chance of success.

Moloney argues that the IRA leaders who accepted partition in the 1920s entered constitutional politics, but "at the cost of serious and bloody splits." Learning lessons from the past, Adams took the same course "but largely kept the organization in tact."[109] Management of fragmentation was vital at every step of the path that brought Sinn Féin to negotiate peace with its former adversaries. It enabled republicans to participate in multiparty peace talks in 1997, to sustain participation for six months, to endorse the Good Friday (Belfast) Agreement to which talks gave rise, and finally to carry out the decommissioning of IRA forces. The population of Northern Ireland voiced strong support for the Good Friday Agreement, with 71 percent endorsing it in a national referendum. Nevertheless, the historic settlement called on the republican hard core to abandon tenets held for generations. It was thus inevitable that some IRA members would fight it. Protesting the peace process, a small group left and formed the Real IRA. Nevertheless, its departure was too late to produce the kind of fragmentation that would return republicans to violence.[110] On the contrary, attacks by the Real IRA and likewise the Continuity IRA tended only to horrify the public. Spoiler violence hence consolidated the pro-peace consensus more than it threatened it.[111]

Analysis of the role of organizational structure in mediating the use of nonviolent protest, violent protest, and constitutional politics helps shed light on puzzles that remain in other accounts of Irish republicanism. Many analysts focus on the role of ideas and values in driving conflict in Northern Ireland. For example, some attribute the traditional prominence of violence in republicans' protest repertoire to a culture of martyrdom[112] or a nearly irrational ideological attachment to physical force.[113] Also highlighting ideas but emphasizing their ability to change, others argue that IRA members genuinely reconsidered violence over the years, and that is what made peace possible.[114]

In contrast to those who offer ideational explanations of this sort, others insist that state policies were the primary engine of shifts in protest to unionist rule.[115] Many conclude that repression of the unarmed civil rights movement in the late 1960s caused the collapse of nonviolent protest and the radicalization of armed struggle.[116] Offering a third perspective, still others argue that protestors in Northern Ireland adapted their strategies in accord with lessons learned from protest occurring elsewhere in the world. They were thus attentive to, and consciously sought to emulate, such models as the American civil rights movement[117] and the protest of leftist students throughout Western Europe in 1968.[118] Finally, a fourth analytical approach to explaining patterns of republican protest draws attention to international circumstances. Assessments in this spirit tend to focus on the peace process, claiming that the road to Good Friday was critically aided by such factors as the end of the cold war,[119] the improvement of Anglo-Irish state relations,[120] and mediation by the United States.[121]

These arguments are important but tell only part of the story. Neither external pressures nor international examples or ideology automatically lead a movement to act in one way or another. Not all members of a complex social movement understand strategic imperatives or tradition in the same way at the same time. When leaders depart from dogma, the question is not only what impelled their actions and why their views evolved, but also how they were able to enforce their preferences in the face of inevitable opposition. The organizational mediation theory of protest shows how fragmentation recurrently undermined the use of nonviolent protest against the status quo in Northern Ireland while increasing motives and opportunities for violent protest. The republican movement's ultimate embrace of political means would not have occurred but for leaders' ability to preempt splits. The turn away from violence was made possible by the rallying of leadership, institutions, and collective purpose to manage fragmentation.

COMPARATIVE ANALYSIS

In South Africa and Northern Ireland, as in the Palestinian national movement, protest strategy has been mediated by movements' organizational structure. Particularly significant has been the varying strength of leadership, institutions, and collective purpose, as well as the capacity of leaders to manage factors that aggravate internal fragmentation. This relationship between organizational structure and protest can be summarized by four paradigmatic patterns. Table 7.1 sketches the characteristics of collective action that result when a cohesive movement engages in nonviolent or violent protest and when a fragmented movement engages in violent protest. It distinguishes a fourth scenario, a fragmented movement using nonviolent protest, as highly unlikely.

This schema illustrates different outcomes associated with the organizational mediation theory of protest, as well as relevant examples from the three self-determination movements examined in this book. Cell (1) indicates that internal cohesion is vital during those times in which movements undertake nonviolent protest. This relationship underlay Palestinians' general strike in 1936 and the first Intifada. It was also apparent in protest by UDF-affiliated groups in South African townships in the mid-1980s and community-based anti-internment protests in Northern Ireland after August 1971. In each instance, an institutional framework based on local committees mobilized sweeping grassroots participation. This both strengthened and was strengthened by an empowering and unifying collective purpose among the population at large. Similarly vital was the role of leadership in offering guidance, political representation, and symbolic unity. Such was the contribution of parliamentarians and other high-level spokespersons from NICRA and SDLP in the Irish case, the ANC in the South African case, and the UNLU–PLO in the Palestinian case.

It is important not to exaggerate either the extent of movement cohesion or the strictly nonviolent character of protest in these examples. Each movement confronted powerful states that refused to grant their goals and used repression that sowed divisions in their ranks. Under such conditions, keeping protest solely within the bounds of nonviolence was a herculean task for even the most tightly unified movements. In all three cases, local communities differed in their ability to rally participation in the face of exhaustion and fear or to prevent restive young people from taking justice into their own hands. Nevertheless, these episodes represent important heights in cohesion and mass-based nonviolent protest in each movement, relative to its own history. Analysis of their dynamics shows why, in the absence of cohesion, nonviolent protest would not have been possible.

TABLE 7.1. *Organizational Mediation Theory of Protest: Predicted Outcomes*

Movement's Organizational Structure	Movement's Protest	
	Nonviolent Protest	Violent Protest
Cohesion	(1)	(2)
	Outcome: Cohesion increases the possibility that protest will be nonviolent	*Outcome:* Cohesion increases the possibility that political violence will be disciplined, targeted, and terminated subject to leadership decision
	Examples: First stage of the Arab Rebellion (1936 General Strike) First Intifada, especially 1987–1988 UDF protest in South Africa, 1980s Northern Ireland anti-interment protests, 1971	*Examples:* Tunnel riots, 1996 ANC guerrilla attacks, 1980s Provisional IRA attacks between ceasefires, 1994–1997
Fragmentation	(3)	(4)
	Outcome: Nonviolent protest is highly unlikely or is limited to isolated, individualized, or localized instances	*Outcome:* Fragmentation increases the likelihood that protest will be violent; violence is prone to escalation, difficult to terminate, and likely to seek private rather than movement goals
		Examples: Second stage of the Arab Rebellion (1937–1939 armed revolt) Second Intifada Palestinian fedayeen outbidding ANC–PAC outbidding IRA factional outbidding Spoiler attacks during peace processes in all three cases

At the opposite extreme, Cell (4) indicates that fragmentation consistently contributes to movements' use of violent protest. Lack of command and control was the context in which Palestinian rebellions in 1937 and 2000 militarized beyond the directives of any leadership, invited individuals to take up arms for a variety of private motives, and eclipsed popular participation in peaceable civic action. Factional competition, whether among PLO groups, IRA splinters, or the ANC and PAC, also spurred groups to adopt greater militancy than they might otherwise have embraced. In all three movements, eventual engagement in peace processes provoked opposition groups to threaten or use violent protest to forestall outcomes that might undermine their interests or goals. However, such spoiler activity was not an automatic result of negotiations. It varied with the personal capacities and institutional resources with which leaders managed fragmentation. In South Africa, the unparalleled authority of Mandela and the ANC, as well as the electoral process that they legitimated, marginalized oppositionists. In Northern Ireland, Adams likewise isolated and divided rivals. He built a base of support, and used ambiguous rhetoric and movement decision-making bodies to sanction controversial changes. Spoiler attacks against the Good Friday Agreement thus remained limited. When they occurred, popular opinion rejected them.

It is in the Palestinian case that movement fragmentation created an organizational structure most conducive to spoiler violence. Compared with the other two movements, Palestinians arguably entered the least favorable peace process in terms of the asymmetry of power and political support from external mediators. Nevertheless, these factors did not alone trigger oppositionists' turn to arms in protest. Protest was also conditioned by the sense of collective purpose in society and the leadership's institutional capacity to exercise command and control. Palestinians who executed attacks against the Oslo process took advantage of opportunities in the PA's weak institutions and the ambivalence of popular backing for an unsatisfactory agreement. In doing so, they exposed the limited effectiveness of Arafat's use of co-optation and other strategies for containing dissent.

Located on the spectrum between fragmented violence and cohesive nonviolent protest are two other outcomes. As Cell (2) suggests, cohesive movements may also use violent protest. However, this violence is qualitatively different from that undertaken when a movement is fragmented. Mediated by a cohesive organizational structure, violence tends to be motivated by pursuit of collective goals more than by particularistic advantages. A cohesive movement has the institutional capacity to direct operations to achieve these goals and to terminate them when political calculations deem appropriate. The antiapartheid struggle offers a telling illustration of this dynamic. The ANC increased guerrilla attacks in the late 1980s as part of a calculated strategy to force the South African government to negotiate, not in an effort to ward off internal challenges. Hegemonic in the liberation movement, the ANC carried out operations to complement and inspire popular mobilization in the townships. There was little risk that this violent protest would overshadow or weaken nonviolent protest. Instead, the military campaign constituted a coup de grâce to further undercut support for apartheid during a time when it was already caving. To that end, the ANC limited its targets to avert killings that might create backlash or undermine its viability as an interlocutor with the state. Such rationalized and disciplined violence would not have been possible had the movement been less internally cohesive. Nor would it have been likely had the ANC faced contradictory pressures created by a need to face down competitors for leadership of the struggle for self-determination.

The IRA similarly illustrates how effective leadership and institutions can be critical in enabling either the escalation or deescalation of violent protest in accord with political calculations. The Troubles offers examples of how violence by cohesive groups differs from that by fragmented ones. Moloney tells of IRA units that were under the control of particularly strong local leaders. On some occasions, the rank and file in units wanted to take up arms, but were prevented from doing so by authoritative commanders who believed that such actions would be counterproductive.[122] Similarly, evidence suggests that the IRA made a deliberate choice not to use any firearms at the civil rights march that ended in Bloody Sunday. Its leaders believed that Britain wanted to lure it into shooting to establish a pretext for a crackdown. Wary of a trap, the IRA ordered its cadres not to bring weapons to the demonstration.[123]

On the flip side, the Provisionals' bombing operations following the collapse of the 1994 ceasefire were intended to force Sinn Féin's inclusion in peace negotiations. They were thus distinct from operations on the part of the Continuity IRA and Real IRA, which aimed at derailing them. As "politics through other means," the Provos' violence assisted Adams's strategy toward Britain. It also helped him to avoid a split in the movement. Attacks therefore served the leadership's overall management of fragmentation. This was apparent in the IRA's ability to bring operations to an effective halt when it called a new ceasefire in 1997. The signature of movement cohesion, therefore, was not the complete absence of armed action. It was leaders' ability to subject the timing, targeting, and intensity of violence to political decision making.

In Palestinian history, episodes of cohesive command and control over the use of force appear to have been fewer and less momentous than episodes of fragmented violence. Still, they were significant at key junctures. After participating in an escalation of hostilities with Israel across the Lebanese border in July 1981, the PLO welcomed a U.S.-negotiated ceasefire. The ceasefire was a reversal for Israel insofar as it represented an unprecedented indirect recognition of the PLO by both Israel and the United States.[124] Arafat understood the political and strategic value of quiet on the border at a time when the Israeli government was signaling its readiness for a major invasion. He thus mustered the institutional capacity to enforce the cessation of hostilities against internal opposition for almost a year. Similar cohesion characterized the demonstrations that broke out against the Jerusalem tunnel in 1996. PA police engaged in gun battles with Israeli security forces, but violence did not spin out of control and doom the peace process. Instead, Arafat was able to call hostilities to a halt when he judged that they had achieved a political objective. Four years later, mounting frustration in society and Fateh rendered the Palestinian movement much less cohesive. When demonstrations again broke out in Jerusalem, therefore, they unfolded in a very different way.

Cell (4) in Table 7.1 identifies the outcome that I argue is unlikely: the use of nonviolent protest by a fragmented movement. When a movement lacks leadership, institutions, and collective purpose, it will be unable to mobilize unarmed, civil protest on any mass scale or sustain it over time. This is not to deny that particular groups or local communities might mount nonviolent protest to the degree that they bring themselves together as a cohesive unit. Yet this small-scale cohesion will be exceptional in the context of the larger fragmented movement. The resulting nonviolent protest will remain isolated, individualized, or localized. It will be unlikely to change the strategy of the movement as a whole.

The village-based protest against Israel's fence/wall in the West Bank provides examples of such cohesion-within-fragmentation aiding the use of nonviolent protest amid violence. The circumstances of republican prisoners' hunger strike offer another example. While intra- and interfactional disputes continued outside the prison walls, prisoners of two rival parties (the IRA and the splinter Irish National Liberation Army) came together and agreed on a clear strategy. They decided that a succession of volunteers would refuse food starting one at a time in staggered intervals. Learning from a previous failed strike, they designed a campaign that would achieve maximum impact by repeatedly shocking the public and the authorities each time a new striker lapsed into coma or breathed his last breath. The cohesion of their effort was apparent in each striker's complete trust that his colleagues would fulfill their commitments. It was likewise manifest in the unwavering dedication of the 10 strikers who starved themselves to death. The protest, perhaps the ultimate example of nonviolent resistance, was thus a historic pocket of cohesion within a movement that long struggled with fragmentation.

CONCLUSION

This chapter does not offer a complete study of the South Africa antiapartheid struggle or the Northern Ireland republican movement. By briefly examining these cases against the backdrop of extensive analysis of Palestinian political history, however, I seek to demonstrate the robustness of the organizational mediation theory of protest. The empirical patterns highlighted here suggest this framework's capacity to explain aspects of protest left unexplained by standard analytical approaches. They also point to its broad applicability in the comparative study of social movements and conflict processes. In the three cases considered here, those who took action in the name of self-determination were driven by instrumental motives, noninstrumental motives, or both simultaneously. Whether they engaged in violent or nonviolent protest, however, was not a straightforward outcome of those motivations. It was also shaped by their movement's organizational structure.

Protest violence might appear the same to outside observers, and be felt as equally brutal by its victims, regardless of its cause. Nevertheless, the analytical distinctions laid out in Table 7.1 indicate that such violence is categorically different depending on the organizational context in which it occurs. Similarly, these distinctions show why a shift from violence to nonviolent protest is not simply a matter of calculation or values. Such a shift requires a move not only from the right- to the left-hand column of the table, but also from the bottom row to the top. Fragmented movements will find it difficult to make this switch, because they do not meet the organizational barrier to entry. Without attention to these matters of organizational structure, analysts cannot fully understand the motivations and constraints that shape movement behavior. Nor can decision makers design appropriate policy responses.

8

Conclusion

Nonviolence ... is mightier than the mightiest weapon.

Mahatma Gandhi

Nonviolence is fine as long as it works.

Malcolm X

Both activists who lead social movements and scholars who study them debate the relative effectiveness of nonviolent versus violent means of protest. This book asks a distinct question. It seeks to understand the conditions under which either form of protest is likely or probable. I propose the organizational mediation theory of protest as a framework for analyzing how movements' internal relationships affect their strategic action. While many factors contribute to a movement's use of violence, one predominant factor makes that use of nonviolent protest possible: the movement's own cohesion. Cohesion is an organizational structure that obtains when the factors that generate cooperation among members outweigh those that propel competitive or antagonistic behavior. It can be measured by assessing the strength of a movement's leadership, institutions, and collective purpose. When a movement is cohesive, it enjoys the organizational capacity to mobilize mass participation, contain disruptive dissent, and rein in violence driven by particularistic motives. In consequence, cohesion increases the possibility that a movement will use nonviolent protest. Inversely, when a movement is unable to centralize authority and institutionalize command and control, it easily becomes racked by divisions. Under conditions of fragmentation, a movement's very organizational structure generates incentives for members to employ force and weakens constraints on its use. It enables the formation of radical splinter and semi-splinter groups, impedes the conclusion and implementation of ceasefires, and reduces the capacity for popular mobilization that is the hallmark of civil disobedience and direct action. Fragmentation thus increases the likelihood that a movement will use violent protest.

Analysis of nearly one hundred years in the history of the Palestinian national movement, as well as comparisons with national movements in South Africa and Northern Ireland, demonstrate the fruitfulness of this approach. When the Palestinian movement used mass unarmed protest, such as during a general strike in the 1930s and the uprising of 1987, internal cohesion proved crucial. In those episodes, a legitimate leadership and grassroots institutional network helped people across social classes, religions, and regions participate in demonstrations, boycotts, and acts of noncooperation and disengagement from the state. While Palestinians did not use nonviolent protest to the exclusion of violence, a structure of coordination and cooperation enabled them to channel much of the will to rebel into unarmed activities and sustain them on a broad scale. Movement cohesion was also essential in facilitating diplomatic initiatives, be they pressure politics in the 1920s or peace negotiations in the 1990s. To the degree that leaders were able to manage fragmentation, they helped impede spoiler violence from derailing those nonviolent initiatives.

At other times the Palestinian national movement lacked the strong central leadership, institutions, or popular consensus that integrated political participation. Under those conditions, fragmentation contributed to the use of violent protest. Various forms of competition along the movement's vertical and horizontal cleavages fed escalation in an armed revolt in the late 1930s, guerrilla warfare in the 1960s, international attacks on civilians in the 1970s, and a militarized uprising beginning in the year 2000. Throughout the history of the national movement, weak authority structures invited the formation of militant splinter groups and obstructed leaders' efforts to reach ceasefires or diplomatic agreements. Cracks in the self-determination struggle invited external actors to intervene and induce or coerce Palestinian parties to act in ways that furthered non-Palestinian interests. This often entailed taking up arms. Fragmentation thus played an irreducible role in encouraging violence. Moreover, it left the movement without the institutional capacity to carry out mass nonviolent protest, even when support for such a strategy existed.

The organizational mediation theory of protest highlights the shortcomings of approaches that posit a range of variables that drive protest but analyze them in isolation from movements' internal structures. Grievances over the denial of self-determination, often worsened by repression, has been the engine of protest throughout Palestinian history. Nonetheless, it alone cannot account for the different forms that protest has taken. Intense feelings of deprivation, anger, and injustice might have triggered violence during every era but did not. That Palestinians instead maintained strikes, boycotts, or pressure politics during some junctures was mediated by their organizational structure. It was testimony to an ideological and organizational discipline inspired by a legitimate leadership, enforced through institutional networks, and affirmed by society's sense of collective purpose.

Physical and material factors have also variously constrained or encouraged different forms of protest activity. In the Palestinian experience, the ability to reach targets affected shifts from cross-border guerrilla warfare to plane hijackings to suicide bombings. There is no doubt that limited access to weapons contributed to the largely unarmed character of the first Intifada, and greater availability influenced the militarization of the second Intifada. Yet resources shape the range of options available to protestors; they do not determine their choices among those options. During some periods, Palestinians possessed more weapons than they used. During others, they devised violent tactics from surprisingly scarce means. Material resources and restrictions alone cannot explain these patterns.

Leaders' particularistic calculations have also affected protest strategies. Some insist that fragmentation in the Palestinian national movement was not structural but deliberate. If there was inconsistency in Palestinians' violent and nonviolent actions, this was because Amin al-Husayni or Yasir Arafat cynically encouraged it. According to this view, they claimed to be prisoners to the will of restive constituents as a ploy to extract the benefits of violence without the costs of overt sponsorship. Yet whether leaders encouraged divisions or divisions instead constrained leaders is largely a question of structure versus agency. Evidence exists to support either interpretation. The organizational mediation theory of protest helps cut through the stalemate of this debate by supporting a novel interpretation: leaders of movements sometimes contribute to violence not by directly feeding it but by failing to provide the leadership that could build a movement's internal cohesion. This may be due to their personalities, skills, or the system of incentives within which they operate. It is not simply a product of their designs toward the external adversary in the overriding self-determination conflict. Without leaders to encourage internal cooperation, command, and control, a movement can become a free-for-all in which violence takes on a life of its own. The Palestinian case reveals how the use of violent protest can bear the imprint of leaders' lack of power over their communities as much as the extent of that power.

Finally, there is no doubt that the straightforward strategic utility of various types of protest influenced their likelihood of being adopted by the Palestinian national movement. Rationalists are correct to insist that the national movement chose protest strategies to achieve political objectives. Yet this begs the question of which of many overlapping external and internal objectives members prioritized at any juncture and why. Analysis of organizational structure offers some answers. There is no constant likelihood that adherents of a movement will act for the benefit of their particular faction as opposed to that of the movement as a whole. Rather, the intensity and significance of factional rivalries vary in accord with the movement's overall cohesion or fragmentation. During periods when the Palestinian movement possessed the leadership, institutional, and popular dimensions of cohesion, competing groups often coordinated their behavior rather than acted at cross-purposes. As those elements weakened, factions became more apt to put narrow interests ahead of national ones. Activists made rational calculations, but the organizational structure of the movement shaped the decisions in which those rationality resulted.

The list of variables that affect protest strategies is long. I propose the organizational mediation theory of protest not to dispute their plausibility, but to illustrate how their effects are mediated by a movement's internal system of rules and relationships. A movement's cohesion or fragmentation is not the only factor impinging upon its strategic choice, but it can make the difference between violence and nonviolence. Movements facing similar sets of incentives and constraints in the overriding struggle for self-determination will act differently depending on how their own structures integrate members for the accomplishment of shared goals.

IMPLICATIONS

This book demonstrates these core causal claims. In addition, it brings to light other empirical and analytical implications of the organizational mediation theory of protest. One implication is that a movement's organizational structure develops over time. Its use of violent or nonviolent protest is thus historically conditioned. The variables and processes governing internal politics at one juncture influence the incentives, perceptions, and opportunities that affect protest choices at later junctures. Nonetheless, a movement's organizational structure is not simply derivative from the past. During the long course of the Palestinian national movement, many episodes appeared to leave the movement in a situation of fragmentation. Yet national unity remained a high value and constant refrain, and activists repeatedly undertook to build cohesion afresh. The degree to which they overcame the internal and external factors that separated rather than united them affected the strategies used in the next round of conflict. Both organizational structure and strategic action were shaped by prior eras, but not determined by them. Individual agency and a dynamic conflict environment also played roles that were vital and often contingent.

Herein lies another important pattern. Actors' choices about how to manage fragmentation give rise to relationships, norms, and expectations that shape the structure of mobilization for years thereafter. In fact, many features of Palestinian national institutions have their roots in earlier efforts to confront fragmentation. Arafat cultivated a mystique as fatherly benefactor that inspired personal loyalty on the part of many Palestinians. This helped bring them together across internal rifts during critical periods in the history of the national movement. Nevertheless, to the degree that Arafat used charismatic legitimacy to substitute for strong institutions, he bequeathed many obstacles to his successor. Lacking personal magnetism, Abbas was left to search for other means to unite the movement behind his direction.[1] That which generated national cohesion at one moment in time thus undermined it at a later point.

As another strategy for managing fragmentation, Palestinian leaders enacted decision-making rules that they believed would bind the movement as a whole. The PLO long sought to decide policy by consensus. The outcome was national goals that represented the lowest common denominator for all groups and their Arab state backers. Consensus decision making helped disparate factions forge a united front. Yet it also established an organizational structure that granted minority voices disproportionate power. It thereby enabled hardline groups to act as veto players and impede the shift from military to diplomatic strategies. Circumventing these limitations, Arafat undertook a third strategy in the management of fragmentation: the neopatrimonial distribution of benefits, jobs, and a range of favors to secure people's allegiance. This political allocation of public monies persuaded many activists at all levels of the nationalist hierarchy to defer to the official leadership and the nationalist project as that leadership defined it. Yet it also produced endemic corruption and a fragile political system vulnerable to collapse under pressure.

The organizational structure of the Fateh movement illustrates some ways in which strategies that are desirable for managing fragmentation in the short term can have perverse effects in the long term. In the 1960s, Fateh's founders favored an open movement and broad ideology with the aim of attracting as many adherents as possible. This strategy for surmounting territorial and ideological fragmentation was functional during an era in which Palestinian nationalism competed against pan-Arabism. At that stage, Fateh faced the challenge of advancing the fedayeen as an alternative to Arab states for leadership of the fight to liberate Palestine. Fateh's catchall character proved less advantageous as Palestinianism became a norm and Fateh found itself one of many groups claiming its mantle. A certain political context thus led Fateh to embrace a loose organizational structure. However, its very success reshaped that context in ways that encouraged the proliferation of rival organizations. Under those conditions, Fateh struggled to discipline its many branches and identify clearly what it represented. The institutional vagueness that was once beneficial for overcoming fragmentation became a liability in the quest to build a more focused movement.

The Palestinian experience demonstrates still other paradoxes. Just as leaders' strategies to fight short-term fragmentation can feed long-term fragmentation, so can opposition groups' efforts to challenge a leadership have the unintended consequence of strengthening that leadership and its policies. When opposition factions stray too far from majority public opinion, they can undercut their legitimacy and doom their quest for political power. In allying themselves too closely with third parties, they may discredit themselves as puppets of foreign interests and betrayers of the national cause. Such was the case in the 1985–1987 War of the Camps, when pro-Syria Palestinian factions were seen as complicit in a brutal siege on innocent civilians. They were thus considered disloyal until they came back into the fold of interorganizational cooperation under Arafat's direction. In this way, opposition groups sometimes marginalize themselves by making erroneous choices or inadvertently exposing their own weakness. Leaders weigh the likelihood of such outcomes in deciding to carry out controversial policies. From the mid-1970s, Arafat calculated that he could gradually shift toward a two-state solution without provoking an irrevocable split in the national movement. His wager paid off. Rejectionists objected but eventually had no recourse but to accommodate the change. Under some circumstances, therefore, the most efficacious way for elites to manage fragmentation may be to tolerate it. This is more likely when opposition factions aspire to mainstream political authority as opposed to independence as a hardline force. As long as groups seek nothing more than autonomy on the margins, they will not be greatly constrained by the quest for popular backing. When they seek recognition as representatives of the national cause, however, public opinion can be the lever determining their political fate.

Ultimately, when other strategies for managing fragmentation fail, movement leaders can try to impose cooperation with internal violence. Such physical intimidation or elimination of challengers has been less commonplace in the contemporary Palestinian national struggle than elsewhere, such as in the Algerian, Vietnamese, and Tamil nationalist movements. Indeed, some might argue that the aversion to internal violence has been one cause of Palestinians' relatively more prominent and enduring political divisions. Under exceptional circumstances, however, Palestinian leaders have resorted to direct confrontation in effort to manage fragmentation. Such was the case when the central leadership faced a politically ambitious or ideologically uncompromising opposition that was confident of its popular appeal. During the first years of the peace process, for example, Arafat attempted to contain Hamas through a combination of repression and bargaining. The Islamist opposition remained defiant until the PA president carried out a sweeping crackdown in 1996. This use of physical coercion severely weakened Hamas. It thus consolidated Arafat's control of the national agenda – at least temporarily.

The inverse may result when fragments use force and a central leadership refrains from meeting the challenge with force of its own. Such might have been the case when PA president Abbas faced resistance within his own Fateh movement. He preferred to try to cajole submission to his authority rather than forcibly impose his pledge to bring the PA areas under a single gun. When fragments test a central leadership's resolve, there may be no substitute for leaders' triumph in a game of wills. This raises questions about the meaning of internal violence in self-determination movements. Is it a sign of fragmentation unleashed? Or is it a step in the process of achieving enduring cohesion? To resolve these questions, it may be appropriate to craft a typology of internal violence. In the Palestinian case, this might identify analytical distinctions between the score settling of the 1936–1939 Arab Rebellion, the killing of collaborators in the first Intifada, and factional battles after 2006.

Analysis of these and other developments over the *longue durée* of Palestinian history reveals how both contingent choices and historic legacies shape the ebbs and flows of a movement's organizational structure. In exploring how organizational structure in turn mediates protest, I hope to make four contributions to the scholarly literature on conflict processes and contentious politics. First, I craft the organizational mediation theory of protest to critique the treatment of movements as if they were unitary actors. It is untenable to analyze insurgents' choices in isolation from the internal structure of insurgent movements. Conventional models and empirical tests that implicitly view movements as single entities should be explicitly modified to take into account movements' varying levels of cohesion. Second, I seek to supplement conflict models that concentrate on actors' ideas and goals by instead emphasizing how actors are organized. The causal link between movement members' preferences and their observable behavior is filtered through the structure of internal cooperation, command, and control within which they make interactive decisions. Third, I critique the tendency to isolate the study of violence and the study of nonviolent protest in different academic literatures. I embrace DeNardo's logic that any explanation of why one strategy (such as violence) is adopted requires an explanation of why another strategy (such as nonviolent protest) is not.[2] I offer the organizational mediation theory as an analytical bridge to do just that. Finally, I extend the scholarly trend that distinguishes between conflict and violence. Violence is not an automatic outcome of conflict. Likewise, nonviolent protest is not automatic whenever social movements forgo violence. Nonviolent protest is a qualitatively distinct phenomenon, and theories of armed and unarmed forms of contention should be formulated accordingly. Due to different organizational requirements, there are many pathways to violence yet one prevailing pathway to nonviolent protest. That latter path requires that a movement be internally cohesive.

NEW QUESTIONS

Repression and Dissent

Decades of scholarship on the impact of state repression on protest have produced contradictory findings. Research has found that countermeasures increase collective dissent, that they decrease dissent, or that their effects are nonlinear, time-lagged, or differ with their character or consistency. As Ekkart Zimmerman concludes, "There are theoretical arguments for all conceivable basic relations between governmental coercion and group protest and rebellion except for no relationship."[3] One reason for this inconclusiveness is that scholars traditionally searched for an overarching relationship between state policies as input and protest as output. In the process, they obscured the dynamics of rebel decision making.[4] Many now call for research to open that "black box" by disaggregating the macro-relationship between coercion and protest into its constituent mechanisms and theorizing how clusters of mechanisms operate in various contexts.[5]

The organizational mediation theory of protest responds to these calls. It shows that the effect of repression on dissent is filtered through a movement's internal structure. A movement's cohesion affects the probability that it will be resilient in the face of external pressure and thus bend like rubber to preserve its institutions and strategy. Alternatively, it conditions the likelihood that it will prove brittle and shatter into internal disputes and rivalries. Even in the most cohesive movements, however, repression typically catalyzes fragmenting processes. When the movement is unable to manage that fragmentation, repression will contribute to precluding nonviolent protest and increasing violent protest.

The Palestinian movement illustrates these relationships. For nearly a century, various states acted in ways that obstructed the development of a cohesive organizational structure. Fundamentally, denial of Palestinians' basic goal of self-determination was the context in which the national movement faced one blocked path after another. Each setback caused some measure of dissension regarding how to proceed. Beyond this, governmental powers sometimes acted to structure the Palestinian political field in ways that abetted fragmentation. For example, the British Mandate's treatment of Palestinian Arabs as Christians or Muslims emphasized religious cleavages at the expense of national integration. The government also enticed Arab elites through public appointments that set their private interests at odds with the collective goals of the national struggle that they were presumed to represent. Granting positions alternatively to the Husaynis and Nashashibis fed rivalries. These in turn trickled down to their allies and clients in the population at large.

When Palestinians turned to protest, both Britain and Israel typically responded with measures to subdue it. One recurrent measure was the arrest, if not deportation or killing, of national and local leaders. Such policies removed those spearheading rebellion but also fragmented the movement's organizational structure in ways that increased its use of violence. Upon the death or imprisonment of a leader, his faction or cell often splintered or became embroiled in internal power struggles. This tended to increase the autonomy of individuals and small groups that were capable of spoiling negotiations over a ceasefire or settlement. It also opened fissures that invited external intervention. Finally, it left the protest initiative to less experienced and disciplined aspirants. They were often more disposed to violence or lacked the organizational skills to mobilize nonviolent protest. In this context, governments sometimes found themselves wondering where "the moderates" had gone or why there was no "partner on the other side" with whom to negotiate peace.

Arab states likewise acted in ways that divided Palestinians. In control of the West Bank and Gaza Strip, Jordanian and Egyptian authorities prohibited independent Palestinian organizations. With the rise of the fedayeen, Arab regimes competed by funding rival Palestinian groups or creating their own proxies. This contributed to the proliferation of factions, subsidized their uncompromising ideological positions, and increased their operational autonomy. In this context, the national movement's official leadership did not impose a unifying strategy as much as negotiate contradictory interests in the search for minimally acceptable compromises. Upon occupying Palestinian territories in 1967, Israel implemented other strategies of divide and rule. Co-optation of traditional elites and new collaborators fueled social divisions. It set the acquiescence of some against the growing nationalist sensibilities of the many. Israel also contributed to rivalries among Palestinian political groups. In the 1980s, it allowed political space for the Muslim Brotherhood and then Hamas to serve as Islamist counterweights to the secular PLO. It would later reverse this position, backing Fateh as a counterweight to Hamas. During the peace process, Israel insisted that the PA suppress its opposition, even in the absence of the political concessions needed to weaken the opposition's appeal. This contradiction widened cracks in the Palestinian polity, and the PA responded by extending undemocratic institutions and norms of bad governance. This was the organizational structure that crumbled under pressure during the second Intifada.

This book cannot resolve the puzzle of whether repression ultimately increases or decreases protest. Yet it makes two contributions to advancing research to that end. It supplements models of strategic interaction between a movement and the state with systematic theorizing about strategic interaction internal to movements themselves. In addition, it shifts the locus of analysis from movements' motivations to their organizational structures. Often the scholarly debate turns on whether repression intensifies the grievances that induce protest or heightens the perceived costs that deter protest. Yet repression does not simply make protestors angry or wary. It also reshapes their relationships to each other. The organizational mediation theory of protest encourages analysts to examine how measures to counter rebellion affect the institutions and power dynamics that structure social or insurgent movements. This is crucial because state policies influence not only *why* a movement acts, but also *who* within the movement decides and to what effect on the decisions of others. Future research can pursue these issues by examining how different state policies have different effects on a movement's organizational structure and under what conditions the same policy might have divergent effects.

Conflict Resolution

The organizational mediation theory of protest also carries implications for theories of conflict resolution. I. William Zartman popularized the idea that protracted conflicts become "ripe" for settlement when circumstances lead warring parties to change their goals, strategies, or calculations.[6] Although scholars have subsequently enumerated a plethora of factors believed to promote ripeness,[7] they have also criticized the concept for being difficult to operationalize, if not ad hoc and tautological.[8] Analysts also critique research on ripeness for neglecting domestic politics and for emphasizing circumstances that affect both antagonists equally instead of considering how each may respond to different sets of factors.[9] I argue that another weakness of the literature on ripeness is its bias toward perception as an explanatory mechanism. It tends to attribute changes in conflict behavior to the notion that people adopt "new ways of thinking" about the utility of fighting. This leaves us to wonder about the organizational structures within which this thinking develops and is translated into action.

The organizational mediation theory offers clues. Throughout the history of the Palestinian national struggle, the circumstances of the overriding conflict with Zionism generated varying incentives to pursue a political settlement. The Palestinian movement was most "ripe" to do so, however, at those times in which it was cohesive due to an authoritative leadership, collective purpose among the population, and institutions capable of curtailing opposition. From the mid-1970s, mainstream leaders increasingly reasoned that it was in Palestinians' interests to endorse an independent state in the West Bank and Gaza Strip. Yet they proceeded only indirectly and inconsistently because autonomous factions threatened to obstruct such a course. Leaders were emboldened as those factions became marginal or subordinate. The more cohesive the national movement became, the less strategic concessions risked tearing it apart. Arafat's perception of domestic challenges undoubtedly helped impel him to embrace Oslo.[10] Nevertheless, his ability to launch the peace process and limit spoiler violence to the degree he did was testimony to the consolidation of politics under his control. Examples from the South African antiapartheid and Northern Ireland republican movements illustrate similar dynamics.

A movement's organizational structure is hence an essential factor shaping its transition from conflict to conflict resolution. An organizational mediation approach compensates for weaknesses in the application of the concept of ripeness because it can be operationalized. Also it shifts focus from actors' perceptions to the structure of their interactions. It focuses analytical attention on domestic politics within a party to conflict rather than simply the binary conflict between parties. It thus accounts for a general observation across cases of conflict. International and military factors are particularly important in motivating leaders to resolve territorial disputes. For challenger parties, however, the main *obstacle* to seeking a settlement tends to be domestic politics.[11]

In this sense, the organizational mediation theory sheds light on how the benchmark of ripeness for a nonstate group differs from that for a state. Due to the vulnerability to fragmentation inherent in statelessness, the former has fewer resources for imposing central decision making and restraining internal dissidents. This relationship between organizational structure and ripeness suggests new questions for research. How can international actors foster unity in a self-determination movement as a step toward conflict resolution? Does the cohesion that enables diplomacy rest equally upon the three elements of leadership, institutions, and collective purpose? If not, which is most important?

Institutions and Order

At the most general level, this book illuminates the components, character, and dynamics of political organization in weakly institutionalized settings.

It thus offers insight on a matter of relevance for nonstate groups and for weak or failed states: How does a community create and enforce "rules of the game" for the achievement of common goals when it not only lacks full sovereignty, but also is penetrated by external powers? Under the British Mandate, Palestinian leaders faced difficulties in building unifying structures because they both used and were used by the colonial power, even as they rebelled against it. The post-1948 diaspora-based movement managed to construct a transborder political project, though it was continually unsettled by rival interests from within and without. After 1993, the PA built an apparatus for self-government. Nevertheless, its institutions remained partial due to the absence of territorial control and a monopoly on coercion.

Palestinian history points to intriguing patterns in how stateless peoples confront the problem of collective action and with what implications. Under variously hostile regimes, Palestinians typically organized themselves with only minimal aid from formal institutions. Personal loyalties held together the small group of young refugees who founded Fateh. Though the PLO and PA later prescribed hierarchies and procedures, real power continued to flow through uncodified exchanges, relationships, and understandings. On the one hand, personal interactions appeared to take precedence over institutions in producing collective action. On the other hand, Palestinian politics may not have been anti-institutional as much as based on *informal* institutions, defined by Gretchen Helmke and Steven Levitsky as socially shared rules that are created, communicated, and enforced outside officially sanctioned channels.[12] The concept of informal institutions is useful for uncovering the incentives and constraints that underlie organizational structure but are neglected by researchers trained to look for formal rules and structures. If, as Helmke and Levitsky advocate, the study of informal institutions represents a cutting-edge research agenda for comparative politics, then the Palestinian case poses a question for future investigations: How do we distinguish between politics that is personalized (as opposed to institutionalized) and politics that functions through informal institutions (as opposed to formal ones)?

A related theme in this book is the relationship between institutions and leadership. In the Palestinian experience, leadership was critical for coordinating members of the national community in the absence of state sovereignty. Yet the biographies of Amin al-Husayni and Yasir Arafat also reveal the obstacles that leaders face in fulfilling this role. Both leaders made fateful choices in their efforts to straddle seemingly irreconcilable external and popular pressures; both arguably undermined long-term institution building by conflating the national cause with a personal interest in holding power.[13] These patterns suggest avenues for further research. How does the character of institutions in a polity shape the character of leadership, and vice versa? To what degree is leadership endogenous to institutions or exogenous? Under what conditions are leadership and institutions substitutes or complements in the processes of nation building and state building?

Cohesion and Social Structure

The organizational mediation approach encourages us to think about the relationship between political fragmentation, meaning the lack of coordination among actors producing unified political action, and social fragmentation, referring to the cleavages that divide a population. Regarding the Palestinian case, many argue that the latter is a main cause of the former. One scholar explains that Palestinians have not unified politically because "they have never overcome the drawbacks of the traditional Middle Eastern social structure as a 'mosaic system' of clannish, tribal, and ethnic in-groups."[14] This view holds weight among many in Israel. A retired Israeli general comments:

> The so-called Arab nations are not really nations. . . . For centuries, in every area there was a ruling family. Each one was like a feudal lord: he had the land and the people were loyal to him. Fragmentation is something very deep in the history of the Middle East. . . . Palestinians have developed this whole culture of fragmentation here in the Middle East into an art.[15]

This book tells a different story. Palestinians' family-based identities sometimes encumbered the institutionalization of politics. Yet they also made nationhood resilient in the face of enormous obstacles. Without a unitary territory or political system after 1948, families became the lynchpin of a social structure within which generations passed on a sense of being Palestinian and a commitment to recovering the lost homeland.[16] The particularistic loyalties that segmented Palestinians socially thus helped the far-flung diaspora keep the national struggle alive. Furthermore, when Palestinians' supra-local institutions broke down under repression, such as during the two Intifadas, many sought refuge in the social cohesion of their village, neighborhood, or clan. The retreat to local forms helped people coordinate and protect themselves until national cohesion could be rebuilt. This pattern challenges the notion that subnational social solidarities are necessarily at odds with national political unity. Rather, the former may bolster or supplement the latter. Future research can probe these relationships by asking under which conditions different kinds of social structure aid or inhibit cohesion in the organizational structure of self-determination movements.

Democratization and Centralization

A final empirical and theoretical concern that this book brings to light is the tension between democratization and centralization under weak institutions. In a state, ideological and organizational pluralism can assist the production of public goods by making citizens better informed, helping decision makers choose the best policies, and ensuring that checks and balances circumscribe the abuse of power. While pluralism can be similarly functional in nonstate groups, such communities face unique risks. Few barriers prevent a contest between political viewpoints from deteriorating into a free-for-all about the basic parameters of political engagement. The Palestinian national movement illustrates the dilemma of pluralism when rules are ambiguous and enforcement incomplete. Factionalism repeatedly hindered the coherence of strategy, yet also contributed to the movement's representativeness and legitimacy. Leaders' need to face domestic challengers created a measure of accountability, even when no elections or other such mechanisms forced them to answer to constituents.

Throughout Palestinian history, small factions resisted the centralization of authority on the charge that it upheld domination by the largest faction and silenced other voices. Unable to challenge Fateh's hegemony within the PLO, other groups frequently advanced their interests by using the most powerful means at their disposal: militant rhetoric and violence. At the same time, the PLO leadership sought to consolidate its power using the most powerful means at its disposal: neopatrimonial co-optation and decision making that circumvented procedures of deliberation and consultation. In this way, the organizational structure of the national movement was wrought by a contest between those who justified fragmentation in the name of democracy and those who justified autocracy in the name of cohesion. Similar contests unfolded in the relationship between the PA and Islamist opposition, as well as within the Fateh and Hamas movements. Future research can examine this friction between democratization and centralization, as well as its ramifications for movement strategy. Research in this direction can also consider how institutional design may resolve the imperatives of both cohesion and contestation.

LOOKING AHEAD

As the Palestinian national movement entered its tenth decade, its main internal split was that between Fateh and Hamas. On the margins of this rivalry, however, new divisions emerged. Rejection of Hamas's electoral victory in 2006 by the international community drove some in Gaza to join ultra-orthodox Salafi-Jihadi groups. This radical current, which some associate with al-Qaeda, had opposed Hamas's electoral bid on the argument that outsiders would never accept an Islamist victory. It grew in political force as events vindicated that prediction.[17] Journalist Khaled Amayreh warned, "Unlike Hamas, which in comparison looks like a group of boy scouts, Al-Qaeda-allied groups don't seek, or care, about popularity, and their actions are not influenced by public opinion."[18] In August 2009, a Salafi group critical of Hamas declared an Islamic emirate in southern Gaza. Hamas responded with a bloody crackdown that left two dozen people dead. In April 2011, other Salafists kidnapped and killed an Italian solidarity activist.

The emerging Salafi presence foretold an entirely new twist in the Palestinian experience with fragmentation and the relationship between fragmentation and violence. Palestinians had battled with factionalism for decades, but factions had always been attentive to popular opinion and the implicit parameters of a struggle for national liberation. Pursuit of political power and the claim to represent the Palestinian people had demanded deference to these two factors. Transnational Islamism, however, observed no such constraints. It therefore threatened a new breed of violence. This violence was not harrowing because it stemmed from fragmentation in the organizational structure of the Palestinian national movement. It was harrowing because it stemmed from an unprecedented fragmentation in Palestinians' loyalties between the national movement and another kind of movement altogether.

As this book has shown, it is within Palestinian society that impetuses to invigorate the unity of the self-determination struggle are recurrently born. In March 2011, thousands of Palestinians rallied on the streets of Ramallah and Gaza City to call for national reconciliation. The following month, Hamas and Fateh representatives announced a far-reaching resolution of their years-long standoff. The historic agreement was a bow to popular frustration with factionalism. In addition, it was a step by the national leadership to bolster its plan to make the case for independent statehood before the United Nations that autumn. Political leaders understood that the national movement had to manage its fragmentation if it were to carry forth with that nonviolent strategy. They had to entrench cohesion if they were to sustain nonviolent protest and keep violent protest at bay. Such cohesion would require Palestinians' continued building of leadership, institutions, and collective purpose in the population at large. It would also require external actors to set aside apprehensions in the understanding that resolution of the Arab–Israeli conflict is impossible without a strong and united Palestinian national movement.

Notes

Chapter 1. The Organizational Mediation Theory of Protest

1. Monty G. Marshall and Ted Robert Gurr, *Peace and Conflict, 2005: A Global Survey of Armed Conflicts, Self-Determination Movements and Democracy* (College Park, MD: Center for International Development and Conflict Management, 2005), 42.
2. Ibid., 21–23.
3. For just a few examples spanning different time periods, see Bard E. O'Neill, *Armed Struggle in Palestine: A Political-Military Analysis* (Boulder, CO: Westview Press, 1978); Issa Khalaf, *Politics in Palestine: Arab Factionalism and Social Disintegration, 1939–1948* (Albany: State University of New York Press, 1991); Rashid Khalidi, *Iron Cage: The Story of the Palestinian Struggle for Statehood* (Boston, MA: Beacon Press, 2006); Graham Usher, "Facing Defeat: The Intifada Two Years On," *Journal of Palestine Studies* 32, no. 2 (Winter 2003): 21–40.
4. Jeff Goodwin and James M. Jasper, "Introduction," in *The Social Movements Reader: Cases and Concepts*, eds. Jeff Goodwin and James M. Jasper (Malden, MA: Blackwell, 2008), 3.
5. Gene Sharp, *The Politics of Nonviolent Action* (Boston, MA: Porter Sargent, 1973).
6. Doug McAdam, John D. McCarthy, and Mayer N. Zald, "Introduction," in *Comparative Perspectives on Social Movements*, eds. Doug McAdam, John D. McCarthy, and Mayer N. Zald (Cambridge: Cambridge University Press, 1996), 1–20.
7. Jeff Goodwin and James M. Jasper, "Caught in a Winding, Snarling Vine: The Structural Bias of Political Process Theory," *Sociological Forum* 14, no. 1 (March 1999): 27–53.
8. See Carol McClurg Mueller, "Building Social Movement Theory," in *Frontiers in Social Movement Theory*, eds. Aldon D. Morris and Carol McClurg Mueller (New Haven, CT: Yale University Press, 1992), 18–19.
9. Goodwin and Jasper, "Winding, Snarling Vine," 41.
10. Anthony Oberschall, *Social Conflict and Social Movements* (Englewood Cliffs, NJ: Prentice Hall, 1973); William A. Gamson, *Strategy of Social Protest* (Homewood, IL: Dorsey, 1975); James DeNardo, *Power in Numbers: The Political Strategy of Protest and Rebellion* (Princeton, NJ: Princeton University Press, 1985).

11. Charles Tilly, *From Mobilization to Revolution* (Englewood Cliffs, NJ: Prentice Hall, 1978); Frances Fox Piven and Richard A. Cloward, *Poor People's Movements: Why They Succeed, How They Fail* (New York: Vintage, 1979).

12. Sharp, *Nonviolent Action*, 16.

13. Martha Crenshaw, "The Causes of Terrorism," *Comparative Politics* 13, no. 4 (July 1981): 379–399; Martha Crenshaw, "The Logic of Terrorism: Terrorist Behavior as a Product of Strategic Choice," in *Origins of Terrorism*, ed. Walter Reich (Washington, DC: Woodrow Wilson Center Press, 1990), 7–24.

14. Robert A. Pape, "The Strategic Logic of Suicide Terrorism," *American Political Science Review* 97, no. 3 (August 2003): 343–361.

15. See Johan L. Olivier, "State Repression and Collective Action in South Africa, 1970–84," *South African Journal of Sociology* 22, no. 4 (December 1991): 109–117; Robert W. White, "From Peaceful Protest to Guerilla War: Micromobilization of the Provisional Irish Republican Army," *American Journal of Sociology* 94, no. 6 (May 1989): 1277–1302; Marwan Khawaja, "Resource Mobilization, Hardship, and Popular Collective Action in the West Bank," *Social Forces* 73, no. 1 (September 1993): 191–220; Donatella della Porta, *Social Movements, Political Violence, and the State: A Comparative Analysis of Italy and Germany* (Cambridge: Cambridge University Press, 1995).

16. Christian Davenport, "Introduction – Repression and Mobilization: Insights from Political Science and Sociology," in *Repression and Mobilization*, eds. Christian Davenport, Hank Johnston, and Carol Mueller (Minneapolis: University of Minnesota Press, 2005), vii–xli.

17. Mark Irving Lichbach, *The Rebel's Dilemma* (Ann Arbor: University of Michigan Press, 1998).

18. T. David Mason, *Caught in the Crossfire: Revolutions, Repression, and the Rational Peasant* (New York: Rowman and Littlefield, 2004); Nicholas Sambanis and Annalisa Zinn, "From Protest to Violence: Conflict Escalation in Self-Determination Movements" (Unpublished manuscript, Yale University, 2006).

19. Karen Rasler, "Concessions, Repression, and Political Protest in the Iranian Revolution," *American Sociological Review* 6, no. 1 (February 1996): 132–152.

20. Charles Tilly, *Popular Contention in Great Britain, 1758–1834* (Cambridge, MA: Harvard University Press, 1998); Doug McAdam, "Culture and Social Movements," in *Culture and Politics: A Reader*, eds. Lane Crothers and Charles Lockhart (New York: Macmillan, 2000), 253–268.

21. David Brooks, "The Culture of Martyrdom," *Atlantic*, June 2002.

22. Ghassan Hage, "'Comes a Time We Are All Enthusiasm': Understanding Palestinian Suicide Bombers in Times of Exighophobia," *Public Culture* 15, no. 1 (2003): 65–89; Christoph Reuter, *My Life Is a Weapon: A Modern History of Suicide Bombing*, trans. Helena Ragg-Kirkby (Princeton, NJ: Princeton University Press, 2004).

23. Robert Benford and David Snow, "Ideology, Frame Resonance, and Participant Mobilization," *International Social Movement Research* 1 (1988): 197–218; James Jasper, *The Art of Moral Protest: Culture, Biography, and Creativity in Social Movements* (Chicago, IL: University of Chicago Press, 1997); Doug McAdam, Sidney Tarrow, and Charles Tilly, *Dynamics of Contention* (Cambridge: Cambridge University Press, 2001).

24. See Mary E. King, *Mahatma Gandhi, and Martin Luther King, Jr., The Power of Nonviolent Action* (Paris: UNESCO, 1999).

25. V. P. Gagnon, Jr., "Ethnic Nationalism and International Conflict: The Case of Serbia," *International Security* 19, no. 3 (Winter 1994–1995): 130–166; Russell Hardin, *One for All: The Logic of Group Conflict* (Princeton, NJ: Princeton University Press, 1995); Jack Snyder, *From Voting to Violence: Democratization and Nationalist Conflict* (New York: W. W. Norton, 2000).

26. Sidney Tarrow, *Power in Movement: Social Movements, Collective Action, and Politics* (Cambridge: Cambridge University Press, 1994), chap. 9.

27. Doug McAdam and William H. Sewell, Jr., "It's about Time: Temporality in the Study of Social Movements and Revolutions," in *Silence and Voice in the Study of Contentious Politics*, eds. Ronald Aminzade, et al. (Cambridge: Cambridge University Press, 2001), 89–125.

28. Lichbach, *Rebel's Dilemma*, 19.

29. Alvin Rabushka and Kenneth Shepsle, *Politics in Plural Societies* (Columbus, OH: Charles E. Merrill, 1972); Donald L. Horowitz, *Ethnic Groups in Conflict* (Berkeley: University of California Press, 2000).

30. Martha Crenshaw, "Theories of Terrorism: Instrumental and Organizational Approaches," in *Inside Terrorist Organizations*, ed. David C. Rapoport (New York: Columbia University Press, 1988), 13–31.

31. Stephen John Stedman, "Spoiler Problems in Peace Processes," *International Security* 22, no. 2 (Fall 1997): 5–53.

32. Stathis Kalyvas, "The Ontology of 'Political Violence': Action and Identity in Civil Wars," *Perspectives on Politics* 1, no. 3 (September 2003): 475–494.

33. See Rui De Figueiredo and Barry R. Weingast, *Vicious Cycles: Endogenous Political Extremism and Political Violence* (Unpublished manuscript, University of California, Berkeley, 2001); Andrew Kydd and Barbara F. Walter, "Sabotaging the Peace: The Politics of Extremist Violence," *International Organizations* 56, no. 2 (Spring 2002): 263–296; Assaf Moghadam, "Palestinian Suicide Terrorism in the Second Intifada: Motivations and Organizational Aspects," *Studies in Conflict and Terrorism*, 26 (March 2003): 65–92; Mia M. Bloom, "Palestinian Suicide Bombing: Popular Support, Market Share, and Outbidding," *Political Science Quarterly* 119 (Winter 2004): 61–88; Ethan Bueno de Mesquita, "Conciliation, Counterterrorism, and Patterns of Terrorist Violence," *International Organization* 59, no. 1 (Winter 2005): 145–176.

34. Tilly, *Mobilization to Revolution*, 156.

35. Jeremy Weinstein, *Inside Rebellion: The Politics of Insurgent Violence* (Cambridge: Cambridge University Press, 2007).

36. See, respectively, Giovanni Sartori, *Parties and Party Systems: A Framework for Analysis* (Cambridge: Cambridge University Press, 1976); Alberto Alesina and Howard Rosenthal, *Partisan Politics, Divided Governments and the Economy* (Cambridge: Cambridge University Press, 1995); and Daniel Posner, "Measuring Ethnic Fractionalization in Africa," *American Journal of Political Science* 48, no. 4 (October 2004): 849–863.

37. Max Weber, "Politics as a Vocation," in *From Max Weber: Essays in Sociology*, eds. H. H. Gerth and C. Wright Mills (New York: Oxford University Press, 1958), 78.

38. See Seymour M. Lipset and Stein Rokkan, eds., *Party Systems and Voter Alignments* (New York: Free Press, 1967).

39. Anders E. Carlsson, "Cohesion (Physics)," in *McGraw-Hill Encyclopedia of Science and Technology*, vol. 4, 8th ed. (New York: McGraw-Hill, 1997), 141–144.

40. Richard McKelvey, "Intransitivities in Multidimensional Voting Models and Some Implications for Agenda Control," *Journal of Economic Theory* 12, no. 3 (June 1976): 472–482.
41. William H. Riker, "Implications from the Disequilibrium of Majority Rule for the Study of Institutions," *American Political Science Review* 74, no. 2 (June 1980): 432–446.
42. Gary W. Cox and Kenneth A. Shepsle, "Majority Cycling and Agenda Manipulation: Richard McKelvey's Contributions and Legacy," in *Positive Changes in Political Science: The Legacy of Richard McKelvey's Most Influential Writings*, eds. John H. Aldrich, James E. Alt, and Arthur Lupia (Ann Arbor: University of Michigan Press, 2007), 35.
43. John W. Gardner, *On Leadership* (New York: Free Press, 1993), 1.
44. Riker, "Implications," 443–445.
45. Douglass C. North, *Institutions, Institutional Change and Economic Performance* (Cambridge: Cambridge University Press, 1990).
46. Samuel P. Huntington, *Political Order in Changing Societies* (New Haven, CT: Yale University Press, 1968), 12, 13–24.
47. Riker, "Implications," 443.
48. Kurt Schock, *Unarmed Insurrections: People Power Movements in Nondemocracies* (Minneapolis: University of Minnesota Press, 2005), 52.
49. Peter Ackerman and Christopher Kruegler, "The Principles of Strategic Nonviolent Conflict," in *Strategic Nonviolent Conflict: Dynamics of People Power in the Twentieth Century*, eds. Peter Ackerman and Christopher Kruegler (Westport, CT: Praeger, 1994), 21–53.
50. Aldon D. Morris, *The Origins of the Civil Rights Movement: Black Communities Organizing for Change* (New York: Free Press, 1984).
51. Doug McAdam, "Tactical Innovation and the Pace of Insurgency," *American Sociological Review* 48, no. 6 (December 1983): 735–754.
52. See Constâncio Pinto and Matthew Jardine, *East Timor's Unfinished Struggle: Inside the Timorese Resistance* (Cambridge, MA: South End Press, 1997).
53. Maria Stephan, "Nonviolent Insurgency: The Role of Civilian-Based Resistance in the East Timorese, Palestinian, and Kosovo Albanian Self-Determination Struggles" (Ph.D. dissertation, Tufts University, 2005).
54. Della Porta, *Social Movements*, 107.
55. Fawaz Gerges, *America and Political Islam: Clash of Cultures or Clash of Interests?* (Cambridge: Cambridge University Press, 1999), 65.
56. See discussion in James Fearon and David Laitin, "Violence and the Social Construction of Ethnic Identity," *International Organization* 54, no. 4 (Autumn 2000): 845–877.
57. International Crisis Group, "Iraq's Muqtada al-Sadr: Spoiler or Stabiliser?" *Middle East Report* 55 (Amman/Brussels, July 2006): 9–10.
58. Otto Kirchheimer, "The Transformation of Western European Party Systems," in *Political Parties and Political Development*, eds. Joseph LaPalombara and Myron Weiner (Princeton, NJ: Princeton University Press, 1966), 177–200.
59. Albert O. Hirschman, *Exit, Voice, and Loyalty: Responses to Decline in Firms, Organizations, and States* (Cambridge, MA: Harvard University Press, 1970); also see Crenshaw, "Theories of Terrorism," 22–23.
60. Lewis Coser, *The Functions of Social Conflict* (New York: Free Press, 1956), 133.

61. John Darby, *The Effects of Violence on Peace Processes* (Washington, DC: United States Institute for Peace, 2001), 8.
62. I am grateful to Hendrik Spruyt for this point.
63. Robert D. Putnam, "Diplomacy and Domestic Politics: The Logic of Two-Level Games," *International Organization* 42, no. 3 (Summer 1988): 427–460.
64. Lichbach, *Rebel's Dilemma*, 205.
65. Samir Khalaf, *Civil and Uncivil Violence in Lebanon: A History of the Internationalization of Communal Conflict* (New York: Columbia University Press, 2002).
66. Theodore McLauchlin and Wendy Pearlman, "Out-group Conflict, In-group Unity? Exploring the Effect of Repression on Movement Fragmentation," *Journal of Conflict Resolution*, forthcoming.
67. Shah M. Tarzi, "Politics of the Afghan Resistance Movement: Cleavages, Disunity, and Fragmentation," *Asian Survey* 31, no. 6 (June 1991): 479–495.
68. See Frank Mark Osanka, ed., *Modern Guerrilla Warfare* (New York: Free Press of Glencoe, 1962); Bard E. O'Neill, William R. Heaton, and Donald J. Alberts, *Insurgency in the Modern World* (Boulder, CO: Westview Press, 1980).
69. Lichbach, *Rebel's Dilemma*, 16–19.
70. Della Porta, *Social Movements*, 107.
71. Frantz Fanon, *Wretched of the Earth* (New York: Grove Press, 1963), 93–94.
72. Karl W. Deutsch, *Tides Among Nations* (New York: Free Press, 1979), chap. 15.
73. See, respectively, George Simmel, *Conflict and the Web of Group-Affiliations* (New York: Free Press, 1955); and Michael Stohl, "The Nexus of Civil and International Conflict," in *Handbook of Political Conflict: Theory and Research*, ed. Ted Robert Gurr (New York: Free Press, 1980), 297–330.
74. Coser, *Social Conflict*, 92.
75. Nayef Hawatmeh, in *Palestinian Lives: Interviews with Leaders of the Resistance*, ed. Clovis Maksoud (Beirut: Palestine Research Center and Kuwaiti Teachers' Association, 1973), 83.
76. Alexander L. George and Andrew Bennett, *Case Studies and Theory Development in the Social Sciences* (Cambridge, MA: MIT Press, 2005), 22–25.
77. Peter Hall, "Aligning Ontology and Methodology in Comparative Research," in *Comparative Historical Analysis in the Social Sciences*, eds. James Mahoney and Dietrich Rueschemeyer (Cambridge: Cambridge University Press, 2003), 373–404.
78. Charles Tilly, "Mechanisms in Political Processes," *Annual Review of Political Science* 4 (2001): 21–41.
79. Donald T. Campbell, "'Degrees of Freedom' and the Case Study," *Comparative Political Studies* 8, no. 2 (July 1975): 178–193.
80. John Gerring, "What Is a Case Study and What Is It Good for?" *American Political Science Review* 98, no. 2 (May 2004): 341–354.
81. Stephen Van Evera, *Guide to Methods for Students of Political Science* (Ithaca, NY: Cornell University Press, 1997), 77–78.
82. Schock, *Unarmed Insurrections*, 171.
83. Charles Tilly, *The Politics of Collective Violence* (Cambridge: Cambridge University Press, 2003).
84. James DeNardo, *Power in Numbers: The Political Strategy of Protest and Rebellion* (Princeton, NJ: Princeton University Press, 1985), 262–263.

85. Rogers Brubaker and David Laitin, "Ethnic and Nationalist Violence," *Annual Review of Sociology* 24 (1998): 426.
86. Stathis N. Kalyvas, *The Logic of Violence in Civil War* (Cambridge: Cambridge University Press, 2006).

Chapter 2. National Struggle under the British Mandate, 1918–1948

1. See Rashid Khalidi, *Palestinian Identity: The Construction of Modern National Consciousness* (New York: Columbia University Press, 1997).
2. Neville J. Mandel, *The Arabs and Zionism before World War I* (Berkeley: University of California Press, 1976), xxiv.
3. Ibid., chap. 2.
4. Ibid., 226.
5. Ann Mosely Lesch, *Arab Politics in Palestine, 1917–1939: The Frustration of a Nationalist Movement* (Ithaca, NY: Cornell University, 1977), 126.
6. Yehoshua Porath, *The Palestinian–Arab National Movement, from Riots to Rebellion, 1929–1939* (London: Frank Cass, 1977), 130.
7. Aziz Shehadeh, *A.B.C. of the Arab Case in Palestine* (Jaffa: Modern Library and Stationery Store, 1936), 34.
8. See Albert Hourani, "Ottoman Reform and the Politics of the Notables," in *Beginnings of Modernization in the Middle East*, eds. William R. Polk and Richard L. Chambers (Chicago, IL: University of Chicago Press, 1968), 41–68.
9. Muhammad Y. Muslih, *The Origins of Palestinian Nationalism* (New York: Columbia University Press, 1989), 156.
10. Ibid., chap. 7.
11. Porath, *Riots to Rebellion*, 127; Muslih, *Origins*, 206.
12. Lesch, *Arab Politics*, 93.
13. Bayan Nuweihid al-Hout, "The Palestinian Political Elite During the Mandate Period," *Journal of Palestine Studies* 9, no. 1 (Autumn 1979): 91.
14. See Lesch, *Arab Politics*, chap. 4.
15. Yehoshua Porath, "The Political Organization of the Palestinian Arabs under the British Mandate," in *Palestinian Arab Politics*, ed. Moshe Ma'oz (Jerusalem: Jerusalem Academic Press, 1975), 10.
16. Cited in David Horowitz and Rita Hinden, *Economic Survey of Palestine, with Special Reference to the Years 1936 and 1937* (Tel Aviv: Economic Research Institute of the Jewish Agency for Palestine, 1938), 204; also see *Government of Palestine Report of Committee on the Economic Condition of Agriculturalists in Palestine and the Fiscal Measures of Government in Relation Thereto*, April 22, 1930; "Extract from Official Gazette no. 258," May 1, 1930, 40–46, Israel State Archives [hereafter cited as ISA], March 7, 1913; J. C. Hurewitz, *The Struggle for Palestine* (New York: Schocken Books, 1976), 32–33.
17. See Salim Tamari, "Factionalism and Class Formation in Recent Palestinian History," in *Studies in the Economic and Social History of Palestine in the Nineteenth and Twentieth Centuries*, ed. Roger Owen (Carbondale, IL: Southern Illinois University Press, 1982), 188–200.
18. Lesch, *Arab Politics*, 60.
19. Khaled al-Hassan, in *Palestinian Lives*, 28.
20. Aaron S. Klieman, "Introduction," in *The Rise of Israel: The Turn Toward Violence, 1920–1929*, ed. Aaron S. Klieman, vol. 18 (New York: Garland, 1987), i.

21. Great Britain, Cmd. 5479, *Report of Palestine Royal Commission ... Peel, Chairman*, in *Political Diaries*, vol. 3 [hereafter cited as *Peel Report*] (London: His Majesty's Stationery Office [hereafter cited as HMSO], 1937), 50.
22. Great Britain, Cmd. 1540, *Palestine Disturbances in May 1921: Reports of the Commission of Inquiry ... Haycraft, Chairman* [hereafter cited as *Haycraft Report*] (London: HMSO, 1921).
23. See Guilain Denoeux, *Urban Unrest in the Middle East: A Comparative Study of Informal Networks in Egypt, Iran, and Lebanon* (Albany: State University of New York Press, 1993).
24. See Yehoshua Porath, *The Emergence of the Palestinian–Arab National Movement, 1918–1929* (London: Frank Cass, 1974), 98.
25. *Peel Report*, 51.
26. Porath, *Emergence*, 131; Lesch, *Arab Politics*, 205–207.
27. *Haycraft Report*, 4.
28. Porath, *Emergence*, 134.
29. Ibid., 101, 213–214; Lesch, *Arab Politics*, 89–90.
30. Khalidi, *Iron Cage*, chap. 2.
31. Cited in Hurewitz, *Struggle*, 52.
32. See Ylana Miller, *Government and Society in Rural Palestine, 1920–1948* (Austin: University of Texas Press, 1985).
33. Khalidi, *Iron Cage*, 85.
34. Great Britain, *The Political History of Palestine under British Administration: Memorandum by His Britannic Majesty's Government presented in July, 1947 to the United Nations Special Committee on Palestine* (Jerusalem, 1947), 8.
35. Great Britain, "Testimony of Mr. E. Mills, Commissioner for Migration and Statistics," in *Palestine Royal Commission: Minutes of Evidence Heard at Public Session*, Colonial no. 134 (London: HMSO, 1937) 9, ISA (Chief Secretary's Office), 2/M/4394; Don Peretz, "Palestinian Social Stratification: The Political Implications," in *The Palestinians and the Middle East Conflict: Studies in Their History, Sociology, and Politics*, ed. Gabriel Ben-Dor (Ramat Gan: Turtledove, 1978), 407.
36. Ilan Pappé, "Historical Features: Haj Amin and the Buraq Revolt," *Jerusalem Quarterly File* 6, no. 18 (June 2003): 11; also see Elia T. Zureik, "Reflections on Twentieth-Century Palestinian Class Structure," in *The Sociology of the Palestinians*, eds. Khalil Nakhleh and Elia Zureik (London: Croom Helm, 1980), 47–63.
37. Lesch, *Arab Politics*, 98, 103.
38. Porath, *Emergence*, 256–257.
39. Great Britain, Cmd 3530, *Report of the Commission on the Palestine Disturbances of August, 1929* [hereafter cited as *Shaw Report*] (London: HMSO, 1930).
40. See Philip Mattar, *The Mufti of Jerusalem: Al-Haj Amin al-Husayni and the Palestinian National Movement* (New York: Columbia University Press, 1988); Zvi Elpeleg, *The Grand Mufti: Haj Amin al-Hussaini, Founder of the Palestinian National Movement* (London: Frank Cass, 1993); Pappé, "Buraq Revolt."
41. Lesch, *Arab Politics*, 210.
42. *Shaw Report*, 54–55; Lesch, *Arab Politics*, 210.
43. *Shaw Report*, 81.
44. Mattar, *Mufti*, 46–49.
45. Cited in Pappé, "Buraq Revolt," 16.

46. *Shaw Report*, 77.

47. Ibid., 76. An alternative interpretation attributes this regional variation to security preparations. See Martin Kolinksy, *Law, Order and Riots in Mandatory Palestine, 1928–35* (London: Macmillan Press, 1993), 76–77.

48. Pappé, "Buraq Revolt," 16.

49. *Shaw Report*, 59, 80–81.

50. Ibid., 66–67.

51. Nels Johnson, *Islam and the Politics of Meaning in Palestinian Nationalism* (London: Kegan Paul International, 1982), 37–38.

52. Mattar, *Mufti*, 121–122.

53. Lesch, *Arab Politics*, chaps. 4, 5.

54. See *Political History of Palestine*, 7; Baruch Kimmerling and Joel Migdal, *The Palestinian People: A History* (Cambridge, MA: Harvard University Press, 2003), 46–54.

55. See "Testimony of Mr. H. E. Bowman, C.M.G., C.B.E.," in *Palestine Royal Commission: Minutes of Evidence Heard at Public Session*, Colonial no. 134 (London: HMSO, 1937), 48, ISA (Chief Secretary's Office), 2/M/4394; "Testimony of Dr. Khalil Totah," in *Palestine Royal Commission: Minutes of Evidence Heard at Public Session*, Colonial no. 134 (London: HMSO, 1937), 352–355; Ghassan Kanafani, *Thawrat 36–39 fi Fillastin* [The Rebellion of 1936–1939] (Jerusalem: Abu Arifa Press Agency, n.d.), 38–39.

56. Adnan Abu-Ghazaleh, *Arab Cultural Nationalism in Palestine* (Beirut: Institute for Palestine Studies, 1973), 50–51.

57. Miller, *Government and Society*, chap. 6.

58. Benedict Anderson, *Imagined Communities: Reflections on the Origin and Spread of Nationalism* (London: Verso, 1991).

59. Kanafani, *Thawrat 36–39*, 38–62; Abu-Ghazaleh, *Arab Cultural Nationalism*, 98–99; Mustafa Kabha, *The Palestinian Press as Shaper of Public Opinion, 1929–39: Writing up a Storm* (London: Vallentine Mitchell, 2007).

60. Doug McAdam, *Political Process and the Development of Black Insurgency, 1930–1970*, 2d ed. (Chicago, IL: University of Chicago Press, 1999).

61. Lesch, *Arab Politics*, 61–64, 106–108; Weldon C. Matthews, *Confronting an Empire, Constructing a Nation: Arab Nationalists and Popular Politics in Mandate Palestine* (London: I. B. Tauris, 2006), chaps. 3, 4.

62. "Testimony of Awni Bey Abdelhadi," in *Palestine Royal Commission: Minutes of Evidence Heard at Public Session*, Colonial no. 134 (London: HMSO, 1937), 305; "Testimony of Mr. George Antonius," in *Palestine Royal Commission: Minutes of Evidence Heard at Public Session*, Colonial no. 134 (London: HMSO, 1937), 360–363, ISA (Chief Secretary's Office), 2/M/4394.

63. Kenneth Stein, *The Land Question in Palestine, 1917–1939* (Chapel Hill: University of North Carolina Press, 1984), chaps. 3, 5.

64. See Matthews, *Confronting an Empire*, 69–71, 171–180.

65. See Porath, *Emergence*, 79, 129.

66. *Peel Report*, 94.

67. Kanafani, *Thawrat 36–39*, 70.

68. "Protests Against Composition of the Arab Delegation to London (April 1936)," ISA (Chief Secretary's Office), 2/M-295/17; 2.11/1–74; Porath, *Riots to Rebellion*, 157–158.

69. Lesch, *Arab Politics*, 217.

70. Akram Zu'aytir, *Yawmiyat Akram Zu'aytir: al-harakah al-wataniyah al-Filastiniyah, 1935–1939* [Diary of Akram Zu'aytir: the Palestinian national struggle, 1935–1939] (Beirut: Institute of Palestine Studies, 1980), 60–61.

71. Ibid., 61.

72. Porath, *Riots to Rebellion*, 164–165.

73. For support of this view, see Antonius, *Arab Awakening*, 405–407; Subhi Yasin, *al-Thawrah al-'Arabiyah al-kubra fi Filastin, 1936–1939* [The Great Arab Revolt in Palestine, 1936–1939] (Damascus: Dar al-Hind, 1961), 22; Taysir Jebarah, *Palestinian Leader, Haj Amin al-Husayni, Mufti of Jerusalem* (Princeton, NJ: Kingston Press, 1985); Yehuda Taggar, *The Mufti of Jerusalem and Palestine Arab Politics, 1930–1937* (New York: Garland, 1986); Mattar, *Mufti*; Muhammad 'Izzat Darwazah, *Mudhakkirat Muhammad 'Izzat Darwazah, 1305 H–1404/1887 M–1984: sijill hafil bi-masirat al-harakah al-'Arabiyah wa al-qadiyah al-Filastiniyah khilala qarn min al-zaman* [Autobiography of Muhammad 'Izzat Darwazah: registrations alongside Arab movements and the Palestinian cause over a century of history], vol. 2 (Beirut: Dar al-Gharb al-Islami, 1993), 17.

74. Robert John and Sami Hadawi, *The Palestine Diary*, vol. 1 (Beirut: Palestine Research Center, 1970), 259.

75. For details, see Porath, *Riots to Rebellion*, 166–173; Darwazah, *Mudhakkirat*, vol. 2, 20–22.

76. Kabha, *Palestinian Press*, chap. 4.

77. "Official Communiqué No. 126/36, June 1936," in *Palestine Riots Official Communiqués* (Jerusalem: Chief Secretary's Office, 1936), ISA (Chief Secretary's Office), 2/M-566/6.

78. Zu'aytir, *Yawmiyat*, 98.

79. See "Official Communiqué No. 36/36, May 5, 1936," in *Palestine Riots Official Communiqués* (Jerusalem: Chief Secretary's Office, 1936); "Report of the High Commissioner's Meeting with AHC Members," ISA (Chief Secretary's Office), 2/M-566/6.

80. Zu'aytir, *Yawmiyat*, 60.

81. For examples, see ibid., 71.

82. Darwazah, *Mudhakkirat*, 52.

83. Zu'aytir, *Yawmiyat*, 611.

84. Ibid., 82–83.

85. Ibid., 92; Darwazah, *Mudhakkirat*, vol. 2, 48.

86. Zu'aytir *Yawmiyat*, 82.

87. Yasin, *al-Thawrah al-'Arabiyah*, 22.

88. Zu'aytir, *Yawmiyat*, 78–80.

89. Tamari, "Factionalism," 192.

90. John and Hadawi, *Palestine Diary*, 260.

91. "Official Communiqué 83/36, May 31, 1936," ISA (Chief Secretary's Office), 2/M-567/3.

92. "Secret Despatch from the High Commissioner for Palestine to the Secretary of State for the Colonies, August 22, 1936," in *Political Diaries of the Arab World: Palestine and Jordan*, ed. Robert L. Jarman, vol. 2 (Cambridge: Cambridge Archive Editions, 2001), 657.

93. "Comments by High Commissioner on Air Marshal Peirse's Secret Memorandum of August 20, 1936," in *Political Diaries*, vol. 2, 665; also see Darwazah, *Mudhakkirat*, vol. 2, 85.

94. See John and Hadawi, *Palestine Diary*, 260–262.

95. Matthew Hughes, "From Law and Order to Pacification: Britain's Suppression of the Arab Revolt in Palestine, 1936–39," *Journal of Palestine Studies* 39, no. 2 (Winter 2010): 10.

96. Yuval Arnon-Ohanna, "The Bands in the Palestinian Arab Revolt, 1936–1939: Structure and Organization," *Asian and African Studies* 15, no. 2 (July 1981): 230–233.

97. Ibid., 233; Porath, *Riots to Rebellion*, 182.

98. Arnon-Ohana, "Bands," 229.

99. See "Secret Despatch from the High Commissioner for Palestine, September 12, 1936," in *Political Diaries*, vol. 2, 671; Taggar, *Mufti of Jerusalem*, 391; Darwazah, *Mudhakkirat*, vol. 2, 246.

100. Taggar, *Mufti of Jerusalem*, 391.

101. Fawzi Qawuqji, *Filastin fi mudhakkirat al-Qawuqji* [Palestine in Qawuqji's memoirs], vol. 2 (Beirut: Palestine Liberation Organization Research Center and Dar al-Quds, 1970), 22, 27, 32.

102. Porath, *Riots to Rebellion*, 191–192.

103. Qawuqji, *Filastin*, 29; also Darwazah, *Mudhakkirat*, vol. 2, 133.

104. Porath, *Riots to Rebellion*, 191–193; Arnon-Ohana, "Bands," 235–236.

105. *Times* (London), September 5, 1936; *Times* (London), September 7, 1936; *Times* (London), September 9, 1936, ISA (George Antonius files), P-65/325/5–65.4/1–6.

106. Darwazah, *Mudhakkirat*, vol. 2, 237, 240.

107. Official Communiqué 287/36, October 13, 1936; Official Communiqué 288/36, October 14, 1936; Official Communiqué 289/36, October 15, 1936, ISA (Chief Secretary's Office), M-567/4.

108. Darwazah, *Mudhakkirat*, vol. 2, 242.

109. Qawuqji, *Filastin*, 52–53.

110. Porath, *Riots to Rebellion*, 215–225.

111. Cited in Lesch, *Arab Politics*, 121.

112. See Hughes, "Pacification."

113. Mustafa Dawud Kabha, *Thawrat 1936 al-kubra, dawafi'uha wa in'ikasatuha* [The Great Revolt of 1936: impetuses and implications] (Nazareth: Maktabat al-Qabas, 1988), 99.

114. Darwazah, *Mudhakkirat*, vol. 3, 37.

115. See Royal Institute of International Affairs Information Department Papers, *Great Britain and Palestine, 1915–1939*, no. 20A (London: Royal Institute of International Affairs, 1939), 104; Hughes, "Pacification."

116. Tom Segev, *One Palestine, Complete: Jews and Arabs under the British Mandate*, trans. Haim Watzman (New York: Owl Books, 2001), 417.

117. Matthew Hughes, "The Practice and Theory of British Counter-insurgency: The Histories of the Atrocities at the Palestinian Village of al-Bassa and Halhul, 1938–39," *Small Wars and Insurgencies* 20, no. 3 (September 2009): 528–550.

118. "H MacMichael, High Commissioner for Palestine, Jerusalem, to Rt. Hon W. Ormsby-Gore, Secretary of State for the Colonies, April 14, 1938," in *Political Diaries*, vol. 3, 171.

119. Porath, *Riots to Rebellion*, 243–245.

120. See W. F. Abboushi, "The Road to Rebellion: Arab Palestine in the 1930's," *Journal of Palestine Studies* 6, no. 3 (Spring 1977): 44.

121. May Seikali, *Haifa: Transformation of a Palestinian Arab Society, 1918–1939* (London: I. B. Tauris, 1995), 253.

122. "District Commissioner's Office, Southern District, Jaffa, Monthly Report for the Month of September 1938, Dated October 8, 1938," in *Political Diaries*, vol. 3, 346; also see Government of Palestine, *A Survey of Palestine: Prepared for the Information of the Anglo-American Committee of Inquiry*, vol. 1 (Jerusalem: Government of Palestine, 1946), 44–45.

123. "Officer Administering the Government, Jerusalem to Rt. Hon W. Ormsby-Gore, Secretary of State for the Colonies, October 14, 1937," in *Political Diaries*, vol. 3, 18.

124. See "Secret Despatch from the High Commissioner for Palestine to the Secretary of State for the Colonies, August 22, 1936," in *Political Diaries*, vol. 2, 657; Lesch *Arab Politics*, 219.

125. Kimmerling and Migdal, *Palestinian People*, 116.

126. Report by General Robert Haining, August 30, 1938, cited in Lesch, *Arab Politics*, 223.

127. "H MacMichael, High Commissioner for Palestine, Jerusalem, to Rt. Hon W. Ormsby-Gore, Secretary of State for the Colonies, January 16, 1939," in *Political Diaries*, vol. 3, 318.

128. See Great Britain, Colonial no. 129, *Report by His Majesty's Government in the United Kingdom of Great Britain and Northern Ireland to the Council of the League of Nations on the Administration of Palestine and Trans-Jordan for the Year 1936* (London: HMSO, 1937), 19; Colonial no. 166, *Report … for the year 1938* (London: HMSO, 1939), 20.

129. Walid Khalidi, ed., *From Haven to Conquest: The Origins and the Development of the Palestine Problem* (Beirut: Institute for Palestine Studies, 1971), 848–849.

130. "H MacMichael, High Commissioner for Palestine, Jerusalem, to Rt. Hon W. Ormsby-Gore, Secretary of State for the Colonies, April 14, 1938," in *Political Diaries*, vol. 3, 170.

131. Porath, *Riots to Rebellion*, 249.

132. "District Commissioner's Offices, Haifa District, October 10, 1938, Two Extracts from Monthly Report for September 1938," in *Political Diaries*, vol. 3, 378.

133. See Mattar, *Mufti*.

134. Darwazah, *Mudhakkirat*, vol. 3, 116.

135. Ibid., 115.

136. Zu'aytir, *Yawmiyat*, 611.

137. See Ted Swedenburg, *Memories of Revolt: The 1936–39 Rebellion and the Palestinian National Past* (Minneapolis: University of Minnesota Press, 1995).

138. Tom Bowden, "The Politics of the Arab Rebellion in Palestine, 1936–39," *Middle Eastern Studies* 2 (May 1975): 147.

139. Porath, *Riots to Rebellion*, 244–247.

140. Kimmerling and Migdal, *Palestinian People*, 131.

141. "H MacMichael, High Commissioner for Palestine, Jerusalem to Rt. Hon Malcolm MacDonald, Secretary of State for the Colonies, September 13, 1938," in *Political Diaries*, vol. 3, 200–202.

142. Ibid., 247.

143. "Secret Despatch from the High Commissioner for Palestine, October 24, 1938," in *Political Diaries*, vol. 3, 222–223.

144. "District Commissioner, Galilee and Acre District, Monthly Administrative Report for December 1938," in *Political Diaries*, vol. 3, 422.

145. "Secret Despatch from the High Commissioner for Palestine, December 29, 1938," in *Political Diaries*, vol. 3, 284; also see "Secret Despatch from the High Commissioner for Palestine, January 16, 1939," in *Political Diaries*, vol. 3, 307–308.

146. "Secret Despatch from the High Commissioner for Palestine, January 16, 1939," in *Political Diaries*, vol. 3, 309.

147. "District Commissioner, Haifa and Samaria District, Monthly Administrative Report for December 1938," in *Political Diaries*, vol. 3, 472.

148. "Extract from District Commissioner, Galilee and Acre District's Monthly Administrative Report for November 1938," in *Political Diaries*, vol. 3, 387.

149. Government of Palestine, *Survey of Palestine*, 48.

150. "Secret Despatch from the High Commissioner for Palestine, December 3, 1938," in *Political Diaries*, vol. 3, 266.

151. Kimmerling and Migdal, *Palestinian People*, 130.

152. Cited in Porath, *Riots to Rebellion*, 293; also see "District Commissioner's Offices, Jerusalem District, June 1, 1939, Report for Fortnight Ended May 31, 1939," in *Political Diaries*, vol. 4, 177.

153. Yasin, *al-Thawrah*, 226.

154. Kabha, *Thawrat 1936*, 97.

155. Porath, *Riots to Rebellion*, 291.

156. Khalidi, *Iron Cage*, 116–117.

157. Mattar, *Mufti*, 84; Khalidi, *Iron Cage*, 117.

158. See Anita Shapira, *Land and Power: The Zionist Resort to Force, 1881–1948*, trans. William Templer (Stanford, CA: Stanford University Press, 1999), chap. 6.

159. See Joseph Nevo, "The Renewal of Palestinian Political Activity, 1943–45 (The Shifting of the Pivot of Dissension from the Husayni-Nashashibi Conflict to the Husayni-Istiqlali Rivalry)," in *Palestinians and the Middle East Conflict*, 59–70.

160. Khalaf, *Politics in Palestine*, 147.

161. Benny Morris, *The Birth of the Palestinian Refugee Problem Revisited*, 2d ed. (Cambridge: Cambridge University Press, 2004), chap 3.

162. Morris, *Refugee Problem*, chap. 4.

163. Martin van Creveld, *The Sword and the Olive: A Critical History of the Israeli Defense Forces* (New York: Public Affairs, 1998), 70.

164. Khalaf, *Politics in Palestine*, 205–209.

165. Ibid., chap. 8.

166. See Avi Shlaim, *Collusion across the Jordan: King Abdullah, the Zionist Movement, and the Partition of Palestine* (Oxford: Clarendon Press, 1988).

167. Morris, *Refugee Problem*, chap. 7.

168. See Issa al-Shuaibi, "The Development of Palestinian Entity-Consciousness: Part I," *Journal of Palestine Studies* 9, no. 1 (Autumn 1979): 67–84.

169. Morris, *Refugee Problem*, chaps. 8–9.

170. Ibid., 603–604.

171. Khalidi, *Palestinian Identity*, 190.

172. Cited in "H MacMichael, High Commissioner for Palestine, Jerusalem, to Rt. Hon W. Ormsby-Gore, Secretary of State for the Colonies, April 14, 1938," in *Political Diaries*, vol. 3, 173.

Chapter 3. Roots and Rise of the Palestine Liberation Organization, 1949–1987

1. George Kossaifi, "Demographic Characteristics of the Arab Palestinian People," in *Sociology of the Palestinians*, 18.

2. See Morris, *Refugee Problem*, xvi–xxii.

3. Boaz Atzili and Wendy Pearlman, "Coercing Strength, Beaten by Weakness: Explaining Deterrence Against States that Host Nonstate Challengers," Paper prepared for delivery at the annual convention of the International Studies Association, New Orleans, February 17–20, 2010.

4. Jonathan Shimshoni, *Israel and Conventional Deterrence: Border Warfare from 1953 to 1970* (Ithaca, NY: Cornell University Press, 1970), 36–39.

5. See, inter alia, Yehoshafat Harkabi, "The Weakness of the Fedayeen," in *Palestinians and Israel* (Jerusalem: Israel Universities Press, 1974), 107–114; Edgar O'Balance, *Arab Guerrilla Power, 1967–1972* (London: Faber and Faber, 1974); William B. Quandt, *Palestinian Nationalism: Its Political and Military Dimensions* (Santa Monica, CA: Rand, n.d.); John W. Amos II, *Palestinian Resistance: Organization of a National Movement* (New York: Pergamon Press, 1980); Aaron David Miller, *The PLO and the Politics of Survival* (Washington, DC: Georgetown University Center for Strategic and International Studies / Wesport, CT: Praeger, 1983).

6. Yezid Sayigh, *Armed Struggle and the Search for State* (Oxford: Oxford University Press, 1997).

7. Cited in Yehoshafat Harkabi, "The Palestinians in the Fifties and Their Awakening as Reflected in Their Literature," in *Palestinian Arab Politics*, ed. Moshe Ma'oz (Jerusalem: Jerusalem Academic Press, 1975), 75; also see Edward Said, "Reflections on Exile," in *Out There: Marginalization and Contemporary Cultures*, eds. Russell Ferguson, Martha Gever, Trinh T. Minh-ha, and Cornel West (Cambridge, MA: MIT Press, 1990), 357–366; Glenn Bowman, "'A Country of Words': Conceiving the Palestinian Nation from the Position of Exile," in *The Making of Political Identities*, ed. Ernesto Laclau (London: Verso Press, 1994), 138–170; Khalidi, *Palestinian Identity*, 1–6.

8. Fawaz Turki, *The Disinherited: Journal of a Palestinian Exile* (New York: Monthly Review Press, 1972), 41, 53.

9. Fawaz Turki, "The Future of a Past: Fragments from the Palestinian Dream," *Journal of Palestine Studies* 6, no. 3 (Spring 1977): 68.

10. Kimmerling and Migdal, *Palestinian People*, 235–239.

11. Moshe Shemesh, "The Palestinian Society in the Wake of the 1948 War: From Social Fragmentation to Consolidation," *Israel Studies* 9, no. 1 (Spring 2004): 88–89.

12. "Fateh," literally meaning "conquest," is the acronym formed by reversing the first letters of its full name, Harakat al-Tahrir al-Watani al-Filastini. See Helena Cobban, *The Palestine Liberation Organization: People, Power, and Politics* (Cambridge: Cambridge University Press, 1984), 23–24.

13. Abu Iyad (Salah Khalaf), *My Home, My Land: A Narrative of the Palestinian Struggle*, with Eric Rouleau, trans. Linda Butler Koseoglu (New York: Times Books, 1981), 30.

14. Ibid., 35.

15. See Moshe Shemesh, *The Palestinian Entity, 1959–1974: Arab Politics and the PLO* (London: Frank Cass, 1988), part 1.

16. Sayigh, *Armed Struggle*, 102.

17. Kimmerling and Migdal, *Palestinian People*, 252.
18. Yezid Sayigh, "Reconstructing the Paradox: The Arab Nationalist Movement, Armed Struggle, and Palestine, 1951–1967," *Middle East Journal* 45, no. 4 (Autumn 1991): 621–622.
19. Malcolm H. Kerr, *The Arab Cold War: Gamal 'Abd al-Nasser and His Rivals, 1958–1970*, 3d ed. (Oxford: Oxford University Press, 1971).
20. See Moshe Shemesh, *Arab Politics, Palestinian Nationalism and the Six Day War: The Crystallization of Arab Strategy and Nasir's Descent to War, 1957–1967* (Brighton: Sussex Academic Press, 2008), 96.
21. Atzili and Pearlman, "Coercing Strength"; Mark Tessler, *A History of the Israeli–Palestinian Conflict* (Bloomington: Indiana University Press, 1994), 377; Fred H. Lawson, *Why Syria Goes to War: Thirty Years of Confrontation* (Ithaca, NY: Cornell University Press, 1996), chap. 1.
22. See Wendy Pearlman, "The Palestinian National Movement and the 1967 War," in *June 1967: The Crisis and Its Consequences*, eds. Roger Louis and Avi Shlaim (New York: Cambridge University Press, 2012).
23. Tom Segev, *1967: Israel, the War, and the Year That Transformed the Middle East*, trans. Jessica Cohen (New York: Metropolitan Books, 2007), 143–144.
24. Sayigh, *Armed Struggle*, 139.
25. Moshe Shemesh, "Did Shuqayri Call for 'Throwing the Jews into the Sea'?" *Israel Studies* 8, no. 2 (Summer 2003): 70–81.
26. Yezid Sayigh, "Turning Defeat into Opportunity: The Guerrillas after the June 1967 War," *Middle East Journal* 46, no. 2 (Spring 1992): 244–265.
27. Rosemary Sayigh, *Palestinians: From Peasants to Revolutionaries* (London: Zed Books, 1979), 144.
28. Don Peretz, "Arab Palestine: Phoenix or Phantom?" *Foreign Affairs* 68, no. 2 (January 1970): 327.
29. Yehoshafat Harakabi, *Fedayeen Action and Arab Strategy*, Adelphi Papers, no. 53 (London: Institute for Strategic Studies, December 1968), 29.
30. Rosemary Sayigh, "Sources of Palestinian Nationalism: A Study of a Palestinian Camp in Lebanon," *Journal of Palestine Studies* 6, no. 4 (Summer 1977): 34.
31. Amos, *Palestinian Resistance*, 35; Ehud Yaari, *Strike Terror: The Story of Fateh*, trans. Esther Yaari (New York: Sabra Books, 1970), 199.
32. Yaari, *Strike Terror*, 198–200.
33. Sayigh, *Armed Struggle*, 227.
34. Amos, *Palestinian Resistance*, 79.
35. Cited in Alain Gresh, *The PLO: The Struggle Within – Towards an Independent Palestinian State*, trans. A. M. Berrett (London: Zed Books, 1985), 12.
36. Amos, *Palestinian Resistance*, 195.
37. Cited in Cobban, *Liberation Organization*, 49; also see Amos, *Palestinian Resistance*, 57; Abu Iyad, *My Home*, 60; Sayigh, *Armed Struggle*, 181.
38. See Cobban, *Liberation Organization*, 26.
39. Pearlman, "1967 War."
40. *Middle East Record, 1969–1970* vol. 5 (Jerusalem: Israel Universities Press, 1977), 1149; Moshe Maoz, *Syria and Israel: From War to Peacemaking* (Oxford: Oxford University Press, 1995), 118.
41. Khaled al-Hassan, in *Palestinian Lives*, 27.
42. Fuad Jabber, "The Arab Regimes and the Palestinian Revolution, 1967–71," *Journal of Palestine Studies* 2, no. 2 (January 1973): 101.

43. Cobban, *Liberation Organization*, 140.
44. O'Neill, *Armed Struggle*, 153.
45. See Amos, *Palestinian Resistance*, 180–191; Sara Bar-Haim, "The Palestine Liberation Army: Stooge or Actor?" in *Palestinians and the Middle East Conflict*, 173–192.
46. See Jamil Hilal, in International Crisis Group, *After Arafat: Challenges and Prospects*, Middle East Briefing (Amman/Brussels, December 2004), 11.
47. Miller, *PLO*, 58–59.
48. Rashid Khalidi, *Under Siege: P.L.O. Decisionmaking during the 1982 War* (New York: Columbia University Press, 1986), 102–103.
49. Amos, *Palestinian Resistance*, 41.
50. Cited in Alan Hart, *Arafat: A Political Biography* (Bloomington: Indiana University Press, 1984), 332–333.
51. Cited in Amos, *Palestinian Resistance*, 41.
52. Cited in Kerr, *Arab Cold War*, 145.
53. I thank Rex Brynen for this point.
54. See Hazem Beblawi and Giacomo Luciani, eds., *The Rentier State* (London: Croom Helm, 1987).
55. Emile D. Sahliyeh, *The PLO after the Lebanon War* (Boulder, CO: Westview Press, 1986), 91–92, 140.
56. Ali Jarbawi and Wendy Pearlman, "Struggle in a Post-Charisma Transition: Rethinking Palestinian Politics after Arafat," *Journal of Palestine Studies* 36, no. 4 (Summer 2007): 4.
57. Rex Brynen, "The Neopatrimonial Dimension of Palestinian Politics," *Journal of Palestine Studies* 25, no. 1 (Autumn 1995): 23–36.
58. John Waterbury, "Endemic and Planned Corruption in a Monarchical Regime," *World Politics* 25, no. 4 (July 1973): 533–555.
59. Paul A. Jureidini and William E. Hazen, *The Palestinian Movement in Politics* (Lexington, MA: Lexington Books, 1976), 51.
60. Abu Iyad, *My Home*, 80.
61. See Sayigh, *Armed Struggle*, 276–279.
62. See Clinton Bailey, *Jordan's Palestinian Challenge, 1948–1983: A Political History* (Boulder, CO: Westview Press, 1984); Rex Brynen, *Sanctuary and Survival: The PLO in Lebanon* (Boulder, CO: Westview Press, 1990), 10–12; Anat Kurz, *Fateh and the Politics of Violence: The Institutionalization of a Popular Struggle* (Brighton: Sussex Academic Press and the Jaffee Center for Strategic Studies, 2005), 63.
63. Hisham Sharabi, "Palestine Resistance: Crisis and Reassessment," *Middle East Newsletter* (Beirut), January 1971.
64. Cited in O'Neill, *Armed Struggle*, 152.
65. Sayigh, *Armed Struggle*, 280–282.
66. Ariel Merari and Shlomo Elad, *The International Dimension of Palestinian Terrorism* (Jerusalem: Jaffee Center for Strategic Studies and Jerusalem Post Press, 1986), 108.
67. Riad El-Rayyes and Durnia Nahas, *Guerrillas for Palestine* (London: Portico Publications, 1976), 58–59; Christopher Dobson, *Black September: Its Short, Violent History* (London: Robert Hale, 1974), 45–46; O'Balance, *Arab Guerrilla Power*, 215.
68. Sayigh, *Armed Struggle*, 306–307; for Khalaf's perspective, see Abu Iyad, *My Home*, 98–120.

69. See O'Neill, *Armed Struggle*, 151.
70. John K. Cooley, *Green March, Black September: The Story of the Palestinian Arabs* (London: Frank Cass, 1973), 123–124.
71. Jureidini and Hazen, *Palestinian Movement*, 84; O'Balance, *Arab Guerrilla Power*, 216; Amos, *Palestinian Resistance*, 226. The major counterpoint to this view is the coerced confession of Muhammad Dawud Awdah, a BSO member arrested by Jordan. See Amos, *Palestinian Resistance*, 315–317.
72. Amos, *Palestinian Resistance*, 144, 226.
73. O'Neill, *Armed Struggle*, 151; Abu Iyad, *My Home*, 96.
74. Sayigh, *Armed Struggle*, 310.
75. Merari and Elad, *International Dimension*, 5–6, 120.
76. Barry Rubin, *Revolution until Victory? The Politics and History of the PLO* (Cambridge, MA: Harvard University Press, 1994), 31–32.
77. See James G. March and Johan P. Olsen, *Rediscovering Institutions* (New York: Free Press, 1989), 24–26.
78. See, respectively, Henry Kissinger, *Years of Upheaval* (Boston, MA: Little, Brown, 1982), 758; and Institute of Palestine Studies, *International Documents on Palestine 1974* [hereafter cited as *IDP*] (Beirut: Institute of Palestine Studies, published annually), 315, 317, 335.
79. Institute of Palestine Studies, *al-Watha'iq al-Filastiniyah al-'Arabiyah 1973* [Palestinian Arab documents] [hereafter cited as *al-Watha'iq*] (Beirut: the Lebanese University, published annually), 430–432, 469–472; *al-Watha'iq 1974*, 19–20; *IDP 1974*, 509.
80. *Al-Watha'iq 1973*, 424–425.
81. *Al-Watha'iq 1973*, 466–467; *IDP 1973*, 517–519; *al-Watha'iq 1975*, 129–130. For discussion see Gresh, *PLO*, 180–182, 220.
82. Kathleen Christison, *Perceptions of Palestine: Their Influence on U.S. Middle East Policy* (Berkeley: University of California Press), 140.
83. See Wendy Pearlman, "Spoiling Inside and Out: Internal Political Contestation and the Middle East Peace Process," *International Security* 33, no. 3 (Winter 2008–2009): 79–109.
84. Sayigh, *Armed Struggle*, 339–341.
85. Ibid., 339.
86. "Who Should Represent the Palestinians?" *Journal of Palestine Studies* 4, no. 3 (April 1975): 143.
87. Abu Iyad, *My Home*, 142.
88. Sayigh, *Armed Struggle*, 341.
89. Gresh, *PLO*, 142.
90. Ibid., 354.
91. Ibid., 349.
92. "From the Hebrew Press," *Journal of Palestine Studies* 3, no. 4 (Summer 1974): 147–155.
93. O'Neill, *Armed Struggle*, 25.
94. Shaul Mishal, *The PLO under 'Arafat: Between Gun and Olive Branch* (New Haven, CT: Yale University Press, 1986), chap. 3.
95. See Kemal Kirisci, *The PLO and World Politics: A Study of the Mobilization of Support for the Palestinian Cause* (London: Frances Pinter, 1986), 183.
96. Khalidi, *Under Siege*, 33.
97. Cited in Brynen, *Sanctuary and Survival*, 173–174.

98. See Brynen, *Sanctuary and Survival*, 67.

99. Sayigh, *Armed Struggle*, 364–369.

100. Ibid., 393.

101. Bar-Haim, "Liberation Army," 174.

102. Sayigh, *Armed Struggle*, 383.

103. Ibid., 430.

104. Ibid., 518.

105. Brynen, *Sanctuary and Survival*, 162.

106. Sahliyeh, *PLO after the Lebanon War*, 142.

107. Sayigh, *Armed Struggle*, 561.

108. Joe Stork, Interview with Rashid Khalidi, "Behind the Fateh Rebellion," *MERIP Reports* 119 (November–December 1983), 12.

109. Sayigh, *Armed Struggle*, 596–597.

110. Kydd and Walter, "Sabotaging the Peace."

Chapter 4. Occupation and the First Intifada, 1967–1993

1. Joost Hiltermann, *Behind the Intifada: Labor and Women's Movements in the Occupied Territories* (Princeton, NJ: Princeton University Press, 1991), 173.

2. Don Peretz, *Intifada: The Palestinian Uprising* (Boulder, CO: Westview Press, 1990), 83.

3. See Ian S. Lustick, "Writing the Intifada: Collective Action in the Occupied Territories," *World Politics* 45, no. 4 (July 1993): 560–594.

4. See Shaul Mishal, *West Bank / East Bank: The Palestinians in Jordan, 1949–1967* (New Haven, CT: Yale University Press, 1978); Joel S. Migdal, "The Effects of Regime Policies on Social Cohesion and Fragmentation – Dispersal and Annexation: Jordanian Rule," in *Palestinian Society and Politics*, ed. Joel S. Migdal (Princeton, NJ: Princeton University Press, 1980), 37; Issa al-Shuaibi, "The Development of Palestinian Entity-Consciousness: Part II," *Journal of Palestine Studies* 9, no. 2 (Winter 1980): 50–70.

5. Benny Morris, *Israel's Border Wars, 1949–1956: Arab Infiltration, Israeli Retaliation, and the Countdown to the Suez War* (Oxford: Oxford University Press, 1993), 91.

6. See Joan Mendell, "Gaza: Israel's Soweto," *MERIP Reports* 136/137 (October–December 1985): 7–19; Sara Roy, *The Gaza Strip: The Political Economy of De-development* (Washington, DC: Institute for Palestine Studies, 1995), chap. 3.

7. *Arab Report and Register*, August 16–23, 1967, 273–274; September 1–15, 1967, 291.

8. Ann Mosley Lesch, *Political Perceptions of the Palestinians on the West Bank and the Gaza Strip* (Washington, DC: Middle East Institute, 1980), 32; Ibrahim Dakkak, "Back to Square One: A Study in the Re-emergence of the Palestinian Identity in the West Bank, 1967–1980," in *Palestinians over the Green Line: Studies on the Relations Between Palestinians on Both Sides of the 1949 Armistice Line since 1967*, ed. Alexander Scholch (London: Ithaca Press, 1983), 70–73; Emile Sahliyeh, *In Search of Leadership: West Bank Politics Since 1967* (Washington, DC: Brookings Institute, 1988), 22–24.

9. Cobban, *Liberation Organization*, 37–39; Rafik Halabi, *The West Bank Story* (New York: Harcourt Brace Jovanovich, 1981), 191–193; *Arab Report and Register*, February 1–15, 1968, 43; Mishal, *PLO under 'Arafat*, 8–9, 32–33.

10. Tessler, *Israeli–Palestinian Conflict*, 473; Lesch, *Political Perceptions*, 41–43; Halabi, *West Bank Story*, chap. 5.
11. See Ann M. Lesch, "Israeli Deportation of Palestinians from the West Bank and the Gaza Strip, 1967–1978," *Journal of Palestine Studies* 8, no. 2 (Winter 1979): 101–131; Rami G. Khouri, "Potential Leaders Expelled: Israel's Deportation Policy," *MERIP Reports* 65 (March 1978): 23–25.
12. Abdul Aziz Hajj Ahmad, "Interview with the Palestine National Front," *MERIP Reports* 50 (August 1976): 16–21.
13. Samir Abdallah Saleh, "The Effects of Israeli Occupation on the Economy of the West Bank and Gaza Strip," in *Intifada: Palestine at the Crossroads*, 46.
14. Glenn E. Robinson, *Building a Palestinian State: The Incomplete Revolution* (Bloomington: Indiana University Press, 1997), 14–15.
15. See Hiltermann, *Behind the Intifada*, 20–26; Moshe Semyonov and Noah Lewin-Epstein, *Hewers of Wood and Drawers of Water: Noncitizen Arabs in the Israeli Labor Market*, Cornell International Industrial and Labor Relations Report no. 13 (Ithaca, NY: ILR Press, 1987).
16. See Bishara A. Bahbah, "A Palestinian View," *Journal of Communication* 35, no. 1 (Winter 1985): 17–21; Dov Shinar, "The West Bank Press and Palestinian Nation-Building," *Jerusalem Quarterly* 43 (Summer 1987): 37–48.
17. See Sahliyeh, *Search of Leadership*, 115–136; Robinson, *Palestinian State*, 19–37.
18. See Fuad Faris, "A Palestinian State?" *MERIP Reports* 33 (December 1974): 20; Ahmad, "Palestine National Front"; The Palestinian National Front," *MERIP Reports* 25 (February 1974): 22–23.
19. Sahliyeh, *Search of Leadership*, 56.
20. See "Seminar: Problems of Palestinian National Struggle," *Journal of Palestine Studies*, 11, no. 2 (Winter 1982): 152–164; Mishal, *PLO under 'Arafat*, 125; Sahliyeh, *Search of Leadership*, 58–60.
21. Sahliyeh, *Search of Leadership*, 61.
22. Moshe Ma'oz, *Palestinian Leadership on the West Bank: The Changing Role of the Arab Mayors under Jordan and Israel* (London: Frank Cass, 1984), 162–163.
23. Former West Bank mayor and NGC member, interview with author, Ramallah, August 16, 2008.
24. Ibid.
25. See *The West Bank Data Project: A Survey of Israel's Policies* (Washington, DC: American Enterprise Institute, 1984), 50–61.
26. Former West Bank mayor and NGC member, interview with author, Ramallah, August 16, 2008.
27. *Arab World Weekly*, August 2, 1980, 7–8.
28. Dakkak, "Square One," 82.
29. Former leader of Jordan Communist Party and Palestine Communist Party, interview with author, East Jerusalem, June 27, 2006.
30. Mishal, *PLO under 'Arafat*, 125.
31. Joel Greenberg, "PLO Splits Reaching Local Palestinians," *Jerusalem Post*, September 17, 1986, 5.
32. See Hiltermann, *Behind the Intifada*, 49–51; Salim Tamari, "The Palestinian Movement in Transition: Historical Reversals and the Uprising," in *Echoes of the Intifada: Regional Repercussions of the Palestinian-Israeli Conflict*, ed. Rex Brynen (Boulder, CO: Westview Press, 1991), 13–28; Robinson, *Palestinian State*, chap. 2.

33. Civil society activist, interview with author, Dheisheh refugee camp, July 24, 2006.

34. See Ziad Abu-Amr, *Islamic Fundamentalism in the West Bank and Gaza: Muslim Brotherhood and Islamic Jihad* (Bloomington: Indiana University Press, 1994); Khaled Hroub, *Hamas: Political Thought and Practice* (Washington, DC: Institute of Palestine Studies, 2000); Shaul Mishal and Avraham Sela, *The Palestinian Hamas: Vision, Violence, and Coexistence* (New York: Columbia University Press, 2000).

35. Jeroen Gunning, *Hamas in Politics: Democracy, Religion, Violence* (New York: Columbia University Press, 2008), 28–31.

36. Beverley Milton-Edwards and Stephen Farrell, *Hamas* (Cambridge: Polity Press, 2010), 210–212.

37. Hroub, *Hamas*, 33.

38. Shaul Mishal and Reuben Aharoni, *Speaking Stones: Communiqués from the Intifada Underground* (Syracuse, NY: Syracuse University Press, 1994), 21.

39. Sayigh, *Armed Struggle*, 609.

40. Joel Beinin, "Marching toward Civil War," *MERIP Reports* 136/137 (October–December 1985): 3–6.

41. Former West Bank mayor and NGC member, interview with author, Ramallah, August 16, 2008.

42. See Ishac Diwan and Radwan A. Shaban, eds., *Development under Adversity: The Palestinian Economy in Transition* (Washington, DC: World Bank and Palestine Economic Policy Research Institute [MAS], 1999).

43. Emile Nakle, "The West Bank and Gaza: Twenty Years Later," *Middle East Journal* 42, no. 2 (Spring 1988): 210.

44. Ann Mosley Lesch, "West Bank and Gaza Political Consensus," *Journal of Palestine Studies* 9, no. 3 (Spring 1980): 187–191.

45. Beshara Doumani, Interviews with Mahmoud and Naji, "Something Was in the Air All of 1987," *Middle East Report* 152 (May–June 1988): 43.

46. Daoud Kuttab, "The al-Fajr Poll," *Journal of Palestine Studies* 16, no. 2 (Winter 1987): 149–151; Mohammed Shadid and Rick Seltzer, "Political Attitudes of Palestinians in the West Bank and Gaza Strip," *Middle East Journal* 42, no. 1 (Winter 1988): 16–32.

47. See "Palestinian Students Unite to Fight Both Israel and Jordan," *Middle East Times*, February 8–14, 1987, 5; Ann Mosley Lesch, "The Palestinian Uprising: Causes and Consequences," *United Field Staff International Reports*, Asia no. 1 (1988–1989): 4.

48. Laetitia Bucaille, *Growing Up Palestinian: Israeli Occupation and the Intifada Generation*, trans. Anthony Roberts (Princeton, NJ: Princeton University Press, 2004), 18.

49. See Waheed Abdel Majeed, "al-Shamuliyah al-ijtima'iyah lil-Intifadah: qira'a awlawiyah" [The social inclusivity of the Intifada: a first reading], *Shu'un Filastiniyah* 193 (April 1988): 3–21; Daoud Kuttab, "The Palestinian Uprising: The Second Phase, Self-Sufficiency," *Journal of Palestine Studies* 17, no. 4 (Summer 1988): 36–45.

50. Daoud Kuttab, "Beyond the Intifada: The Struggle to Build a Nation," *The Nation*, October 17, 1988, 336–340; Hunter, *Palestinian Uprising*, 63–64.

51. See Rabae Madhoun, *al-Intifadah al-Filastiniyah: al-haykal al-tanzimi wa-asalib al-'amal* [The Palestinian uprising: structure and activities] (Acre: Dar al-Aswar, 1989), 29–44; Robinson, *Palestinian State*, chap. 5.

52. Fayez Sara, "al-Bunyah al-ijtima'iyah lil-Intifada al-Filastiniyah" [The social structure of the Palestinian Intifada], *Shu'un Filastiniyah* 189 (December 1988): 7–8; also see Hannan Mikhail Ashrawi, *The Coming of Age: An Anatomy of the Palestinian Intifada* (Tunis: Palestine Liberation Organization Unified Information, 1988), 5–6.

53. Ashrawi, *Coming of Age*, 10.

54. Mishal and Aharoni, *Speaking Stones*, 74, 106, 139, 173.

55. Roger Heacock, "From the Mediterranean to the Gulag and Back Again: The Palestinian Intifada and the Gulf War," *Arab Studies Quarterly* 13, no. 1–2 (Winter–Spring 1991): 68.

56. Jamal R. Nassar and Roger Heacock, "The Revolutionary Transformation of the Palestinians Under Occupation," in *Intifada: Palestine at the Crossroads*, eds. Jamal R. Nassar and Roger Heacock (New York: Praeger, 1990), 191.

57. Ibid., 197–198.

58. Meir Litvak, *Palestinian Leadership in the Territories* (Tel Aviv: Moshe Dayan Center for Middle Eastern and African Studies Shiloah Institute, 1991), 4.

59. Ali Jarbawi, *al-Intifadah wa-al-qiyadat al-siyasiyah fi al-Diffah al-Gharbiyah wa-Qita' Ghazzah: bahth fi al-nukbah al-siyasiyah* [The Intifada and political leadership in the West Bank and Gaza Strip: a study of political elites] (Beirut: Dar al-Taliyah, 1989), 73–74.

60. Rashid Khalidi, "The Palestinian People: Twenty-two Years after 1967," in *Intifada: The Palestinian Uprising against Israeli Occupation*, eds. Zachary Lockman and Joel Beinin (Boston, MA: South End Press / Washington, DC: Middle East Research and Information Project, 1989), 117–118.

61. Jamal Zaqout, "al-Intifadah wa-shurut injaz al-mashru'a al-wataniyah" [The Intifada and conditions for realizing the national project], *Majallat al-Dirasat al-Filastiniyah* 56 (Summer 2002): 42.

62. DFLP official, interview with author, Ramallah, June 14, 2006.

63. Academic, interview with author, East Jerusalem, July 12, 2006.

64. Jarbawi, *al-Intifadah wa-al-qiyadat al-siyasiyah*; Robinson, *Palestinian State*, chap. 2; Bucaille, *Growing Up Palestinian*; John Collins, *Occupied by Memory: The Intifada Generation and the Palestinian State of Emergency* (New York: New York University Press, 2004).

65. Daoud Kuttab, "A Profile of the Stonethrowers," *Journal of Palestine Studies* 17, no. 3 (Spring 1988): 14–23; Julie Peteet, "Male Gender Rituals of Resistance in the Palestinian Intifada: A Cultural Politics of Violence," *American Ethnologist* 21, no. 1 (February 1994): 31–49.

66. See James Ron, *Frontiers and Ghettos: State Violence in Serbia and Israel* (Berkeley: University of California Press, 2003).

67. Aryeh Shalev, *The Intifada: Causes and Effects* (Tel Aviv: Jaffee Center for Strategic Studies, *Jerusalem Post*, and Westview Press, 1991), 76.

68. Ze'ev Schiff and Ehud Ya'ari, *Intifada: The Palestinian Uprising: Israel's Third Front*, trans. Ina Friedman (New York: Touchstone, 1989), 31.

69. Jerusalem Media and Communication Centre [hereafter cited as JMCC], *The Stone and the Olive Branch: Four Years of the Intifada – From Jabalia to Madrid* (Jerusalem, 1991), 19.

70. Souad Rashed Dajani, *The Intifada* (Amman: University of Jordan Center for Hebraic Studies, 1990), 73.

71. Shalev, *Intifada*, 76.

72. Joe Stork, "The Significance of Stones: Notes from the Seventh Month," in *Intifada: The Palestinian Uprising against Israeli Occupation*, 74.
73. See Joel Beinin, "From Land Day to Peace Day … and Beyond," in *Intifada: The Palestinian Uprising against Israeli Occupation*, 205–216.
74. See Salim Tamari, "Limited Rebellion and Civil Society: The Uprising's Dilemma," *Middle East Report* 164–165 (May–August 1990): 5.
75. Academic, interview with author, Ramallah, June 19, 2006.
76. Former West Bank mayor and NGC member, interview with author, Ramallah, August 16, 2008.
77. Community activist, interview with author, Dheisheh refugee camp, July 4, 2006.
78. Lesch, "The Palestinian Uprising," 6.
79. Mishal and Aharoni, *Speaking Stones*, 62, 139, 160, 177.
80. Islah Jad, "From Salons to the Popular Committees: Palestinian Women, 1919–89," in *The Israel/Palestine Question: Rewriting Histories*, ed. Ilan Pappé (London: Routledge, 1999), 225.
81. Ziad Abu 'Amr, "The 'Personalities' of the Occupied Territories: Notes on Palestinian Political Leadership," *Middle East Report* 154 (September–October 1988): 23–25.
82. Hunter, *Palestinian Uprising*, 68.
83. See Hanan Ashrawi, *This Side of Peace* (New York: Touchstone, 1995), 50–51.
84. See Kuttab, "Second Phase," 38.
85. Abdel Majeed, "al-Shamuliyah al-ijtima'iyah," 12.
86. Hunter, *Palestinian Uprising*, 141.
87. J. Kristen Urban, "Blueprint for a Democratic Palestinian state: UNLU Communiqués and the Codification of Political Values for the First Two Years of the Intifada," *Arab Studies Quarterly* 16, no. 3 (Summer 1994): 74; also see Phyllis Bennis, *From Stones to Statehood: The Palestinian Uprising* (Brooklyn, NY: Olive Branch Press, 1990), 24.
88. Cited in Hiltermann, *Behind the Intifada*, 175.
89. Hunter, *Palestinian Uprising*, 66.
90. Doumani, "Something Was in the Air," 44.
91. Kuttab, "Beyond the Intifada," 340.
92. Ibid., 340; UNLU Leaflet no. 19, in Mishal and Aharoni, *Speaking Stones*, 105.
93. Urban, "Blueprint," 71.
94. Mishal and Aharoni, *Speaking Stones*, 96, 133, 138.
95. Ibrahim Abu Lughod, "Introduction: On Achieving Independence," in *Intifada: Palestine at the Crossroads*, 10.
96. Dajani, *Intifada*, 116; also see UNLU Leaflet no. 45, in Mishal and Aharoni, *Speaking Stones*, 170.
97. Lesch, "Palestinian Uprising," 7; Kuttab, "Second Phase," 39; Salim Tamari, "Eyeless in Judea: Israel's Strategy of Collaborators and Forgeries," *Middle East Report* 164–165 (May–August 1990), 44.
98. Citizen from Tulkarem, interview with author, Ramallah, June 20, 2006.
99. Kuttab, "Stonethrowers," 16–17.
100. See Eitan Y. Alimi, *Israeli Politics and the Palestinian Intifada: Political Opportunities, Framing Processes, and Contentious Politics* (London: Routledge, 2006), chap. 5.

101. See Mary E. King, *A Quiet Revolution: The First Palestinian Intifada and Nonviolent Resistance* (New York: Nation Books, 2007).
102. See Abu-Amr, *Islamic Fundamentalism*, 71.
103. See Institute for Counter-Terrorism – Merari terrorist incidents database, Interdisciplinary Center, Herzlia, Israel, http://www.ict.org.il/, accessed February 8, 2005.
104. Former UNLU member, interview with author, Ramallah, June 21, 2006.
105. Ibid.
106. Tessler, *Israeli–Palestinian Conflict*, 695.
107. Hunter, *Palestinian Uprising*, 67, 207.
108. Hroub, *Hamas*, 101.
109. See Peretz, *Intifada*, 89; Nassar and Heacock, "Revolutionary Transformation," 198.
110. Rex Brynen, "The Neopatrimonial Dimension of Palestinian Politics," *Journal of Palestine Studies* 25, no. 1 (Autumn 1995): 30.
111. See Ashrawi, *Side of Peace*, 84.
112. Sayigh, *Armed Struggle*, 623.
113. Ibid.
114. Cited in Bennis, *From Stones to Statehood*, 123.
115. Sayigh, *Armed Struggle*, 624.
116. Ashrawi, *Side of Peace*, 155–157.
117. See Pearlman, "Spoiling Inside and Out."
118. Former UNLU member, interview with author, Ramallah, June 21, 2006.
119. Schiff and Ya'ari, *Intifada*, 150.
120. James Garbarino and Kathleen Kostelny, "The Effects of Political Violence on Palestinian Children's Behavior Problems: A Risk Accumulation Model," *Child Development* 67, no. 1 (February 1996): 34.
121. B'Tselem, *Activity of the Undercover Units in the Occupied Territories* (Jerusalem, May 1992).
122. Tessler, *Israeli–Palestinian Conflict*, 701.
123. U.S. Department of State, "Country Reports on Human Rights Practices for 1988, 'The Occupied Territories,'" *Journal of Palestine Studies* 18, no. 3 (Spring 1989): 114–116.
124. See B'Tselem, *Interrogation of Palestinians During the Intifada: Ill-Treatment, "Moderate Physical Pressure" or Torture?* (Jerusalem, March 1991); B'Tselem, *The Interrogation of Palestinians During the Intifada: Follow Up to March 1991 Report* (Jerusalem, March 1992).
125. Al-Haq (Law in the Service of Man), *Punishing a Nation: Human Rights Violations During the Palestinian Uprising, December 1987–December 1988* (Boston: South End Press, 1990), 124.
126. See Shalev, *Intifada*, 118–119.
127. Al-Haq, *Punishing a Nation*, 154–155.
128. JMCC, *Stone and the Olive Branch*, 34.
129. Ibid., 40.
130. U.S. Department of State, "Country Reports," 117.
131. Al-Haq, *Punishing a Nation*, chap. 3.
132. Shalev, *Intifada*, 90.
133. Tamari, "Limited Rebellion."

134. Former civil disobedience activist, interview with author, Beit Sahour, July 13, 2006.
135. Dajani, *Intifada*, 117.
136. Bucaille, *Growing Up Palestinian*, 23.
137. Robinson, *Palestinian State*, 124–126.
138. Tamari, "Limited Rebellion," 4.
139. Bucaille, *Growing Up Palestinian*, 25.
140. Ibid., 25; Joost R. Hiltermann, "The Enemy inside the Intifada," *The Nation*, September 10, 1990, 232; Andrew Rigby, *Living the Intifada* (London: Zed Books, 1991), 53.
141. Cited in Deborah J. Gerner, "Palestinians, Israelis, and the Intifada: The Third Year and Beyond," *Arab Studies Quarterly* 13 (Summer–Fall 1991): 36.
142. Robinson, *Palestinian State*, 98–99.
143. Jamil Hilal, "PLO Institutions: The Challenge Ahead," *Journal of Palestine Studies* 23, no. 1 (Autumn, 1993): 54.
144. See Meir Litvak, "Inside Versus Outside: The Challenge of the Local Leadership, 1967–1994," in *The PLO and Israel: From Armed Conflict to Political Settlement, 1964–1994*, eds. Avraham Sela and Moshe Ma'oz (New York: St. Martin's Press, 1997), 171–196.
145. Lamis Andoni, "The Decline of the PLO in the Occupied Territories," *Middle East International*, February 4, 1994.
146. See Graham Usher, Interviews with Marwan Barghouti and Ghazi Abu Jiab, "Arafat and the Opposition," *Middle East Report* 191 (November–December 1994): 22.
147. Sayigh, *Armed Struggle*, 689.
148. Fateh leader, interview with author, Bethlehem, July 13, 2006; for similar perspectives, see Collins, *Occupied by Memory*, 173–175.
149. Ali Jarbawi and Penny Johnson, "The PLO Is Still Waging a Struggle for Recognition Rather Than a Solution," *Middle East Report* 164–165 (May–August 1990): 23.
150. Citizen from Tulkarem, interview with author, Ramallah, June 20, 2006.
151. Former UNLU member, interview with author, Ramallah, June 21, 2006.
152. Institute for Counter-Terrorism – Merari terrorist incidents database.
153. See Hroub, *Hamas*, 100, 119–120.
154. G. H. Jansen, "Victims of Despair," *Middle East International*, July 23, 1993.
155. Abu-Amr, *Islamic Fundamentalism*, 75.
156. See Boaz Ganor, "Hamas: The Islamic Resistance Movement in the Territories," *Survey of Arab Affairs* (Jerusalem Center for Public Affairs), February 2, 1992; Michel Jubran and Laura Drake, "The Islamic Fundamentalist Movement in the West Bank and Gaza Strip," *Middle East Policy* 2, no. 2 (Spring 1993): 13; Abu-Amr, *Islamic Fundamentalism*, 74; Graham Usher, *Dispatches from Palestine: The Rise and Fall of the Oslo Peace Process* (London: Pluto Press, 1999), 20–21; Robinson, *Palestinian State*, 167.
157. See Hillel Cohen, *Army of Shadows: Palestinian Collaboration with Zionism, 1917–1948* (Berkeley: University of California Press, 2008); Hillel Cohen, *Good Arabs: The Israeli Security Agencies and the Israeli Arabs, 1948–1967* (Berkeley: University of California Press, 2010).
158. Hiltermann, "Enemy Inside," 232; Nassar and Heacock, "Revolutionary Transformation," 200–201; Robinson, *Palestinian State*, 121–122.

159. Tamari, "Eyeless in Judea," 44.
160. B'Tselem, *Collaborators in the Occupied Territories: Human Rights Abuses and Violations* (Jerusalem, January 1994), 60; Tessler, *Israeli–Palestinian Conflict*, 747.
161. B'Tselem, *Collaborators*, 1.
162. IDF Spokesman's Unit Information Branch, *Incidents in Judea, Samaria, and the Gaza District since the Beginning of the Uprising* (Jerusalem, December 1992), 3.
163. See UNLU Leaflet no. 55, in Mishal and Aharoni, *Speaking Stones*, 183–184; Robinson, *Palestinian State*, 127–130.
164. Jansen, "Victims of Despair," 5.
165. Rema Hammami, "Women, the Hijab, and the Intifada," *Middle East Report* 164–165 (May–August 1990): 24–28, 71, 78; Eileen S. Kuttab, "Palestinian Women in the Intifada: Fighting on Two Fronts," *Arab Studies Quarterly* 15, no. 2 (Spring 1993): 69–85.
166. Cited in B'Tselem, *Collaborators*, 14; also see "From Dream to Nightmare," *Economist*, June 29, 1991.
167. Sara M. Roy, "Gaza: New Dynamics of Civic Disintegration," *Journal of Palestine Studies* 22, no. 4 (Summer 1993): 23–25.
168. Mouin Rabbani, "Why Arafat Has Embarked on a Desperate Gamble," *Middle East International*, September 10, 1993.
169. Cited in Collins, *Occupied by Memory*, 177.

Chapter 5. The Oslo Peace Process, 1993–2000

1. Sara Roy, "Why Peace Failed: An Oslo Autopsy," in *Failing Peace: Gaza and the Palestinian–Israeli Conflict* (London: Pluto Press, 2007), 239.
2. Sara Roy, "Palestinian Society and Economy: The Continued Denial of Possibility," *Journal of Palestine Studies* 30, no. 4 (Summer 2001): 10.
3. B'Tselem, *Oslo: Before and After, the Status of Human Rights in the Occupied Territories* (Jerusalem, May 1999), 7.
4. See, inter alia, Edward Said, *Peace and Its Discontents: Gaza-Jericho, 1993–1995* (New York: Vintage, 1995); Edward Said, *The End of the Peace Process: Oslo and After* (New York: Pantheon Books, 2000).
5. Mouin Rabbani, "'Gaza-Jericho First': The Palestinian Debate," *Middle East International*, September 24, 1993.
6. Salim Tamari, "Fading Flags: The Crises of Political Legitimacy," *Middle East Report* 194–195 (May–August 1995): 10–12.
7. Mona Naim and Joe Stork, Interview with Mahmoud Darwish, "My Opposition to the Terms of the Accord Is a Measure of My Attachment to Real Peace," *Middle East Report* 194–195 (May–August 1995): 18.
8. Center for Palestine Research and Studies (CPRS) and Palestine Center for Survey Research (PSR), Public Opinion Polls, February 1994–April 2000; see http://www.pcpsr.org/survey/survey.html, accessed April 2, 2005.
9. CPRS and PSR, Public Opinion Polls, February 1995–April 2000; see http://www.pcpsr.org/survey/survey.html, accessed April 2, 2005.
10. CPRS and PSR, Public Opinion Polls, July 1995–April 2000; see http://www.pcpsr.org/survey/survey.html, accessed April 2, 2005.
11. Yezid Sayigh, "Redefining the Basics: Sovereignty and Security of the Palestinian State," *Journal of Palestine Studies* 24, no. 4 (Summer 1995): 5–19.
12. Cited in Usher, *Dispatches*, 17.

13. Cited in Sara Roy, "'The Seed of Chaos, and of Night': The Gaza Strip after the Agreement," *Journal of Palestine Studies* 23, no. 3 (Spring 1994): 91–92; also see "Consent and Discontent in Khan Yunis," *News from Within*, October 13, 1993.

14. Jamil Hilal and Mushtaq Husain Khan, "State Formation under the PA: Potential Outcomes and Their Viability," in *State Formation in Palestine: Viability and Governance during a Social Transformation*, ed. Mushtaq Husain Khan with George Giacaman and Inge Amundsen (New York: Routledge, 2004), 85.

15. Rabbani, "Gaza–Jericho."

16. Ron Pundak, "From Oslo to Taba: What Went Wrong," in *Israeli–Palestinian Peace Process: Oslo and the Lessons of Failure – Perspectives, Predicaments, and Prospects*, eds. Robert L. Rothstein, Moshe Ma'oz, and Khalil Shikaki (Brighton: Sussex Academic Press, 2002), 88–113.

17. See B'Tselem, *Divide and Rule: Prohibition on Passage between the Gaza Strip and the West Bank* (Jerusalem, May 1998); Amira Hass, "Israel's Closure Policy: An Ineffective Strategy of Containment and Repression," *Journal of Palestine Studies* 31, no. 3 (Spring 2002): 5–20; Roy, "Continued Denial of Possibility," 10–11.

18. See Amira Hass, *Drinking the Sea at Gaza: Days and Nights in a Land Under Siege* (New York: Henry Holt, 1996), chap. 10.

19. See Sara Roy, "De-Development Revisited: Palestinian Economy and Society since Oslo," *Journal of Palestine Studies* 28, no. 3 (Spring 1999): 64–82.

20. CPRS, Public Opinion Poll No. 1, September 10–11, 1993; CPRS, Public Opinion Poll No. 2, October 5–10, 1993; CPRS, Public Opinion Poll No. 9, May 31, 1994; see http://www.pcpsr.org/survey/survey.html, accessed April 2, 2005.

21. Salem Aljuni, "The Palestinian Economy and the Second Intifada," *Journal of Palestine Studies* 32, no. 3 (Spring 2003): 69.

22. Roy, "De-Development Revisited," 69.

23. Leila Farsakh, "Economic Viability of a Palestinian State in the West Bank and Gaza Strip: Is It Possible without Territorial Integrity and Sovereignty?" *MIT Electronic Journal of Middle East Studies* 1 (May 2001): 43–48.

24. See "What Happened to the Dream? A Roundtable Discussion with Longtime Ex-Prisoners," *News from Within* 11, no. 1 (January 1995): 3–13; Dan Connell, "Palestine on the Edge: Crisis in the National Movement," *Middle East Report* 194–195 (May–August 1995): 6–9; Naseer Aruri, "The Serious Challenges Facing Palestinian Society," *Middle East International*, August 25, 1995, 3–13; Fouad Moughrabi, "A Year of Discovery," *Journal of Palestine Studies* 26, no. 2 (Winter 1997): 5–15; Christopher Parker, *Resignation or Revolt? Socio-political Development and the Challenges of Peace in Palestine* (London: I. B. Tauris, 1999); Toufic Haddad, "Retrospective: Without Illusion – Interview with the Intifada Generation," *News from Within* 25, no. 3 (March 1999): 16–21; Said, *End of the Peace*; Collins, *Occupied by Memory*.

25. Mustafa Barghouti, "Posteuphoria in Palestine," *Journal of Palestine Studies* 25, no. 4 (Summer 1996): 90–91.

26. Rema Hammami, "NGOs: The Professionalisation of Politics," *Race and Class* 37, no. 2 (October–December, 1995): 51–63.

27. Amaney Jamal, *Barriers to Democracy: The Other Side of Social Capital in Palestine and the Arab World* (Princeton, NJ: Princeton University Press, 2007).

28. Ghazi A. Hamad, "The Relationship between Hamas and the Palestinian National Authority (PA): The Conflictual Past and the Unknown Future," in *Palestinian Perspectives*, ed. Wolfgang Freund (Frankfurt am Main: Peter Lang, 1999), 177.

29. Laetitia Bucaille, *Gaza: La violence de la paix* (Paris: Presses de Science Po, 1998); Nigel Parsons, *The Politics of the Palestinian Authority: From Oslo to al-Aqsa* (London: Routledge, 2005).

30. Interview with Demetri Dilyani, October 27, 2004, http://www.justvision.org/portrait/76079/interview, accessed June 5, 2007.

31. Cited in J. Kirsten Urban, "Palestine's Paradoxical Search," *Peace Review* 10, no. 2 (June 1998): 192.

32. Cited in Roy, "Seeds of Chaos," 92.

33. Rose-Marie Barbeau, "Crisis or Not: The Trend toward Peace," *Palestine Report*, March 21, 1997.

34. The lower rate in the West Bank could be attributed to impediments to voting in Hebron and East Jerusalem, which remained under Israeli control.

35. Nathan J. Brown, *Palestinian Politics after the Oslo Accords: Resuming Arab Palestine* (Berkeley: University of California Press, 2003), chap. 2.

36. Academic, interview with author, Ramallah, June 19, 2006.

37. Hroub, *Hamas*, 132–133; Graham Usher, "Arafat and the Opposition," *Middle East Report* 191 (November–December 1994): 25.

38. See Moughrabi, "Year of Discovery"; Graham Usher, "The PLO Opposition: Rebels Without a Constituency," *Middle East International*, October 7, 1994; Jamil Hilal, *al-Nizam al-siyasi al-Filastini ba'da Uslu: dirasah tahliliyah naqdiyah* [The Palestinian political system after Oslo: a critical assessment] (Ramallah: Muwatin, 1998), 102–108.

39. Muhammad Jadallah, *al-Mu'aridah wa-al-Sultah al-Wataniyah* [The Opposition and the National Authority] (Nablus: Center for Palestine Research and Studies, 1994).

40. "An Interview with Salim Tamari," *Middle East Report* 186 (January–February 1994): 18; "Interview with Azmi Bishara," in Usher, *Dispatches*, 63.

41. Sayigh, *Armed Struggle*, 691.

42. See Graham Usher, "An Interview with Salah Abd al-Shafi," *Middle East Report* 186 (January–February 1994): 11–13; Joe Stork, "An Interview with Charles Shammas," *Middle East Report* 186 (January–February 1994): 15–17; Joe Stork, "Interview with Salim Tamari," 17–19.

43. "Five out of 10 Palestinians Want to Quit Peace Talks: Poll," *Agence France Presse*, August 4, 1993.

44. See Amnesty International, *Annual Report* (London, 1995–2000).

45. Hilal, "Oslo Agreement," 125.

46. See Palestinian Independent Commission for Citizen's Rights (PICCR), *Annual Report* (Ramallah: 1996–2000); Hilal, *al-Nizam al-siyasi*; JMCC, *The Palestinian Council*, 2d ed. (Jerusalem: JMCC, 1998); Ali Jarbawi, *al-Bunyah al-qanuniyah wa-al-tahawwul al-dimuqrati fi Filastin* [Legal structures and the transition to democracy in Palestine] (Ramallah: Muwatin, 1999); David Schenker, *Palestinian Democracy and Governance: An Appraisal of the Legislative Council* (Washington, DC: Washington Institute for Near East Policy, 2000); Brown, *Palestinian Politics*, chap. 3.

47. *Strengthening Palestinian Public Institutions: Report of an Independent Task Force Sponsored by the Council on Foreign Relations, Michel Rocard, Chairman; Henry Siegman, Project Director; Yezid Sayigh and Khalil Shikaki, Principal Authors* (New York: Council on Foreign Relations, 1999), 51.

48. Lawyer, interview with author, Ramallah, July 26, 2006.

49. See *Strengthening Palestinian Public Institutions*, 81–86.
50. "Interview with Charles Shamas," 15.
51. Academic, interview with author, Ramallah, June 19, 2006.
52. Bashir Barghouti, *Tatawur al-haraka al-wataniyah al-filastinyah* [Development of the Palestinian national movement] (Nablus: Center for Palestine Research and Studies, 1996), 10–11.
53. Islah Jad, "Tribalism and the Municipal Elections: A Feminist Perspective," *News from Within* 11, no. 11 (November 1995): 32–34; Wafaa 'Amru, "Fateh 'al-dakhil': hiwarat sarihah ma'a qaada maydaniyin" [Fateh "insiders": frank talk with field leaders], *Majallat al-Dirasat al-Filastiniyah* 66 (Winter 1995): 64–78; Graham Usher, "The Return of the Tribes," *al-Ahram Weekly*, October 30–November 5, 1997; Hillel Frisch, "Modern Absolutism or Neopatriarchal State Building? Customary Law, Extended Families and the Palestinian Authority," *International Journal of Middle East Studies* 29, no. 3 (August 1997): 341–358; Robinson, *Palestinian State*, 178–179; "Interview with Azmi Bishara," 62.
54. I am grateful to Nathan Brown for this point.
55. See David Samuels, "In a Ruined Country," *Atlantic Monthly*, September 2005.
56. Frisch, *Countdown*, 133; Gal Luft, "The Mirage of a Demilitarized Palestine," *Middle East Quarterly* 8, no. 3 (Summer 2001): 53.
57. Graham Usher, "Fateh Tearing Itself Apart," *Middle East International*, February 18, 1994; Graham Usher, "Uneasy Marriages," *Middle East International*, December 15, 1995.
58. Khalil Shikaki, "Palestinians Divided," *Foreign Affairs* 81, no. 1 (2002): 89–105.
59. Usher, "Arafat and the Opposition"; Graham Usher, "Back to the Old Days," *Middle East International*, February 4, 1994; 'Amru, "Fateh 'al-dakhil.'"
60. Connell, "Palestine on the Edge"; Graham Usher, *Palestine in Crisis: The Struggle for Peace and Political Independence after Oslo* (London: Pluto Press, 1995), 74–75.
61. Graham Usher, "Fateh's Tanzim: Origins and Politics," *Middle East Report* 217, (Winter 2000): 6–7; Parsons, *Palestinian Authority*, 137–138; Eitan Y. Alimi, "Contextualizing Political Terrorism: A Collective Action Perspective for Understanding the Tanzim," *Studies in Conflict and Terrorism* 29, no. 3 (May 2006): 263–283.
62. Interviewed in 'Amru, "Fateh 'al-dakhil,'" 67.
63. Daniel Lieberfeld, *Talking with the Enemy: Negotiation and Threat Perception in South Africa and Israel/Palestine* (Westport, CT: Praeger, 1999).
64. Karen Rasler, "Shocks, Expectancy Revision, and the De-escalation of Protracted Conflicts: The Israeli–Palestinian Case," *Journal of Peace Research* 37, no. 6 (November 2000): 699–720.
65. Philip A. Schrodt, Ömür Yilmaz, and Deborah J. Gerner, "Evaluating 'Ripeness' and 'Hurting Stalemate' in Mediated International Conflicts: An Event Data Study of the Middle East, Balkans, and West Africa," Paper presented at the annual meeting of the International Studies Association, Portland, OR, February 2003.
66. I. William Zartman, "Explaining Oslo," *International Negotiation* 2, no. 2 (February 1997): 195–215.
67. Herbert C. Kelman, "Some Determinants of the Oslo Breakthrough," *International Negotiation* 2, no. 2 (February 1997): 183–194.

68. See Stuart Cohen, "How Did the Intifada Affect the IDF?" *Conflict Quarterly* 24, no. 4 (Summer 1994): 7–22; David Makovsky, *Making Peace with the PLO: The Rabin Government's Road to the Oslo Accord* (Boulder, CO: Westview Press, 1996); Mira Sucharov, *The International Self: Psychoanalysis and the Search for Israeli–Palestinian Peace* (Albany: State University of New York Press, 2005).

69. Muhammad Muslih, "A Study of PLO Peace Initiatives, 1974–1988," in *The PLO and Israel: From Armed Conflict to Political Solution, 1964–1994*, eds. Avraham Sela and Moshe Ma'oz (New York: St. Martin's Press, 1997), 37–53.

70. Academic, interview with author, Ramallah, June 19, 2006.

71. Jeroen Gunning, "Peace with Hamas? The Transforming Potential of Political Participation" *International Affairs* 80, no. 2 (March 2004): 243.

72. See Hroub, "*Harakat Hamas*," 28–29; Graham Usher, "Hamas Seeks a Place at the Table," *Middle East International*, May 13, 1994; Mishal and Sela, *Palestinian Hamas*, 73.

73. CPRS, Public Opinion Poll No. 1, September 10–11, 1993; see http://www.pcpsr.org/survey/survey.html, accessed April 2, 2005.

74. CPRS and PSR, Public Opinion Polls, March 1995–April 2000; see http://www.pcpsr.org/survey/survey.html, accessed April 2, 2005.

75. Barry Rubin, "The Future of Palestinian Politics: Factions, Frictions, and Functions," *Middle East Review of International Affairs Journal* 4, no. 3 (September 2000), http://meria.idc.ac.il/journal/2000/issue3/jv4n3a7.html, accessed April 4, 2011; Khaled Hroub, "Hamas after Shaykh Yasin and Rantisi," *Journal of Palestine Studies* 33, no. 4 (Summer 2004): 23.

76. Lamis Andoni, "Palestinian Islamist Group Signals Shift in Strategy," *Christian Science Monitor*, September 13, 1994.

77. Graham Usher and Bassam Jarrar, "The Islamist Movement and the Palestinian Authority," *Middle East Report* 189 (July–August 1994): 28–29; also see Khaled al-Hindi, "Fahm al-harakah li-taba'iyat al-sira'a ma'a al-mashru'a al-sahiyuniyah wa-falsafat idaratihu" [The movement's understanding of the nature of the conflict with the Zionist project and its philosophy for managing it], in *Dirasah fi al-fikr al-siyasi li-Harakat al-Muqawama al-Islamiyah (HAMAS), 1987–1996* [A study of the political thought of the Islamic Resistance Movement (Hamas)], eds. Jawad el-Hamad and Iyad al-Barghouti (Amman: Middle East Studies Centre, 1997), 131–135; Mishal and Sela, *Palestinian Hamas*, 2.

78. See Khaled Hroub, "Harakat Hamas bayn al-Sulta al-Filastiniyah wa-Israil: min muthallath al-qiwa ila al-mitraqa wal-sandan" [The Hamas movement between the Palestinian Authority and Israel: from the triangle of forces to the hammer and anvil], *Majallat al-Dirasat al-Filastiniyah* 18 (Spring 1994): 30–34; Mishal and Sela, *Palestinian Hamas*, 71–72; Charmaine Seitz, "Coming of Age: HAMAS's Rise to Prominence in the Post-Oslo Era," in *The Struggle for Sovereignty: Palestine and Israel, 1993–2005*, eds. Joel Beinin and Rebecca L. Stein, (Stanford, CA: Stanford University Press and Middle East Information and Research Project, 2006), 113–117.

79. See Azzam Tamimi, *Hamas: A History from Within* (Northampton, MA: Olive Branch, 2007), chap. 7.

80. Cited in Andoni, "Group Signals Shift in Strategy."

81. Hroub, "Harakat Hamas," 28–29.

82. Mishal and Sela, *Palestinian Hamas*, 56, 58–59.
83. See Khaled Amayreh, "PNA and Hamas: Signs of rapprochement," *Middle East International*, October, 20, 1995.
84. Mishal and Sela, *Palestinian Hamas*, 73–74.
85. Gunning, *Hamas*, 40.
86. Ibid., 41.
87. "Hamas Leaders Call for End to Violence," *Palestine Report*, March 8, 1996.
88. Hamad, "Relationship," 182.
89. Salwa Kanaana and Stephanie Nolan, "Bombs Bring Chaos," *Palestine Report*, March 8, 1996; also see Salwa Kanaana, "The End of Armed Operations?" *Palestine Report*, May 31, 1996; Muhammed El-Hassan, "Internal Divisions Still Plague Hamas," *Palestine Report*, August 23, 1996; Usher, *Dispatches*, 86.
90. Anis F. Kassim, ed., *The Palestine Yearbook of International Law, 1996–1997*, vol. 9 (The Hague: Kluwer Law International, 1998), 302.
91. CPRS, Public Opinion Poll No. 22, March 29–31, 1996; see http://www.pcpsr.org/survey/survey.html, accessed April 2, 2005.
92. JMCC, Public Opinion Polls, February 1996, August 1996, http://www.jmcc.org/polls.aspx, accessed March 25, 2005.
93. Former General Security Service officer, interview with author, July 30, 2006.
94. "Interview with Hamas Leader Shaykh Ahmed Yasin," *Delo* (Slovenia), October 27, 1997, as cited in FBIS/WNC, insert November 2, 1998.
95. Ori Slonim, "The Hamas and Terror: An Alternative Explanation for the Use of Violence," *Strategic Assessment* 2, no. 3 (December 1999), http://www.inss.org.il/publications.php?cat=21&incat=&read=621, accessed April 4, 2011.
96. "Interview with Islamic Jihad Movement Secretary General Dr. Ramadan 'Abdallah Shallah," *al-Sharq al-Awsat*, October 18, 1996, as cited in FBIS/WNC, insert October 24, 1996.
97. Stephanie Nolen, "Was This a Hamas Bombing?" *Palestine Report*, March 28, 1997; Asya Abdul Hadi, "Hamas Divided over Strategy," *Palestine Report*, March 28, 1997; Graham Usher, "The Death of the Oslo Process?" *Middle East International*, April 4, 1997; Stephanie Nolen, "PA Leads Israel to Surif Hamas Cell," *Palestine Report*, April 18, 1997.
98. See Joharah Baker, "Bombings Prompt Brutal Closure," *Palestine Report*, August 8, 1997; Stephanie Nolen, "Bombers, and Motives, Unknown," *Palestine Report*, August 8, 1997; Graham Usher, "Arafat's Slender Lifelines," *Middle East International*, August, 8, 1997.
99. Sara Roy, "The Transformation of Islamic NGOs in Palestine," *Middle East Report* 214 (Spring 2000): 24–26.
100. Palestinian Academic Society for the Study of International Affairs (PASSIA), *Annual Report 1996* (Jerusalem, 1997).
101. Barghouti, "Posteuphoria," 87.
102. B'Tselem, *Playing with Fire on the Temple Mount: Use of Lethal and Excessive Force by the Israel Police Force* (Jerusalem, December 1996).
103. Andrea Levin, "The Media's Tunnel Vision," *Middle East Quarterly* 3, no. 4 (December 1996): 3–9; also see Efraim Karsh, *Arafat's War: The Man and His Battle for Israeli Conquest* (New York: Grove Press, 2003), 147–151.
104. Mamdouh Nofal, "Yasir Arafat, the Political Player: A Mixed Legacy," *Journal of Palestine Studies* 35, no. 2 (Winter 2006): 34; also see Karsh, *Arafat's War*, 147–151.

105. Graham Usher, "Picture of War," *Middle East International*, October 4, 1996;
Graham Usher, "Madness in Ramallah," *Middle East International*, October
4, 1996; Manal Jamal, "Birzeit Students Recall Clashes," *Palestine Report*,
October 4, 1996; Mouin Rabbani, "Palestinian Authority, Israeli Rule: From
Transitional to Permanent Arrangement," *Middle East Report* 201 (October–
December 1996), 2–6, 22; Charles Enderlin, *Shattered Dreams: The Failure of
the Peace Process in the Middle East, 1995–2002*, trans. Susan Fairfield (New
York: Other Press, 2002), 55–56.

106. Rabbani, "Permanent Arrangement."

107. "IPS Forum: The Tunnel Crisis," *Journal of Palestine Studies* 26, no. 2 (Winter
1997): 95–101.

108. Rabbani, "Palestinian Authority, Israeli Rule."

109. Ilene R. Prusher, "Palestinians Talk of a New Intifadah," *Christian Science
Monitor*, August 19, 1996.

110. See Ghassan Khatib, "A Bloody Peace Process?" *Palestine Report*, October
4, 1996; Stephanie Nolen, "Arafat Moves to Consolidate Renewed Support,"
Palestine Report, October 4, 1996; Graham Usher, "Resistance and
Negotiations," *News from Within* 12, no. 10, (November 1996): 7–9.

111. Enderlin, *Shattered Dreams*, 62, 136.

112. Ibid., 137; Ben Kaspit, "Israel Is Not a Country with an Army, but an Army
with an Attached Country," *Ma'ariv*, September 6, 2002, as cited in FBIS, insert
September 9, 2002; Yoram Peri, *The Israeli Military and Israel's Palestinian
Policy*, Peaceworks Paper 47 (Washington, DC: United States Institute of Peace,
November 2002), 30.

113. Rose-Marie Barbeau, "Unity over Settlement Issue," *Palestine Report*, March
14, 1997.

114. Usher, "Death of the Oslo Process?"

115. Ibid.; Khader Abusway, "Palestinian Police Do a 'Good Job'," *Palestine Report*,
April 4, 1997.

116. CPRS, Public Opinion Poll No. 30, November 29, 1997; see http://www.pcpsr.
org/survey/survey.html, accessed April 2, 2005.

117. Ghassan Khatib, "The Peace Process: Between Non-collapse and Non-success,"
Palestine Report, April 4, 1997.

118. Emile Sahliyeh and Zixian Deng, "The Determinants of Palestinians, Attitudes
towards Peace with Israel," *International Studies Quarterly* 47, no. 4 (December
2003): 693–708.

119. CPRS and PSR, Public Opinion Polls, December 1996–April 2000; see http://
www.pcpsr.org/survey/survey.html, accessed April 2, 2005.

120. CPRS and PSR, Public Opinion Polls, November 1994–April 2000; see http://
www.pcpsr.org/survey/survey.html, accessed April 2, 2005.

121. Toufic Haddad, "In the Crucible of Rebellion," *News from Within* 16, no. 6
(June 2000): 12–15.

122. Nimer, "Service Providers," 47.

123. Graham Usher, "Fateh and the Peace Process: An Interview with Marwan
Barghouti," *News from Within* 11, no. 5, (May 1997): 22–24.

124. See Islah Jad, "Bir Zeit Elections: Why the Shabiba Won," *News from Within*
11, no. 5 (May 1997): 25–26.

125. Fateh leader, interview with author, Ramallah, July 26, 2006.

126. Graham Usher, "Waiting for Fateh," *Middle East International*, April 18, 1997.
127. Cited in 'Amru, "Fateh 'al-dakhil'," 73.
128. Husayn Agha and Robert Malley, "Camp David: The Tragedy of Errors," *New York Review of Books*, August 9, 2001.
129. Mark A. Heller, "Implications of the Withdrawal from Lebanon for Israeli–Palestinian Relations," *Strategic Assessment* 3, no. 1 (June 2000), http://www.inss.org.il/publications.php?cat=21&incat=&read=634, accessed April 4, 2011; Shlomo Brom, "The Withdrawal from Southern Lebanon: One Year Later," *Strategic Assessment* 4, no. 2 (August 2001); Ronen Sebag, "Lebanon: The Intifada's False Premise," *Middle East Quarterly* 9, no. 2 (Spring 2002); for analysis see Ben Kaspit, "The Army Will Decide and Approve," *Ma'ariv*, September 13, 2002, as cited in FBIS/WNC, insert September 16, 2002; Peri, *Israel's Palestinian Policy*, 33.
130. Clayton E. Swisher, *The Truth about Camp David: The Untold Story about the Collapse of the Middle East Peace Process* (New York: Nation Books, 2004), 242; Agha and Malley, "Camp David."
131. See Aluf Benn, "The Selling of the Summit," *Ha'aretz*, July 27, 2001; Meron Benvenisti, "Challenging the Camp David Myth," *Ha'aretz*, August 2, 2001.
132. Agha and Malley, "Camp David"; Swisher, *Camp David*; Deborah Sontag, "Quest for Mideast Peace: How and Why It Failed," *New York Times*, July 26, 2001.
133. Jeremy Pressman, "Visions in Collision: What Happened at Camp David and Taba?" *International Security* 28, no. 2 (Fall 2003): 5–43.
134. See PLO Negotiations Affairs Department, "Camp David Peace Proposal of July 2000," http://www.nad-plo.org/inner.php?view=nego_nego_camp_cmp_ncampdavid1p, accessed February 14, 2007.
135. Agha and Malley, "Camp David."
136. See Swisher, *Camp David*; Ahron Bregman, *Elusive Peace: How the Holy Land Defeated America* (New York: Penguin, 2005).
137. Academic, interview with author, West Jerusalem, August 7, 2006.
138. *Ha'aretz*, July 26, 2000.
139. *Jerusalem Post*, September 13, 2000.
140. "IDF Studying Possibility of Cancelling Joint Patrols with Palestinian Policemen," *Ma'ariv*, September 24, 2000, as cited in FBIS/WNC, insert September 27, 2000.
141. See Benny Morris, "Camp David and After: An Exchange (1. An Interview with Ehud Barak)," *New York Review of Books*, June 13, 2002, 42–45; Karsh, *Arafat's War*.

Chapter 6. The Second Intifada, 2000

1. Kaspit, "Not a State"; Reuven Pedatzur, "More Than a Million Bullets," *Ha'aretz*, June, 29, 2004.
2. *Jerusalem Post*, October 3, 2000; "Chronology," *Journal of Palestine Studies* 30, no. 2 (Winter 2001): 198.
3. United Nations Economic and Social Council Commission on Human Rights (UN-ECOSOC), "Question of the Violation of Human Rights in the Occupied

Arab Territories, Including Palestine: Report of the Human Rights Inquiry Commission Established Pursuant to Commission Resolution S–5/1 of 19 October 2000," E/CN.4/2001/121, March 16, 2001, 15.

4. Thomas Friedman, "Arafat's War," *New York Times*, October 13, 2000; Charles Krauthammer, "Arafat's Strategy," *New York Times*, October 20, 2000; Ely Karmon, "Arafat's Strategy: Lebanonization and Entanglement," International Institute for Counter-Terrorism, Herzliya, Israel, November 16, 2000, http://www. ict.org.il/apage/5374.php, accessed August 9, 2007; Karsh, *Arafat's War*; Michael Herzog, "The Palestinian Intifada: Lessons and Prospects (Part I)," *Washington Institute for Near East Policy Peacewatch* 474, September 29, 2004.

5. See *Ha'aretz*, October 10–15, 2004.

6. PSR, Public Opinion Polls, June 2001–March 2005, see http://www.pcpsr.org/ survey/survey.html, accessed April 2, 2005.

7. Lori Allen, "There Are Many Reasons Why: Suicide Bombers and Martyrs in Palestine," *Middle East Report* 223 (Summer 2002): 34–37; Wendy Pearlman, *Occupied Voices: Stories of Everyday Life from the Second Intifada* (New York: Nation Books, 2003).

8. *Al-Quds*, June 20, 2002, available at http://www.bitterlemons.org/docs/suicide. html, accessed April 8, 2011.

9. Taysir Qub'ah, "Protection and Continuation of the Blessed Intifada Is a Top Priority of All Palestinian Forces," *al-Ayyam*, October 6, 2000, as cited in FBIS/ WNC, insert October 13, 2000.

10. Cited in David Schenker, "Palestinian National Unity: Formalizing the Informal?" *Washington Institute for Near East Policy Peacewatch* 34, August 15, 2001; also see Talal Awkal, "The Jerusalem Intifada: Lessons and Examples," *al-Ayyam*, October 2, 2000, as cited in FBIS/WNC, insert October 6, 2000; Lamia Lahoud and AP, "Arafat Loyalists, Opposition Run Uprising Together," *Jerusalem Post*, October 26, 2000.

11. Amira Hass, "Blurring the Dividing Lines," *Ha'aretz*, August 27, 2001.

12. Cited in Usher, "Facing Defeat," 28.

13. Coser, *Functions of Social Conflict*, 92.

14. Yezid Sayigh, "Palestine – Where To?" PASSIA Roundtable Meeting and Discussion, July 9, 2002, http://www.passia.org/meetings/2002/round0907. htm, accessed August 19, 2007; also see "For the Record: Interview with Yezid Sayigh," *Palestine Report*, March 7, 2001.

15. Graham Usher, "The Intifada Next time," *al-Ahram Weekly*, September 27– October 3, 2001.

16. Rema Hammami and Salim Tamari, "The Second Uprising: End or New Beginning?" *Journal of Palestine Studies* 30, no. 2 (Winter 2001): 18.

17. Cited in James Bennet, "Isolated and Angry, Gaza Battles Itself, Too," *New York Times*, July 16, 2004; also see comments by Kamil Mansur and Imad Ghayaza in Parsons, *Palestinian Authority*, 274–275.

18. Roy, "Continued Denial of Possibility," 9; also see Toufic Haddad, "A Portrait of Sociocide: The Challenge of Khan Yunis, the Gaza Strip," *Between the Lines* 1, no. 5 (March 2001), 2–10.

19. Rema Hammami and Jamil Hillal, "An Uprising at a Crossroads," *Middle East Report* 219 (Summer 2001): 2–7, 41.

20. See Edward Said, "The Tragedy Deepens," *al-Ahram Weekly*, December 7–13, 2000; Ashraf al-Agrami, "National Unity: The Need to Reconsider," *al-Ayyam*, January 13, 2003, as cited in FBIS/WNC, insert January 16, 2003.

21. Yezid Sayigh, "Arafat and the Anatomy of a Revolt," *Survival* 43, no. 3 (2001): 47–60.
22. Fateh leader, interview with author, Ramallah, July 26, 2006.
23. NIFHC member, interview with author, Ramallah, June 22, 2006.
24. See Mustapha Barghouthi, et al., *Wijhat nathar: fi tatawurat al-Intifada wa-Ahdaafiha.* [Roundtable: on the development of the Intifada and its goals]. *Majallat al-Darasat al-Filistiniyah* 47 (Summer 2001): 42.
25. Fateh leader, interview with author, Ramallah, June 15, 2006; also see Parsons, *Palestinian Authority*, 276.
26. See "Chronology," *Journal of Palestine Studies* 30, no. 2 (Winter 2001): 191–217.
27. Fateh leader, interview with author, Ramallah, July 26, 2006; also see Ghazi Hamad, "The Islamist Catch-22," *Palestine Report*, December 13, 2000.
28. Fateh leader, interview with author, Ramallah, July 26, 2006.
29. Haydar 'Abd al-Shafi, "Looking Back, Looking Forward: An Interview with Haydar 'Abd al-Shafi," *Journal of Palestine Studies* 32, no. 1 (Autumn 2002): 28–35.
30. Jamil Hilal, "al-Harakah al-wataniyah al-Filastiniyah amam su'al sa'ab" [The Palestinian national movement faces difficult questions], *Majallat al-Dirasat al-Filastiniyah* 56 (Fall 2003): 20.
31. Hani al-Masri, "Filastin amam muftaraq turuq" [Palestine at a crossroads], *Majallat al-Dirasat al-Filastiniyah* 51 (Summer 2002): 50; also see Barghouti et al., "Wijhat Nathar"; Ali Jarbawi, *Li-kay natakhatta al-azmah: nahwa khittah istratijiyah jadidah lil-'amal al-Filastini* [Overcoming the crisis: toward a new Palestinian strategy] (Birzeit: Brizeit University, 2001); Zaqout, "al-Intifadah wa shurut injaz"; also see Azmi Bishara, *Ma ba'da al-ijtiyah: fi qadaya al-istratijiyah al-wataniyah al-Filastiniyah* [In the wake of the Israeli invasion: on issues of Palestinian national strategy] (Ramallah: Muwatin, 2002).
32. Lawyer, interview with author, Ramallah, July 26, 2006.
33. Cited in Graham Usher, "Still Seeking a Vision" *al-Ahram Weekly*, September 30–October 6, 2004; also see Hadeel Wahdan, "Who Is in Control? *Palestine Report*, December 13, 2000; Ali Jarbawi, "Critical Reflections on One Year of the Intifada," *Between the Lines* 1, no. 12 (October 2001): 9–14; Azmi Bishara, "The Quest for Strategy," *Journal of Palestine Studies* 32, no. 2 (Winter 2003): 41–49.
34. Cited in Graham Usher, "The Assassination of Shaykh Yasin," *Middle East International*, April 1, 2001.
35. Cited in Bucaille, *Growing Up Palestinian*, 125.
36. Husayn Agha and Robert Malley, "The Lost Palestinians," *New York Review of Books*, June 9, 2005; also see James Bennet, "A People Adrift, Part I: In Chaos, Palestinians Struggle for a Way Out," *New York Times*, July 15, 2004; Anat Kurz, "Fateh's Struggle for Institutionalization," *Strategic Assessment* 3, no. 4 (January 2001), http://www.tau.ac.il/jcss/sa/v3n4p4.html, accessed August 9, 2007.
37. Fateh leader, interview with author, Ramallah, June 12, 2006.
38. Ibid.
39. B'Tselem, *Illusions of Restraint: Human Rights Violations during the Events in the Occupied Territories, 29 September–2 December 2000* (Jerusalem, December 2000).
40. Toufic Haddad, "The Changing Face of Southern Gaza Popular Resistance Committees," *Between the Lines* 1, no. 8 (July 2001): 11–16; Saleh al-Masri, "Interview with Awni Za'noun, PRC Leader," *Between the Lines* 1, no. 8 (July 2001): 16–18.

41. Fateh leader, interview with author, Ramallah, July 26, 2006.
42. Jarbawi, "Critical Reflections."
43. Sayigh, "Anatomy of a Revolt."
44. Abdel Jawad, "Intifada's Military Lessons."
45. See "Press Briefing by Colonel Daniel Reisner – Head of the International Law Branch of the IDF Legal Division," Jerusalem, November 15, 2000, http://www.mfa.gov.il/MFA/MFAArchive/2000_2009/2000/11/Press+Briefi ng+by+Colonel+Daniel+Reisner-+Head+of.html, accessed August 9, 2007; Kaspit, "Not a State"; Kaspit, "Army Will Decide"; Pedatzur, "Million Bullets"; Yoram Peri, *Generals in the Cabinet Room: How the Military Shapes Israeli Policy* (Washington, DC: United States Institute of Peace Press, 2006).
46. "Press Briefing by Colonel Daniel Reisner"; Amira Hass, "Don't Shoot Till You Can See They're over the Age of 12," *Ha'aretz*, November 20, 2000.
47. Kaspit, "Not a State."
48. See UN-ECOSOC, "Question of the Violation of Human Rights," 23; al-Mezan Center for Human Rights, *The Intifada in Figures: Statistics on Israel's Violations of Human Rights in the Occupied Palestinian Territories, September 28, 2000– September 28, 2003* (Gaza, 2003); Amnesty International, *Israel and the Occupied Territories: Under the Rubble – House Demolition and Destruction of Land and Property*, May 18, 2004; B'Tselem, *Policy of Destruction: House Demolitions and Destruction of Agricultural Land in the Gaza Strip* (Jerusalem, January– February 2002); Human Rights Watch, *Razing Rafah: Mass Demolitions in the Gaza Strip* (New York, October 2004).
49. See B'Tselem, *Excessive Force: Human Rights Violations during IDF Actions in Area A* (Jerusalem, December 2001); The Palestinian Human Rights Monitoring Group (PHRMG), "Overkill: Israeli Bombardment and Destruction of Palestinian Civilian Homes and Infrastructure," *Monitor* 5, no. 1 (Jerusalem, February 2001).
50. UNICEF Press Release, Geneva, November 15, 2001; see http://www.unicef.org/ newsline/01pr87.htm, accessed April 8, 2011.
51. Office of the United Nations Special Coordinator for the Middle East Peace Process, (UNSCO), "The Impact on the Palestinian Economy of Confrontation, Border Closures and Mobility Restrictions" (October 2000–September 30, 2001), http://www.un.org/News/dh/mideast/econ-report-final.pdf, accessed April 8, 2011.
52. See Leila Farsakh, "Under Siege: Closure, Separation and the Palestinian Economy," *Middle East Report* 217 (Winter 2000): 22–25; World Bank Group, *West Bank and Gaza Update: One Year of Intifada, Closures and Palestinian Economic Crisis* (West Bank and Gaza Strip, November 2001), http:// lnweb18.worldbank.org/mna/mena.nsf/Attachments/Update+Nov+2001/$File/ World+Bank+update+Nov+2001+Eng.pdf, accessed August 9, 2007.
53. UNSCO, *Annual Economic Report 2000, Executive Summary* (August 23, 2001); World Bank, "West Bank and Gaza Update: One Year of Intifada, Closures and Palestinian Economic Crisis" (November 2001).
54. Hass, "Israel's Closure Policy."
55. See "Statement by Ambassador Yehuda Lancry, Permanent Representative of Israel to the United Nations, at the Tenth Emergency Special Session of the General Assembly," October 18, 2000; "Briefing by Colonel Daniel Reisner."

56. Apart from reports and press releases by Palestinian human rights organizations, see Physicians for Human Rights (USA), *Evaluation of the Use of Force in Israel, Gaza and the West Bank: Medical and Forensic Investigation*, November 2000, http://physiciansforhumanrights.org/library/documents/reports/report-useofforce-israel.pdf, accessed August 9, 2007; B'Tselem, *Illusions of Restraint*; UN-ECOSOC, "Human Rights Inquiry Commission," 15; B'Tselem, *Excessive Force*; Human Rights Watch, *Center of the Storm: A Case Study of Human Rights Abuses in the Hebron District* (New York, April 2001); Amnesty International, *Broken Lives: A Year of Intifada* (London, 2001), 17; B'Tselem, *Trigger Happy: Unjustified Shooting and Violation of the Open-Fire Regulations during the al-Aqsa Intifada* (Jerusalem, March 2002); International Committee of the Red Cross, "Implementation of the Fourth Geneva Convention in the Occupied Palestinian Territories: History of a Multilateral Process (1997–2001)," *International Review of the Red Cross* 847 (September 30, 2002): 661–698.
57. Fateh leader, interview with author, East Jerusalem, June 27, 2006.
58. Program on International Policy Attitudes, "The Potential for a Nonviolent Intifada: A Study of Palestinian and Israeli Jewish Public Attitudes," August 28, 2002, http://www.worldpublicopinion.org/pipa/articles/international_security_bt/136.php?lb=brme&pnt=136&nid=&id=, accessed April 5, 2011.
59. Toufic Haddad, "Overcoming the Culture of Petitions: Critiquing the Role and Influence of Palestinian 'Secular, National, Democratic' Forces," *Between the Lines* 11, no. 14 (March 2002): 30–36.
60. PLC member, interview with author, Ramallah, June 20, 2006.
61. Ghassan Andoni, "A Comparative Study of Intifada 1987 and Intifada 2000," in *The New Intifada: Resisting Israel's Apartheid*, ed. Roane Carey (London: Verso Books, 2001), 218.
62. Abdel Jawad, "Intifada's Military Lessons."
63. Journalist, interview with author, Ramallah, June 29, 2006.
64. Former civil disobedience activist, interview with author, Beit Sahour, July 13, 2006.
65. Community activist, interview with author, Dheisheh refugee camp, July 4, 2006.
66. See Haddad, "Sociocide."
67. See Jeff Halper, "Paralysis over Palestine: Questions of Strategy," *Journal of Palestine Studies* 34, no. 2 (Winter 2005): 55–69.
68. Parsons, *Palestinian Authority*, 265.
69. See Penny Johnson and Eileen Kuttab, "Where Have All the Women (and Men) Gone? Reflections on Gender and the Second Palestinian Intifada," *Feminist Review* 69 (Winter 2001): 21–43.
70. See International Court of Justice, *Legal Consequences of the Construction of a Wall in the Occupied Palestinian Territory*, July 9, 2004.
71. Coordinator, Bil'in Campaign against the Wall, interview with author, Ramallah, July 25, 2006.
72. See Bil'in village website, http://www.bilin-village.org/english/discover-bilin/, accessed April 8, 2011.
73. Coordinator, Bil'in Campaign against the Wall, interview with author, Ramallah, July 25, 2006.

74. Security force officer, interview with author, Dheisheh refugee camp, July 13, 2006.
75. Doug McAdam, "Political Opportunities: Conceptual Origins, Current Problems, Future Directions," in *Comparative Perspectives on Social Movements*, 26.
76. AMB member, interview with author, Nablus, December 4, 2004.
77. Bloom, "Palestinian Suicide Bombing"; also see Moghadam, "Palestinian Suicide Terrorism"; Mohammed Hafez, *Manufacturing Human Bombs: The Making of Palestinian Suicide Bombers* (Washington, D.C.: United States Institute of Peace, 2006); Alimi, "Contextualizing Political Terrorism."
78. Fateh leader, interview with author, East Jerusalem, June 27, 2006.
79. AMB member, interview with author, Nablus, December 4, 2004.
80. "The Nature and Extent of Palestinian Terrorism, 2006," Intelligence and Terrorism Information Center at Israel Intelligence's Heritage and Commemoration Center, March 1, 2007, Israeli Ministry of Foreign Affairs, http://www.mfa.gov.il/MFA/Terrorism-+Obstacle+to+Peace/Palestinian+terror+since+2000/Palestinian+terrorism+2006.htm, accessed August 19, 2007.
81. See Ghazi Hamad, "Divisions Emerge over Qassams," *Palestine Report*, August 11, 2004; Laila El-Haddad, "Bitter Harvest in Gaza's Breadbasket," *al-Jazeera.net*, August 20, 2004, http://english.aljazeera.net/English/archive/archive?ArchiveId=5918, accessed August 19, 2007.
82. Cited in Arnon Regular, "Palestinian Inquiry Blames Yasser Arafat for Anarchy," *Ha'aretz*, August 10, 2004.
83. Cited in Hamad, "Divisions."
84. Aluf Benn, "The Qassam Connection," *Ha'aretz*, July 2, 2004.
85. "Between the Corrupt and the Corrupt," *Palestine Report*, July 28, 2004.
86. See Pinhas Inbari, "Nablus: The Locus of Palestinian Civil War?" International Institute for Counter-Terrorism, January 1, 2004, http://www.ict.org.il/apage/5293.php, accessed August 19, 2007; PHRMG, "The 'Intra'fada: The Chaos of Weapons – An Analysis of Internal Palestinian Violence," *Monitor* 7, no. 1 (Jerusalem, April, 2004); Graham Usher, "Still Seeking a Vision," *al-Ahram Weekly*, September 30–October 6, 2004; Katya Adler, "Police Chief Promises Change in Nablus," *BBC News*, April 29, 2007, http://news.bbc.co.uk/2/hi/middle_east/6598813.stm, accessed August 19, 2007; United Nations Office for the Coordination of Humanitarian Affairs (UN-OCHA), *Nablus after Five Years of Conflict* (Jerusalem, December 2005).
87. AMB member, interview with author, Nablus, December 4, 2004.
88. Fateh leader, interview with author, Ramallah, August 8, 2006; also see Center for Defense Information, "Terrorism: In the Spotlight: al-Aqsa Martyrs Brigades," http://www.cdi.org/friendlyversion/printversion.cfm?documentID=1100&from_page=../program/document.cfm, accessed August 19, 2007.
89. International Crisis Group, "Who Governs the West Bank? Palestinian Administration Under Israeli Occupation," *Middle East Report* 32 (Amman/Brussels, September 2004), 24–25; also see Parsons, *Palestinian Authority*, 267–268.
90. Human Rights Watch, *Erased in a Moment: Suicide Bombing Attacks Against Israeli Civilians* (New York, October 2002), 62–63.
91. AMB member, interview with author, Jenin, October 23, 2004.
92. See Haddad, "Petitions."
93. See Joshua Hammer, *A Season in Bethlehem: Unholy War in a Sacred Place* (New York: Free Press, 2003).

94. See respectively, International Crisis Group, "Who Governs the West Bank?" 26; Usher, "Facing Defeat," 27.

95. Cited in "Fateh Can Be Rescued from Itself," *Mideast Mirror*, October 25, 2004; also see "Al-Aqsa Commander: No One Can Unilaterally End De-escalation," *Financial Times*, April 28, 2005.

96. These figures are according to B'Tselem, which notes that 272 bystanders were killed in the process. The Palestinian Human Rights Monitoring Group recorded 209 assassinations during the same period. See www.phrmg.org/aqsa/list_of_assassination_english.htm, accessed August 19, 2007.

97. See Hammer, *Season in Bethlehem*, 127.

98. Bennet, "People Adrift."

99. Usher, "Facing Defeat," 34.

100. International Crisis Group, "Who Governs the West Bank?" 25.

101. Community activist, interview with author, Dheisheh refugee camp, July 4, 2006.

102. Hamas member, interview with author, Ramallah, June 18, 2006; also see International Crisis Group, "Dealing with Hamas," *Middle East Report* 21 (Amman/Brussels, January 26, 2004): 11; Bradley Burston, "Hamas vs. Abbas: The Lethal Wild Card, a Profile" *Ha'aretz*, January 22, 2005.

103. Graham Usher, "Dead End," *Middle East International*, September 12, 2003.

104. See Zvi Bar'el, "Women's Work," *Ha'aretz*, January 23, 2004.

105. Journalist, interview with author, Gaza City, August 9, 2005.

106. Strategic Assessments Initiative, *Planning Considerations for International Involvement in the Palestinian Security Sector* (Washington, DC: Strategic Assessments Initiative, July 2005), 13, http://www.strategicassessments.org/ontherecord/sai_publications/SAI-Planning_Considerations_for_International_Involvement_July_2005.pdf, accessed August 19, 2007.

107. Ibid., 13.

108. Political analyst, interview with author, Gaza City, July 30, 2005.

109. See *Report of the Secretary-General Prepared Pursuant to General Assembly Resolution ES-10/10*. Available at http://www.un.org/peace/jenin/index.html, accessed May 1, 2007.

110. Amira Hass, "Operation Destroy the Data," *Ha'aretz*, April 24, 2002.

111. See Jarbawi and Pearlman, "Post-Charisma," 5.

112. Fateh leader, interview with author, Ramallah, June 13, 2006.

113. JMCC, Public Opinion Poll No. 51, June 2004, http://www.jmcc.org/polls.aspx, accessed March 25, 2005.

114. International Crisis Group, "Who Governs the West Bank?" 18; also see Azmi Bishara, "Beyond Belief," *al-Ahram Weekly*, July 25–31, 2002; "Fateh Can Be Rescued from Itself."

115. Rami G. Khouri, "Gaza's Crisis Mirrors Palestinian and Wider Arab Failures," *Daily Star*, July 21, 2004; Danny Rubinstein, "Internal Conflict in Gaza May Scuttle Withdrawal," *Ha'aretz*, September 20, 2004. "Palestinians Say Can't Arrest Americans' Killers," *Reuters*, September 22, 2004; Danny Rubinstein, "Apparently Dahlan Was the Target," *Ha'aretz*, November 11, 2004.

116. See PICCR, *Hawla su' istikhdam al-silah min qibal al-'amilin fi al-ajhiza al-amniyah al-Filastiniyah khilala al-'am 2001* [Misuse of weapons on the part of Palestinian security force personnel, 2001] (Ramallah, 2002); PHRMG, "The 'Intra'fada"; PHRMG, "Gaza in Turmoil: The Power Struggle within the

Palestinian Authority," *Monitor* 8, no. 1 (Jerusalem, May, 2005); PICCR, *Hawla halat al-inflat al-amni wa-da'f siyadat al-qanun fi aradi al-Sultah al-Wataniyah al-Filastiniyah* [The security lapse and weak rule of law under the Palestinian National Authority] (Ramallah, 2005); on the PLC inquiry into this internal situation, see Arnon Regular, "Palestinian Inquiry Blames Yasser Arafat for Anarchy," *Ha'aretz*, August 10, 2004.

117. Ferry Biedermann, "Crime Soars in Palestinian Areas," *Inter Press Service News Agency*, February 3, 200; also see Ahmad Sub Laban, "Victims of Violence," *Palestine Report*, March 16, 2005; Human Rights Watch, *A Question of Security: Violence against Palestinian Women and Girls* (New York, November 2006).

118. PLC member, interview with author, Ramallah, June 20, 2006.

119. Staff member at al-Najah University, conversation with author, Nablus, December 4, 2004; also see Salim Tamari, "Review Essay: Who Rules Palestine?" *Journal of Palestine Studies* 31, no. 4 (Summer 2002): 102–113; International Crisis Group, "Who Governs the West Bank?"

120. See Yossi Olmert, "Arafat's Little Game of Cease-Fires," *Jerusalem Post*, June 10, 2001; Yoel Marcus, "Dr. Cease-Fire and Mr. Terror," *Ha'aretz*, June 12, 2001.

121. See Rema Hammami, "Interregnum: Palestine after Operation Defensive Shield," *Middle East Report* 223 (Summer 2002): 18–27; Parsons, *Palestinian Authority*, 277–278.

122. *Ha'aretz*, October 6, 2000; "Fateh al-Tanzim Leader in West Bank Marwan al-Barghuthi Interviewed on Intifadah," *al-Majallah*, October 29, 2000, as cited in FBIS/WNC, insert November 6, 2000; "'Peaceful intifada' Will Go On," *Mideast Mirror*, November 2, 2000; "PFLP, Other Palestinian Forces Reject Unconditional Talks," *al-Hayat al-Jadidah*, December 19, 2000, as cited in FBIS/WNC, insert December 27, 2000; Mouin Rabbani, "Negotiating over the Clinton Plan," *Middle East Report*, Press Information Note no. 43, January 6, 2001, http://www.merip.org/pins/pin43.html, accessed August 9, 2007.

123. Citizen from Tulkarem, interview with author, Ramallah, June 20, 2006.

124. Graham Usher, "Arafat and the Armed Resistance," *Middle East International*, May 4, 2001; also see "Peace Monitor," *Journal of Palestine Studies* 30, no. 1 (Autumn 2001): 138.

125. Charmaine Seitz, "Ceasefire Receives Mixed Reviews," *Palestine Report*, September 19, 2001; Charmaine Seitz, "The Dissenters," *Palestine Report*, October 17, 2001.

126. Charmaine Seitz, "Palestinian Anger Turns Inward," *Palestine Report*, October 10, 2001.

127. Fateh leader, interview with author, Ramallah, June 15, 2006.

128. Beverly Milton-Edwards and Alastair Crooke, "Waving, Not Drowning: Strategic Dimensions of Ceasefires and Islamic Movements," *Security Dialogue* 35, no. 3 (September 2004): 295–310.

129. Graham Usher, "Cease-fires That Cannot Be," *Middle East International*, August 16, 2002.

130. James Bennet, "Palestinian Focus: The Internal Fight," *New York Times*, July 1, 2003.

131. Cited in Khaled Abu Toameh, "Talking at Cross Purposes," *Jerusalem Post*, January 31, 2003.

132. Fateh leader, interview with author, Ramallah, July 26, 2006.

133. Graham Usher, "Third Parties," *al-Ahram Weekly*, March 3–9, 2005.

134. Matthew Levitt, "Hizballah's West Bank Foothold," *Washington Institute for Near East Policy PeaceWatch* 429, August 20, 2003; Khaled Abu Toameh, "New Fateh Groups Controlled by PLO Dissident in Lebanon," *Jerusalem Post*, August 26, 2002; Human Rights Watch, *Erased in a Moment*, 85–86.

135. Cited in Levitt, "Hizballah's West Bank Foothold."

136. Ibid.

137. Abu Toameh, "Cross Purposes."

138. Dan Murphy, "Egypt Plays Mideast Peace Broker," *Christian Science Monitor*, November 15, 2004.

139. Alastair Crooke, "Apply Sparingly," *Bitterlemons International*, May 12, 2005; also see Omar Karmi, "Tinkering Will No Longer Help," *Bitterlemons International*, May 12, 2005, http://www.bitterlemons-international.org/previous.php?opt=1&id=83, accessed August 16, 2007.

140. Jean-Francois Legrain, "The Successions of Yasir Arafat," *Journal of Palestine Studies* 28, no. 4 (Summer 1999): 5–20; Barry Rubin, "After Arafat," *Middle East Quarterly* 11, no. 2 (Spring 2004): 13–21; Glenn E. Robinson, "After Arafat," *Current History* 104 (January 2005): 19–24.

141. Graham Usher, "Letter from the Occupied Territories: The Palestinians after Arafat," *Journal of Palestine Studies* 34, no. 3 (Spring 2005): 51.

142. Cited in Usher, "Palestinians after Arafat," 54–55.

143. See Ali Jarbawi, "Filastin wa al-marhalah al-jadidah" [Palestine and the new phase], *Majallat Dirasat al-Filastiniyah* 66 (Spring 2006): 7–20; Khalid Hroub, "Hamas Is Being Punished for Moderate Behavior," *Daily Star*, October 26, 2006.

144. Greg Myre, "Palestinian Gunmen Storm Election Offices," *New York Times*, December 13, 2005; Khaled Abu Toameh, "Fateh Gunmen Threaten Election Chaos," *Jerusalem Post*, December 29, 2005; also see "The Crisis of Fateh," PASSIA Political Landscape Meeting, July 27, 2005, http://www.passia.org/meetings/2005/Crisis-of-Fateh.htm, accessed August 19, 2007.

145. World Bank, *West Bank and Gaza Update* (Washington, DC, September 2006).

146. Hamas member, interview with author, Ramallah, June 18, 2006.

147. PLC member, interview with author, Ramallah, June 20, 2006.

148. Academic, interview with author, West Jerusalem, August 7, 2006.

149. PFLP leader, interview with author, Ramallah, June 15, 2006.

150. International Institute for Strategic Studies, "Hamas Coup in Gaza: Fundamental Shift in Palestinian Politics," *Strategic Comments* 13, no. 5 (June 2007); David Rose, "The Gaza Bombshell," *Vanity Fair* 50, no. 4 (April 2008): 192–197.

151. Ronny Shaked, "Palestinian National Struggle Faces Deep Crisis over Fateh–Hamas Rift," *Ynetnews*, 27 July 2007, http://www.ynetnews.com/articles/0,7340,L-3430590,00.html, accessed July 27, 2007.

152. "Political Chaos Takes Its Toll: A New Poll Says Palestinians Are Losing Faith in Their Political Leaders and Want Reconciliation between Hamas and Fateh," *Fafo Press Release*, July 18, 2007. http://www.fafo.no/ais/middeast/opt/opinion polls/180707palestinapresseeng.htm, accessed July 27, 2007.

153. Amos Harel, "Will Hamas–Israel Truce Come to an End in January?" *Ha'aretz*, October 19, 2008.

154. Israel Defense Forces Spokesperson's Unit, http://idfspokesperson.com/category/idf-statistics/, accessed January 24, 2009.

155. United Nations Office of the Coordinator of Humanitarian Affairs (UN-OCHA), *The Humanitarian Monitor: Occupied Palestinian Territory*, June–December 2008, http://www.ochaopt.org/?module=displaysection&section_id=118&static=0&edition_id=&format=html, accessed January 24, 2009.

156. Israeli General Security Services Director Yuval Diskin cited in ICG, "Round Two in Gaza," *Middle East Briefing* 24 (Brussels, September 11, 2008), 12.

157. Avi Isacharoff and Yuval Azoulav, "Hamas: Continued Rocket Fire by Fateh Armed Group Harms Palestinian Interests," *Ha'aretz*, June 27, 2008; Intelligence and Terrorism Information Center, *The Six Months of the Lull Arrangement* (Ramat Hasharon: Israel Intelligence Heritage and Commemoration Center, December 2008), 2, http://www.terrorism-info.org.il/malam_multimedia/English/eng_n/pdf/hamas_e017.pdf, accessed January 24, 2009.

158. "Report: Gaza Hamas Heads Furious with Meshal Decision to End Lull," *Ha'aretz*, January 31, 2009.

159. United Nations Office of the Coordinator of Humanitarian Affairs (UN-OCHA), *Protection of Civilians Weekly Report*, January 16–20, 2008, http://www.ocha-opt.org/documents/ocha_opt_protection_of_civilians_weekly_2009_01_20_english.pdf, accessed January 24, 2009.

Chapter 7. Comparisons: South Africa and Northern Ireland

1. Leonard M. Thompson, *A History of South Africa* (New Haven, CT: Yale Nota Bene, 2001), 171.

2. Ibid., 173–174.

3. Peter Walshe, *The Rise of African Nationalism in South Africa: The African National Congress, 1912–1952* (Berkeley: University of California Press, 1971), 34.

4. Thompson, *History*, 156, 176.

5. ibid., 178.

6. Dan O'Meara, "The 1946 African Mine Workers' Strike and the Political Economy of South Africa," *Journal of the Commonwealth and Comparative Politics* 12, no. 2 (1975): 153.

7. Mona N. Younis, *Liberation and Democratization: The South African and Palestinian National Movements* (Minneapolis: University of Minnesota Press, 2000), 51.

8. Cited in Jeff Goodwin, "'The Struggle Made Me a Non-Racialist': Why There Was So Little Terrorism in the Antiapartheid Struggle," *Mobilization* 12, no. 2 (June 2007): 198.

9. Stephen Ellis and Tsepo Sechaba, *Comrades against Apartheid: The ANC and the South African Communist Party* (London: James Currey, 1992), 11.

10. Tom Lodge, *Black Politics in South Africa since 1945* (Johannesburg: Ravan Press, 1983), 24–25; Walshe, *African Nationalism*, 385–387.

11. O'Meara, "Mine Workers' Strike," 168.

12. Edward Feit, "Generational Conflict and African Nationalism in South Africa: The African National Congress, 1949–1959," *International Journal of African Historical Studies* 5, no. 2 (1972): 184–185.

13. Thomas Karis and Gwendolen M. Carter, *From Protest to Challenge: A Documentary History of African Politics in South Africa* (Stanford, CA: Hoover Institution Press, 1973), vol. 2, 412, 418.

14. Ibid., 415.

15. Ibid., 485–486.

16. Ibid., 490.

17. Feit, "Generational Conflict," 193.

18. Ibid., 198; Karis and Carter, *Protest to Challenge*, vol. 3, 329.

19. Karis and Carter, *Protest to Challenge*, vol. 3, 331; Rob Davies, Dan O'Meara, and Sipho Dlamini, *The Struggle for South Africa* (London: Zed Books, 1984), vol. 2, 299–300.

20. Gail M. Gerhart, *Black Power in South Africa: The Evolution of an Ideology* (Berkeley: University of California Press, 1978), 227.

21. Ibid., 227, 229.

22. Cited in Feit, "Generational Conflict," 199.

23. Karis and Carter, *Protest to Challenge*, vol. 3, 333.

24. Ibid., 335; Gerhart, *Black Power*, 239.

25. Elisabeth Jean Wood, *Forging Democracy from Below: Insurgent Transitions in South Africa and El Salvador* (Cambridge: Cambridge University Press, 2000), 130.

26. Sheridan Johns, "Obstacles to Guerrilla Warfare – A South African Case Study," *Journal of Modern African Studies* 11, no. 2 (June 1973): 272.

27. Wood, *Forging Democracy*, 130–131.

28. Robert Price, "Race and Reconciliation in the New South Africa," *Politics & Society* 25, no. 2 (June 1997): 149–178.

29. Feit, "Generational Conflict," 197.

30. Davies, O'Meara, and Dlamini, *Struggle for South Africa*, 300–302.

31. Amnesty International, *South Africa: Torture, Ill-Treatment and Executions in African National Congress Camps*, AFR 53/027/1992, December 2, 1992, http://www.amnesty.org/en/library/info/AFR53/027/1992/en.

32. Todd Cleveland, "'We Still Want the Truth': The ANC's Angolan Detention Camps and Post-Apartheid Memory," *Comparative Studies of South Asia, Africa and the Middle East* 25, no. 1 (2005): 63.

33. See Raymond Suttner, *The ANC Underground in South Africa: A Social and Historical Study* (Auckland Park: Jacana, 2008), 33–36.

34. Ellis and Sechaba, *Comrades*, 6.

35. Suttner, *ANC Underground*, 77–79.

36. Wood, *Forging Democracy*, 135.

37. Gregory F. Houston, *The National Liberation Struggle in South Africa: A Case Study of the United Democratic Front, 1983–1987* (Aldershot: Ashgate, 1999), 42.

38. Stephen M. Davis, *Apartheid's Rebels: Inside South Africa's Hidden War* (New Haven, CT: Yale University Press, 1987), 57.

39. Suttner, *ANC Underground*, 160.

40. Houston, *Liberation Struggle*, 46.

41. Gay Seidman, "Guerrillas in Their Midst: Armed Struggle in the South Africa Anti-Apartheid Movement," *Mobilization* 6, no. 2 (Fall 2001): 124.

42. Jeremy Seekings, *The UDF: A History of the United Democratic Front in South Africa, 1983–1991* (Athens: Ohio University Press, 2000), 9.

43. Houston, *Liberation Struggle*, 45
44. Seekings, *UDF*, 15–16, 189.
45. Houston, *Liberation Struggle*, 41.
46. Ibid., 1.
47. Younis, *Liberation and Democratization*, 139.
48. Robert M. Price, *The Apartheid State in Crisis: Political Transformation in South Africa, 1975–1990* (New York : Oxford University Press, 1991), 199–202.
49. Houston, *Liberation Struggle*, 83.
50. Seekings, *UDF*, 106–107.
51. Wood, *Forging Democracy*, 137.
52. Jeremy Seekings, "The Development of Strategic Thought in South Africa's Civic Movements, 1977–90," in *From Comrades to Citizens: The South African Civics Movement and the Transition to Democracy*, eds. Glenn Adler and Johnny Steinberg, (London: Macmillan, 2000), 52.
53. Lieberfeld, *Talking with the Enemy*, 109.
54. Peter Ackeman and Jack DuVall, *A Force More Powerful* (New York: Palgrave Macmillan, 2000), 354.
55. Ibid., 361; Price, *Apartheid State*, 190–219.
56. Seekings, "Strategic Thought," 73.
57. Houston, *Liberation Struggle*, 197.
58. Price, *Apartheid State*, 203.
59. Anthony W. Marx, *Lessons of Struggle: South African Internal Opposition, 1960–1990* (New York: Oxford University Press, 1992), 157.
60. Ibid., 158.
61. Cited in Goodwin, "Non-Racialist," 195–196.
62. Ibid.
63. Stephen Zunes, "The Role of Non-violent Action in the Downfall of Apartheid," *Journal of Modern African Studies* 37, no. 1 (March 1999): 148.
64. See Seidman, "Guerrillas."
65. Darby, *Violence on Peace Processes*, 56.
66. Timothy D. Sisk, "The Violence-Negotiation Nexus: South Africa in Transition and the Politics of Uncertainty," *Negotiation Journal* 9, no. 1 (January 1993): 77–94.
67. Roger Mac Ginty and John Darby, *Guns and Government: The Management of the Northern Ireland Peace Process* (New York: Palgrave, 2002), 94.
68. Ed Moloney, *The Secret History of the IRA* (New York: W. W. Norton, 2002), 49.
69. J. Bowyer Bell, *The Secret Army: A History of the IRA, 1916–1979* (Cambridge, MA: MIT Press, 1980), 255–256.
70. Brian Feeney, *Sinn Féin: A Hundred Turbulent Years* (New York: O'Brien Press, 2002), 203.
71. Richard English, *Armed Struggle: The History of the IRA* (London: Macmillan, 2003), 72; Bell, *Secret Army*, 316; *An Phoblacht*, October 27, 2005.
72. Bell, *Secret Army*, 275.
73. Moloney, *Secret History*, 310.
74. Feeney, *Sinn Féin*, 204.
75. Moloney, *Secret History*, 310; also see English, *Armed Struggle*, 72; Bell, *Secret Army*, 316; Thomas Hennessey, *A History of Northern Ireland, 1920–1996* (London: Macmillan, 1997), 107.

76. Hennessey, *Northern Ireland*, 107.
77. Gerard Murray and Jonathan Tonge, *Sinn Féin and the SDLP: From Alienation to Participation* (London: Hurst, 2005), 7.
78. Paul Bew, Peter Gibbon, and Henry Patterson, *Northern Ireland, 1921–2001: Political Forces and Social Classes* (London: Serif, 2002), 139.
79. Enda Staunton, *The Nationalists of Northern Ireland, 1918–1973* (Dublin: Columbia Press, 2001), chap. 11.
80. Hennessey, *Northern Ireland*, 100–101.
81. Paul F. Power, "Civil Protest in Northern Ireland," *Journal of Peace Research* 9, no. 3 (September 1972): 225.
82. See Michael Farrell, *Northern Ireland: The Orange State* (London: Pluto Press, 1980).
83. Jonathan Tonge, *Northern Ireland: Conflict and Change* (Harlow: Pearson Education, 2002), 24–25.
84. Bew, Gibbon, and Patterson, *Northern Ireland*, 146.
85. Hennessey, *Northern Ireland*, 138.
86. Simon Prince, *Northern Ireland's '68: Civil Rights, Global Revolt and the Origins of the Troubles* (Dublin: Irish Academic Press, 2007), 124–25.
87. See Conflict Archive on the Internet (CAIN), "The Civil Rights Campaign: A Chronology of Main Events," http://cain.ulst.ac.uk/events/crights/chron.htm, accessed April 10, 2011
88. *Disturbances in Northern Ireland: Report of the Commission Appointed by the Governor of Northern Ireland*, Honourable Lord Cameron, D.S.C., Chairman. Cmd. 532 (Belfast: Her Majesty's Stationery Office, 1969), chap. 15, 193.
89. Moloney, *Secret History*, 59–60.
90. Gerry Adams, *Before the Dawn* (Kerry: Brandon, 1996), 131.
91. Sutton Index of Deaths, see http://www.cain.ulst.ac.uk/sutton/book/index.html#append, accessed April 13, 2011.
92. *Report of the Bloody Sunday Inquiry*, Honourable Lord Saville, Chairman, vol. 1, chap. 8.52, http://report.bloody-sunday-inquiry.org/volume01/chapter008/, accessed April 13, 2011.
93. Murray and Tonge, *Sinn Féin and the SDLP*, 12.
94. Hennessey, *Northern Ireland*, 195.
95. John McGuffin, *Internment* (Tralee, County Kerry: Anvil Books, 1973), chap. 10; *Bloody Sunday Inquiry*, vol. 8, chap. 8.52.
96. Cited in Hennessey, *Northern Ireland*, 196.
97. *Bloody Sunday Inquiry*, vol. 8, chap. 8.52.
98. CAIN, "The Civil Rights Campaign."
99. Bob Purdie, *Politics in the Streets: The Origins of the Civil Rights Movement in Northern Ireland* (Belfast: Blackstaff Press, 1990), 4.
100. Michael Addison, *Violent Politics: Strategies of Internal Conflict* (Hampshire: Palgrave, 2002), 98.
101. Addison, *Violent Politics*, 85.
102. Moloney, *Secret History*, 160.
103. Jonathan Tonge, "From VNSAs to Constitutional Politicians: Militarism and Politics in the Irish Republican Army," in *Violent Non-state Actors in World Politics*, ed. Klejda Mulaj (London: Hurst, 2010), 52–53.
104. See Moloney, *Secret History*, chap. 10.
105. Ibid., chaps. 16, 17.

106. Cathy Gormley-Heenan, "Chameleonic Leadership: Towards a New Understanding of the Northern Ireland Peace Process," *Leadership* 2, no. 1 (February 2006): 3–75.
107. See Moloney, *Secret History*, 436–441.
108. Mac Ginty and Darby, *Guns and Government*, 88.
109. Moloney, *Secret History*, 289.
110. Ibid., 479.
111. Mac Ginty and Darby, *Guns and Government*, 104.
112. Padraig O'Malley, *Biting at the Grave: The Irish Hunger Strikes and the Politics of Despair* (Boston, MA: Beacon Press, 1991).
113. M. L. R. Smith, *Fighting for Ireland? The Military Strategy of the Irish Republican Movement* (London: Routledge, 1995), 220.
114. English, *Armed Struggle*, 307–315.
115. Anthony McIntyre, "Modern Irish Republicanism: The Product of British State Strategies," *Irish Political Studies* 10, no. 1 (1995): 101.
116. Robert W. White, "From Peaceful Protest to Guerrilla War: Micromobilization of the Provisional Irish Republican Army," *American Journal of Sociology* 94, no. 6 (May 1989): 1277–1302.
117. Brian Dooley, *Black and Green: The Fight for Civil Rights in Northern Ireland and Black America* (London: Pluto Press, 1998).
118. Prince, *Northern Ireland's '68*.
119. Michael Cox, "Bringing in the 'International': The IRA Ceasefire and the End of the Cold War," *International Affairs* 73, no. 4 (October 1997): 671–693.
120. Eamonn O'Kane, *Britain, Ireland, and Northern Ireland since 1980* (London: Routledge, 2007).
121. Roger Mac Ginty, "American Influences on the Northern Ireland Peace Process," *Journal of Conflict Studies* 17, no. 2 (Fall 1997): 31–50.
122. Moloney, *Secret History*, 97.
123. Ibid., 110–111.
124. Avner Yaniv, *Dilemmas of Security: Politics, Strategy, and the Israeli Experience in Lebanon* (New York: Oxford University Press, 1987), 89.

Chapter 8. Conclusion

1. Jarbawi and Pearlman, "Post-Charisma."
2. DeNardo, *Power in Numbers*, 262–263.
3. Ekkart Zimmerman, "Macro-Comparative Research on Political Protest," in *Handbook of Political Conflict: Theory and Research*, ed. Ted Robert Gurr (New York: Free Press, 1980), 191.
4. Mark Lichbach, "Deterrence or Escalation? The Puzzle of Aggregate Studies of Repression and Dissent," *Journal of Conflict Resolution* 31, no. 2 (June 1987): 266–297; Ronald Francisco, "The Relationship Between Coercion and Protest: An Empirical Evaluation in Three Coercive States," *Journal of Conflict Resolution* 39, no. 2 (June 1995): 263–282; Ronald Francisco, "Coercion and Protest: An Empirical Test in Two Democratic States," *American Political Science Review* 40, no. 4 (November 1996): 1179–1204.
5. See Charles Tilly, "Repression, Mobilization, and Explanation," in *Repression and Mobilization*, 211–226; Mark Lichbach, "How to Organize Your Mechanisms: Research Programs, Stylized Facts, and Historical Narratives," in *Repression and Mobilization*, 227–243.

6. I. William Zartman, *Ripe for Resolution: Conflict and Intervention in Africa*, 2d ed. (New York: Oxford University Press, 1989).

7. See Rasler, "Shocks," 700.

8. Stephen J. Stedman, *Peacemaking in Civil War: International Mediation in Zimbabwe, 1974–1980* (Boulder, CO: Lynne Rienner, 1991), 240.

9. See, respectively, ibid., 235; and Dean G. Pruitt and Paul V. Olczak, "Beyond Hope: Approaches to Resolving Seemingly Intractable Conflict," in *Conflict, Cooperation and Justice: Essays Inspired by the Work of Morton Deutsch*, eds. Barbara Benedict Bunker, Jeffrey Z. Rubin, and Associates (San Francisco, CA: Jossey-Bass, 1995), 70.

10. Lieberfeld, *Talking with the Enemy.*

11. Paul K. Huth, *Standing Your Ground: Territorial Disputes and International Conflict* (Ann Arbor: University of Michigan Press, 1996), 183–184.

12. Gretchen Helmke and Steven Levitsky, "Informal Institutions and Comparative Politics: A Research Agenda," *Perspectives on Politics* 2, no. 4 (December 2004): 725–740.

13. See Khalidi, *Iron Cage*, 117.

14. David Th. Schiller, "A Battlegroup Divided: The Palestinian Fedayeen," in *Inside Terrorist Organizations*, ed. David C. Rapoport (New York: Columbia University Press, 1988), 92.

15. Retired general, Israeli Defense Forces, interview with author, Tel Aviv, June 16, 2006.

16. See Shafeeq Ghabra, *Palestinians in Kuwait: The Family and the Politics of Survival* (Boulder, CO: Westview Press, 1987).

17. Steven Erlanger and Hassan M. Fattah, "Jihadist Groups Fill a Palestinian Power Vacuum," *New York Times*, May 31, 2007; International Crisis Group, "Radical Islam in Gaza," *Middle East Report* 104 (Amman/Brussels, March 29, 2011).

18. Khaled Amayreh, "Enter Al-Qaeda," *al-Ahram Weekly*, May 10–16, 2007.

Index

Printed in Great Britain
by Amazon